Shakespeare Spelt Ruin

SHAKESPEARE SPELT RUIN

The Life of Frederick Balsir Chatterton,
Drury Lane's Last Bankrupt

Robert Whelan

Published by Jacob Tonson

www.jacobtonson.com

Copyright © Robert Whelan 2019

First published November 2019

Robert Whelan asserts the moral right
to be identified as the author of this work

ISBN 978-0-9575980-1-0

All rights reserved. No part of this publication may be reproduced, stored in a retrieval system, or transmitted, in any form or by any means, electronic mechanical, photocopying, recording or otherwise without the prior written permission of the publisher.

Design and layout: Luke Jefford

Printed and bound in Great Britain by One Digital, Brighton

For Penny

By the same author

The Other National Theatre: 350 Years of Shows in Drury Lane

*I am neither a literary missionary nor a martyr;
I am simply the manager of a theatre, a vendor of
intellectual entertainment to the London public, and I
found that Shakespeare spelt ruin and Byron bankruptcy.*

**Frederick Balsir Chatterton, Letter to *The Times*,
24 August 1869**

*Mr Chatterton has in his misfortune only followed in the road
trodden by plenty of bankrupt Drury Lane managers before him…
Mr Chatterton will probably be remembered chiefly
by the epigram that 'Shakespeare spelt ruin'.*

***The Theatre*, March & September 1879**

*Drury Lane was a vampire and sucked
the life-blood out of everyone.*

James Anderson, actor and one-time lessee of Drury Lane, 1902

Contents

Illustrations — x

Acknowledgements — xii

Preface — 1

1. The Youth of Chatterton — 5
2. The Lyceum Years — 9
3. A Stroll Down Drury Lane — 29
4. A Partnership at the National Theatre — 39
   - 1862/63: Falconer as house playwright — 39
   - 1863/64: The prestige of nationality — 50
   - 1864/65: Open for the legitimate drama — 61
   - 1865/66: That fatal quicksand Drury Lane — 69
5. Sole Lessee and Manager — 77
   - 1866/77: Shakespeare in his proper home — 77
   - 1867/68: Shakespeare and legitimacy — 85
6. Success — 95
   - 1868/69: Swerving from the legitimate course — 95
   - 1869/70: The tawny siren of Hyde Park — 100
   - 1870/71: The people's theatre — 109
   - 1871/72: Scott is synonymous with success — 114
7. The Cracks Begin to Show — 124
   - 1872/73: The best lessee ever — 124
   - 1873/74: The judicious few looked coldly on — 128
   - 1874/75: The meretricious aid of dogs and horses — 142

8.	Indian Summer	149
	1875/76: Apollo, Pan and paying the piper	149
9.	Drury Lane in Decline	163
	1876/77: The most repulsive Richard III	163
	1877/78: The estimation in which Mr Chatterton is held	175
10.	The Collapse	185
	1878/79: Cold and wintry enough in all conscience	185
11.	The Last Years	200
12.	Man and Manager	208

Epilogue: Drury Lane as the National Theatre	225
Appendix 1: Chatterton's Drury Lane Seasons	235
Appendix 2: Cast of Characters	238
Bibliography	246
Notes	251
Index	288

Illustrations

Frontispiece: Frederick Balsir Chatterton from 'Touchstone Portrait Gallery', *Touchstone*, 1 March 1879, 2 © British Library Board, LOU.LON.16 (1879)

Nitocris, Drury Lane 1855	1
The St James's Theatre	15
Henry Sinclair as Roderick Dhu in *The Lady of the Lake* at Drury Lane (1872)	20
The poster for *Woman or Love Against the World*, Lyceum, 1861	23
The 'sensation scene' in *Peep o' Day*. *The Illustrated London News*, 14 December 1861	25
The pit of Drury Lane being boarded over	35
The stage of Drury Lane converted to a circus ring	37
'Preparing for the Pantomime: Notes at Drury Lane. Mr Beverly's Painting Room.' *The Illustrated Sporting and Dramatic News*, 19 December 1874	43
The Steinbach Falls from *Manfred*. *The Illustrated London News*, 17 October 1863	51
Pantomime 'big heads' being prepared in the Drury Lane workshop. *The Illustrated London News*, 17 December 1870	55
The Battle of Shrewsbury from Shakespeare's *Henry IV Part 1*. *The Illustrated London News*, 30 April 1864	59
The betrothal of Princess Blanche and the Dauphin outside Angiers from *King John*. *Illustrated Times*, 29 September 1866	72
Returning from the pantomime. *The Illustrated London News*, 6 January 1866	73
The beheading of Marino Faliero on the Giants' Staircase of the Doge's Palace. *The Illustrated London News*, 23 November 1867	88
The destruction by fire of Her Majesty's Theatre in the Haymarket on 6 December 1867. *The Illustrated London News*, 14 December 1867	89
'Engaging Children for the Christmas Pantomime at Drury Lane.' *The Illustrated London News*, 7 December 1867	92
The rising of the apprentices in Fleet Street from *King o' Scots*. *The Illustrated London News*, 17 October 1868	96
The Vokes family. *The Illustrated Sporting and Dramatic News*, 26 December 1874	106
Andrew Halliday, Chatterton and E. L. Blanchard grinding money out of Drury Lane. From *The Life and Reminiscences of E. L. Blanchard*, 1891, vol. 1, opp. 349	116

'F. B. Chatterton Esq. A shrewd demonstration of
"The Rule of Three"'. *The Entr'Acte*, 9 November 1872,
5 © British Library Board, LOU.LON.173   122

The Battle of Actium from *Antony and Cleopatra*. *The Graphic*,
8 November 1873   130

E. L. Blanchard as Aladdin. From *The Life and Reminiscences
of E. L. Blanchard*, 1891, vol 2, opp. 445   145

Tommaso Salvini as Othello. Used by permission of the Folger
Shakespeare Library, Washington   147

The Shaughraun. *The Illustrated Sporting and Dramatic News*,
18 September 1875   151

'One word for the Fenian prisoners and how many for
The Shaughraun?' Cartoon by Alfred Bryan. *The Entr'Acte*,
15 January 1876, 7 © British Library Board, LOU.LON.115   156

Chatterton dances for joy when his lease is renewed.
Cartoon by Alfred Bryan. *The Entr'Acte*, 20 July 1878,
8 © British Library Board, LOU.LON.187   185

The statue scene from *The Winter's Tale*.
The Illustrated London News, 12 October 1878   189

'Master Gussy Harris: What Will He Do With It?'
The Entr'Acte, 1 November 1879   198

Colour illustrations between pages 148 and 149

Edmund Falconer as Danny Mann and Agnes Robertson as Eily O' Connor in *The Colleen Bawn*, Adelphi Theatre, 1861. Watercolour by Egron Sellif Lundgren. Royal Collection Trust/© HM Queen Elizabeth II 2019

Dundag Bay with the Royal Family in the foreground, one of six scenes in the panorama of the Lakes of Killarney, *Little Red Riding Hood*, Lyceum Theatre 1861. Watercolour by William Telbin © Victoria and Albert Museum, London

Watercolour of the auditorium of Drury Lane as it was in the 1860s/1870s. Houghton Library, Harvard Library, Harvard University

Frederick Balsir Chatterton, pencil and watercolour by Frederick Sem ('Sem'), 1869, National Portrait Gallery, London © National Portrait Gallery, London

Dion Boucicault, pencil and watercolour by Frederick Sem ('Sem'), 1869, National Portrait Gallery, London © National Portrait Gallery, London

Acknowledgements

The name of the London Library appears on the acknowledgements page of many books, accompanied by tributes to its unique character and helpful staff. In my case, I must give it precedence over all others as this book could not have been written without access to its bound collection of *The Times* from 1807 onwards. The bedrock of my research was a series of spreadsheets that I compiled from *The Times* showing every performance at Drury Lane from 1862 to 1879. I initially thought this would simply be a matter of looking at the theatre listings for each day and noting down the names of the various pieces in the bill. However I soon realised that a wealth of further information was contained in the classified advertising that preceded these listings. Managers used this additional space to tell readers about the play, the stars, the running times and the details of booking seats. Of course, *The Times* has been digitised and all of this information is now accessible online, but it's not the same. First of all, it takes longer to find small classified advertisements within the file for each day's paper than it takes to turn the pages. Secondly, you don't get the same sense of where the advertisements are in the paper and on the page, and how much advertising other theatres were taking. This was particularly important to me as Chatterton pioneered the use of newspaper advertising in marketing shows, and as I turned the pages through the years I could see the Drury Lane section of the column grow and grow. I found myself entering a sort of trance-like state which enabled me to spot small changes as new material was added or bits were cut. On alternate Monday evenings, when London Library staff conduct tours for prospective members, I listened to them explaining the advantages of being able to access the paper in hard copy form. I heard the talk so often I could easily give it myself, and I was once asked by a reader working beside me if I was an actor paid by the Library to demonstrate the usefulness of the Times Room. I must thank the Society for Theatre Research for a grant to turn this database into a Drury Lane Calendar on my website (www.jacobtonson.com/repertoire).

I have drawn heavily on the resources of the Theatre and Performance Collection of the Victoria and Albert Museum and of the British Library, especially the newspaper section where I was able to inspect what I suspect is the last remaining set of copies of Chatterton's vanity publishing project *Touchstone or The New Era*. The performing arts collection at the Westminster Reference Library provided a rich vein of material to mine, especially its invaluable run of *The Era*. Moira Goff, librarian of the Garrick Club, made me welcome, as did the librarians and staff of the Medway Archives and Local Studies Centre; Special Collections, University of Kent Library; Wandsworth Heritage Services; Lambeth Archives; Bishopsgate Institute; Royal Institute of British Architects; Killarney Library; and Queen Mary College, University of London. I was helpfully supplied with material by the Folger Shakespeare Library, Washington, the University of Nottingham Library and the Houghton Library at Harvard University, which seems to have the only copy in the world of Chatterton's pamphlet containing the complaint and answer between himself and Edmund Falconer in the 1865 court case. Melanie Bunch, hon. archivist and historian of St George's Cathedral, Southwark, told me about the memorial window to John Oxenford. I found The Adelphi Theatre Calendar (part of the London Stage Project 1800 – 1900) very helpful and Arthur Lloyd's Music Hall and Theatre website (www.arthurlloyd.co.uk) has been a mine of information. I am grateful to Görel Garlick for generously sharing her incomparable knowledge of nineteenth-century theatre architecture. My proof-readers, Jonathan Axworthy and Mark Fox, saved me from many errors. All remaining mistakes are, of course, my own.

Chatterton is the invisible man in most histories of Drury Lane, recalled only for his famous aphorism, but the late American scholar Daniel Barrett paid him the unusual compliment of taking him seriously as a producer of Shakespeare in his article '"Shakespeare spelt ruin and Byron bankruptcy": Shakespeare at Chatterton's Drury Lane', published in *Theatre Survey* in 1988.

Thanks are due to the President and Fellows of Harvard University for permission to reproduce the monochrome watercolour depicting the auditorium of Drury Lane in the colour section. It is one of a series of thirty-eight such images of London theatre interiors signed 'A. B.', assigned to A. Boycott, although no artist of that name is known. They form part of the theatre collection of Harvard University and are held in the Houghton Library, Harvard Library, Harvard University (MS Thr 434). They carry dates between 1864 and 1871 although some, including the Drury Lane illustration, are undated. They were first published in an article by Richard Southern that appeared in *Theatre Notebook*, the journal of the Society for Theatre Research, in 1950. Southern drew attention to the fact that the style of the watercolours does not suggest the dates attributed to them. He commented on the 'severe and highly conventionalised – almost Japanese – tone effect instead of the elaborate multiplicity of detail seen in most of the work of the time' (Southern, 59) and suggested that their style was closer to that of Aubrey Beardsley, the Beggarstaff Brothers or Edward Gordon Craig. He speculated that they represent an early-twentieth-century reworking of a set of presumably lost mid-Victorian images. The watercolours were acquired from a bookseller in the Charing Cross Road who had in turn acquired them from Edward Anthony Craig, the son of Edward Gordon Craig, so Southern's hypothesis is plausible.

The modern equivalents (2018 values) of monetary amounts are taken from the Bank of England's Inflation Calculator.

Finally, I am indebted to John Balsir Chatterton for letting me read and quote from letters written by his ancestor. They provided a rare opportunity to hear the authentic voice of FBC, unmediated by the flowery prose of his publicist Charles Lamb Kenney.

Preface

In October 1855, a young actor called John Coleman went with two friends to Drury Lane to see its latest offering: a spectacular drama set in ancient Egypt called *Nitocris*. The dress circle was full and Coleman didn't want to sit in the pit, so he and his friends took three seats at the back of the first circle. Finding that he had left his opera-glasses at home, and wanting to get a good look at sets and costumes that were said to be the most lavish ever seen at Drury Lane, Coleman asked the box-keeper to find him some. The young man obliged him, but as soon as he had left, three more men turned up claiming the seats as their own. A fight ensued during which Coleman received a black eye and gave two. The police were called and the three interlopers were charged. The next morning they were fined forty shillings each plus costs.

Coleman remembered the incident well when he turned theatrical biographer many years later, because the twenty-one-year old box-keeper who found him the opera glasses was Frederick Balsir Chatterton. The next time Coleman saw him at Drury Lane, he was running the theatre.

Nitocris, Drury Lane, 1855

Chatterton is the subject of this book, but it seems only fair to begin by saying something about Coleman since, without him, a biography of Chatterton would have been an almost impossible task.

Coleman wrote an autobiography called *Fifty Years of an Actor's Life* that was published in 1904, a few weeks after his death. It is a remarkable document, recording a long career in the theatre working under circumstances that were so different from those pertaining at the time of publication that he must have seemed like a dinosaur to younger readers.

Born into an Irish Catholic family in Derby in 1830,[1] Coleman was destined for the priesthood but had to be removed from the seminary when his mother died as there was no money to pay the fees. After reading a biography of William Betty, the child-star known as 'The Infant Roscius' who had been the theatrical sensation of the first decade of the century, Coleman decided to become an actor. He managed to get himself to London where he presented himself at the stage door of Sadler's Wells on the first day of Samuel Phelps's legendary eighteen-year management, asking for a job. He was turned away for being too young at fourteen. He got the same answer at Drury Lane. He got work in Windsor, then Leicester, Manchester and other cities. In the nineteenth century, with films, radio and TV many decades in the future, there was a flourishing theatre culture all around the country: most towns had a theatre and cities had several. This would become Coleman's world, first acting in and then managing these regional theatres. They were often grouped in circuits, with the acting company moving from one town to another on a weekly basis if there wasn't enough demand for a full-time theatre in each town. He managed the Worcester circuit, moving between Worcester, Shrewsbury and Coventry, and tried to revive Tait Wilkinson's famous York circuit, buying the theatre in Leeds and leasing the one in York. He formed the 'Famous Company of the Great Northern Circuit', including Hull, Doncaster, Lincoln, Liverpool, Glasgow and the Isle of Man. By the end of the nineteenth centuries these circuits had long since closed down, and the larger regional theatres were no longer producing managements for most of the year, acting as receiving houses for touring productions of West End hits. Coleman's book is the last glimpse we can catch of this vigorous regional theatre culture before its demise.

Coleman is frank about his flops but he also had some big hits, like a spectacular production of *Uncle Tom's Cabin* which opened in Leeds in the 1850s and which he was still presenting in Glasgow and

Edinburgh twenty years later. However, then as now, London was the pinnacle of all theatrical ambition and Coleman was keen to get into the West End. In 1876 he took the lease of the Queen's Theatre in Longacre, Covent Garden, with disastrous results that will be recounted later. After this, he returned to the provinces, where his career as an actor/manager went into decline.

The lure of the West End remained strong, and in 1882 Coleman produced Robert Buchanan's stage version of his own novel *The Shadow of the Sword* at Brighton. He took it into the Olympic Theatre, off Drury Lane, where it flopped.[2] By this stage, Coleman's wife was seriously ill and he needed a position in London to be near her doctors. He claims to have turned down job offers from Augustus Harris, Herbert Beerbohm Tree and Richard D'Oyly Carte as unsuitable, then set up as an author.

Coleman had already written some plays, either translations or adaptations of novels, and a short novel of his own,[3] but he now focused on dramatic biography. In 1886 he published his first attempt in the genre: *Memoirs of Samuel Phelps*, co-written with his son Edward. Coleman had worked with Phelps on the York circuit and regarded him as a friend. The two men had spent a long holiday together on the Isle of Man during which Phelps told Coleman the story of his life. Coleman wrote these narratives down and after Phelps's death turned them into a memoir, in which the subject tells his story in his own words.

It must have occurred to Coleman that, at the end of a long career in the theatre, he knew enough about other famous 'names' to produce a series of short biographies, or brief lives, that would focus on his own encounters with his subjects without necessarily doing the full biographical rigmarole. This turned into *Players and Playwrights I Have Known* in 1888.

In two volumes, Coleman gave brief overviews of the careers of eighteen actors and playwrights, most of whom he had known personally. They are unbalanced in the sense that they focus on the periods when their careers overlapped with Coleman's, with other periods glossed over, but they form a valuable source of information about people who were 'names' in their day but are largely forgotten now. All of Coleman's subjects were dead at the time he started work on the book with one exception: Frederick Balsir Chatterton. Coleman and Chatterton had never worked together, as Chatterton's career had been in the West End and Coleman's mainly in the provinces, and they had fallen out at the time of Coleman's management of the Queen's in

1876. However, after Chatterton's bankruptcy in 1879, Coleman heard that he was being shunned by those who had formerly courted him, and was living a lonely life in a lodging-house off the Strand. Coleman sought him out and they made up the rift, after which Chatterton developed a fondness for dropping in on Coleman in the evening when they would have a drink and talk about old times. Chatterton's accounts of his own career were so interesting that Coleman began writing them down. He became the Boswell to Chatterton's Johnson, compiling transcripts of Chatterton's narratives which he then gave to Chatterton to correct. When Chatterton died in 1886, Coleman decided to work these transcripts up into a chapter for his book. As a result, most of the chapter on Chatterton appears between quotation marks, like Coleman's memoir of Phelps. It is the only chapter in the book that is mainly autobiography rather than biography, and without it we would know very little about the last man who ran Drury Lane as the National Theatre.

Coleman divided his subjects into 'Victors' and 'Vanquished', with Chatterton's sad story concluding the latter section. Chatterton survived for only seven years after his downfall in 1879, dying at the age of fifty-one. However, he lived long enough to see Augustus Harris, his successor at Drury Lane, turn the theatre into a successful, profit-making venture by throwing overboard all concepts of Drury Lane as the National Theatre and home of the higher drama. Chatterton told Coleman that he feared his work would be forgotten, and that he felt almost forgotten already. He was right about that. His funeral was sparsely attended, with none of London's theatre managers turning up to honour the man who had been for so long the most powerful of them all. He was buried in the same grave as his father and mother, but his name was never cut into the tombstone. When I wrote a history of Drury Lane,[4] I discovered that he was one of only two people who had been in charge of the Lane over three-and-a-half centuries who was not commemorated in the *Oxford Dictionary of National Biography*. (The other one was Arthur Collins.) I was asked to rectify the omission, which I was happy to do, but I felt that more was owing to the memory of the man for whom Shakespeare spelt ruin and Byron bankruptcy. This book is the result.

1

The Youth of Chatterton

Frederick Balsir Chatterton was born on 17 September 1834 in Seymour Street (now Eversholt Street) beside Euston Station, the eldest child of Edward and Amelia. His father Edward was one of the sons of Frederick Chatterton, a professor of music in Portsmouth. (It was a family tradition to have a Frederick in each generation. Where there is a danger of confusion, the subject of this biography, who called his eldest son Frederick, will be referred to as FBC.) This Portsmouth Frederick had inherited a fortune that was supposed to be entailed, but he managed to un-entail it and spend the lot. His idea for restoring the family fortunes was to turn his sons into famous harpists, and he was successful in two cases. The eldest, John Balsir Chatterton (1804 – 1871) and the youngest, Frederick Chatterton (1814 – 1894), both responded to the challenge and became the two leading harpists in the country. John Balsir became harpist by appointment to Queen Victoria, but Frederick was regarded as the better player. The rivalry between the two of them became so poisonous that their brother Edward never ceased to warn FBC of the terrible consequences of family feuds. FBC was closer to his Uncle Frederick, who would be in the Drury Lane orchestra pit for many of his nephew's productions, whilst: 'I never see my Uncle John by any chance, and we never take any notice of each other when we do meet.'[1]

Edward Andrew Chatterton (1809/10 – 1875) refused to go down the harpist route. He resisted all attempts to steer him into a profession and became, in his son's words, a Jack-of-all-trades including music publisher and vendor of musical instruments.[2] He was described on his son's birth certificate as a tailor, but he does not appear to have done that for long. For most of his career he was working in the front-of-house of various London theatres, which is how his son came to think about a career on the stage.

This was not his father's plan for him at all. Edward Chatterton might have resisted his own father's attempts to make a harpist of him, but he wanted his own son to enjoy a professional status that would ensure that he was not socially inferior to his cousins. Young FBC was to be a professor of music, and was put to train under William Aspull, brother of a musical child prodigy called George Aspull. Apart from this musical instruction, Frederick's education was distinctly patchy, as his father's uncertain income meant that he was constantly being withdrawn from schools in the absence of the money for fees. Aspull did his best to encourage his young pupil to improve his literacy by going to the British Museum Reading Room and devouring as many books as possible. However, according to FBC, his gateway to the world of literature was through a penny edition of Shakespeare that was being published in weekly parts. 'I used to invest in a "penn'orth" each week and carry it about in my jacket pocket, morning, noon and night, reading it in the streets, or anywhere I could get a chance, till I had learnt the "bard" almost by heart.'[3] Whatever gaps there may have been in his education, the young Chatterton acquired a deep love of Shakespeare that would profoundly affect his career in theatre management.

FBC had four younger siblings: Isabella, Percy, Kate and Horace. There was a gap of fifteen years between him and Horace, the baby of the family, to whom he became deeply attached while nursing him through a serious childhood illness. As soon as he was earning, FBC took charge of the education of his younger brothers and made sure they were trained for the professions, unlike himself. They looked up to him, partly because of the age-gap and partly because he grew up extraordinarily quickly. He determined at a young age to restore the fortune of his family that had been squandered by his grandfather, and his siblings trusted him to do it. The question was how. At the age of fourteen FBC was listed in the Post Office directory as a 'Professor of the Harp', earning his living as a music teacher by day whilst helping his father with the front-of-house management of the Marylebone Theatre by night. However, the day-job didn't appeal: he was no more eager to make his mark as a harpist than his father had been. He wanted a career in the theatre, but this would be in the teeth of opposition from his family.

When FBC was small, his father was box office manager of Sadler's Wells Theatre in Islington, run by Tom Greenwood. His earliest memories were of growing up behind the scenes there, and he was desperately keen to appear in the pantomime. His parents were opposed to the idea, but he badgered Greenwood until he was given a small part at the rate of sixpence a night. When his uncles, who were establishing themselves as the leading harpists of the day, heard of this, they rebuked Edward Chatterton for disgracing the family name by allowing his eldest son to be 'kicked and cuffed about by the clown' and, after a very few performances, FBC left the cast.

Denied the chance to go on the stage professionally, he gratified his Thespian yearnings with amateur dramatics. The Victorian passion for amateur dramatics was so widespread that there were several theatres in London catering specifically for them.[4] Anyone could hire one of these theatres by the day or the week and recoup the cost by selling parts to other amateurs. When he was seventeen, Chatterton became acquainted with a young man three years older than himself called Henry Jennings who was eking out his eighteen-shillings-a-week salary as a solicitor's clerk by acting as an amateur impresario. Chatterton and Jennings decided to stage a production of Henry Spicer's drama *The Lords of Ellingham* at the Cabinet Theatre in King's Cross. As part of the deal Chatterton was given twelve shillings-worth of tickets to sell, for which he had to pay three shillings. He had no difficulty in disposing of them, so he made a profit of nine shillings as well as getting his part in the play for nothing. 'From that moment… I made up my mind to be a manager.' He then decided to turn impresario on his own account and produced *Othello* with himself as the Moor. A clerk in the railway clearing house paid £2 for Cassio, an ironnmonger in the Edgware Road was Iago for 30 shillings, Roderigo paid 7s. 6d., while Brabantio, Montano and Lodovico went for 3s. 6d. As his total outgoings amounted to £2 15s., he had made a profit of £1 13s. before he even started selling tickets.

Whilst leading this double life as music teacher by day and amateur impresario by night, Chatterton married Mary Ann Williams at St George's Church in Bloomsbury on 13 October 1853. He was nineteen and she was twenty-five. His profession was given on the marriage certificate as 'Professor of Music', whilst his father's, rather optimistically, was given as 'gentleman'. Edward Chatterton's career in the front-of-house of various London theatres came nowhere near to qualifying him as a gentleman, but the vicar of St George's probably didn't know the family, who lived in Lisson Grove. It may have been an attempt to impress the in-laws, as the bride's father, Samuel Williams, was a dairyman in Waterloo.

Gentleman or not, Edward Chatterton eventually had to accept that his eldest son was never going to be a harpist (although his daughter Kate would carry on the family tradition) and that opposition to his theatrical ambitions was pointless. Edward was running the box office at Drury Lane and managed to get FBC a job in the front of house for the 1855/56 season, which is where he met John Coleman on the night of the disturbance at *Nitocris*. Still only twenty-one, FBC was regarded within his family as 'a very promising young man' who 'before long… will be independent of anyone'.[5] After the close of the Drury Lane season, FBC was hired by the actor Charles Dillon, who had just taken the lease on the Lyceum, to be his acting manager.

2

The Lyceum Years

During Samuel Phelps's eighteen-year management of Sadler's Wells Theatre in Islington, in which he staged all but six of Shakespeare's plays, he would occasionally let the theatre to visiting companies when he needed a break. One of these lettings occurred in the spring of 1856, when George Webster took the Wells for two months. During this brief management, Webster presented a production of *Belphegor*, a drama by Charles Webb about a strolling mountebank who suffers the loss of his wife and child but has to keep on performing for coins donated by passers-by. Webster took the opportunity to introduce to London audiences in the title role an actor who had been enjoying success in the provinces called Charles Dillon. The extraordinary success of Samuel Phelps's management of Sadler's Wells had attracted West End theatregoers and critics who would not normally venture as far as Islington, but it was still unusual for a national paper to review a show in what was described as 'that almost suburban temple of the drama… little regarded beyond its own immediate neighbourhood'.[1] However, George Webster was the nephew of Benjamin Webster, who ran the Haymarket and the Adelphi Theatres for many years, and he was able to use his connections as a scion of a theatrical dynasty to get John Oxenford, theatre critic of *The Times*, to review his production of *Belphegor*.

Oxenford started his review by emphasising the wide gap that separated something that was acceptable in the provinces from the standard required in London. However, he went on to give Dillon's performance an excellent review, praising him for his sincerity, his naturalness and his pathos.[2] The review made Dillon a star overnight.

On the strength of his success at Sadler's Wells, Dillon was able to set himself up as a manager, obtaining the lease of the Lyceum Theatre, where he opened in September 1856. Chatterton was hired as his acting manager, in charge of the box office. A classified advertisement in *The Times*, just before the season began, directed those wishing to book tickets to 'Mr Chatterton junior' in the box office.[3] The 'junior' was necessary because his father Edward was already well known to theatregoers as the box office manager at Drury Lane,[4] and the fact that FBC had been put in charge of the Lyceum box office before his twenty-second birthday certainly suggests that he would be relying on his experienced senior to show him how things were managed in that important theatrical space.

Belphegor provided the backbone of the repertoire at the Lyceum until December, but on 5 December Dillon appeared for the first time in London as William Tell. The performance was a benefit, but the most surprising thing about it was the identity of the beneficiary, who was none other than Mr Chatterton junior.

Benefit performances had been introduced on the English stage in the last part of the seventeenth century. The beneficiary, who would have been one of the most popular members of the acting company, received the takings of the house minus a deduction for the running costs. This could represent a very large amount of money, and it had the advantage of being paid immediately, whereas salaries were often weeks or months in arrears. Star status was reflected in the terms the star could extract for his or her benefit, such as the timing of it and the extent of the deductions (none in some cases) from managers anxious to secure their services. This was still the case at the start of the nineteenth century, but benefit performances became less frequent as the century progressed. By the mid-to-late nineteenth century, the terms on which actors were employed had changed radically with long runs replacing the repertory system. Actors were often hired on run-of-the-play contracts instead of being contracted for the whole theatrical season, and benefits were a casualty of these changes. However the same period saw the emergence of benefits for theatre managers – not just actor-managers but managers who never appeared before the public. This seems strange as the receipts from a benefit – the night's takings minus the running costs – would have belonged to the manager anyway. Nevertheless, such benefits became routine. Sometimes benefits would be held for other members of the production team who had fallen on hard times, such as May the costumier who suffered heavy losses when Her Majesty's Theatre went up in flames.[5] However, to hold a benefit for anyone below the level of the manager or lessee was so rare as to be almost unheard of,[6] so how did Chatterton obtain this favour within three months of starting in his first responsible position in a London theatre? One possible explanation is that Chatterton, young and inexperienced as he was, had already made himself useful to Dillon on the financial side of things.[7] Dillon was, and would always remain, hopeless with money. Chatterton helped him out, even to the extent of lending Dillon money, which he would have cause to regret. His benefit was probably the pay-back for one of these loans.

The night after Chatterton's benefit saw another play joining the Lyceum repertoire: a new blank-verse drama in five acts called *The Cagot*. Its author, so completely unknown that his name did not appear on any of the publicity, was an Irish actor called Edmund O'Rourke whom Dillon had brought into London from the provinces to join his Lyceum company. The plot of the play drew heavily on *Il Trovatore* and was so complicated that the first night audience struggled to follow it. Nevertheless, it was well received and there was a call at the end for the author. This resulted in:

> … the appearance of a modest-looking gentleman, who bowed his acknowledgements as he crossed the stage. The actors were then called in succession, and Mr Barrett, in his capacity as stage manager, announced the piece for repetition tomorrow… amid universal applause. He was then called upon to name the author… The name of Falkner was accordingly given, with the addition that its owner had written several poems, and was a distinguished provincial actor.[8]

Edmund O'Rourke had taken Falconer as his stage-name, and his meeting with Chatterton at the Lyceum would change the courses of both of their lives. *The Cagot* received seven performances over the course of the season, so it wasn't a great success, but it wasn't a flop either. Falconer had established his London credentials as a playwright.

Dillon's first season at the Lyceum went well, with the actor-manager appearing as Belphegor, as D'Artagnan in an adaptation of *The Three Musketeers* and as Othello. The 'country actor' was well received, despite the fact that he was entering a competitive market, with Samuel Phelps at Sadler's Wells, Charles Kean presenting spectacular Shakespearean revivals at the Princess's Theatre, and John Buckstone's prestigious management at the Haymarket. Nevertheless, the seeds of the destruction of Dillon's management were already sown. On top of his inability to handle money and manage debt, Dillon lived a louche lifestyle, drinking heavily and paying too little attention to his duties as a manager. Coleman gives him a chapter in *Players and Playwrights I Have Known* which is included in the section of the book called 'The Vanquished'. Dillon comes across as a sort of Dickensian character, hopelessly disorganised, dishonest, drunk and unreliable. At a time when actors were trying to get away from their 'rogues and vagabonds' image to become respectable, Dillon refused to conform to the ordinary rules of social conduct. He sub-let the Lyceum for opera and magic acts during the summer and autumn of 1857, not opening his own productions until Boxing Day. His management finally collapsed in March 1858.

Dillon petitioned for bankruptcy on 8 April and there was a hearing on 27 May, postponed for six weeks to allow Dillon to present his accounts. It took Dillon until September to do this, when he disclosed a long list of creditors, including £2,076 (over a quarter of a million pounds in modern values) owed to his father-in-law Benjamin Conquest, landlord of the famous Eagle Tavern on City Road. When Dillon married Conquest's daughter Clara, who was an actress, Conquest had been happy to finance his son-in-law's ventures, but when Dillon began an affair with another actress during the Lyceum season and his marriage to Clara broke down, Conquest became a demanding creditor.

The *Times*'s report of the bankruptcy proceedings reveals that Chatterton had engaged counsel to represent him, and his counsel requested clarification of a statement made by Dillon's counsel to the effect that Chatterton had not paid any rent for the box office during the last season. A document was produced, signed by Dillon, stating that Chatterton had indeed duly accounted for all proceeds arising from the weekly rental of the box office up to 25 March 1858 (the last day of Dillon's management). This is interesting for several reasons. First, it shows how Chatterton was ready to instruct counsel, even in cases that did not directly affect him; secondly, it reveals that Chatterton had not been simply an employee, but was running the box office on some sort of franchise arrangement (perhaps devised by his father); and thirdly, it shows how sensitive Chatterton was to any insinuation of dishonest dealing. Whatever failings he may have had, Chatterton was scrupulously honest and would not allow anyone to say otherwise.[9]

The suggestion that he was in any way responsible for Dillon's failure would have been especially galling as he was himself one of the disappointed creditors. He had lent Dillon every penny he could raise to keep his management afloat and now had very little chance of seeing his capital again. 'I do not despair,' he wrote to a relative. 'I can tell you I have all the Chatterton pluck and can take a rare quantity of beating before I cry enough.'[10]

When Dillon's management collapsed, Falconer's next play was actually in rehearsal. It was a three-act comedy called *Extremes* and Falconer, unwilling to lose his work, suggested to Chatterton that they should go into partnership and hire the Lyceum themselves to present his play. Chatterton agreed and they opened with *Extremes* on 26

August 1858. The play lasted for four hours (Falconer's plays were all criticised for their excessive length) but the audience liked it. John Oxenford gave it a good review in *The Times*, praising its witty dialogue which got better as the play went on.[11] It ran until 23 October, when it had to come off because the theatre had been booked for a series of promenade concerts by Louis Jullien throughout November and December. However, a winter season, 'under the same management', was promised, opening on 26 December.

Chatterton had taken a benefit performance on 4 October, choosing Sheridan Knowles's drama *The Hunchback* instead of another performance of *Extremes*, but the public must have wondered who this beneficiary was. Chatterton's name did not appear in the management billing, which simply stated 'Manager Mr E. Falconer', and we only find out from later classified advertisements that his role was that of 'treasurer' – we would say finance director. From the very beginning of his relationship with Falconer, he was the money man, and he had to get his father to guarantee £500 (over £60,000 today) for the rent, in spite of the success of *Extremes*. Edward Chatterton now recognised that his son had a real talent for theatre management and from this point on did everything possible to assist him.

Chatterton and Falconer opened their second spell in charge of the Lyceum on Boxing Day 1858 with a burlesque of Homer's *Iliad* called *The Siege of Troy* followed by a pantomime called *Harlequin Toy Horse*. The show was a financial disaster. Falconer had told Chatterton that he could produce *The Siege of Troy* for £500 but it cost £1,500. It had over sixty speaking parts, thirty of which were cut after the third performance to reduce the excessive length – the *Times* review had complained of three-and-a-half hours without a break. The review also mentioned that the machinery jammed on the first night, spoiling the scenic effects, and that there was little to say about the pantomime, 'the tricks being few and not very novel'.[12] Falconer and Chatterton had taken the unusual step of opening with a Boxing Day matinee, and the first two houses were good – £200 for the matinee and £215 for the evening performance – but word-of-mouth killed the bookings, which went down to £50 on the second day and continued to fall. Chatterton had already borrowed money from his father to mount the show and had to borrow a further £300 (over £36,000 today) to pay salaries. Falconer was in talks with two potential backers, so Chatterton said that, if they would guarantee the next week's salaries, he would withdraw altogether. This offer was accepted.

Falconer continued with the management of the Lyceum, trying to cover the deficiencies of *The Siege of Troy* by putting on melodramas starring Madame Céleste. Madame Céleste was a popular and successful actress, especially in melodramas, as well as having a long track record of theatre management at the Adelphi which she ran with her long-term partner Benjamin Webster. After a serious disagreement with Webster (who held the freehold of the Adelphi) she was looking for opportunities elsewhere. She appeared at the Lyceum in *Marion de Lorme, The Sister's Sacrifice* and a trusty old standby called *The Child of the Wreck*. Falconer then organised a season of Irish-themed plays starring Irish-American actor Barney Williams (described by one critic as a 'conventional Paddywhack, stuffed-stick Irishman')[13] who lasted for only two weeks, after which Falconer put in some more performances of *Extremes* to keep the theatre open while he prepared his next play: *Francesca: A Dream of Venice*. It opened on 31 March and ran for only four performances. On 16 April the theatre closed and was advertised to be let with immediate possession. Madame Céleste offered Falconer £500 for the remainder of his lease, which he was glad to accept.

Chatterton, meanwhile, was by no means deterred from theatrical management by his bad experience at the Lyceum. 'I had tasted blood, and could not keep out of speculation.'[14] He persuaded his father to back him in taking the lease of the St James's Theatre in King Street. Built in 1835 for the successful tenor John Braham, the St James's soon became known as 'Braham's Folly'. The main problem was its location which, in spite of being in one of the most fashionable parts of London, was considered too far west of the theatre district to attract audiences.[15] As a result, it was available for a low rent, so Chatterton became the lessee, but with his father really in charge. At twenty-five, he was the youngest manager in the West End and still very inexperienced for such a venture. Edward Chatterton gave up his position in the box office at Drury Lane and moved to the St James's box office to keep a close eye on things. They were probably jointly responsible for the decision to offer low prices – described as 'transpontine prices' in a West End theatre (transpontine being the term used to described less prestigious theatres south of the Thames) – of five shillings in the stalls, three shillings in the dress circle, one shilling in the pit and sixpence in the gallery. FBC also tried to counter the perception of the theatre's poor location by emphasising in his classified advertising that the St James's was the 'nearest theatre to Chelsea, Pimlico, Westminster, Knightsbridge, Brompton, Kensington and Bayswater, the park being open to carriages and foot passengers all hours of the night'.

Chatterton opened on Saturday 1 October 1859 with a triple bill: *The Widow's Wedding*, a comedy by Edward Fitzball, followed by

Leicester Buckingham's burlesque *Virginius*, followed by a farce called *A Dead Shot*. *The Times* reported a successful evening with an enthusiastic audience who were prepared to applaud everything, in spite of the fact that the pieces themselves were weak and far below the level of the company Chatterton had assembled: 'With drama that would to any extent develop the resources of his company he might probably reverse the ill fortune so long associated with the most Western theatre in London.' The critic did, however, note the excellence of the *corps de ballet*, and in particular 'Miss Lydia Thompson, who… is well known as one of the most eminent of English dancers… The new manager evidently intends that Terpsichorean art shall be duly cultivated at this theatre.'[16]

The critic was in a position to know whereof he spoke, because three nights later Chatterton put on a ballet-farce with songs called *Magic Toys*, starring Lydia Thompson and adapted from the French vaudeville *Les Pantins de Violette* by none other than *Times* critic John Oxenford. Oxenford wrote a favourable notice for *The Times*, praising Lydia

The St James's Theatre

Thompson who appeared in four different costumes performing four different styles of dance in a piece that only lasted forty-five minutes. 'With such a dancer as Miss Lydia Thompson, and such vocal actresses as Miss St. Casse and Miss Eliza Arden, the manager is well supplied with supporters of the highest kind of drama.'[17] Although reviews were unsigned in those days, everyone involved with the London theatre would have known that Oxenford was reviewing his own work, or at the very least getting it reviewed by his assistant who would not have dared to offend him.[18] This would be considered a serious conflict of interest today, but at the time 'those amphibious authors – half journalist, half dramatist – who become their own insurers by writing the critiques of their own works'[19] were not breaking any rules. The position of dramatic critic was low-status and poorly paid: even Oxenford, the acknowledged leader of the *corps dramatique* who was always provided with a private box on opening nights, received only five pounds a week.[20] Reviewers were therefore expected to have other sources of income and most dramatic critics were also playwrights and translators of plays, which meant that they were selling their wares to the managers whose shows they were reviewing. As one theatregoer complained, impartial dramatic criticism was a vain hope while 'the dramatic critics of the leading journals… are more or less dramatic authors'.[21] In spite of the recognised drawbacks, the situation was accepted as inevitable since, as the playwright and critic Shirley Brooks told a parliamentary committee: 'unless the critic is mixed up with theatrical people, he will hardly be qualified for his task, and if he is much mixed up with them, he seems very liable to all such influences'.[22]

Oxenford wrote over seventy melodramas, comedies, farces, libretti and ballets, many of them adaptations or translations.[23] Most of these are now forgotten, although his farce *A Day Well Spent* (Lyceum, 4 April 1836) inspired Thornton Wilder's *The Merchant of Yonkers* which in turn became *Hello Dolly!* He was far from alone in adopting the dual role of critic and dramatist, but the stature of *The Times* as the most important paper in Europe, coupled with Oxenford's length of tenure from 1839 to 1875, meant that he could set the tone for relationships between critics and managers.[24]

Oxenford had a genius for summarising the important elements of complex plots, which makes his reviews useful to theatre historians. They were less useful to readers who were wondering if a show was actually worth seeing, because he tried to avoid giving bad reviews. According to Edmund Yates, who knew him well, Oxenford had, in his very early days at *The Times*, given a bad review to an actor who responded with a letter of protest to John Delane, the editor.

Delane showed Oxenford the letter and told him to write his reviews in such a manner as to prevent any further letters of that nature from being addressed to the editor of *The Times*. Theatre, he told Oxenford, 'is of very little consequence to the great body of our readers, and I could not think of letting the paper become the field for argument on the point'.[25]

Oxenford preferred to give a less embarrassing reason for the blandness of his reviews, boasting that 'it was the brightest remembrance of his life that during [his] long career he had never written a word which would send a man home to find his wife and children crying'.[26] A more cynical interpretation of the unwillingness to write killer reviews would be that Oxenford was selling his plays to the managers who provided him with his first night box, so he was unlikely to bite the hand that was signing his cheques. His relationship with Chatterton was hopelessly compromised from the start because Chatterton, realising the importance of getting *The Times* onside, produced pieces by Oxenford throughout his career in management: at the Lyceum, the St James's, Rochester, Drury Lane, Hull, the Adelphi and the Princess's. Oxenford would become a personal friend and a guest at Chatterton's house.[27] Even when Oxenford wasn't selling his own plays, he was known to accept substantial 'retainers' from managers to read and edit a play before it was put into rehearsal, thus virtually guaranteeing a good review in *The Times*.[28]

Burlesque was at the height of its popularity when Chatterton took over the St James's, and in so far as his management could be described as having a tone, burlesque was it. Burlesque was a parody or spoof of some well known narrative from classical mythology, English history, Shakespeare or some other respectable source. It shared some elements of pantomime, such as men dragged up as absurd female characters and heroes played by pretty girls in tights, but it was a bit more literary, assuming some knowledge of the source material in the audience. Chatterton opened with *Virginius*, a burlesque of Sheridan Knowles's ponderous tragedy about a Roman senator; followed a few weeks later by *The Swan and Edgar*, based on the Swan Lake story that later became Tchaikovsky's ballet; followed in February by *Dido*, the first piece for the stage written by Frank Burnand, just down from Cambridge, and based on the Dido and Aeneas episode from *The Aeneid*.[29] These shows had respectable runs – sixteen performances for *The Swan and Edgar*, forty-six for *Virginius* and sixty for *Dido* – and provided the backbone for the repertoire, as there were three or four items on the bill every night, so these popular short pieces could be kept rotating throughout the season.

The 'legitimate drama' was not completely neglected, and on 9 November Chatterton staged *London Pride*, a comedy by James Kenney who had died in 1849 after a successful forty-year career as a playwright. The play had been written in five acts, which was by this time considered an outdated format, so it was cut to three by the author's son, Charles Lamb Kenney (named after his godfather Charles Lamb who had been a family friend). Charles Lamb Kenney was also the co-author (with Sutherland Edwards) of *The Swan & Edgar* that was staged as the afterpiece to *London Pride*. This would be the beginning of a long association between Chatterton and Kenney.

Chatterton's management of the St James's was described as the most successful in its twenty-five-year history.[30] In March he indulged his own taste for the higher drama by presenting his old boss Charles Dillon for a few nights in *Belphegor*, *The King's Musketeers* and *The Lady of Lyons*, then in August twelve nights of the Irish Shakespearean actor Barry Sullivan in *Macbeth*, *Hamlet* and *Richard III*. The theatre was sub-let to a company of French actors who appeared in plays performed in French (a tradition at the St James's) between 28 May and 1 August. The season was still running in September, nominally under FBC, but in reality he was depending on his father to keep the ship afloat by this stage. 'I came a cropper,' he told John Coleman, 'mainly owing to an unfortunate lawsuit with [the actor] Sam Emery.'[31] He doesn't say what the lawsuit was about but it would be the first of many. Edward Chatterton saved the day by disposing of the lease of the St James's to actor-manager Alfred Wigan. The Chattertons were probably relieved to be clear of the St James's which had an association with failure so strong as to almost become a self-fulfilling prophecy. Charles Lamb Kenney later described it as: 'an establishment whose history seems as naturally and indissolubly connected with abortive dramatic schemes as an orthopaedic hospital with distortions of the human frame, and which has sheltered them in almost as great and instructive variety'.[32]

Young Chatterton's next experiment in management took place outside London, without any assistance from his father, and turned into a disaster. He took on the lease of the Theatre Royal, Rochester, where he opened on 17 November 1860 with a triple bill of *A Friend in Need*, *The Daughter of the Regiment* and *The Middy Ashore*. He was billed as 'Lessee and Manager Mr F. B. Chatterton (late Lessee of the Royal St James's Theatre London)'. The review in the local paper was not encouraging: 'We wish we could congratulate Mr Chatterton on the success of his new undertaking; but the performances on Saturday evening and during the early part of the week were but thinly attended... We sincerely wish Mr Chatterton much greater success than he has hitherto experienced.'[33]

This wish was not to be granted. For two months Chatterton struggled on with thin houses that didn't cover his costs. The only good house he had was on 13 December when Charles Dillon was meant to be appearing. Dillon failed to show up and Chatterton had to offer the patrons their money back or tickets for another night.[34] Undeterred by poor houses, Chatterton was determined to maintain standards and his pantomime, *Guy Faux or Harlequin and the Fairy of the Land of Loyalty*, was described as: 'one of the best ever witnessed on the Rochester boards... The transformation scene took the audience by surprise, nothing approaching it having been witnessed on these boards for years'.[35] Chatterton tried everything. He gave away cakes to the audience on Twelfth Night and half of one night's takings to the poor of the town.[36] When he staged *Gustavus III or the Masked Ball*,[37] the occupants of the dress circle were allowed to come onto the stage in the last act as 'guests' at the ball. His uncle Frederick played a harp solo for his benefit.[38] Still the public stayed away.

It is hard to know why Chatterton decided to go to Rochester in the first place. The theatre had been built in 1791 as part of Sarah Baker's Kent circuit. This was inherited by her grandson William Dowton, the Drury Lane actor, who was said to spend his life shuttling between Drury Lane and Kent trying to keep everything going. After Dowton it went through a series of short-lived managements that were all defeated by the very small theatregoing public in Rochester. Its main claim to fame was as the site of Charles Dickens's first introduction to Shakespeare as a boy living in Chatham, but even this brush with literary immortality was doom-laden. Dickens revisited the theatre shortly before Chatterton's management and mentioned it in an essay published in *All the Year Round* in June 1860. 'To the Theatre... I repaired for consolation. But I found very little, for it was in a bad and declining way... It was To Let, and hopelessly so, for its old purposes; and there had been no entertainment within its walls for a long time, except a panorama... No, there was no comfort in the Theatre. It was mysteriously gone, like my own youth.'[39] As a keen Dickensian, Chatterton probably read *All The Year Round*, and it may have been this article that gave him the idea of reopening the Theatre Royal, Rochester. If so, it was an unfortunate one.

The season came to an end with Chatterton's benefit for himself – the third in his two-month management – on 16 January. He chose *Othello*, with himself in the title role. He had played Claude Melnotte in *The Lady of Lyons* for his first benefit on 3 December and Tactic in John Oxenford's farce *My Fellow Clerk* in the second on 14 January. The experience seems to have convinced him that his genius lay in management, because he never tried his luck as an actor again. He was so broke by the end of his Rochester stint, that he had to walk back to London, together with Henry Sinclair, his leading man.[40] Whatever they found to talk about on their thirty-mile trek, they must have formed a close bond because Sinclair would act for Chatterton in almost every year of his subsequent career in management.

Henry Sinclair (with the dagger) as Roderick Dhu in *The Lady of the Lake* at Drury Lane (1872)

While Chatterton was developing as a manager, Falconer was pursuing his career as an actor and landed the role of the villain Danny Mann in the first London production of Dion Boucicault's Irish melodrama *The Colleen Bawn*. The play, first seen in the USA, had its London premiere at the Adelphi on 10 September 1860. Its success was so great that it ran continuously for the next ten months, bar a five-week break in March/April when Boucicault took the show to Dublin, becoming London's first long run in the modern sense of continuous performances. Boucicault appeared himself as the loveable rogue Myles-na-Coppaleen who saves the life of the heroine he adores, although she loves another.

One day Falconer met Chatterton as he was walking down the Strand. Since the breakdown of their management of the Lyceum, relations between Chatterton and Edmund Falconer had been cool, but on this occasion Falconer said something civil to Chatterton, who responded civilly, and they agreed to go into partnership again. Madame Céleste's management of the Lyceum had come to an end, so the theatre was empty, and Falconer was looking for somewhere to stage his new drama *Woman or Love Against the World*, based on the Yelverton divorce case which changed the law regarding marriages between Catholics and Protestants in Ireland. (They had previously been null and void if conducted by a Catholic priest.) Chatterton and Falconer decided to produce the play at the Lyceum but they were not ready to commit to a long-term lease (or perhaps the proprietor

Samuel Arnold was not willing to give them one after their last attempt) so they took the theatre at a weekly rental of £60 (over £7,000 today) while Arnold continued to advertise for a tenant. Chatterton borrowed £100 from his father, allowing them to begin their management on Monday 19 August 1861 with a working capital of £40.

'We opened with *Woman* and, by Jove, I thought we were going to shut with it, business was so awfully bad', Chatterton told Coleman.[41] They struggled to pay the salaries on Saturday, and on the following Monday night the two of them stood beneath the Lyceum's huge portico in the moonlight wondering how they were going to pay suppliers' bills that were due the next day.

'Fred,' said Falconer, 'I fear it's all up with us. I'm just afther thinking hwat the divil we're to do for tomorrow's threasury.'

Chatterton replied that his main concern was holding on to the theatre until the following year when the second Great Exhibition was to be held. The Exhibition of 1851 had brought millions of visitors to London, and Chatterton expected a similar influx in 1862, which would be good for theatres.

'Ah, g'long; you might just as well think of collaring the moon yonder, and shutting her up in a lanthern like a farthing rushlight.'[42]

(Apparently Falconer actually spoke the stage-Oirish he wrote for his characters.)

Chatterton refused to be defeatist about it and promised that he would get his father to take care of the bills the next day if Falconer would go to Arnold and offer a guarantee from Chatterton for £1,000 (£113,000 today) to secure the Lyceum for 1862. Arnold wouldn't accept this, but said that if they could pay him £500 in two weeks, he would accept a guarantee for the other £500 and stop advertising the theatre. Chatterton managed to scrape together the £500 and on 25 September the *Times's* classified section carried an announcement that:

> The Manager, Mr Edmund Falconer, having taken the theatre for a term extending over the year 1862, begs to announce several novelties in preparation, and in particular a new and original drama entitled *Peep o' Day or Savourneen Deelish*,[43] in the production of which all the resources of the theatre will be employed.

The surprising thing about these negotiations is that, while Chatterton was the driving force, everything was done in Falconer's name. It was Falconer who went to see Arnold and who was listed in the advertisements as 'Sole lessee and manager'. Chatterton's job description was acting manager, but his name didn't appear in the publicity.

The most probable explanation is that, as an actor and playwright, Falconer was a 'name', albeit a minor one, whereas Chatterton had no public profile. To get theatrical projects off the ground, star names are important, no matter how little they actually do. However, the deal was done, and on 9 November 1861 *Peep o' Day* opened. It would be the turning point in the lives of both men.

While the negotiations for the lease were going on, against a background of poor houses for *Woman*, there was an interesting development in the classified columns of *The Times*. In the third week of its run, the advertisements for the Lyceum took up more space than those for rival theatres, as extracts from reviews were included to promote the show.

> Triumphant success of the new comedy *Woman*... A reference to the opinions of the press will prove the high estimate set upon it as a work of art. 'A clever and interesting play, equally distinguished for force of character, vigour of thought, and felicity of expression' – *Morning Post*. 'The new comedy is a good, healthy-toned and smartly written addition to our modern English plays' – *Daily News*. 'The merits of Mr Falconer's comedy are not small' – *Athenaeum*.... 'The author's case is amply proved by the manifest delight with which his comedy has been witnessed by a crowded audience' – *Saturday Review*.[44]

The poster for *Woman* was similarly stuffed with critical compliments. This was not the first time that favourable phrases had been plucked from reviews for the purposes of marketing – the practice seems to have been developed by Benjamin Webster at the Adelphi in the last years of the 1850s – but it had never been done to such an extent before. As Falconer and Chatterton were in partnership, we cannot be sure whose idea it was, but for the rest of Chatterton's career, his shows would routinely dominate the classified columns with numerous and lengthy advertisements.[45] As other managers imitated him, the theatre classifieds in *The Times* grew from about half a column at the beginning of Chatterton's career to about two columns by the end.

Falconer's involvement with the hugely successful *Colleen Bawn*, which was based on an 1829 novel called *The Collegians* by Gerald Griffin, may have caused him to think about looking at other Irish stories to adapt for the stage. He found a story called 'John Doe' in *Tales by the O'Hara Family* (1825) by John and Michael Banim who wrote under the name of the O'Hara brothers. Their aim was to write stories about the lives of ordinary Irish people that would be acceptable to English readers without involving excessive sentimentality. They wanted to be the Irish equivalent of Walter Scott.

'John Doe' is a story about the ruthless exploitation of a family of Catholic farmers called Kavanagh by an unscrupulous Protestant land-agent called Purcell. Purcell has enriched himself by stirring up peasants to rebel against the authorities, then informing on them as rebels. When they had been executed or banished, Purcell was able to seize their land, thus becoming rich. He had young Harry Kavanagh branded a traitor and chased out of Ireland, from which he escaped to America. Harry's elderly and infirm mother was thrown out of her cottage on a stormy night and died from exposure. His beautiful sister Kathleen was seduced by Purcell who promised to marry her but never did. When Purcell tired of Kathleen, he threw her out into another stormy night, together with their baby, so that he could pursue the beautiful heiress Mary Grace. Mary is the childhood sweetheart of

On 8 November 1872, Chatterton placed thirty classified advertisements in *The Times* for the three theatres under his control: fourteen for Drury Lane, thirteen for the Adelphi and three for the Princess's.

Harry Kavanagh who has, unknown to anyone, returned from America, now a rich man, to claim her. Harry calls himself John Doe – a well-known legal fiction – and becomes the leader of a group of rebels who are being pursued by a British army officer called Captain Howard. Howard falls in love with Mary and she with him. In the story's dramatic conclusion, Purcell and a gang of thugs kidnap Mary Grace, her father and Captain Howard. The plan is to take them to a remote spot where Mary will be forced to marry Purcell. Kavanagh and the rebels follow them, save the captives and overpower the soldiers. All are forced to stand in front of Purcell's magnificent house – originally Harry's house but now much enlarged – which is set alight. Purcell is handed by Harry to his followers. A struggle ensues in which Purcell, knowing what is coming to him, shoots himself. Harry asks Mary if she still loves him. She says no, they were only children when she said she loved him, and now she loves Captain Howard. Harry says he will return to America, taking with him his disgraced sister Kathleen.

Falconer worked this up into a play called *The Green Hills* which was performed at the Adelphi Theatre in Liverpool, where he had been a member of the company just before joining Charles Dillon at the Lyceum. He revised this as *Peep o' Day*, making various changes to his source material to make it acceptable to theatre audiences. First of all, his Kathleen has really been married to Purcell, but Purcell refuses to acknowledge it. Unlike the book, which is vague about dates, *Peep o' Day* is set specifically in 1798 – the year of the Irish rebellion against the British – and is described as being 'illustrative of the transition state of society in Ireland fifty years ago',[46] as if it could have no bearing on the current state of relations between England and Ireland. Fr O'Cleary, the parish priest, has applied for a pardon for all the rebels – now known as the Peep o' Day boys[47] – and this arrives in the last scene, so they can live as loyal subjects to the Queen and avoid any suspicion that Falconer was encouraging rebellion against the crown. The kidnap of Mary Grace and her father, which forms the longest sequence of the novel, is reduced in importance, but the part of poor wronged Kathleen is enlarged, and it was this which gave the play its 'sensation scene'. In the play, Kathleen is lured to an old quarry by one of Purcell's murderous henchmen by means of a letter she thinks comes from Harry. Once she is at the bottom of the quarry, the would-be murderer cuts down the bridge which forms the only access point, so that no one else can get down. Harry arrives in time to see that his sister is about to be murdered, so he grabs the top of a tree which is growing up from the floor of the quarry. His weight causes the tree to bend, lowering him to the quarry floor where he saves his sister. This scene was Falconer's invention: there is nothing like it in the novel. Finally, in the play Mary reveals that she does indeed still love Harry, so his efforts are rewarded and poor Captain Howard has to 'go back to England without an Irish conquest for your wife'.[48]

Falconer directed the production and wrote for himself the part of Barney O'Toole, a loveable Irish rogue who is not in the novel and bears a striking resemblance to Myles-na-Coppaleen, Dion Boucicault's part in *The Colleen Bawn*. Falconer knew that much of the success of *The Colleen Bawn* was owing to Boucicault's performance as Myles, the rascal on the wrong side of the law who cherishes a hopeless passion for the Colleen and saves her from a watery grave. In the same way, Falconer's loveable rogue Barney O' Toole saves the hero Harry Kavanagh by shooting the villain Purcell just as he is about to shoot Harry, thus drawing a great cheer from the audience.

As ever with Falconer, the play was too long and the first performance didn't end until midnight, but it was a great success. *The Times* review predicted a long run if only Falconer would cut the dialogue, and reported that the sensation scene produced 'a shout of admiration that shook the theatre to its base'.[49] The other big scene in the show was the pattern fair (the name was supposed to derive from 'patron')

The 'sensation scene' in *Peep o' Day* in which Harry Kavanagh grasps the top of a tree to lower himself to the floor of the quarry

and faction fight which concluded Act II. A faction fight, the Banim brothers explained on the first page of 'John Doe', was a violent skirmish between 'factions of fifty or a hundred, met, by appointment, to wage determined war', simply for want of something better to do.[50] In the play the fight is given slightly more purpose by having the wicked Purcell rebuffed by the Peep o' Day boys when he tries to get them to kidnap Mary Grace. They turn on him with abuse and he exits promising to send his thugs to beat them up. The act concludes with a massive fight between the two peasant factions which ends immediately when the parish priest arrives and holds up his hands. All the men fall to their knees before him. This sequence was staged by the choreographer Oscar Byrne, who also arranged a lively Irish jig to proceed it.

The success of *Peep o' Day* was overwhelming. As Christmas drew near, Falconer and Chatterton had no intention of taking it off for the pantomime, *Little Red Riding Hood*, which had to follow it as an afterpiece. *Peep o' Day* had originally run for five hours on its own so, even allowing for cuts by December, the pantomime must have been finishing at an uncomfortably late hour for parents of small children.

The pantomime script, by Leicester Buckingham, bore very little resemblance to the traditional story of Red Riding Hood, and had Baron Wolf pursuing the heroine through England, Scotland and Ireland. This provided the opportunity for a great many scenic displays, and the sequence in Ireland contained a panorama of the Lakes of Killarney painted by the leading scene-painter William Telbin. The Lakes had been a famous beauty spot since the eighteenth century, but the visit of Queen Victoria and Prince Albert in August of 1861 had turned them into a major tourist destination – hence the panorama. Telbin included the Royal family in one of his views, but Prince Albert died on 15 December. It was decided not to paint out the group, as 'it now embodies a memory of a happier time'.[51]

Panoramas, also known as dioramas, were popular scenic effects in the Victorian theatre. They required a very long sheet of canvas that was scrolled between two vertical rollers at the back of the stage, moving from one side to the other. They usually represented a journey, but in this case there were six separate scenes, side by side, which glided across the stage.[52] According to *The Times*: 'Nothing so perfect of its kind has ever been produced on the stage... the effect is impossible to describe.'[53] *The Times* was not alone in hailing Telbin's work as a masterpiece. Following the practice used to promote *Woman*, *Peep o' Day* had been publicised in the classifieds by advertisements quoting press reviews, especially in relation to the sensation scene in the quarry.[54]

Now, following the excellent reviews of the pantomime, the classified advertising for the Lyceum became even longer:

> Extracts from press notices of the scenery for panorama. 'A series of six panoramic views of the Lakes of Killarney constitutes a sight which no one should omit the opportunity of seeing; it is no exaggeration to say that these views of the most lovely scenery in Ireland are unsurpassed in beauty by anything that has been seen' *The Observer*. 'Nothing so perfect of its kind has ever been produced on the stage. The effects of light, shade and perspective are literally magical.' *Morning Paper*.[55]

The last quotation came from the *Times* review, but it would appear that the editor of that publication had reservations about the name of his august organ appearing in an advertisement. For years to come, all quotations from reviews in *The Times* that appeared in the paper would be attributed to 'Morning Paper'. (This did not apply to other forms of advertising over which the editor exerted no control: the name of *The Times* was freely used in posters and playbills.)

In March *Peep o' Day* reached its hundredth performance, with the pantomime still running. By April *Little Red Riding Hood* had been running for longer than any pantomime in London theatre history, and Chatterton and Falconer must have felt that they would be pushing their luck by continuing it into the summer. However, the panorama of the Lakes showed no sign of losing its appeal, so it was carved out of the pantomime and made the centrepiece of a ballet, simply called *Killarney*, with music by Irish composer Michael Balfe and choreography by Oscar Byrne.[56] Lydia Thompson was the principal *danseuse* and Telbin painted yet another view of the Lakes (making seven). Falconer wrote a song, also called *Killarney*, which became popular and formed part of the concert tenor's repertoire well into the twentieth century.

The ballet proved to be as popular as the pantomime. It ran and ran as the afterpiece to *Peep o' Day*, which passed 200 performances in July and 300 in October. On Monday 10 November 1862 *Peep o' Day* became the first play to run continuously in London for a year.[57] Chatterton and Falconer must have been feeling that the good times would last, if not forever, at least for the foreseeable future, when they received some bad news. Samuel Arnold had issued a lease on the Lyceum, starting in January 1863, to the French actor Charles Fechter. They were given notice to quit.

Fechter had decided, after a long and successful career in Paris, to try his luck in London, acting in English. He opened at the Princess's Theatre in Oxford Street, then managed by Augustus Harris senior (father of the future lessee of Drury Lane), in October 1860. In March of the following year he appeared as Hamlet to great acclaim. His interpretation was regarded as naturalistic and emotionally convincing, free from the formal poses and verbal traditions that had become attached to the part, and he enjoyed a successful run of appearances at the Princess's throughout 1861 and 1862. Unfortunately Fechter had an explosive temper which blighted his career. After a row with Harris he walked out of the Princess's and decided to set up in management on his own account. With the backing of a coterie of writers and intellectuals led by Charles Dickens, he must have looked like a promising prospect to Arnold, who told Chatterton and Falconer that their lease would not be renewed when it expired in December.

This must have come as an unpleasant surprise to the two men, who needed another theatre quickly if they were to continue in management. On Saturday 20 December 1862 *Peep o' Day* reached its 345th continuous performance. Falconer took his benefit on the following Monday with a performance of *Woman*. There was one more performance of *Peep o' Day* on Tuesday, followed by the 209th performance of the ballet *Killarney*, then on Christmas Eve Falconer and Chatterton closed their management of the Lyceum with a final performance of *Woman*. Two days later they opened a new management in the most historic and prestigious theatre in London: the Theatre Royal, Drury Lane.

3

A Stroll Down Drury Lane

The Theatre Royal, Drury Lane, which Falconer and Chatterton were moving into, was the fourth building on the site. The first theatre had opened in 1663 and burnt down nine years later. The second theatre, supposedly designed by Sir Christopher Wren, opened in 1674 and lasted for 117 years. This was the Drury Lane which David Garrick turned into the most important theatre in Europe and which he passed on to the brilliant but improvident Richard Brinsley Sheridan. Sheridan was a playwright of genius who was, in theory, the ideal person to take on Drury Lane. In his first year in charge he wrote *The School for Scandal*, which became the most successful play ever known at that time. Had Sheridan kept on writing plays, he could not only have given Drury Lane another golden age but might have enriched the development of English drama in the nineteenth century, which would prove to be a lean period. Unfortunately, Sheridan entertained a vigorous dislike for the theatre and all those associated with it, and was only interested in using Drury Lane as a piggy bank to fund his political career. The stage he wanted to dominate was not in Drury Lane but the Palace of Westminster: he saw himself above all as an orator and statesman.

His early years at Drury Lane were profitable but not profitable enough for his increasing needs. Sheridan therefore took the decision to pull down the old building and replace it with something on a much grander scale. The original theatre had been built on a very awkward site, in the back gardens of four streets of houses (Drury Lane, Russell Street, Brydges Street and Vinegar Alley) with no street frontage. The ground landlord was the Duke of Bedford, whose ancestors had received the Covent Garden estate from Henry VIII and Edward VI after the dissolution of the monasteries. (Covent Garden was the *convent* garden belonging to Westminster Abbey.) However, during the early part of the seventeenth century the Earls of Bedford (as they then were) had sold some plots under an arrangement known as fee-farm, not unlike our 999-year leases, which meant that they effectively passed out of the control of the family. The Drury Lane site was surrounded by these fee-farm plots, which made expansion extremely difficult.

Garrick had tried to get round the problem by taking leases on some of the surrounding properties and incorporating them into the theatre as dressing rooms, offices and foyers, but they were still separate buildings with a door knocked in the back wall. Sheridan envisaged something different: a completely new block of buildings that would fill the whole island site, entailing the demolition of all the houses and enabling the creation of a much larger theatre. The spaces at either end of the site would become houses, shops and taverns in the same architectural style.

To achieve this, it was necessary to persuade the Duke of Bedford to buy back the plots sold on fee-farm, as no one would put up money for such a grand development if it stood on plots owned by different landlords. The Duke was enthusiastic about a 'metropolitan improvement' that would add value to the now rather seedy Covent Garden estate, and gave Sheridan the larger site he needed. Sheridan's architect, Henry Holland, produced a magnificent plan which would encase the much larger theatre in a shell of neo-classical design. Unfortunately, as always with Sheridan, the finances became chaotic. He raised £150,000 to clear all debts and loans on the old building, pull it down and erect a new one. The money ran out before the project was completed, so Sheridan, desperate to get some money coming into the treasury, opened the theatre before the rest of the development was complete. It never was completed, so the theatre stood surrounded by areas of waste land throughout its short existence, to the annoyance of the Duke of Bedford and the fury of the architect.

When it burnt down in 1809, it looked as if that might be the end for Drury Lane. Sheridan had enmeshed the theatre in such a web of loans and mortgages that no one (not even Sheridan) knew what the real level of its indebtedness was. However Sheridan, who was always at his best in a crisis, was determined that Drury Lane should rise from the ashes, and he asked Samuel Whitbread to chair a rebuilding committee. Whitbread was a distant relative on Sheridan's wife's side, a fellow Whig MP and a very wealthy man, as he was heir to the brewery. Even more important, he was known to be a man of the utmost integrity, whose word could be relied upon – the complete opposite of Sheridan. Whitbread soon discovered that whenever he approached anyone about investing in the new Drury Lane, the first question they asked was: 'Will Mr Sheridan be involved at all?' Unless he could give a definite 'No', there would be no funds forthcoming, so Sheridan was prevailed upon to sell his stake and retire from Drury Lane.

Samuel Whitbread and his Theatre Royal Drury Lane Company of Proprietors managed to sort out the financial muddle bequeathed to them by Sheridan and to open the fourth (and current) Drury Lane on 10 October 1812. The original idea was that they would run the theatre themselves, but none of them had any relevant experience and the theatre was losing money. When Samuel Whitbread experienced a severe mental breakdown and took his own life in 1815, many people blamed the stress involved in sorting out Sheridan's financial mismanagement of Drury Lane. On 5 June 1819 the theatre closed without warning, announcing debts of £90,922,[1] and the proprietors decided to hand over its running to a professional. They advertised for applications to take the theatre on lease, bringing the joint-stock principle of management to a close. Drury Lane would be run by lessees for the rest of the nineteenth century.

The position of the lessee was a difficult one. He had to pay rent to the proprietors which would cover the ground rent they paid to the Duke of Bedford as well as dividends to those who had invested in the building. The proprietors played no part in running the theatre, they merely received the rent. However, they retained the right to order repairs and redecorations which had to be carried out at the expense of the lessee, under the supervision of their own architect. The lessee had to provide all scenery and costumes for productions, but these remained in the theatre at the end of his lease.

The lessee had the right to sub-let the theatre, with the agreement of the proprietors. These sub-letters paid rent to the lessee, who in turn paid rent to the proprietors, who paid rent to the Duke of Bedford. Strictly speaking, the lessee should have been referred to as the sub-lessee, as the head lease was held by the Company of Proprietors from the Duke, but this would have been confusing.

The position of the lessee of Drury Lane became more difficult after the passing of the Theatres Regulation Act of 1843 which removed the patent privileges. Following the restoration of the monarchy in 1660, Charles II had issued patents to his courtiers Thomas Killigrew and William Davenant, giving them the exclusive right to present plays in London. Killigrew had used his patent to establish Drury Lane while the Davenant patent was first used for a theatre in Lincoln's Inn Fields, then for the theatre we now call Covent Garden in Bow Street. As the population of London grew and the city spread out, the idea that two theatres could meet the entertainment needs of such a vast and diverse metropolis was challenged, and people began to find ways of getting round the patent restrictions. Opera was in any case regarded as a special case, and a separate patent had been issued to the theatre in the Haymarket (now called Her Majesty's) conferring the exclusive right to perform Italian opera. Separate patents were issued to 'summer' theatres – the Haymarket, then the Lyceum – allowing them to open in the summer months when Drury Lane and Covent Garden were closed. Concerts and musical entertainments were considered outside the patents' terms of reference, so people then had the idea of putting on shows in which there would be little or no dialogue but lots of songs, miming and holding up of signs to explain the plot to the audience. These entertainments were known as burlettas, and were flexible enough to allow for the performance of Shakespeare's plays in the format.

By the early part of the nineteenth century, the situation was so obviously absurd that a political head of steam started to build up for the abolition of patent privileges. A bill introduced in 1833 passed in the Commons only to be defeated in the Lords, but ten years later, despite furious and predictable protestations about property rights from interested parties, those two patents issued by Charles II 180 years before were scrapped.

By this stage Covent Garden had virtually ceased to function as a theatre, being used for meetings, dinners and concerts, and four years later it became an opera house (which it remains). Drury Lane was therefore left in a unique position, as a large theatre in the central London area that would increasingly have to compete with smaller theatres more suited to the dramatic taste of the times. As if that wasn't challenging enough, there was the residual problem of National Theatre status.

The patents conferred certain privileges on their possessors, but raised certain expectations in return. The rationale for a monopoly – or at least a duopoly – had been the desire to maintain standards. If Covent Garden and Drury Lane were protected from competition, they should have been able to put on good plays and elevate public taste. Of course, it had never worked like that, partly because they were in competition with each other, but mainly because they received no public subsidy and good plays didn't bring in enough money to pay the bills. Putting on straight plays had never been as profitable as putting on pantomimes, which is why the latter were so often scheduled to run after the former. People could be persuaded to sit through Shakespeare if the evening concluded with Harlequin. Spectacle was always more of a draw than poetry, which is why both Covent Garden and Drury Lane had been rebuilt on a large scale at the turn of the nineteenth century.

The Drury Lane that Garrick handed on to Sheridan in 1776 had seated about 2,300 people,[2] but the auditorium Henry Holland designed for Sheridan sat 3,600 – an increase of over fifty per cent.[3] When Covent Garden was rebuilt after the fire of 1808, it accommodated over 2,800.[4] These auditoria were described by Richard

Peake, the Drury Lane treasurer, as 'covered Salisbury Plains'[5] and the popular playwright Richard Cumberland complained that henceforth there would be 'theatres for spectators rather than playhouses for hearers... The splendour of the scenes... now in a great degree superseded the labours of the poet.'[6]

Any manager of Drury Lane or Covent Garden could have pointed out to these complainants that, in the absence of subsidy, managers had little option but to give the public what they wanted. Nevertheless, there was concern about the state of the drama, and it was humorously captured by J. R. Planché in an 'extravaganza' for the Olympic Theatre in April 1838 called *The Drama's Levée*. The central characters in Planché's plot were The Drama ('in a critical state of health') and her two sons The Legitimate Drama and The Illegitimate Drama, described as being 'on the worst possible terms with each other'. The Legitimate Drama, representing comedy and tragedy and dressed in a Roman toga, complains that his illegitimate brother has impoverished him. The Illegitimate Drama, representing pantomime and sensation dramas, dressed 'half-harlequin and half melodramatic', replies that his legitimate brother has been stealing his toys ever since they were children:

> Stole from the nursery of my best hopes,
> My rocking horses and my skipping ropes,
> And took my harlequins from loss to save you,
> And now you blame the punches that I gave you.[7]

The separation of theatrical entertainments into legitimate and illegitimate passed immediately into common usage, and in 1840 Alfred Bunn, the bankrupt lessee of Drury Lane, published an autobiography that contained a furious defence of his management against 'the gravest charge... that has been preferred against me... of my having neglected the legitimate drama, and infected its dominions with gewgaw and pageantry, wherein SENSE had been compelled to give way to SHOW'.[8] Bunn spent many pages laying out lists of all the legitimate dramas he had presented, as a proportion of all the nights on which the theatre was open, and he concludes this angry tirade with the observation that: 'one legitimate drama was played nearly as often as all the rest put together, and that was THE ROAD TO RUIN!'[9]

Almost without exception, the nineteenth-century lessees of Drury Lane took this road, ending up either in the bankruptcy courts or losing their life's savings or both. As the wrecks of ruined managements piled up, the rent that the Drury Lane Proprietors could demand was falling:

**Rent charged for the lease by the Drury Lane Company
of Proprietors (selected years)**

YEAR	LESSEE	RENT PER ANNUM
1819	Robert Elliston	£10,200
1826	Stephen Price	£10,600
1830	Captain Polehill/ Alexander Lee	£9,000
1833	Captain Polehill	£8,000
1835	Alfred Bunn	£6,500
1836	Alfred Bunn	£6,000
1839	William Hammond	£5,000
1841	William Charles Macready	£3,400
1843	Alfred Bunn	£4,000
1847	Louis Jullien	£3,500
1853	E. T. Smith	£4,000
1859	E. T. Smith	£4,500

Drury Lane was described by one of its lessees as a vampire that 'sucked the life-blood out of everyone'. One journalist facetiously suggested that the terms for hiring the theatre included possession of a strait-jacket. Another compared taking on Drury Lane to making a pact with the devil, except that those who sell their souls to Satan are traditionally showered with riches – unlike the poor manager of Drury Lane.[10] Nevertheless, it was still the National Theatre. In the early part of the century, it has been customary to refer to both Drury Lane and Covent Garden as national theatres, but, when Covent Garden became an opera house, Drury Lane became the sole claimant of the title. Whoever was in charge was expected to respect its status by staging Shakespeare and the legitimate drama, which almost always lost money, and for which no one was offering a subsidy.

In 1847 the Company of Proprietors let Drury Lane to Louis Jullien for a rent of only £3,500 per annum.[11] The fact that he was paying less than a third of the rent demanded in the 1820s shows how unprofitable the theatre had become. Jullien was a flamboyant composer and conductor who had made his fortune with a series of extremely successful promenade concerts which he staged in a spectacular style. Many of these had been held at Drury Lane where he would board over the pit to create the promenade, allowing those attending to stroll around between potted plants and statues while the orchestra played. Jullien had rented the theatre for periods of a few weeks at a time to give these concerts, but now he had decided to go up-market and set himself up as an opera impresario. His opera season opened in December 1847 and closed in February 1848 with losses of £15,000 that pushed him into bankruptcy. Remarkably, in spite of his bankruptcy he remained the lessee of Drury Lane, which shows how desperate the proprietors were to find anyone at all to run it. Jullien presented an equestrian troupe from from the *Cirque National de Paris*, followed by the *Theâtre Historique* from Paris presenting the stage version of Alexandre Dumas' *The Count of Monte Cristo*. French actors speaking French at the National Theatre provoked riots that closed the play after two nights. Jullien brought back the *Cirque National* which was uncontroversial (French actors were accused of taking the bread out of the mouths of British actors, but there was no animosity towards French horses) then a series of German operas.

The proprietors were conscious of the fact that they were being censured for allowing the hallowed boards of Drury Lane, once trodden by Garrick, to be strolled on by promenaders and trotted on by horses. They wanted to see the drama return to Drury Lane, so they came up with the idea of 'double-letting'. As Jullien presented his promenade concerts in the autumn, he didn't need the theatre all the year round. He was therefore offered a shoter period of July to December, with the actor James Anderson taking January to June for dramatic performances at a rent of £2,500 for each six-month period. It was understood that Anderson had to be able to get in early enough to open his pantomime on Boxing Day, so Anderson opened on 26 December 1849 with Shakespeare's *The Merchant of Venice* and the pantomime *Harlequin and Good Queen Bess, or Merrie England in the Olden Times* as the afterpiece. Under the terms of the agreement with Jullien, Anderson could not

The pit of Drury Lane was boarded over to create the promenade for Louis Jullien's concerts

produce operas or concerts, but that didn't bother him: he was only interested in the 'legitimate' theatre. His first season consisted of Shakespeare and 'legitimate' stalwarts like *The Lady of Lyons* and *The Hunchback* with some new plays; it closed in May with losses of £5,500.[12] The second season opened on 26 December 1850 with Shakespeare's *The Winter's Tale* and *Humpty-Dumpty or the First Lord Mayor of London*. Anderson continued his 'legitimate' programme as before and found himself in debtors' prison in June. He received his discharge from the bankruptcy court on 5 August 1851, having run through his life's savings of nearly £10,000 and incurred debts on top of that of over £5,000 – a loss of over £2m in modern values.[13] Drury Lane was let to an American circus during the Great Exhibition of 1851, then to Alfred Bunn, returning to the Lane for the third time. Bunn withdrew in March 1852, and the proprietors decided that this 'double-letting' arrangement was more trouble than it was worth. Rent was unpaid or not paid in full and the Duke of Bedford was being advised by his London agent to pull the theatre down and erect buildings on the site from which he might actually collect some rent.[14] At this point the proprietors issued a seven-year lease to E. T. Smith at £4,000 per annum.[15]

Edward Tyrell Smith, always styled E. T. Smith, was described by John Coleman as a man 'whose audacity was as astonishing as his enterprise, and whose ignorance was more astounding than either'.[16] He was at different times a Bow Street Runner, restaurateur, picture-dealer and pub landlord. His smattering of French was picked up when he was driving the stagecoach between Waterloo and Brussels.[17] He acquired a reputation as a big businessman by hiring a one-thousand-pound note from a moneylender for a pound a day which he would proffer when cash was demanded for goods at auction or to secure the lease of a property As no one could change the note, he was able to get things on credit for which no credit had been offered, resell at a profit and pocket the difference without ever laying out any capital.

He was said to have taken Drury Lane, as Britain took the empire, in a fit of breezy absence of mind.[18] It was a bold move as Drury Lane had been a problem in the London theatre world for so long that the *Times* described it as 'the disowned among the metropolitan theatres'.[19] Turning it around would be difficult, and most people would have regarded this as a full-time job, but that was not Smith's style: his restless energy meant that he could never be content with doing only one thing at a time. During what proved to be a remarkably long ten-year tenancy at the Lane, Smith also took on Her Majesty's Theatre and Cremorne Gardens, bought *The Sunday Times* and built the Alhambra music hall in Leicester Square.

Smith was well-liked: 'an honest, straightforward and kind-hearted man... a plucky manager... and a jovial companion'.[20] Nevertheless, there was a feeling that this 'shrewd, uneducated, good-natured vulgarian'[21] wasn't right for Drury Lane, where he was responsible for the 'lowest decline in [its] standing and... dignity'.[22] He had no respect for Drury Lane's cultural status and pursued an unashamedly populist policy, slashing prices and staging whatever sold tickets. Whilst styling his company Her Majesty's Servants and being happy to invoke National Theatre status when he occasionally put on Shakespeare, Smith was never going to be a martyr to the legitimate drama. The box office dictated artistic policy and Shakespeare had to give way to performing dogs and a man who could walk on the ceiling when a new attraction was needed.[23]

In 1859 his original lease on Drury Lane expired and in October he signed a new lease at a rental of £4,500 per annum[24] that contained a clause requiring him to refurbish the building according to the specifications of the committee's architect. This was like signing a blank cheque that was clearly going to be filled in for a large sum. Smith was seriously over-extended at Her Majesty's and Cremorne Gardens and began to look for someone who would take Drury Lane off his hands before the redecoration was ordered. The obvious candidate was Dion Boucicault, the most successful dramatist of the century, but Boucicault was wary. 'Only six thousand pounds, my boy,' said Smith. 'You walk in, I walk out.' 'Very good, Smith,' replied Boucicault. 'I should want you to give me six thousand, and then I should not walk in but keep out.'[25] However, Boucicault did take a sub-lease towards the end of 1862 when he needed a theatre at very short notice.

The stage of Drury Lane was often converted into a circus ring by E. T. Smith

His melodrama *The Colleen Bawn* had become the longest-running play ever seen in London since its opening at the Adelphi on 10 September 1860. The owner of the Adelphi, Benjamin Webster, was delighted by receipts that exceeded anything he had ever known before, but Boucicault felt that he was making a lot of money for Webster and not enough for himself. After a year he insisted on a new agreement under which they would enter into a partnership to run the Adelphi, with Boucicault responsible for the stage and Webster for the front-of-house. Boucicault and his wife Agnes, who were starring in the play, would receive £5 each for each night of performance, and Boucicault would receive £1 per act per night for any play of his that was acted. This agreement was revolutionary as it was the first time that a playwright had received a royalty for every performance, and it changed the whole financial basis of the dramatist's profession. However, the more annoying aspect, from Webster's point of view, was that he had effectively lost control of his own theatre, as Boucicault could decide what was to be presented.

As Chatterton would observe many years later, everyone who worked with Boucicault fell out with him eventually, and this arrangement between two strong-willed characters was doomed from the start. Boucicault's arrogant behaviour backstage and vocal criticisms of Webster split the staff into factions, either for him or for Webster. Boucicault claimed that he and Agnes needed a break from continuous performances of *The Colleen Bawn* and replaced it with his play *The Octoroon* that was less successful, followed by others. Webster was so frustrated that they were losing money by withholding *The Colleen Bawn* that he published a poster announcing it for the next Monday night, 9 June 1862. Boucicault claimed he had breached their agreement and went to court. The judge refused to rule for either party and advised the complainants to reach an agreement, but Boucicault had no intention of compromising. As far as he was concerned, the partnership with Webster was over. He had been negotiating with E. T. Smith for a short lease on Drury Lane, where he and Agnes opened on 23 June 1862 in *The Colleen Bawn*. They played to packed houses for twelve weeks, after which Boucicault replaced it with another of his plays, *The Relief of Lucknow*. This ran for eight weeks, in a double-bill with *The Colleen Bawn* for the last four.[26] By the time Boucicault's season closed on 8 November 1862, Smith had found a new tenant for Drury Lane who would pay for the redecoration. *The Times* carried the announcement: 'Theatre Royal, Drury Lane, after having been entirely redecorated and embellished, will be opened for a dramatic season on the 26th of December next under the sole management of Mr Edmund Falconer.'[27]

4

A Partnership at the National Theatre

1862/1863: Falconer as house playwright

It is a truism of theatrical biography that success can be harder to handle than failure, and that was certainly true of Edmund Falconer. The record-breaking success of *Peep o' Day* had generated enormous profits – of £16,000 (over £1.9m. in modern values) according to Chatterton – and Falconer had celebrated by living in style. He took a large house in Fulham, ran his own carriage and pair, and started collecting art. He also hit the bottle. As Chatterton told Coleman later: 'He, who had hitherto been the most temperate… of men, became suddenly afflicted with an insatiable thirst, which for some years acted like a poison on his blood and brains.'[1] The descent into alcoholism was rapid and destroyed Falconer's career just as it seemed to be taking off. As the author and producer of the most successful play ever seen in London, Falconer no doubt felt that he would be able to pay for his mansion in Fulham and his carriage and pair with a string of future hits. In fact, he would produce flop after flop.

Under the terms of their agreement for taking the lease of the Lyceum in September of 1861, Chatterton was to receive a salary of £6 per week as acting manager plus one-third of the profits. This was in recognition of the fact that Chatterton had raised the money and persuaded Falconer to sign the lease when Falconer himself had wanted to abandon the project. However, money coming in to the theatre was paid directly into Falconer's private bank account, as this was not a legal partnership, so Chatterton had to wait to receive his one-third share from Falconer, who was spending the money as fast as it was coming in. On 15 August 1862 Falconer gave Chatterton an I.O.U. for £1,453, and by the close of the Lyceum season in December he owed a further £1,433, totalling £2,886 (over £344,000 today).

Falconer paid E. T. Smith £5,000 for the remaining term of his seven-year lease, during which he would pay rent at the same rate that

Smith had been paying of £4,500 per annum.[2] He also had to take on the responsibility, contained in Smith's lease, to completely redecorate the theatre according to the specifications of the theatre's architect. This was done in a style that was described as Louis XIV, which entailed lots of gilding on white paintwork. Falconer claimed that it cost him £8,000.[3] Audiences were delighted by the result, as Drury Lane had been a byword for dirt and dinginess for some time, but there was more involved than just the painting. The partitions that had divided sections of the dress circle to create a number of boxes were removed, so that the seating ran uninterrupted from one side of the auditorium to the other. Dress circle patrons sat in imitation mahogany upholstered chairs, but the more significant change was in the cheaper parts of the theatre. The benches were removed from pit and galleries to be replaced by individual seats – an innovation in London. This affected the behaviour of the audience as there was no need to scramble for a place on a bench. 'Even in the upper or sixpenny gallery,' according to the architect, 'the character of the audience is completely changed and the seats are principally occupied by quiet, respectable persons and their children, rendering the presence of the police almost a form'.[4] The proscenium was given a massive gilt surround and the royal box was moved back to its original position, up against the proscenium on the dress circle level. The suite of rooms behind the royal box, for many years used for lumber, was restored and the box facing it across the stalls became the Prince of Wales's box for the use of the future Edward VII.[5]

When Drury Lane re-opened on Boxing Day 1862 in its splendid new guise, the managerial billing was: 'Lessee and Manager Mr Edmund Falconer'. However the negotiations for the transfer of the lease were not complete, and it seems that Smith did not intend to transfer it to Falconer completely. Falconer and Chatterton were paying rent to Smith, who was in turn paying rent to the Company of Proprietors. Smith had been in a hurry to escape the liability to redecorate the theatre, but he wanted to retain some sort of presence there and insisted on keeping the manager's office and retaining his own box. The situation became so confusing that even the shareholders were puzzled. At the AGM on 31 January 1863, one of them asked: 'Is Mr Smith our lessee or Mr Falconer?' and was told that: 'this was a question that it was extremely improper to discuss. It was a matter that was now under consideration.' The shareholder was unwilling to let the matter rest there, as he was complaining about sometimes being denied his right of free admission to any part of the theatre (a long-running source of complaints at these meetings). 'Suppose I should determine to take proceedings, on account of being refused admission, whom am

I to take proceedings against, Mr Falconer or Mr Smith?' 'At present Mr Smith,' replied the chairman. Smith, who was present at the meeting, added: 'Negotiations are pending between Mr Falconer and myself.'[6] He added that Mr Chatterton could sort out any disputes regarding seats.

If Smith was only sub-letting, it is hard to understand why Falconer, with no long-term lease to rely on, would have paid £8,000 to redecorate the theatre. The most likely explanation is that he did a deal with Smith when they were both in their cups, and when Falconer was under pressure to find another theatre quickly, having been given notice to quit the Lyceum. By the time they opened, Chatterton and Falconer had scraped together every penny they could raise to pay for the first productions, and there was nothing in the kitty.[7] Fortunately for them, they were opening on Boxing Day with a pantomime: *Little Goody Two Shoes*. Whatever criticisms people might have made of E. T. Smith's management of Drury Lane, everyone acknowledged that he had made it supreme in the field of pantomime. Other London theatres presented them, but the Drury Lane pantomime was in a league of its own, a great British institution like Magna Carta and Habeas Corpus.[8] 'So great a reputation has the National Theatre for [pantomimes],' wrote one critic, 'that many persons wouldn't believe they had seen one, unless it was Mr E. L. Blanchard's Christmas Annual.'[9]

E. L. Blanchard was the acknowledged king of pantomime in the second half of the nineteenth century. He wrote his first Drury Lane pantomime in 1852 for E. T. Smith and his last in 1889 for Augustus Harris, as well as every year in between – an unbroken run of thirty-seven pantomimes (or 'annuals' as he called them). He also wrote pantomimes for Sadler's Wells, the Crystal Palace and other theatres, so he sometimes had two or three running at the same time. 'Pantomimes are not so funny as they used to be,' *The Illustrated London News* told its readers, but they 'aim at a moral purpose and elegance of composition unattempted in the olden time.'[10] Blanchard was named as the leading exponent of the new style, and rightly so. His pantomimes wove together fairy tales, nursery rhymes and legends to create shows that were both clever and funny, magical for children and delightful for grown-ups. The stories were told in rhyming couplets that were compared to Alexander Pope's for elegance.[11] There was no smut ('we have cause to be thankful that there is one writer who can supply our children with jokes that are not coarse'[12]) and he avoided the political gags that cropped up in many pantomimes. Blanchard was able to boast, after decades of writing for the stage, that not a single line of his dialogue had ever been deleted by the Lord Chamberlain's Examiner of Plays.[13]

The pantomimes made serious points. 'Mr Blanchard always puts some meaning into his work,' wrote one critic, 'and... upsets the theory that, in order to be amusing... , it is also necessary to be stupid.'[14] One favourite message was the need to hold on to the good old customs whilst welcoming the fruits of progress. In the 1869/1870 pantomime *Beauty and the Beast*, Old Tradition complains to Mother Bunch that the fine old traditions like Twelfth Night, Valentine's Day and Guy Fawkes are dying out. Mother Bunch promises to take good care of them but reminds Tradition that Progress is changing the lives of people for the better: the Thames Embankment, the Holborn Viaduct, Blackfriars Bridge ('colossal tasks completed') and the Suez Canal. 'Such transformations, wrought by modern science,/May set all Mother Bunch's at defiance.' Each of these wonders was represented by an elaborately costumed performer to remind the audience that we should celebrate the new whilst preserving the best of the old.[15]

Recognising Blanchard's value to their management, Falconer and Chatterton altered his terms. E. T. Smith had been paying him a flat rate of £30 for a pantomime script, but this changed to a royalty of one pound per performance. Thus, he received £76 for *Little Goody Two Shoes*, and his earnings increased as the runs of the pantomimes became longer.[16]

Since 1855, the scenery for the Drury Lane pantomimes had been designed by William Beverley. William Roxby Beverley was one of the greatest scene-painters of the century, described as 'the Watteau of scene-painters... the Claude Lorrain of pantomime... the scenic artist of the present day'.[17] He came from a theatrical family, his father being an actor-manager and proprietor of the Durham circuit of theatres. The family name was really Roxby but his father started using Beverley after the town in Yorkshire where his own father had been born.[18] William Beverley began painting scenery for his father's productions, then in 1839 he travelled to London where he worked at the Coburg Theatre (now the Old Vic) and the Princess's Theatre in Oxford Street. In 1847 he joined the management of Madame Vestris and Charles Matthews at the Lyceum where he designed a series of extravaganzas, written for them by J. R. Planché, and this was when his career really took off. Extravaganzas, popular in the 1830s and 1840s, were like very genteel pantomimes with no harlequinade, no low comedy and no coarseness. They appealed to a more educated audience who could recognise references to Shakespeare and classical mythology and who would enjoy knowing references to contemporary events and personalities. Planché was the great creator of extravaganzas and Beverley gave them such strikingly beautiful visual expression that, to Planché's dismay, the scenery became the main feature of the production rather than the words. 'As to me, I was positively painted out,' he complained in his memoirs.[19] Beverley combined a high level of pictorial ability with a thorough understanding of stage machinery and was able to achieve effects no one had seen before. He pioneered the transformation scene, which involved an elaborate arrangement of sliding shutters, flying gauzes and opening vistas that, over the space of fifteen or twenty minutes, revealed visions of striking beauty, often involving dream-like evocations of fairyland peopled by dozens of fairies shimmering in jewels and moonlight.

Beverley was forever associated with fairyland ('Titania's own artist'[20]) to the extent that a journalist, sent to interview him at home in prosaic Russell Square, was sad to discover that: 'Even the architects of fairyland must dwell in houses built by mortal hands.' However, Beverley insisted that he owed his success to his love of nature, acquired as a boy: 'The ozone freshened the atmosphere of the footlights. I revelled in fairyland, but I never forgot Nature.'[21]

Victorian audiences placed great emphasis on the look of a show and the most successful designers became stars in their own right, with their names in large letters on the posters. Beverley was the brightest of these stars and was regularly called before the curtain on first nights, sometimes more than once, to receive plaudits for his magical visions. He was one of the last great scene-painters to retain the tradition of

'Preparing for the Pantomime: Mr Beverly's Painting Room'

flat scenery – wings and backcloths – rather than the 'built-out' three-dimensional sets that came into fashion towards the end of the nineteenth century. Oscar Wilde thought that Beverley's canvas cloths were more artistic than structural sets and that he should have been made a Royal Academician.[22]

In 1855 the Vestris/ Matthews management at the Lyceum collapsed and Beverley crossed the road to Drury Lane, together with his brother, the actor Robert Roxby, who became the Lane's stage manager. By the time Falconer and Chatterton moved in, they were both well-established there, but they found their services were not required for the 1862/63 pantomime as the new managers had brought most of their team with them from the Lyceum. William Telbin and Thomas Grieve were commissioned to design the scenery in the hope that they would achieve another triumph like the panorama of the Lakes of Killarney but, although the scenery for *Little Goody Two Shoes* was praised, it wasn't sensational. There was a view of the interior of that year's International Exhibition in South Kensington but, as the exhibition had already closed, that wasn't particularly exciting. Grieve and Telbin weren't called to take a bow, which had become routine for Beverley.

The curtain-raiser for the pantomime was a short play, written by and starring Falconer, called *Next of Kin* and described by Chatterton as a fiasco,[23] but it didn't really matter because there was a tradition at Drury Lane that on Boxing Night the gallery made so much noise until the pantomime started that not a word of the curtain-raiser could be heard. Boxing Night at Drury Lane was marked by traditions, and no one appreciated this more than John Oxenford, theatre critic of *The Times*, for whom it had acquired a significance such as we now attach to the last night of the Proms. He began his review by pointing out that the patent privileges had long since been abolished, but, on Boxing Night, Drury Lane came into its own: 'its old *prestige*... still in full lustre... Drury Lane is the theatre which everyone should select who wishes to study the customs of the English people'.[24]

Oxenford would become the principal cheerleader in the press for Falconer and Chatterton's management at Drury Lane, then for Chatterton on his own. It is easy to dismiss his support as a return for the favours he received when they staged his various dramatic pieces – five in the first three seasons – but this would be unfair. Oxenford had a keen appreciation of the cultural importance of Drury Lane which he saw as not just one theatre amongst many in London, but as the National Theatre, the place where, as in former times, all classes could come together to watch a play in a sort of symbolic community. For many years Covent Garden and Drury Lane had been national theatres, protected by their patents, but since the abolition of the patents in 1843 they had struggled to survive in the new competitive environment. Newer, smaller theatres had been built that were more comfortable and more suitable for domestic dramas; the music hall had made inroads into the working-class audiences; the middle classes were reluctant to go out after their late dinners; the upper classes preferred the opera. Covent Garden had been lost to the drama altogether, becoming an opera house in 1847. For Oxenford, it was important to make Drury Lane work, and he identified himself so closely with its fortunes that after his death there was a campaign to erect a statue of him in the foyer.[25]

Little Goody Two Shoes ran with *Next of Kin* as the curtain-raiser until February, when it became customary to add a bit more ballast to the evening's entertainment by presenting a full-length play, followed by a cut-down version of the pantomime. On 9 February the three-act comedy *Don Caesar de Bazan* opened for a two-week run, leading up to the first full-scale drama to be presented by Falconer and Chatterton: *Bonnie Dundee*, written and directed by Falconer. This was a big production about the Jacobite uprising against William III after he had taken the crown from the deposed James II. The Scottish Highlanders, led by John Graham, 1st Viscount Dundee (known as Bonnie Dundee) sought to restore James II to the throne, but Dundee was killed in battle in 1689 and the Jacobites were defeated. The Massacre of Glencoe, which followed in 1692, was an attempt to break the clan system that supported rebellion against the crown. The big scene in the drama showed the descent of four hundred tartan-clad warriors from the Highlands to gather round the Jacobite standard.[26]

John Oxenford's review in *The Times* was shocking for two reasons. First, it consisted of one paragraph, whereas a major Drury Lane production would normally have warranted the best part of a column. Second, it began: 'The new spectacular drama entitled *Bonnie Dundee, or the Gathering of the Clans*, requires much modification before any hope can be entertained of its permanent success' and it ended: 'At the fall of the curtain the expression of opinion by the audience by no means indicated general satisfaction.'[27] For the kindly John Oxenford to tell readers that the audience was booing at the end was about as bad as it could get. According to Chatterton, the fate of the play was sealed when one of the cast, 'an effeminate young man', looked over the sea of dead and dying men after the Massacre of Glencoe and 'lisped in the most ladylike manner, "Oh, how dreadful!" whereupon some wag in the pit responded, "Right you are, old man, it is dreadful!" This evolved into a yell which sealed the fate of the piece.'[28]

Bonnie Dundee staggered along for three weeks, playing to almost empty houses.[29] It closed on 14 March, to be followed by a two-week revival of Falconer's earlier play *Extremes*. In an attempt to salvage some of the enormous costs of *Bonnie Dundee*, the second act, which contained the gathering of the clans, was performed on its own after *Extremes*, but the experiment only lasted a week. The theatre closed for Passion Week then re-opened on Easter Monday with what was described as the 347th performance of *Peep o' Day*. It lasted for only sixteen performances with another actor in Falconer's old part of Barney O' Toole. The reason for Falconer's non-appearance was explained by Charles Dickens in a letter to Wilkie Collins: 'That wretched Mr Falconer is at the end of his tether at Drury Lane – which he closes this week – and goes about in a state of delirium tremens, grasping at imaginary spectres, pots of porter, or glasses of brandy and water.'[30]

Falconer and Chatterton's first season at Drury Lane had been a financial disaster. The pantomime had done less well than expected, but the real problem was Falconer's insistence on producing his own plays. *Bonnie Dundee* lost £1,507, the revival of *Extremes* lost £883 and the revival of *Peep o' Day* lost £180.[31] In March, during the *Bonnie Dundee* fiasco, Falconer had asked Chatterton to raise £2,000 urgently to pay the rent arrears. Chatterton had still not received any of the £2,886 due to him from the Lyceum season and he had been borrowing money from his father Edward, back in charge of the Drury Lane box office after taking time out to manage Chatterton's season at the St James's, to keep them afloat. He decided that if he were to raise any more money for Drury Lane, he wanted his relationship with Falconer to be on a more formal basis. He was no longer going to be an employee but a partner. His terms would remain the same – £6 per week plus one third of the profits – but Falconer would no longer be able to treat whatever came in at the box office as his own, and all expenditure as well as monies raised against the business would have to be agreed between the two men. Chatterton was also to receive equal billing with Falconer in the publicity.

The rent was owed not to the Company of Proprietors of Drury Lane but to E. T. Smith who had still not transferred his lease to Falconer. Chatterton, who was never easy working in partnership with anyone else, found it infuriating that Smith was still hanging around Drury Lane and interfering with things. 'He took care to make it as hot as he could for us,' Chatterton would later tell Coleman, 'and I had to devise the means for check-mating him.'[32] Smith invited Chatterton to dinner and proposed that the two of them should go into partnership, dropping Falconer altogether. Chatterton refused, whereupon Smith said that if Chatterton could raise the whole amount he owed to the proprietors (£1,800) plus a sweetener of £250 for himself, he would retire from Drury Lane altogether. Falconer would then hold the lease directly from the proprietors.[33]

Chatterton raised £1,000 from John Knowles, the proprietor of the Theatre Royal, Manchester, who was known as the 'theatrical pawnbroker' for his willingness to bail out cash-strapped fellow managers.[34] Knowles had a low opinion of Falconer – 'What reet had yon Irish idiot to go and set up carriages, and horses, and flunkeys, and that sort of muck?' – but he realised that Chatterton was more business-like. As security, Chatterton gave him the rights to produce *Peep o' Day* in Manchester up to Christmas, from which the profits would pay off the loan. Knowles wanted more, so Chatterton threw in Telbin's panorama of the Lakes of Killarney, which clinched it.[35] Chatterton, who contributed the remaining £800 for the rent himself, decided that the time had come to get a written statement of what he was owed by Falconer, whose descent into alcoholism made him a risky creditor. The deed of partnership recorded that the £800 Chatterton had just provided, added to the £2,886 owed from the Lyceum management, made a total of £3,686. After some small deductions which Chatterton agreed to, the sum of £3,675 was recorded as Chatterton's stake in the company – over £450,000 in modern values. The articles of partnership were dated 28 March and signed on 7 April 1863.[36]

As a partner, Chatterton now had more say in what the theatre was to present. Seeing that Falconer's policy of vanity-producing his own plays would soon bankrupt them, Chatterton 'insisted upon our reverting at once to the legitimate and classic drama'.[37] By coincidence, developments at the Lyceum, which they had just vacated, played into his hands.

When the French actor Charles Fechter replaced Chatterton and Falconer at the Lyceum, he wanted to promote himself as an interpreter of Shakespearean roles. He needed to surround himself with talented actors who were known for their work with the Bard and so he signed up Samuel Phelps as a member of his company at £40 a week for three performances a week. At least that was his version of events.

Samuel Phelps had been a member of Macready's legendary companies at Covent Garden (1837–1839) and Drury Lane (1841–1843) which were looked back on by many people as the high-water mark of theatrical achievement in the nineteenth century. Macready had wanted to show that the two patent theatres could be run as they had been designed to be run, presenting quality productions of good plays with strong casts. He gathered about himself, in both cases, stellar casts, most of whom agreed to work for less than their normal rates because they believed in what he was doing. Macready had put on superb productions of Shakespeare as well as new plays, using methods that anticipated many aspects of play production that we take for granted. He insisted on long rehearsals to make sure that everyone was good in their part and he gave his productions a 'look', with sets and costumes designed to be coherent. However, he still had enough of the old actor-manager in him to want to be sure of keeping the attention fixed on himself. When Phelps proved to be extremely good, and in the opinion of some people better than Macready, he responded by removing Phelps from leading parts and keeping him in subordinate roles. Phelps resented this but accepted it as the way things were. Macready was quite blunt with him about his determination to stay at the top of the profession, and Phelps would later say that he would have done exactly the same thing in Macready's position. Nevertheless, Macready had a high opinion of Phelps and advised him to accept his lot for the time being, as his time would come. A year after the close of his Drury Lane management, Macready offered Phelps a large sum to accompany him on a tour of America, but Phelps declined. He thought that, with Macready out of London, his time had come.

In 1844 Phelps formed a partnership with Tom Greenwood, the manager of Sadler's Wells, and the actor Amelia Warner, to do at Sadler's Wells what Macready had tried to do at the patent houses: put on good productions of good plays, especially those of Shakespeare. It was a risky undertaking as Islington was regarded (then as now) as being a long way out of town in theatrical terms. West End theatregoers were unlikely to be drawn to what dramatic critics facetiously described as 'a sort of colonial outpost of the drama' in 'the remote waste of Islington',[38] productions were unlikely to be reviewed in the national press, and the large auditorium (2,600 capacity) had to be filled with the shopkeepers, clerks and artisans who lived in the area. The theatre was associated with pantomimes and nautical dramas, for which a huge water-tank had been installed under the stage to allow British naval victories to be re-enacted by fleets of models boats, but the 'legitimate drama' was almost unknown there, as the power of the patents had reserved it to Covent Garden and Drury Lane. The 1843 Theatres Regulation Act had changed all that, allowing any theatre to put on any kind of show, subject to getting a licence from the Lord Chamberlain. Phelps's management at Sadler's Wells was a direct result of that legislative change of the previous year.

In spite of the risks, this management, which lasted for eighteen years, was triumphantly successful. Phelps mounted all of Shakespeare's plays apart from *Troilus and Cressida* and *Titus Andronicus* (which were regarded as unactable on grounds of indecency[39]), *Richard II*, and the *Henry VI* trilogy. Plays that hadn't been seen for decades, and in some cases centuries, like *Love's Labours Lost* and *Pericles*, were revived. Phelps gave one of the earliest successful productions of *A Midsummer Night's Dream*, which had never been popular with actor-managers because it didn't contain a big star part. He played Bottom, and it became one of his signature parts. Like Macready, he insisted on long rehearsals and wanted everyone to feel they were doing their best. There was tremendous loyalty within the company to his vision and also within the audience. When the West-Enders began to make their way to distant Islington they were amazed by the quiet attentiveness of people they had expected to be raucous and uncomprehending in the face of high culture. Audience members would take it upon themselves to explain to newcomers that Sadler's Wells was not like other theatres: you were meant to sit quietly and listen to the play. Phelps's audience was too limited for long runs so he had to keep productions in repertory. Ticket prices were low, as his audience were predominantly working-class or lower middle-class, so there was never enough money for spectacle, but the sets and costumes were well designed to support the text. When the critics did eventually find their way to Islington, they acknowledged that tight budgets which rule out eye-popping spectacle can be an advantage: 'Shakespeare is not fairly heard when he is made to speak from behind masses of theatrical upholstery.'[40] The whole thing was an important step along the road towards a national theatre, showing that good theatre appeals to all classes.

Amelia Warner withdrew from the management after the first two years and in 1860 Tom Greenwood retired. This left Phelps with the business management as well as the artistic direction, and he began to find it too much. His beloved wife was diagnosed with breast cancer that would require long years of nursing, so Phelps gave his last performance at Sadler's Wells on 15 March 1862. This meant that he was available when Fechter was putting together his company for the Lyceum.

If Fechter was planning a Shakespearean season, it was natural that he would want to have Phelps in the company, but it soon became clear that he had another game in mind. Fechter opened in January 1863 with a play called *The Duke's Motto*, in which Phelps didn't appear. The play was a success and ran for months, during which Phelps had nothing to do. He asked Fechter to release him from his contract but Fechter refused. His real purpose in employing Phelps had been to keep his most serious rival off the stage, and he intended to continue that policy. He told Phelps that he was planning a production of *Hamlet*, so Phelps naturally assumed he would be playing the Dane. When Fechter told him he was intending to take that part himself, Phelps asked what he would be playing. 'I thought, perhaps, you would play the Ghost,' was the reply. Phelps refused and then made matters worse by telling Fechter's acting manager that he had no intention of playing the Ghost 'to a blasted Frenchman'.[41] Charles Dickens, who was a friend of both men, was asked to mediate but relations between the two men had deteriorated to the point at which no reconciliation was possible. Fechter terminated Phelps's contract which meant that Phelps was available again, just as Chatterton was telling Falconer that Drury Lane was going to revert to 'the legitimate and classic drama'. The timing couldn't have been better. He was offered £80 a week to play leading roles and to be what we would call artistic director.

1863/1864: The prestige of nationality

Falconer and Chatterton opened their second season at Drury Lane on Saturday 12 September 1863 with new managerial billing: 'Managers Messrs. Edmund Falconer and F. B. Chatterton'. There was no mention of the lease, still in Falconer's sole name, as Chatterton had insisted on equal billing.

The first production was Falconer's new three-act comedy *Nature's Above Art* which was so confused that, when one of the characters said he was puzzled by what was going on, the audience roared with laughter. One critic said it was hard to know if they were laughing with or at the author.[42] It ran for twenty-three performances and lost £729,[43] after which it was replaced by what Chatterton regarded as the main event of the season: a spectacular staging of Lord Byron's dramatic poem *Manfred*, starring Samuel Phelps in the title role.

Byron had always insisted that his dramas were meant to be read, not performed, as they were not suited to the conditions of the stage of his time. His judgement has, on the whole, been validated by posterity and, since Byron's reputation suffered a striking eclipse in the twentieth century, it is probably true to say that his plays have not only been unperformed but largely unread as well. There is very little in them that could be described as dramatic, and *Manfred*, which Byron described as a 'metaphysical drama', is a striking example of this. It is his version of the Dr Faustus legend, with a central character whose great learning has enabled him to conjure up and command demons, only to find that this does not bring him happiness. He carries the guilt of great sins but we don't know what they are. An Abbot tries to save his soul but without success. In an unspectacular death scene, Manfred tells the Abbot: 'Old man, tis not so difficult to die'.[44] When Byron sent it to his publisher, John Murray, he wrote that, whatever its failings, 'I have at least rendered it *quite impossible* for the stage, for which my intercourse with Drury Lane has given me the greatest contempt'.[45] Before scandalous rumours about his private life caused him to flee the country, Byron had been a member of the management sub-committee of Drury Lane and had not much enjoyed the experience, in spite of being a keen theatregoer. 'It is like being at the whole process of a woman's toilet – it disenchants.'[46]

The Steinbach Falls from *Manfred*

Byron's confidence in the impossibility of staging *Manfred* was misplaced. There was a production at Covent Garden in 1834, and the first night of Chatterton's Drury Lane production, nearly thirty years later, was a triumph, mainly owing to the appearance of Samuel Phelps. There was a large contingent from Islington in the first-night audience, determined to support their man now that he was finally being given his due in the West End. As Oxenford put it in his *Times* review: 'his exertions in the cause of the legitimate drama at Sadler's Wells have earned him a veneration which in some persons almost borders on idolatry... Mr Phelps is one of the great benefactors of the age.'[47] There was a roar of approbation as Phelps made his first entrance and everything went well from then on. This was a big show, with an enlarged orchestra playing Henry Bishop's score for the 1834 production[48] and choir of fifty voices, plus scenery that included the summit of the Jungfrau, the Steinbach waterfall and the Hall of Arimanes in the Netherworld (the latter based on John Martin's epic painting *Satan in Council*). Byron's rather subdued ending was replaced by one in which a bolt of lightning destroyed Manfred's castle and caused an avalanche. Oxenford gave it a good review in *The Times* on 13 October but then took the unusual step of reviewing the show again two weeks later. He wanted to draw attention to the significance of the success of *Manfred* for Drury Lane, a large theatre that, in terms he would use many times in the years to come, still maintained 'the *prestige* of nationality'.[49]

> In endeavouring to restore this establishment to the importance which traditionally belongs to it, Messrs Falconer and Chatterton have a somewhat delicate task to perform. One the one hand… they cannot be expected to resist the temptation of performing spectacles; on the other hand, if they devote themselves to mere glitter, they are gradually undermining the classical *prestige* of this property, which, much as it has been compromised by miscellaneous entertainments, is still of inestimable value. It is thus their obvious policy to make spectacle respectable by associating it with works of recognised literary merit and with the best histrionic talent that the times will afford.[50]

For the sake of appearances, Oxenford talks as if the change in managerial policy were the result of a joint decision by Falconer and Chatterton, when in reality it had been Chatterton's alone. Oxenford was in a position to know this as he was a Drury Lane insider. His one-act farces *Gone to Texas* and *Beauty or the Beast* were both used as curtain-raisers for *Manfred*. He even praised his own work (or had his assistant praise it), describing *Beauty or the Beast* as an: 'uproarious piece of extravagance… eliciting the most boisterous shouts of laughter'.[51]

One of the characteristics of Chatterton's managerial style was the extensive use of printed material 'explaining and extolling the objects he has in view',[52] to keep in touch with supporters, in very much the same way that the theatre companies today use their networks of 'Friends'. He used his programmes, season prospectuses, classified advertisements and flyers to set out his artistic policy. The flyers were especially useful as they were quite large in format, being four-page quarto-sized pamphlets with details of the cast and scenes on the first two pages, leaving two more pages for philosophising about art or (quite often in Chatterton's career) attacking rivals and critics. 'Mr Chatterton's manifesto has for some weeks formed a striking portion of our mural literature' wrote one critic sniffily, meaning that these flyers had been pasted on walls all over London.[53]

There was just such a flyer for *Manfred*. Pages three and four carried an extract from John Oxenford's *Times* review of the production followed by an essay written by 'A Dilletante Behind the Scenes'. This told expectant theatregoers:

> Though... Messrs Falconer and Chatterton have put forth no manifesto declaring their resolve... there can be little doubt that in witnessing the revival... of Byron's dramatic poem of *Manfred*, the public will be taking part in a laudable and spirited attempt to restore some dignity and some elevation to the productions of the English Stage, the success of which, and the consequent revival of the bygone glories of Drury Lane Theatre, will mainly depend upon their appreciation of this important step.[54]

If this isn't a manifesto, it certainly sounds very like one. For Chatterton, the production of *Manfred* was a watershed moment. He later told John Coleman: 'I was now enabled to realise the dream of my life – to restore Old Drury to its position as the home of the poetic drama, from which it had been deposed by E. T. Smith.'[55]

John Oxenford told his readers that the 'Dilletante Behind the Scenes' was actually Charles Lamb Kenney.[56] Kenney had first come into contact with Chatterton when he adapted *London Pride*, written by his father, the Irish playwright James Kenney, for production by Chatterton at the St James's in 1859. Growing up in a theatrical family, Kenney had enjoyed free access to the London theatres and spent many evenings in the pit of Drury Lane and the Adelphi watching plays with his schoolfriend Dion Boucicault. In 1841 he was appointed assistant to John Oxenford at *The Times*, although he didn't last long in the position.[57] Kenney was known as a wit and a toiler in the vineyard of literature in various capacities, his chief claim to fame being his translations into English of the libretti for several of Offenbach's operettas, including *La Belle Hélène*.[58] He never achieved any great success, probably because he was constitutionally lazy.[59] According to John Hollingshead: 'Charles Lamb Kenney... was a clever journalist on *The Times*, but he had one great peculiarity. When you wanted him in Printing House Square [the address of *The Times*] he was on the top of Snowdon; and when you wanted him on the top of Snowdon he was always in Printing House Square. When he became "literary adviser" to… F. B. Chatterton, of Drury Lane Theatre, this peculiarity was probably found to be a useful qualification.'[60] This last remark refers to Chatterton's volcanic temper, which made it advisable for people to make themselves scarce when it erupted. 'His outbursts of wrath… were terrible,' according to one leading lady. 'The humbler members of the company quailed before him.'[61]

'Literary adviser' was rather a grand title for Kenney's role at Drury Lane, which was closer to publicist. Chatterton claimed that, whilst he often used Kenney (and sometimes his younger brother Horace) to put his messages to the theatregoing public into good English, the content was always his own. Nevertheless, Chatterton must have respected Kenney's abilities, as he used him from the opening of *Manfred* to the collapse of his management sixteen years later.

Although Falconer was still the lessee, Chatterton dated his management of Drury Lane from the opening of *Manfred*. It established the template for all of his subsequent seasons: a big autumn drama followed by a big Christmas pantomime. It was fortunate for him, therefore, that the show was a great success. It ran for sixty-one performances until it had to be taken off to make way for the pantomime, which this year was *Sinbad the Sailor*. For *Sinbad*, William Beverley was brought back to Drury Lane with an assurance to the public that his services had been exclusively contracted for the Drury Lane pantomime. This year's scenes included the source of the Nile by moonlight (with a real waterfall), the Valley of Diamonds (from which Sinbad is carried in the claws of the Great Roc) and the great transformation scene of the Basaltic City of the Dwarfs into a beautiful garden peopled by fays in long silver robes. Robert Roxby returned to Drury Lane with his brother to stage manage (i.e. direct) the pantomimes until his death three years later. The script was by Blanchard (his twelfth for Drury Lane) and another regular, who had been at Drury Lane for as long as Blanchard, was on the bills: R. W. (Richard Wynne) Keene, whose pantomime work was always credited to Dykwynkyn. Keene was a designer of costumes and props who specialised in masks and what were called 'big heads' – large, papier-maché heads that represented demons, monsters and sometimes well-known characters such as leading politicians. Described as the 'Michel Angelo of pantomime mask inventors',[62] Keene was a highly skilled specialist prop-maker whose credits varied from year to year, but, while he sometimes designed the costumes, he always produced not only the big heads but armour, regalia and anything unusual.[63] His greatest claim to fame is that he was commissioned to produce the animals and monsters for the original production of Wagner's Ring

Cycle in 1876, including the dragon which was sent in three sections. Unfortunately the middle section was delivered to Beirut instead of Bayreuth, which spoiled the effect on the first night.

Pantomime 'big heads' being prepared in the Drury Lane workshop

One newcomer was Master Percy Roselle, a child prodigy who played the Old Man of the Sea – a part written specially for him. He was so popular that the next four Drury Lane pantomimes would be built around him, but his age was a matter of controversy. The management never stated his exact age in publicity, but the *Times* review described him as 'not... above seven years of age'.[64] Chatterton must have known that this couldn't be true because, when his management of the Theatre Royal, Rochester, had collapsed two years before, he had been followed into the theatre by a Mr Henning who presented Master Percy Roselle 'the little wonder'.[65] However prodigious Master Percy's talents might have been, it is unlikely that he would have been able to carry a show at the age of five. It seems probable that Percy Roselle was not a child but a midget.

For twelve performances the pantomime was preceded by *A Roland for an Oliver*, Thomas Morton's two-act musical farce, but on 9 January 1864 Falconer's new 'serio-comic drama' *Night and Morn* was introduced before *Sinbad*, with Samuel Phelps in the lead. 'Go to Drury,' Blanchard wrote in his diary, 'and see a dreary piece, three acts, by Falconer, called *Night and Morning* [sic]; very bad – say so.'[66]

One wonders to whom he said so; probably not to the author, who was also the lessee. John Oxenford wrote a review in which he tried to avoid saying what he thought of the play by simply describing the plot, which was manifestly absurd. He did express the view that, although it was short, it could benefit by being much shorter.[67] It was given forty-one performances and came to an end with the run of the pantomime on 5 March.

Manfred was then revived for eleven performances, with *The Four Mowbrays* as a curtain-raiser. *The Four Mowbrays*, devised forty years before to display the talents of Miss Clara Fisher, another child prodigy, was now a vehicle for Master Percy Roselle. Drury Lane closed for Passion Week and re-opened on Easter Monday, 28 March 1864, with a production that meant a great deal to Chatterton, because it was his first of a play by Shakespeare: *Henry IV Part 1*.

The commemoration of the tercentenary of Shakespeare's birth in 1864 was a milestone in the development of the idea of Shakespeare as not only the greatest playwright in the history of the theatre but a great national treasure and a sign of God's special care for the English nation. The first centenary in 1664 had passed unremarked, as did the second in 1764. However, in 1769 David Garrick organised a Shakespeare Jubilee in Stratford-upon-Avon that took Bardolatry to a new level. There was an oratorio in the church and a rotunda was erected beside the Avon for the performance of an Ode to Shakespeare, written by Garrick and set to music by Thomas Arne. There was to be a procession of actors dressed as Shakespearean characters, but that was rained off, and a firework display turned into a literal damp squib. The Avon burst its banks and revellers at the grand ball had to leave the rotunda in a hurry when it was in danger of being swept away by the flood. However, whilst it was not completely successful, the 1769 Jubilee did at least establish Stratford as a place for Shakespeare-lovers to visit, and a place that should be involved in anniversary commemorations.

By the middle of the nineteenth century, Shakespeare's national status was so well established that it would have been unthinkable not to commemorate the tercentenary on a large scale. A committee was formed in Stratford with another, called the National Shakespeare Committee, in London. They both had plans to erect a memorial, as well as organising the usual round of dinners, concerts and processions. The Stratford committee, well aware that Garrick had been mocked for not having a single line of Shakespeare's immortal verse recited during his Jubilee, took care to build a theatre for the performance of some plays. This theatre, called the Pavilion, was built on Southern Lane, on the other side of the road from the river, to avoid the risk of flooding.

It was a large building with a capacity of 5,000 and had excellent acoustics and sightlines. It was suggested that someone should consider bringing the Pavilion to London and erecting it in Leicester Square to confer on the London play-going public 'the rare English luxury of being comfortable in a theatre'.[68] However, there was the question of which plays and which players would be presented in the Pavilion, and here the Stratford committee were at a disadvantage. They needed people in London who were in touch with the theatre scene to act on their behalf, so they appointed Robert Hunter as their secretary and Revd J. C. M. Bellew, a theatre-loving Anglican clergyman, as their London representative. Hunter wrote to Phelps asking if he would appear in Stratford and offering the parts of Hamlet, Macbeth or Othello. Phelps said he would be happy to appear as Hamlet. Unfortunately Revd Bellew had already offered the part to his friend and near neighbour Charles Fechter, who had gratefully accepted. When Bellew discovered the mistake, he wrote to Phelps offering him Iachimo in *Cymbeline* and saying that Hunter had acted without authority in offering Hamlet.

Phelps was furious to be offered such an inferior part while the greatest part in English dramatic literature was to be played by a Frenchman, and a Frenchman who had treated him badly at the Lyceum the year before. He wrote an angry letter of protest describing his services to Shakespeare at Sadler's Wells and saying: 'I claim the right... to be considered the foremost man in my profession in a demonstration meant to honour Shakespeare... the Stratford committee have insulted me by asking any man in this country to play Hamlet on such an occasion, without having first offered me a choice of characters.'[69] He refused to have anything more to do with the Stratford celebrations and threatened to publish his correspondence with the committee.

As Phelps was the star of the Drury Lane season and a key figure in Chatterton's determination to be 'legitimate', Chatterton allowed Phelps to use one of his promotional pamphlets to express his sense of outraged dignity. To announce the forthcoming production of *Henry IV Part 1*, therefore, Chatterton produced a four-pager with the cast and scenes of the production on the first two pages, leaving pages three and four for the account of 'Mr Phelps and the Stratford-upon-Avon Committee'.[70] This was an error of judgement as Phelps came across as petulant and self-regarding. In fact, he was a modest man, almost too modest for his own good, but he became very sensitive wherever his services to Shakespeare were concerned. He soon discovered that the publication of his correspondence had caused offence owing to his claim to be considered 'the foremost man in my profession'. It was not universally agreed that Phelps *was* the leader of the profession. He was highly respected for his work at Sadler's Wells, but he did not have the status of Macready before him or Henry Irving after him. He was a solid, dependable actor with high ideals, but he was regarded as old-fashioned and he lacked star quality.[71] When Phelps learnt of the reaction to the publication of his correspondence, he was mortified and wanted to backtrack. Chatterton, no doubt feeling protective of his star, set his literary adviser to work, and within days Charles Lamb Kenney had produced a sixpenny pamphlet called *Mr Phelps and the Critics of His Correspondence with the Stratford Committee*. It was written in Kenney's worst style – sneering, arch and snobbish – but it made the reasonable point that Phelps had not claimed to be first in his profession, but the first who should have been consulted with regard to a national celebration of Shakespeare. He concluded by saying that Mr Phelps wished 'to retire from the field of controversy, determined to obtrude himself no more upon the attention of the public, save in a strictly professional capacity'.[72]

By this time, the dispute had inevitably taken on nationalistic overtones. 'The foremost of English tragedians is not to be put off with a paltry Iachimo, while a frog-eating Frenchman presents the noble Dane!' thundered *The Saturday Review*.[73] In the end there was no Hamlet at all at Shakespeare's birthday celebrations because Fechter, no doubt anticipating further references to frogs, snails, garlic and so on, backed out two weeks before the start of the celebrations.[74]

When *Henry IV Part 1* opened at Drury Lane on Easter Monday, directed by Phelps who also appeared as Falstaff, it was a triumph, hailed as the work of 'a national theatre which may now take rank as really one of the finest in the world'.[75] It was, by a long way, the most impressive and successful of the various Shakespearean productions marking the tercentenary. Phelps was a good Falstaff and the cast was strong. The text showed Phelps's reverence for the Bard, restoring the Owen Glendower scene and Lady Mortimer's Welsh song (arranged for the harp by Chatterton's Uncle Frederick) that had traditionally been cut. The production had new scenery by Beverley with costumes and armour designed by R. W. Keene (Dykwynkyn) 'taken from illustrated MSS of the period and other authorities'. The big scene was the Battle of Shrewsbury, fought by three hundred extras in real armour and described as 'simply the only battle scene we have ever seen on the English stage… Stage illusion has never been carried to a higher point, nor have the resources of our national stage ever been devoted to a worthier object'.[76] However, Blanchard noted in his diary: 'Phelps good as Falstaff, but, beyond the rush of supers at the end, not very expensively produced.'[77] Beverley's scenery was beautiful, especially the road to Gadshill by moonlight, but not overwhelming – 'appropriate to the plot' as one critic put it.[78] The text was still the most important thing.

The Battle of Shrewsbury from *Henry IV Part 1*

During the preparations for the tercentenary, there had been a good deal of metropolitan snobbery about whether a bunch of country folk in Warwickshire could be expected to do anything that would sufficiently honour the national poet. In fact, the Stratford committee was considerably more successful than the London committee, which achieved very little. When Charles Fechter dropped out, George Viner offered his productions of *The Comedy of Errors* and *Romeo and Juliet* from the Princess's Theatre and John Buckstone took his *Twelfth Night* from the Haymarket. As a devout Bardolater, Chatterton would no doubt have liked to be involved with the performances at Stratford, but the very public spat between his star and the Stratford committee ruled that out. Instead, he wished a plague on both committees. When the unwise reproduction of Samuel Phelps's correspondence was pulled from the Drury Lane programme, it was replaced by a contribution from 'A Dilettante' (Charles Lamb Kenney, under dictation) headed 'Shakespeare's Tercentenary'. This poured scorn on the 'occasional junketings organised by municipal brains in the delirium of a tercentenary fever, whether or no a French *chef de cuisine* contribute his condimental science to heighten the relish of the principal dish'. The sneering and Francophobia leave a sour taste, but the Dilletante went on to make a valid point. Both the London and Stratford committees had been focused on creating a physical memorial to Shakespeare in terms of a monument or statue.[79] Neither succeeded, and the failure was made more conspicuous by the fact that statues of the late Prince Albert were sprouting like mushrooms all over the Empire, but Chatterton's position was that there was no need for a graven image in any case. The best memorial to Shakespeare is the performance of his plays – and not just the half-dozen most popular ones that offered star parts to actor-managers:

> Until we have seen more of Shakespeare's works acted – the early, and the middle, and the late; the fanciful, the historical and the psychical… we cannot yet say that we thoroughly know this Shakespeare, of whom… we feel ourselves at liberty so lavishly to sing the praises.

The Dilletante saw the production of *Henry IV Part 1* at Drury Lane as 'the first stone for such a monument… and on the encouragement received from the public… will depend whether it become finally set up.' Chatterton wanted his audience to understand that the project to restore the fortunes of Drury Lane was a co-operative one.[80]

Henry IV Part 1 enjoyed a run of forty-eight continuous performances until the season closed on 21 May 1864, representing twenty-three per cent of all evening performances during the season. No other Shakespeare production at Drury Lane had enjoyed such a successful first run. Oxenford gave the management a glowing end-of-season report:

> On Saturday night Messrs Falconer and Chatterton closed Drury Lane for the season with the first part of *Henry IV*… They opened on the 10th of September, and the season just terminated is said to have been the longest for thirty years. Their policy has been to rely chiefly on works of literary celebrity, and thus turn to account the old *prestige* of their establishment… the soundness of this policy has been proved by the results.[81]

Oxenford maintained the fiction that Falconer and Chatterton were running Drury Lane jointly, but he must have been aware of the increasing tensions. In March 1864 Chatterton had insisted on a new partnership agreement with Falconer, who was by that time playing no significant part in running the theatre. Chatterton was constantly having to raise money to cover losses that he claimed were the result of putting on Falconer's plays which 'were not suited to the tastes of the Drury Lane audience'.[82] Under the terms of the new agreement, the profits were to be split fifty/fifty instead of two-thirds/one-third. In September 1864 Falconer gave Chatterton authorisation to sign cheques and documents on his behalf as the bank was refusing to accept Falconer's cheques, owing to the deterioration in his handwriting resulting from drink.[83]

1864 – 1865: Open for the legitimate drama

Prior to opening the 1864/1865 season, Falconer and Chatterton published a season prospectus 'which they trust will be found in keeping with the dignity of the National Theatre', announcing twelve plays by Shakespeare, a new play by Edmund Falconer, a new play by Theodore Martin called *Madonna del Pia* and the *Antigone* of Sophocles.[84] Although a detailed prospectus was expected for opera seasons, it was rare to publish one for a dramatic season since, in the absence of subsidy or subscription, the 'run' of a production was entirely dependent on the box office, making it difficult to predict the number of shows in a season. It seemed too good to be true – 'Mr Falconer has put too many plums in one pudding' according to one critic[85] but ten of the twelve Shakespeare plays were produced (plus *Julius Caesar*, which wasn't on the list), as well as two new plays by Falconer.[86]

The prospectus was accompanied by a pamphlet written by Kenney entitled 'The Legitimate Drama at Drury Lane Theatre' which began by claiming that: 'To find the Legitimate Drama triumphantly rearing its head again within the walls of Old Drury… is something to make an old playgoer rub his eyes with incredulous wonder'. It goes on to acclaim Falconer and Chatterton as 'halcyons of the National Drama' who:

> …have built your nest within her oldest temple [where] the people have returned, reverently, to her profaned altars; and the cynical misbelievers who would have had us deem her beneficent influence forever ended and replaced by the degrading orgies of the worshippers of that wicked deity of the nether world Sensation, are utterly confounded![87]

A little of this sort of thing goes a long way, but Kenney kept up the breathless hyperbole for fourteen pages.

The emphasis, from the start, was on legitimacy, and publicity for the season carried the strapline: *Open for the performance of legitimate drama*. Samuel Phelps was announced as stage manager, which in our terms would mean director or artistic director. A less welcome announcement was that the prices were going up.

Falconer and Chatterton had inherited from E. T. Smith a regime of low prices. When Smith took over Drury Lane in 1852, he had made drastic reductions in seat prices to: stalls 4s.; dress circle 3s.; pit 2s.; galleries 1s. and 6d. These prices were too low to be viable and Smith soon raised the stalls to 5s. and the dress circle to 4s. He varied his prices frequently, depending on the attraction – more for opera, less for circuses – but they were always low compared with other West End theatres. 'Reduced prices as usual' was the standard rubric in his advertising. In the last year of his management Smith was charging 6s. for stalls and 5s. for dress circle, but when Boucicault took Drury Lane for the last half of 1862 to present *The Colleen Bawn* he put prices back to 5s. stalls and 4s. dress circle. For their first two seasons, Falconer and Chatterton were charging: stalls 6s.; dress circle 4s.; pit 2s.; galleries 1s. and 6d. From the opening of the 1864/65 season, this became: stalls 7s.; dress circle 5s.; pit 2s.; galleries 1s. and 6d.

The season opened on 24 September with a revival of *Henry IV Part 1* which ran for six performances, making way for the much less frequently performed *Henry IV Part 2*. There had been no production of this in the West End since Macready played the King at Covent Garden in 1821, but Samuel Phelps had produced it at Sadler's Wells in 1853, doubling as the King and Justice Shallow. He repeated this double-act at Drury Lane and it was well received, particularly his performance as the foolish old Justice pathetically reminiscing about his wild youth. In his *Times* review, Oxenford drew an interesting comparison between the current managers of Drury Lane and Phelps as manager of Sadler's Wells:

> Drury Lane is to central London what Sadler's Wells was to a particular district. Regaining for their theatre a character for 'legitimacy', possessed of an ample stock of well-painted scenes, and by no means pledged to a system of costly 'revivals', they are able to present a series of Shakespearean plays without constantly aiming at a long 'run' or an intense sensation.[88]

William Beverley was in charge of the scenic department at Drury Lane, but was not expected to produce new sets for every production. When theatres were let on lease, they came with all of the scenery and costumes that had been created by previous managements and these were expected to furnish almost any play the new manager put on, with a little touching up.[89] In the days before three-dimensional or 'built-out' sets, it was an easy matter to get backcloths and wings out of storage, allowing for a rapid change of productions. A review of 1864/65 season noted that: 'Where new scenery has been required, Mr Beverley has supplied it; while some of the best of the old scenes, many magnificently painted, have been brought forward from their hiding places.' Even when it wasn't new, the scenery never looked shoddy, and one critic waxed lyrical over a Forest of Arden which comprised 'a notable display of the fine forest scenery which successive artists have left within these walls to keep their talents, if not their names, green in our memory'.[90] The system made it possible to put on plays like *Henry IV Part 2* that were interesting but not destined for a long run.

After a few more performances of the two *Henry IV* plays, plus some of *Othello* with Phelps in the title role, came another Shakespearean play with another big star. On 17 October *Cymbeline* opened with Phelps as Posthumus and Helen Faucit as Imogen. Helen Faucit was by this stage the *grande dame* of British theatre, the biggest female star Chatterton could have found to act opposite Samuel Phelps. Unfortunately they couldn't stand each other.

Helen Faucit, born into an acting family, had made her London debut at Covent Garden in 1836. She had been a member of Macready's companies at Covent Garden and Drury Lane in which she had starred in plays by Shakespeare (including *The Winter's Tale, Romeo and Juliet, As You Like It* and *Macbeth*) as well as creating the female leads in new plays including *The Lady of Lyons* and *Richelieu* by Bulwer Lytton, regarded as two of the best plays of the century. This all happened before her twenty-eighth birthday, so she had been Macready's leading lady at a very young age. Her relationship with the great man was so intense that, when she took time off for health reasons, it was said that she was pregnant by him, and she had to protect her reputation by threatening legal action against anyone repeating the rumour. Her career went from strength to strength as she built up a large and loyal following, not only in London but in major cities around the country. By the time she signed up with Chatterton for Drury Lane she was unquestionably the leading leading lady, the rivals of her youth having either died, like Amelia Warner and Louisa Nisbett, or reached the end of their careers, like Mrs Charles Kean (Ellen Tree). Aged fifty, she was a little old for Juliet and Rosalind, but it would have been regarded as very ungallant to point that out. In 1851 she had married Theodore Martin, a lawyer, parliamentary lobbyist and aspiring author.

They had a beautiful house in Onslow Square and moved in the best circles. Martin was eventually chosen to write the official biography of the late Prince Albert, which so pleased the Queen that he was knighted. Lady Martin became a very grand person indeed, but she had not lacked for the manner before the actual conferring of the title. She let it be known from the time of her marriage that she didn't need to act and would only accept roles that suited her love of the poetic drama.[91] Managers adopted a craven tone in their publicity, as if to thank her for the condescension she displayed in agreeing to appear. She was thus able to bring very considerable status to Chatterton's attempts to associate Drury Lane with the legitimate drama, but the engagement was good for her too. She had not been seen in London since 1858, so there was considerable anticipation of her re-appearance.

Unfortunately, she decided to treat Phelps to her grandest manner. 'She gave herself airs,' he complained, 'and a little of that went a long way with me. We didn't get on well together, and I fear we have never been just to each other; still she is a great actress.'[92] Mrs Martin was not so generous to him. Her friend Arthur Munby recorded in his diary, after taking tea with her in Onslow Square: 'I was a little amused to see however that Helen Faucit is not above the usual jealousies of the profession: she spoke with airy laughing scorn of Phelps's acting.'[93] The problem was that she could not forget that Phelps had been kept by Macready in small roles when she was playing leads. She was not inclined to take direction from him over twenty years later.

In spite of these unpromising omens, the production was a success. The day after the first night, John Oxenford, who disliked writing overnight reviews, inserted a brief paragraph to inform his readers that: 'Miss Helen Faucit… was greeted with a tumult of enthusiasm… The piece is strongly cast and admirably put upon the stage, after the precedent set by Mr Macready during his management of Drury Lane.'[94] Helen Faucit was no doubt also thinking of Macready's production of twenty-one years before, as the scenery was the same and she had been playing the same part.[95] Phelps, on the other hand, who had been given the small part of Belarius in Macready's production, was now playing the lead.

There were eight performances of *Cymbeline*, in repertory with *Henry IV* and *Othello*, which made way on 3 November for the big production of the season: *Macbeth* with Phelps and Faucit as the murderous couple. The scenery, by Beverley, was completely new and on a grand scale: it was the most spectacular production Helen Faucit ever appeared in,[96] but the scenery was still in keeping with the text. The poetry wasn't overwhelmed by what some Victorian critics termed the 'upholstery'. John Oxenford delivered one of his big set-piece reviews on the significance of the production four days after its opening (which was late even for him)[97] in which he described the plight of Melpomene, the Muse of Tragedy, wandering homeless around London since Macready's retirement. Phelps had put her up at Clerkenwell (Sadler's Wells), but if she wanted a berth in the West End she could only go to the Haymarket where her sister Thalia (the Muse of Comedy) was already in occupation. Charles Kean welcomed her to the Princess's Theatre in the 1850s, until he had to part with his expensive guest. Now, to everyone's surprise, she has taken up residence at Drury Lane:

> Although Drury Lane has now been for nearly two years under the management of the present lessees, Messrs Falconer and Chatterton, those gentlemen were not at first so clear about their principles of action as they are at present. Of late, they have adhered to 'legitimacy', and have succeeded. Drury Lane is now indisputably the house of the poetical drama… A *prestige* is restored that has much of the practical virtue of a patent.[98]

Hundreds were turned away on the first night and the demand for tickets was such that *Macbeth* had a continuous run of 38 performances (apart from a benefit performance of *Othello* just as the run was coming to an end). Neither Phelps nor Faucit was prepared to do six performances a week, so two other actors took over as the Macbeths on Tuesdays and Thursdays. There were two more performances of *Cymbeline* to accommodate pent-up demand, then the theatre closed for five days to get ready for the pantomime. By this stage, Drury Lane had been presenting Shakespeare on every night that it was open from Easter to Christmas – an extraordinary and still unrivalled record in the long history of the theatre.

The pantomime was *Hop o' My Thumb*, built around the juvenile talents of Master Percy Roselle, with scenery by William Beverley 'whose personal services will be exclusively devoted to this theatre, for the illustration of the Grand Christmas Pantomime'.[99] This ran to the end of January with John Oxenford's farce *A Young Lad From The Country* as the curtain-raiser. (This had also been the curtain-raiser for the last four weeks of *Macbeth*, making it Oxenford's most successful piece for Chatterton.) On 30 January, however, the pantomime became the afterpiece to Shakespeare's *Henry VIII* with Phelps in his signature role as Cardinal Wolsey. Although it now seems strange to follow a production of one of Shakespeare's plays with a pantomime, that was normal at the time. Ever since pantomimes had been introduced at the beginning of the eighteenth century, they had been afterpieces, starting at around 9.30 p.m. after a full-length play and ending between 11.00 p.m. and midnight. As Victorian pantomimes became bigger and longer, this arrangement seemed less satisfactory, especially as it meant keeping children up very late and making them sit through something else that they really didn't want to see. E. T. Smith had been addressing this problem when he introduced matinee performances of the pantomime on its own at 2.00 p.m. on Wednesdays in 1853. The practice was quickly adopted by other managers. Also, in recognition of the fact that most of the audience only wanted to see the pantomime, managers began to use short, one-act pieces, usually farces, as the first part of the evening programme, so that the pantomime began at 7.45 p.m. or 8.00 p.m. However, there was still a feeling that, while this was acceptable for the school holiday period, there should be a return to the practice of having a full-length play as the first item on the bill at some point during January or at the latest February, so that serious theatregoers would not be starved of intellectual nourishment.

Falconer and Chatterton moved into Drury Lane at this transitional phase and, for the four seasons that they were jointly in charge, the pantomime was preceded by a one-act farce for the first few weeks, then by a full-length play for the last part of its run. (Pantomimes usually closed at the end of February or the beginning of March.). Oxenford's review of *Henry VIII* sets out the thinking behind this:

> During the Christmas holydays the importance of the pantomime so completely outweighs all other considerations, and the holyday-makers are so anxious to see the entertainment of the season begin as soon as possible, that a short farce suffices for the earlier part of the evening. 'Legitimacy' is thus in abeyance till about the end of January, when affairs theatrical resume their normal state and the pantomime is regarded as a glittering supplement to a more serious form of recreation.[100]

He goes on to say that *Henry VIII* is not a spectacle, as 'an audience which before 10 o'clock is about to witness the splendours of Mr W. Beverley's scenes in the pantomime does not require... decorative splendours.' So *Henry VIII*, which began at 7.00 p.m., ran for less than three hours. It was customary in the nineteenth century to drop the final act of the play, closing with the death of Queen Katharine, and Phelps cut this even further to close with the death of Wolsey. *Henry VIII* was followed by Bulwer Lytton's *Richelieu* which also ended around 10.00 p.m.[101] When the pantomime became the afterpiece, it was shortened and ended with the transformation scene, omitting the whole of the harlequinade. Nevertheless, it must have been a late night for the kiddies, assuming that parents were still bringing their children to the pantomime in February.

Richelieu ran for two weeks, and on 4 March Helen Faucit returned for a five-week engagement during which she would appear on three nights a week as the heroines of *Romeo and Juliet, As You Like It* and *Cymbeline*. By this stage Phelps had had enough of acting with her and gave the part of Posthumus in *Cymbeline* to Walter Montgomery. *Macbeth* wasn't revived, so Phelps appeared in his popular roles on the nights Faucit wasn't acting.

Drury Lane was closed for Passion Week, as it had been ever since Falconer and Chatterton moved in. From the re-opening of the theatres that followed the restoration of the monarchy in 1660, there had been nights when theatres had to remain closed, particularly during Lent. Over the years these restrictions had gradually been lifted and the requirement to close for Passion Week came to an end in 1862 (apart from Good Friday). Nevertheless Chatterton, who was a deeply religious man, insisted on observing the old restriction and would usually arrange to be rehearsing a new production, thus giving an excuse for closure. In this case, the new production was to be Milton's masque *Comus*.

Like the plays of Lord Byron, Milton's *Comus* was not written for the public stage. It was commissioned for a private performance before the first Earl of Bridgewater by members of his family in 1634. Conceived as a eulogy on chastity, it was more of a pageant than a play and not, therefore, very promising material for a London manager. Nevertheless, also like Byron, Milton was considered a symbol of high culture, which meant that, from time to time, people would try to increase their stock of cultural capital by staging *Comus*. In 1843 Macready had put on a production at Drury Lane, adding bits from *L'Allegro* and *Arcades*, and it was this text that Chatterton used. Comus was a sort of minor god of debauchery and the best parts of the production were the 'Bacchanalian dances and revel rout' of his followers, with lots of ballet girls showing their legs. There was new scenery by Beverley with costumes and masks by R. W. Keene 'from classical authorities'. A choir of fifty included soloists from the Paris Conservatoire and an increased orchestra included Chatterton's Uncle Frederick playing his own arrangements on the harp. Nevertheless, a paean of praise to chastity was always going to be a hard sell in Drury Lane – an address famous for its brothels in the eighteenth century –

and the show was a flop.[102] 'The public would not come to see it,' Chatterton admitted later. 'They praised it and kept away.'[103]

Nevertheless, *Comus* ran for thirty nights as the afterpiece for various plays starring Samuel Phelps, as well as a new French Revolution drama in blank verse by Falconer (who played Robespierre with a heavy Irish brogue) called *Love's Ordeal*. Blanchard described it as 'very long [four hours] and very dull'.[104] It lasted for seven performances.

The season closed on 20 May with Edmund Falconer's benefit, consisting of his own farce *The O'Flaherty's* followed by *Cymbeline* followed by *Comus*. There was a feeling that something extraordinary had happened at Drury Lane. A theatre that had struggled for years to keep the doors open with circuses and operas was now acclaimed as the home of 'the poetic drama', as if nothing could be more natural. The season had run for 194 nights, of which 123 (63 per cent) had been given to Shakespeare. The sense of the historic moment was sufficient to persuade Samuel Phelps to overcome his antipathy towards Helen Faucit and rejoin the cast of *Cymbeline* for one last performance opposite the *grande dame*. Falconer delivered a curtain speech (probably written for him by Chatterton) thanking his company and team, and promising that, since the success of the season had proved that 'the relish of the public for good plays... is as great as ever', the 'legitimate drama' was in no danger at Drury Lane, and that he and his partner would be back with more of the same in September.[105]

Once again, the season received a glowing assessment from John Oxenford. He praised the Shakespearean productions, 'executed without startling magnificence, but generally with appropriate decorations, a valuable stock of old scenery having been renovated', and the assembling of a permanent company headed by Phelps. 'The soundness of their system,' he told his readers, 'is proved by the fact that the last two seasons of Drury Lane have been the longest within the reach of the longest memories.'[106] Another critic compared the effect on public taste of presenting the works of great authors at Drury Lane to the removal of filth from the Thames by the construction of the London sewers.[107]

It was an extraordinary moment for Chatterton. As far as most of the theatregoing public were concerned, Falconer, as lessee, was in charge of Drury Lane,[108] but Chatterton had been able to take advantage of Falconer's decline to seize control and return Drury Lane to 'legitimacy'. Only weeks before that start of the first 'legitimate' season, *The Illustrated London News* had warned that the prospects for the legitimate drama were so bleak that it might have to be taken out of the commercial sector to survive. Now, two years later, it could report that: 'The public has declared, in most unmistakable terms, its entire appreciation of a management that has so undauntedly and successfully enlisted under the banners of legitimacy.'[109] At the age of only thirty, Chatterton had achieved his goal of making Drury Lane the home of the poetic drama. He had succeeded where the great Macready had failed, and he had done it without a subsidy and whilst coping with an alcoholic partner who insisted on staging his own increasingly unpopular plays. The next season would see the end of this partnership and Chatterton's assumption of full control as 'Sole Lessee and Manager', but this moment in 1865, as the second 'legitimate' season came to its end, was the highpoint of his career at Drury Lane. Things would never go so well again.

1865 – 1866: That fatal quicksand Drury Lane

The 1865/66 season got off to a bad start – in fact, it nearly didn't start at all. On 1 September 1865 Chatterton published the bills announcing the new season and Falconer applied for an injunction to prevent him from opening the theatre. Falconer claimed that Chatterton had agreed to dissolve their partnership and therefore had no further authority at Drury Lane.

The dispute, which marked the final stage of the now collapsing relationship between the two men, had begun in January when Chatterton discovered that Falconer was trying to raise money by issuing forward-dated cheques drawn against Drury Lane. Under the terms of the partnership agreement, both partners had to agree on any loans taken out or liabilities incurred, and Chatterton had no intention of allowing Falconer to raise money in such a risky way. Falconer took his refusal as an expression of his intention to dissolve the partnership, and Chatterton was not averse to this. However he insisted that he had to receive the £3,675 that he had invested in the business, most of which was represented by the money still owing to him from the 1861/62 season at the Lyceum. Falconer disowned this debt, so Chatterton would not agree to the dissolution. However Falconer proceeded on the assumption that Chatterton had agreed to dissolve the partnership for which six months' notice was required. On Friday 22 September 1865 – the day before the season was due to open Falconer's application for an injunction was heard in the Court of Chancery.

Falconer's complaint was based on a portrait he painted of himself as an artistic soul who wasn't good with money and was easily misled by others into signing documents he hadn't read. He admitted that he had agreed to take Chatterton into partnership in March 1863, sharing profits on a two-thirds/one-third basis. However he repudiated the clause in the partnership agreement that gave Chatterton's investment in the partnership as £3,675. He claimed that he had asked for the clause to be removed, that the removal had been agreed, but that he had been so ill at the time that he didn't read the document before signing it, so he was unaware that the clause objected to was still included. He was feared to be in danger of death or insanity as a result of the stress incurred in running Drury Lane, so he had to trust his partner and his solicitor, who had been recommended to him by Mr Chatterton. A year later, the partnership needed to raise even more money, which Falconer thought was surprising as business had been good, but he was so ill that he left the running of the theatre almost entirely to Chatterton, who was responsible for the money. Under the terms of this second partnership document of March 1864, Chatterton was to receive one-half of the profits rather than one-third. The partners were to also have an equal share in debts and losses. Falconer agreed to everything, but was so ill at the time that his hand had to be guided as he signed his name, again without reading the document.[110] By the beginning of the following year, Falconer was once again surprised to discover that further funds were needed, but perhaps this was because Mr Chatterton had been taking money out of the business that he was not entitled to.[111] Falconer therefore requested that the partnership be declared dissolved; that Drury Lane should be prevented from opening on the next day; and that a receiver should be appointed to handle its affairs.

    Chatterton's answer to the complaint was lengthy and robust. He denied that Falconer had ever been so ill as to be in danger of death or insanity. He regretted to have to inform the court that Mr Falconer's incapacity for business was due to his addiction to wine and spirits, and that his intemperance had done great damage to the conduct of the theatre's business until it became a public scandal. When he wasn't drunk, Mr Falconer was perfectly capable of understanding what was going on. The contents of both of the partnership agreements had been explained to him and Chatterton had given him a detailed account of how the sum of £3,675 had been arrived at, to which Falconer had good-humouredly replied: 'Well, a man certainly cannot dispute his own signature'.[112] It was not the case that Chatterton had been solely responsible for finances and had concealed information from his partner. The company's accounts and financial statements were kept at the theatre by the treasurer and were available for inspection by both partners, who had to sign off accounts jointly. The losses sustained by the business were occasioned by Mr Falconer's insistence of staging and starring in his own plays 'and also on insisting on engaging so many members of his own family who are incapable of sustaining the parts in which they appear'.[113]

Courts tend to take a dim view of people who sign documents without reading them and Falconer gave a very poor account of himself. Chatterton came across as an efficient man of business, which he was, who was able to produce documentary evidence to support his case. The judge refused to grant the injunction or to appoint a receiver, so Drury Lane did in fact open the following night.[114]

After this courtroom drama, there was a danger that the actual drama might come as an anti-climax. However, Oxenford reported that the opening of the season, with a revival of *Macbeth* followed by a revival of *Comus*, went well and came as a relief to those who feared that 'Melpomene might flee the earth, as Astraea did in days of yore' once the 'very disjunctive preposition *versus*' replaced 'the conjunctive conjunction *and*' between the names of Falconer and Chatterton.[115]

Helen Faucit was no longer in the cast and Phelps was now alternating with James Anderson as Macbeth. Anderson had found himself bankrupt with the loss of all his savings when his management of Drury Lane collapsed in 1851, but he had restored his fortunes by several successful tours of the USA. In 1863 he went back into management, taking over the Surrey Theatre on Blackfriars Road in partnership with Richard Shepherd. Once again, his managerial attempts were doomed, but for a different reason: the Surrey burnt down during the night of 30 January 1865. Anderson estimated his losses at £2,000, including his costumes, armour, jewellery and his irreplaceable theatrical library.[116] There was a charity matinee of *The School for Scandal* at Drury Lane on 16 February 1865 for all those affected by the fire, but Anderson was fortunate enough to get some more permanent relief for himself: Chatterton hired him for Helen Faucit's forthcoming five-week stint, opening with *Cymbeline* on 6 March, and he remained with the company for the autumn season.

This opened on 23 September 1865 with the *Macbeth/Comus* programme which ran for thirty nights. This was followed by six performances of *Julius Caesar*, leading up to the new autumn production of *King John*, which opened on 4 November. This was a big production 'which for splendour... has never been surpassed',[117] with new scenery by Beverley, props and banners by R. W. Keene and costumes (including two hundred suits of armour) based on historical sources.[118] Phelps played the King, James Anderson was Faulconbridge (the same part he had played in Macready's production at Drury Lane twenty-three years earlier) and Master Percy Roselle 'of pantomime celebrity'[119] was Prince Arthur, the rightful king who dies attempting to escape from the clutches of his wicked Uncle John. John Oxenford noted that Percy Roselle was younger than Shakespeare's Prince Arthur, who in turn was younger than his historical counterpart. In fact, the historical Prince Arthur was sixteen when he died, and Percy Roselle ('the little fellow acts with great intelligence') was probably already older than that. Although *King John* is rarely performed now, it was one of Shakespeare's most popular plays in the eighteenth and nineteenth centuries, partly because its rabid anti-Catholicism was felt to reflect 'the national character, natural progress, and the national spirit'.[120] Oxenford thought that no play was better suited to a national theatre than *King John* 'which is impregnated with nationality throughout, everywhere appealing to the feelings, and even to the prejudices, of the English masses'.[121]

King John ran for thirty-seven performances, after which the theatre closed for a week for the get-in of the pantomime. This year it was *Little King Pippin*, once again created to showcase the talents of Percy Roselle who was having a busy year for a supposed nine-year-old. The theatre

The betrothal of Princess Blanche and the Dauphin outside Angiers from *King John*

historian John Doran visited Drury Lane on the afternoon of Boxing Day to describe the production for the readers of *Temple Bar Magazine*. He recorded 900 people employed on the show, including front-of-house and backstage crew, with over 200 children, 60 ballet girls, 48 wardrobe staff, 45 dressers, 6 hairdressers and 17 gasmen.[122] The growing dominance of the Drury Lane pantomime in London can be seen in the increased number of matinees. Falconer and Chatterton had inherited from E. T. Smith a tradition of pantomime matinees on Wednesday. For *Hop o' My Thumb* that increased to Wednesdays and Saturdays, and for *Little King Pippin* to Mondays, Wednesdays and Saturdays, with matinees every day apart from Boxing Day in the opening week. *The Illustrated London News* welcomed the increased number of matinees as a sort of public service for children:

> … who ought not to be subjected, even for a single night, to the unwholesome influences of late sitting, foul air, flaring gas, and unwonted excitement from seven o'clock to nearly twelve… it is better for them to be at Drury Lane Theatre from two o'clock till five than romping in the drawing room, or moping in the nursery… the pleasant sight at the doors of the good old playhouse, when such an audience… of boys and girls, with their parents, governesses, and other domestic guardians, are coming out, in a mood of unmixed gratification… will plead most effectively, we trust, in favour of this rational custom of morning performances.[123]

'Returning from the pantomime'

This commendable urge to protect children from the foul air and unwholesome influences of a late night in the theatre did not extend to the very large numbers of children who appeared in the pantomimes. Doran saw 200 at the rehearsal for *Little King Pippin* (1865/66) but this cohort would grow. *Puss in Boots* (1868/69) featured 300 'miniature marines' on the deck of a man of war, while *Aladdin* (1874/75) had 400 children recreating the Lord Mayor's Show. These children were in the theatre until nearly midnight every night from Boxing Day until some point in February or March, with two or three matinees a week, so it must have interfered with their schooling. There were occasional calls for restrictions on their employment but defenders of the system, like the journalist George Augustus Sala, maintained that the experience did them no harm and taught them much that was useful, as well as bringing their families a few shillings a week. Sala found that there was a hierarchy within these juvenile troupes, with career-conscious children unwilling to play vegetable characters such as a stick of celery or – the lowest of the low – a potato.[124]

On 21 February 1866, during the run of *Little King Pippin*, there was an AGM of the renters (i.e. shareholders) of Drury Lane. A vote of thanks was given to the managers for a season that had produced the highest dividend (£7, over £800 today) for many years. Prior to the arrival of Falconer and Chatterton it had been £2 or £3 and sometimes nothing. The renters were delighted that an amicable solution had been found to the recent 'misunderstanding' between the managers, 'as a contrary course must have proved detrimental to the interests of the renters'.[125] Nine days later, Falconer was incarcerated in Whitecross Street Prison for debt. James Anderson, who knew what it felt like to be taken from the Drury Lane manager's office to debtors' prison, lamented: 'I did think that an Irishman's luck would have saved him from the fate that has befallen so many of his predecessors. But no! That fatal quicksand, Drury Lane, swallowed up Edmund Falconer.'[126]

Falconer's bankruptcy proceedings dragged on for months, and he was actually imprisoned for eleven weeks because of his failure to produce accounts and reach agreement with his creditors. He made wild accusations against his partner, claiming that Chatterton owed him £9,296. Chatterton was furious about the aspersions being cast on his integrity and insisted on their withdrawal before Falconer was discharged.[127] As the surviving (non-bankrupt) partner, Chatterton, was now paying off the partnership's debts. He claimed that he paid every penny and that it cost him £10,000 – well over a million pounds in modern values.[128]

The fact that performances at Drury Lane continued without interruption, with Falconer's name still appearing in the advertisements as joint manager, until the season closed on 24 March, shows how little he had to do with running the theatre by this stage. With his bankruptcy, the lease reverted to the Company of Proprietors, who advertised for applicants. There were a lot of people wanting to run Drury Lane, so Chatterton strengthened his chances by giving himself a benefit. There was nothing out of the ordinary about the performance – Phelps was appearing as Richelieu once again – but there was an unusual advertisement announcing it in the theatrical newspaper *The Era*. The paper's classified columns carried details of an organising committee for Chatterton's benefit of over forty people, headed by an admiral and including many of Chatterton's close associates at Drury Lane, expressing 'their sense of the ability and integrity which have characterised the managerial career of Mr F. B. Chatterton'.[129] The wording was carefully chosen because integrity was a quality that no one, by this time, would have attributed to Edmund Falconer. The afterpiece for the evening was a performance of *The Beggar's Opera*. If any of the proprietors were in the house for Gay's 'Newgate pastoral', they must have been reminded of the current lessee of Drury Lane, languishing at that moment in debtors' prison.

The proprietors awarded the lease to Chatterton, not because his offer was the highest but because he had impressed them with his management of the theatre during Falconer's lesseeship when, as everyone knew, he had really been in charge. 'Whilst his efforts were bold, his experience was great; and these things combined had led to his success.'[130] Chatterton was granted a seven-year lease at £5,000 per annum – an increase of £500 – for a season of up to 200 nights; nights over 200 would be charged at £5 extra up to a maximum rent of £5,350 for 270 nights.[131]

Chatterton, meanwhile, had lost all of the money Falconer owed him from the run of *Peep o' Day* four years before and he was saddled with £10,000 of debt. Nevertheless, it was his dream come true, like one of Beverley's wonderful transformations of darkness into light. He had gone from being yoked to a spendthrift alcoholic who insisted on starring in his own rotten plays to being the man who had inherited the mantle of Macready. He was going to succeed where the great man had failed and show that Drury Lane could once again be the National Theatre, the temple of Shakespeare and the home of the poetic drama. Following his by-now established precedent, Chatterton published a prospectus for the season in which he promised to stick to 'the course which during the last few years has revived the old renown of Drury

Lane Theatre as a home of the Legitimate Drama', resolving 'to place his main reliance on a series of Shakespearean performances'.[132] It was a bold vision of which the risks would have been obvious to anyone who knew the history of the building, but the commitment was warmly received. 'No one has ever shown a healthier spirit of enterprise,' declared *The Era* encouragingly, and *The Illustrated London News*, while mocking the prolixity and poor grammar of the manifesto, promised 'a hearty welcome' for Chatterton 'who now wields the baton alone' and has promised that 'at the national theatre the legitimate drama is the decided attraction'.[133]

Chatterton was so pleased with his manifesto that he sent a copy of it to Macready, now living in retirement in Cheltenham. Macready's reply was a model of tact and restraint:

> In acknowledging the very handsome tribute that you offer to my humble endeavours to maintain the dignity of my late profession, I can only wish you, as I most cordially do, every possible success in the honourable and arduous task you have undertaken.[134]

Chatterton described this letter as 'one of proudest possessions of my life',[135] but we can only speculate as to what Macready must have been thinking when he wrote it. When Macready took on Drury Lane in 1841, he had been the acknowledged leader of his profession: a great actor, a great interpreter of Shakespeare and a great director. He had gathered at Drury Lane a brilliant company representing the best of the profession, and he had the support of an influential coterie of writers, artists and intellectuals. The failure of the venture had cost him his savings. Chatterton was embarking on his lesseeship with few of these advantages and at a time when shows were more expensive to produce because production values were higher. In spite of this, Chatterton went into it with a heart full of pride. 'I determined to play a high game and to start with a flourish of trumpets.'[136]

5

Sole Lessee and Manager

1866 – 1867: Shakespeare in his proper home

On Saturday 22 September 1866, Chatterton opened his first season as sole lessee and manager of the Theatre Royal, Drury Lane. At the age of thirty-two, he was in charge of the largest theatre in the West End with an official capacity of 3,800, although more could be crammed in on a busy night.[1]

Having disposed of his alcoholic partner, he was determined to make a splash with this opening, and had the whole house, which had been completely redecorated only four years before, repainted and regilded. The rotunda was decorated with potted plants and the saloon now had a counter displaying newspapers and magazines. Drury Lane had originally been known as the King's Theatre and had enjoyed the unusual privilege, in the days when theatre riots were an occupational hazard, of being able to call upon a division of guards to defend its entrances. This custom had long since fallen into abeyance, but Chatterton revived it for his big first night, so the patrons were greeted with military splendour.

The opening production was a revival of the previous season's *King John* with the same cast except that the Irish actor Barry Sullivan took over as Faulconbridge. In his *Times* review John Oxenford gave Chatterton's efforts the sort of boost that far exceeded anything that Charles Lamb Kenney could come up with for the printed publicity:

> The days when 'Old Drury'... was one of the most insignificant of playhouses have passed away... Drury Lane has in the sight of the people gained an exceptional nationality... There is a widely spread feeling that Shakespeare at Drury Lane is in his own proper home, and... there is a large multitude that loves to associate with the national poet the belief in a national theatre.[2]

King John was followed by the one-act version of *The Comedy of Errors* that had been presented at the Princess's Theatre two years before, with the uncannily similar Webb brothers – Henry and Charles – as the Dromios.[3]

All of the principal actors were 'called', with a final call for Chatterton himself, who stood in the centre of the company and led them in a rousing rendition of the National Anthem. It was a night to remember.

Chatterton was fully aware of the value of William Beverley to his management and put him under exclusive contract to Drury Lane, rather than – as previously – exclusive for the pantomime only.[4] The poster for *King John* carried Beverley's name in enormous letters – larger than the font used for Phelps, for Chatterton and for Shakespeare. This would become the norm for the rest of Chatterton's management. With very few exceptions, Beverley would have his name in larger letters than anyone else's.[5]

A week of *King John* was followed by a week of *Macbeth*, with Phelps and Barry Sullivan alternating as Macbeth, then another week of each play leading up to the big production of the autumn season: Goethe's *Faust*. This was not an obvious choice for Drury Lane, but Chatterton must have been sufficiently encouraged by the success in 1863 of *Manfred*, Byron's take on the Faust legend, to feel that he might as well go for the most famous version of all. Byron had been a great admirer of Goethe, although he claimed never to have read his *Faust*, and Goethe was generous in his praise of *Manfred*, describing it as 'a wonderful phenomenon'.[6] Goethe's *Faust* was acknowledged to be not only his own greatest work, but one of the greatest works of German literature. Unfortunately it was scarcely any easier to stage than Byron's plays, running to two complete five-act dramas full of philosophy and mysticism. The first part took Goethe thirty years to write and the second part wasn't published until after his death. Chatterton set Bayle Bernard to work on an adaptation that would work for the London stage.

Bernard, who was the author of over one hundred plays, wisely decided that there was no point in trying to abbreviate Goethe's two plays, which had never been intended for the stage anyway, so he created a new framework into which he shoe-horned as many bits from the original as possible. This was not the first attempt to adapt the German masterpiece: in 1825 Robert Elliston had staged at Drury Lane a version by George Soane (son of the famous architect) which was successful on the basis of its spectacular scenery and the fact that it virtually ignored Goethe's text;[7] Dion Boucicault had adapted a French version, which he called *Faust and Margaret*, for Charles Kean to stage at the Princess's in 1854; and Gounod's popular opera, also based on the French version, had appeared in 1859. However, Chatterton claimed that his version was effectively the first appearance of Goethe's masterpiece on the English stage because it stuck more closely to the original than any of the other adaptations. He acknowledged the concern that might arise from having 'Goethe enthroned with Shakespeare... on equal terms',[8] but he believed that 'the arena of a National Stage, such as that of Drury Lane theatre, cannot be better or more gracefully occupied than in presenting... the productions of great writers of other nations'. He clinched the matter by calling Goethe 'the German Shakespeare' and referring to 'the many affinities between the races from which the genius of Shakespeare and Goethe arose'.[9] Patrons were confronted, as they arrived, by a colossal bust of Goethe in the foyer.

The production was on a large scale, with Beverley's pencil (the everlasting metonym for his design skills) supplying quaint medieval architecture, the ascent of Margaret into the Empyrean, and – most spectacular of all – the summit of the Brocken on Walpurgis Night, a sort of Hieronymous Bosch-style vision of demonic decadence:

> The orgies of the Walpurgis mob are of a kind novel to the stage. Witches and their familiars creep through the chinks and crevices of jagged rocks, till the scene is peopled by a wild unruly mass.[10]

Costumes and props were by R. W. Keene and there was an 'increased orchestra and numerous chorus' performing a score that comprised the work of Weber, Spohr, Mendelssohn and Haydn (but not Gounod). Samuel Phelps was Mephistopheles, his son Edward was Faust and Mrs Hermann Vezin was Margaret. The first night was a great success and Chatterton received two curtain calls for his efforts.

A week after the opening, Chatterton was running extracts from press notices in the classified advertising and on the posters. He was also using the classifieds to explain his artistic policy to the public, which meant that the Drury Lane classifieds dominated the theatre classified columns to a marked degree. *Faust* had an uninterrupted run of twenty-five performances, after which it alternated with performances by Helen Faucit in *As You Like It, The Lady of Lyons* and *The Hunchback*. (These would be her last performances in London, apart from occasional benefits.) For the first few weeks of its run, *Faust* was being followed (rather incongruously, we would feel) by *The Comedy of Errors*, until that was replaced as the afterpiece by *Catherine and Petruchio*, David Garrick's shortened, sentimental version of *The Taming of the Shrew*. The last performance was on 19 December, after which the theatre closed until the opening of the pantomime on Boxing Day.

While Faust was selling his soul to the devil at Drury Lane, Edmund Falconer was experiencing his own problems at Her Majesty's Theatre in the Haymarket, which he had rented to produce his new play *Oonagh*.

Falconer's verbosity was legendary and he was described by the theatre critic Clement Scott as 'the most long-winded author that the stage has ever known',[11] but he really excelled himself with *Oonagh*. The first performance on 19 November dragged on past eleven o'clock, past midnight and past one o'clock in the morning. There was a trial scene which seemed to take longer than the real thing, with speeches for the prosecution and the defence, after which the judge told the jury that as some of the evidence had been contradictory, he would read them his notes. 'No, don't', shouted a man in the pit, 'Hang the old duffer at once!'[12] At two in the morning the stage crew took matters into their own hands and brought down the curtain. A legend developed around this disastrous first night to the effect that the first performance of *Oonagh* was also the last, as Falconer fled to the USA the next day to escape his creditors.[13] In fact, it staggered on for two weeks, after which Falconer really did depart for America. *Oonagh* was known in the business as Falconer's Shipwreck.[14]

The Drury Lane pantomime this year was *Number Nip*, based on a mid-European fairy tale about a mischievous Gnome King who can change his shape and has to be tamed by marriage. It was the usual over-the-top affair with scenes of The Retreat of Romance, The Palace of the Gnome King in the Centre of the Earth and a magnificent transformation scene of The Earth's Treasures as the Wedding Dowry of Number Nip. There were a hundred ballet girls as River Fairies and a hundred children as little elfin creatures who crawl through the keyhole of a poor cobbler's shop and spend the night making wonderful fairy shoes to boost his business. Percy Roselle was Number Nip, supported by what had become Chatterton's regular team: script by Blanchard, sets by Beverley, costumes by Dykwynkyn, James Tully as musical director and John Cormack as choreographer. Edward Stirling, who had worked at Drury Lane under E. T. Smith, returned as stage manager (we would say director) to replace William Beverley's brother Robert Roxby, who had died in July. Oxenford's review in *The Times* acknowledged the problems that faced Chatterton in trying to revive the ancient glories of Drury Lane in a rapidly changing theatrical environment:

> Within the last few years there have, indeed, been wonderful changes in the topography of the drama. Old 'institutions' have threatened to sink into oblivion; obscure nooks have become places of fashionable resort; saloons, by the magic of the Lord Chamberlain's licence, have been converted into theatres; music halls have expanded into gorgeous temples of the ballet; but no

change can affect 'Old Drury' as the theatre typical of Christmas. On ordinary occasions, fashion is rather disposed to favour theatrical edifices of dimensions so small that they would have been utterly despised by our fathers; but a large pantomime at a large house is like the Christmas pudding, an acknowledged holiday treat.[15]

Number Nip ran until 4 March, clocking up sixty-three evening performances and twenty-two matinees (Mondays, Wednesday and Saturdays to the end of January). It ran with a farce called *A Day After the Wedding* as the curtain-raiser until 21 January, after which Samuel Phelps began to appear in full-length plays like *The Man of the World* and *The Merchant of Venice* with a shortened version of *Number Nip* as the afterpiece. There was a sad benefit matinee on 21 February to raise money for the widow and five children of Henry Webb who had died in January, just weeks after delighting Drury Lane audiences as one of the Dromios in *The Comedy of Errors*. It featured the companies of several London theatres in extracts from their latest hits, ran for four hours and raised £460.[16]

Following the closure of the pantomime, there was a revival of *Faust*, which only lasted for two weeks, after which Chatterton produced Henry Bishop's operatic version of *Rob Roy*, with Phelps as Baillie Nicol Jarvie. The part of Sir Francis Osbaldistone was to have been played by Sims Reeves, the most popular tenor of the day, but he went sick at the last moment and, after postponing the opening for a week, Chatterton was forced to cast someone else until Reeves recovered. Audiences were well used to no-shows from Reeves, who pleaded a sore throat to an increasingly sceptical public,[17] but this time he refused to join the cast at all as he objected to the way in which a replacement had been found. He felt Chatterton should have waited. Without its star, *Rob Roy* closed after eighteen performances with heavy losses and Chatterton sued Reeves for breach of contract. He was awarded £1,500 in damages, but it was a hollow victory: if Reeves had appeared, he would have gained much more than that in ticket sales.[18]

Chatterton gave himself a benefit performance on 13 April, the last night of the season. The programme consisted of Sheridan's *The School for Scandal* followed by a concert in which his Uncle Frederick and his sister Kate both played the harp. At the end of the performance, Chatterton made a speech from the stage, in which he spoke of the difficulties under which he had embarked on his first season as sole lessee of Drury Lane, burdened with the debts of the partnership with Falconer. In spite of this: 'I felt that the only course to achieve success would be to perform the works of standard authors, and to engage artistes of high reputation.'[19]

We have an account, written by Charles Lamb Kenney in 1875, of the first ten years of Chatterton's sole management, which gives the financial outcome of this policy of performing 'the works of standard authors'. During the 1866/67 season, the revival of *Macbeth* had lost money and *Faust* only just covered its expenses in the pre-Christmas run. The revival of *Faust* after the pantomime was a disaster, playing to houses worth as little as £50. Helen Faucit's performances had been successful, but she only appeared on twelve nights, so the only source of solid profits had been the pantomime:

> The pantomime safely reached, the Manager of Drury Lane Theatre leaves for a time all his troubles and anxieties behind him... the annual rising of the Nile fructifying the Egyptian valley and covering the arid soil with golden harvests is not looked forward to with more eager anticipation... than is the advent of the Christmas holiday season by the lessee of this Temple of the Drama, especially if he has been sacrificing too freely to its all devouring idols, Shakespeare and Legitimacy. In fact, but for the golden tide which now flows into the exchequer to fill up ugly deficits, and make all smooth and pleasant again, it would be impossible to pay the least regard to the exacting requirements of those local deities.[20]

This was not a very encouraging first solo season for Chatterton, especially after the successes of the previous two years with Falconer. However, he must have been moved when his colleagues presented him with a silver salver, a tea and a coffee service, claret jug and cigar case worth 250 guineas in recognition of his efforts. The salver was engraved: 'Presented to F. B. Chatterton Esq. by the members of the company of the Theatre Royal, Drury Lane, and a few of his personal friends, as a token of the esteem in which they hold him, and as a mark of their admiration for the ability and honourable conduct which has distinguished his career as the lessee and manager of the Theatre Royal, Drury Lane. April 18th, 1867.'[21] In spite of his famous temper, Chatterton was a sentimental man, and this tribute from his company would have meant a lot to him. The presentation took place on Maundy Thursday when Drury Lane was closed for Passion Week, in accordance with Chatterton's religious principles. However, he was getting ready for an opening on Easter Monday that would be significant for him, as it represented his first attempt at a summer season.

When making his curtain speech at his benefit performance, Chatterton had told the audience that: 'I have not broken one of the announcements I made except in regard to Mr Sims Reeves, who failed to fulfil his engagement with me.'[22] In fact, there was one other. In his season prospectus, Chatterton had promised a new play by Dion Boucicault. This never materialised, but the fact that Chatterton was even contemplating something by this famous author of crowd-pleasing melodramas shows that, even at the beginning of his lesseeship, Chatterton had an inkling that an exclusive diet of 'the works of standard authors' might not pay the bills.

Instead of Boucicault, Chatterton put on a new play that had been brought to him by the Scottish journalist and playwright Andrew Halliday, called *The Great City*. Halliday was already known to Chatterton as the co-author (with William Brough) of some short farces staged by Chatterton and Falconer at the Lyceum and Drury Lane,[23] but *The Great City* was a full-length play and his own unaided work (albeit borrowing some of the plot from Dickens's *Great Expectations*). The heroine, Edith, is the daughter of a convict transported to Australia, where he has made a great fortune. Edith finds herself set up as a great lady, although she has no idea of where the money is coming from. Mogg, the father she believes to be dead, returns to London to see his daughter in the gorgeous clothes and splendid house he has paid for, where he discovers that the villain, Jacob Blount MP, has swindled a young gentleman out of a fortune and intends to get his hands on Edith's by marrying her. Mogg threatens to expose Blount as a fraud and Blount threatens to have Mogg arrested as an illegally returned convict. All is resolved after an exciting chase across the rooftops of London from which Mogg falls, sustaining fatal injuries. Beverley came up with some impressive sets, representing the Charing Cross Hotel, Waterloo Bridge by gaslight and a recreation of Frith's famous painting of *The Railway Station*. There was a dance of Jolly Beggars in a night-hostel and the appearance on the stage of a real horse-drawn hansom cab. (The latter provoked a discussion which has continued to the present day about why audiences are delighted to see on a stage 'bad imitations of what they can see elsewhere for nothing'.)[24]

The Great City might not have been great literature ('*Great City*, great rubbish' was E. L. Blanchard's verdict)[25] but it achieved unprecedented success by exploiting the fascination, which would last to the end of the century, with London as the world's most enormous, awful, diverse and tempting city. As Mogg (the equivalent of Magwitch in *Great Expectations*) puts it: 'This town of London, though it's fuller of poverty and misery than it is of wealth and pleasure, is a devilish sight…

The very misery of this town has a sort of fascination for those who have suffered most by it.'[26] Moving between a ballroom in Belgravia and the entrance to a workhouse, where a Jewish character berates a so-called Christian society for allowing such suffering, Halliday tapped into what *The Spectator* called 'a new-born desire to idealise the unique metropolis in which we live and work'.[27]

Chatterton ran extensive press quotes in the classified columns and on the printed publicity: the four-page handbill had a whole page of rave reviews from almost every major paper.[28] *The Great City* ran and ran, through the summer and into the autumn. Its success was so extraordinary that Chatterton began to publish in the classified advertisements the ordinal number of the night's performance and the total number of people who had seen the play so far. Monday 5 August represented the 91st night, by which time the show had been seen by 362,000 people. The following Monday was the 97th night, with a total audience of 387,000 people. By subtracting the first total from the second and dividing by six (there were no matinees) we get an average audience of 4,167.[29] The final performance took place on 17 August 1867, announced as the 102nd performance with the total audience numbers given as 406,000 people. In fact, it was the 101st performance, as Chatterton had not included *The Great City* in his own benefit performance on 24 July, for which he had chosen scenes from Shakespeare. Nevertheless, *The Great City* was the first show in the history of Drury Lane to run continuously for one hundred nights. Chatterton's first summer season had been an astonishing success: added to the main season of 169 nights, Drury Lane had been open for 271 nights over eleven months of the theatrical year, which was unprecedented. *The Great City* transferred to the Grecian Theatre in East London then went on tour to Manchester, Sunderland, Portsmouth, Glasgow, Leeds and Birmingham.

Almost by accident, Chatterton had stumbled on the formula that would turn Drury Lane into a goldmine for his successor: an exciting drama of modern life involving complicated schemes, a suave villain, an innocent heroine, a 'sensation scene' (the horse and cab) and the recreation onstage of well-known London locations. However, Chatterton was sensitive to 'the banter showered on him by the small wits of the press… for his hansom-cab excursion into the realms of sensational drama'.[30] Effective plays often deploy symbolism, using small things to represent big things, and the hansom cab came to symbolise what many people regarded as the degradation of the stage. Six years after *The Great City*, this effect – a very modest one by the standards of Drury Lane – was still fresh in memory when Chatterton had a real-life cabby brought before a magistrate for refusing to take him home to Kennington. The cabman was fined forty shillings and had his licence suspended for a month. Chatterton thought this was too harsh but he pleaded in vain with the magistrate for a more lenient sentence. One of 'the small wits of the press' observed that he had the remedy in his own hands: 'he can easily make amends by getting Mr Halliday to write a part for him and his vehicle in the next spectacular drama to be produced at Old Drury'.[31] Chatterton decided, for the time being at least, to give 'sensation' a wide berth at Drury Lane and to regard *The Great City* as 'a summer frolic – a midsummer night's dream – to be followed by an awakening to the stern reality of the classic muse.'[32]

1867 – 1868: Shakespeare and legitimacy

Few muses are sterner than Goethe's, and the new season opened with the second revival of *Faust*. Although the last revival, after the pantomime, had been a failure, Chatterton chose to attribute that to the unfavourable time of year. He was also determined to show that he 'would not easily be deterred from his announced design of identifying his management with the higher drama'.[33] This stubborn defiance of the box office did not bode well for the future.

He backed up Faust with a revival of a famous old melodrama, *The Miller and his Men*. This had never been performed at Drury Lane, although the original production at Covent Garden in 1813 had been a great success and the play became part of the stock repertoire for years. It also became one of the most popular plays of the 'juvenile drama', the toy theatres so popular with little boys in the early part of the nineteenth century, and one of the little boys who staged this melodrama in miniature was Charles Dickens. Putting on a show for his schoolfriends, the young Dickens was dissatisfied with the last scene in which the mill was blown up by gunpowder. He asked a fellow pupil who was good at drawing to redesign the scene for him and the resulting cardboard catastrophe was a great hit. The mill was designed to fall to pieces when some fire-crackers exploded, and it was said that Dickens gave so many performances of this explosive finale that on one occasion the police were called. The artistic schoolfriend was William Beverley. However, the grown-up Beverley didn't design the Drury Lane production as he was busy with the sets for the big autumn drama, and Dickens was seriously displeased with Chatterton's version which sent up the old Penny Plain, Tuppence Coloured barnstormer he remembered so fondly. He sat in silence, 'a little shocked at seeing his old idol shattered', until in the middle of the second act he stood up and said he could stand it no longer.[34]

The Miller and His Men lasted for six weeks but *Faust* came off after only two weeks, to be replaced by one week of *King John* and then two weeks of *Macbeth*, with Phelps and Barry Sullivan alternating in the title part. There was a week of Bulwer Lytton's *The Lady of Lyons*, with Sullivan in the lead, followed by the big production of the autumn season: an adaptation by Bayle Bernard of Lord Byron's *Marino Faliero*, retitled *The Doge of Venice*.

Marino Faliero, the story of the treacherous Doge who tried to overthrow the Republic of Venice, had a history at Drury Lane, and it was anything but encouraging. Byron had written it whilst living in scandalous exile, and when he sent it to his publisher John Murray he was proud of its unsuitability for the stage. It had no melodrama, he boasted, no trap-doors, no 'outrageous ranting villains', no opportunities for actors to prance about 'tossing their heads and kicking their heels', and no love – a passion he considered unsuitable for tragedy.[35] He knew that it would not be popular, but 'did I ever write for *popularity*?'[36] This rhetorical question sounded slightly strange coming from the man who woke up famous after the publication of *Childe Harold's Pilgrimage* and enjoyed rock-star celebrity, even in exile. However it pleased Byron, who was a tremendous snob, to be snooty about the state of the theatre and to declare that the last thing he wanted for his plays was to see them produced. He was dismayed to discover, therefore, that Robert Elliston, the lessee of Drury Lane, had got sheets of the play from his printer even before it was published and intended to stage it at Drury Lane. Byron told his publisher, John Murray, to take out an injunction, but Elliston had already applied for a licence from the Lord Chamberlain. The Lord Chamberlain's licence for performance of *Marino Faliero* arrived at Drury Lane on the morning of what was supposed to be the first night, followed, thirty minutes later, by the injunction forbidding it. Elliston searched throughout London until he found Lord Eldon, the Lord Chamberlain, and persuaded him to lift the injunction so that the play could open that night. It was scarcely worth the trouble as it closed after seven poorly attended performances.[37] His inability to prevent its production made Byron even more hostile towards Drury Lane: 'It is like Louis XIV, who insisted upon buying at any price Algernon Sydney's horse, and, on his refusal, on taking it by force, Sydney shot the horse. I could not shoot my tragedy, but I would have flung it into the fire rather than have had it represented.'[38]

The cause of its failure was easily found. First, the plot was absurd. Marino Faliero, the Doge of Venice, is outraged when a Venetian nobleman writes defamatory graffiti about his wife on the ducal throne and then receives a very light sentence for his crime. Faliero enters into a conspiracy to destroy the entire government of Venice and murder the senators purely for this affront to his family honour. As the *Quarterly Review* put it: 'It is little to the purpose to say that this is all historically true. A thing may be true without being probable.'[39] Byron then made things harder for himself by observing the classical unities and confining the action to the passage of twenty-four hours. The revolution is planned and executed at breakneck speed, which makes it seem even more improbable. All the drama takes place offstage, there are too many long speeches, and the leading lady speaks of nothing but her virtue. William Hazlitt described it as being: 'without plot, without characters… and without the spirit of dialogue'.[40] Even for the literary gentleman in his library, for whom Byron claimed to have written it, this was very dull stuff.

If Robert Elliston couldn't make money out of this at Drury Lane while Byron was still the hottest of celebrities, it is hard to see why any other manager would want to stage *Marino Faliero*. However, Byron's status as a touchstone of high culture made his plays catnip for theatre managers who sought the palm of 'legitimacy', and no one would become more closely associated with this quest than Chatterton. Byron had the same status in the nineteenth century that Thomas Otway had enjoyed throughout the eighteenth: he was the playwright you *ought* to appreciate, even if you would rather be watching something more entertaining. The fact that Otway's reputation rested almost entirely on *Venice Preserv'd*, to which *Marino Faliero* bore strong similarities, just strengthened the parallel. Macready attempted a production of *Marino Faliero* during his Drury Lane management in 1842 but it received only four performances.[41] Chatterton, who idolised Macready, decided to see what he could do with it.

He asked Bayle Bernard to put together a script, allowing him considerable leeway with the original. Byron's play had inspired another version of the story by the French dramatist Casimir Delavigne who injected a bit of passion into the dry classicism of Byron's text. The Delavigne version became, in turn, the source for Donizetti's opera of the same name. In this treatment, the Doge's wife entertains a passion for his nephew which leads to the offensive graffiti. The young man challenges the author of the graffiti to a duel and is killed, which provides a stronger motive for the Doge's revenge. Bernard used this additional romantic material and did away with the twenty-four-hour timeframe, opening up the front of the story to show the development of the conspiracy amongst workers in the Arsenal. He also provided the opportunity for the display of Beverley's talents in sets that included the Arsenal, Leoni's Palace overlooking the Grand Canal, the Giant's Staircase of the Doge's Palace on which Marino Faliero is beheaded and – most spectacularly – the Venetian Carnival in the Piazzetta of St Mark's. This was the big setpiece of the show, 'unanimously pronounced… to be one of the grandest spectacular effects to be witnessed on the stage'.[42] Chatterton advertised the time of the carnival scene – 7.45 p.m. – in case people were coming just to see that bit.

Oxenford's review in *The Times* acknowledged the overpowering nature of Beverley's contribution to the production: 'Venice, almost done to death under every form of pictorial art, lives anew through Mr Beverley, the scene-painter… Her canals sparkle in the moonbeams as they never sparkled before, and her sons plunge into the riots of the Carnival with a sensual vigour for which there is no precedent.'[43] He praised Bernard for steering a middle course between Byron – no passion at all – and Delavigne – rather too much of it. (In Bernard's version, the illicit passion of the Duchess and her husband's nephew becomes an unrequited infatuation on the part of his adopted son, thus removing the whiff of incest.) Following his by-now established custom, Chatterton used extracts from Oxenford's review, as well as others, in the classified advertisements under the heading: 'Opinions of the press of the brilliantly successful, spectacular, musical and romantic play *The Doge of Venice*':

William Beverley's recreation of the Giants' Staircase of the Doge's Palace on which Marino Faliero was beheaded

> 'The decided success of *The Doge of Venice* was finally declared by acclamations which have rarely been more enthusiastic' (*Daily Telegraph*); 'The magnificence of the scenery, the splendour and rich variety of the costumes, the dazzling character of the mise en scène, and the powerful acting cannot fail' (*Standard*).

Chatterton had certainly put everything into it. Costumes and carnival masks were by R. W. Keene and there was a lush musical score comprising bits of Donizetti, Verdi, and even a Requiem by Pope Gregory. The musical element, with its rousing choruses, was so strong that the *Pall Mall Gazette* critic said it was like listening to an opera in which the principal characters have suddenly lost their singing voices, 'although the actors, to do them justice, by their vehement ranting and mouthing, do their best to compete with the trombones and the big drums'. Samuel Phelps did what he could with the verse, but the audience could only endure 'such large excerpts from Lord Byron' by reflecting that 'the efforts of the scene-painter and the ballet-master would again be speedily called into action'.[44] One critic, observing that the bust of Goethe in the foyer had been replaced by a colossal bust of Byron, said that this was strange way of honouring a poet whose text was being mangled on the stage.[45]

The production looked stunning and certainly had its admirers. There was a vote of thanks to Chatterton at the annual meeting of the Drury Lane proprietors for sustaining 'the character of the building which was now the only national theatre in existence (hear, hear!) [by] the manner in which he brought out *The Doge of Venice* [which] entitled him to the thanks not only of the proprietors but of the outside public (hear, hear!).'[46] However, it was a financial disaster, losing £5,000 – over half-a-million pounds in modern values.[47] Chatterton kept it running for forty-one performances until it had to make way for the pantomime, but losses on this scale threatened the survival of his management.

The destruction by fire of Her Majesty's Theatre in the Haymarket on 6 December 1867

Towards the end of the run, an event took place that would serendipitously improve the profitability of Chatterton's operation: late in the evening of Friday 6 December 1867 Her Majesty's Theatre in the Haymarket burnt to the ground. For a century and a half it had been the principal opera house in London, and during most of that time it had been protected by a royal patent giving it the exclusive right to present Italian opera in London. However, the Theatres Regulation Act of 1843 abolished the patent privileges, leaving the managers of theatres free to put on whatever shows they wanted to produce, subject to getting a licence from the Lord Chamberlain. In 1847 Covent Garden, which had effectively ceased to function as a theatre, became an opera house, staging Italian opera in competition with Her Majesty's.

Now that opera is regarded as a loss-making activity requiring large subsidies from public bodies, it is hard to appreciate the way in which, throughout the eighteenth and nineteenth centuries, in Britain and the USA, it was a commercial enterprise with the capacity to make fortunes. Like modern musicals, opera seasons were expensive and risky to mount, but, if they were successful, they could make their promoters rich. This led to the emergence of a breed of buccaneering opera impresarios, reckless, ruthless and savagely competitive. Their colourful biographies are more reminiscent of Hollywood moguls than anything seen in the opera houses of the world today.

The lessee of Her Majesty's, since 1862, had been James Mapleson. Mapleson had trained as a singer and musician, then set up as an agent, supplying singers to both opera houses. He managed opera seasons for E. T. Smith, both at Drury Lane and at Her Majesty's, of which Smith also held the lease at the time. When Smith was forced to cancel his season at Her Majesty's in 1861, Mapleson decided to go into business as an opera impresario on his own account and tried to take over Her Majesty's. He was unable to get it, as Smith was still the lessee and was making himself scarce to avoid creditors. However, Mapleson met him by chance one day in the street and asked if he could rent Drury Lane from him for a season. Smith said yes but refused to allow him to put on Italian opera there, so Mapleson took the Lyceum instead.[48] The Lyceum season was a financial failure but a critical success, and Mapleson, bitten by the bug, lost no time in taking a twenty-one year lease of Her Majesty's once Smith had been ejected for non-payment of rent.

Mapleson's main rival was Frederick Gye who had been in charge of Covent Garden since 1849. Covent Garden was a smaller house than Her Majesty's and a comparative newcomer to the operatic scene. However, Gye was twenty years older than Mapleson, with more experience and a reputation for being a gentleman whose word was his bond. He had been forced to raise money to rebuild Covent Garden after the fire of 1857, so money was tight and, even with very careful management, Gye only generated small profits. He would have had a much easier time with no competition from Her Majesty's.

There was no performance at Her Majesty's on the night of the fire and Mapleson was having dinner with his *prima donna* when the servant rushed in to tell him that the glow on the horizon was not the dawn, it was his theatre going up in flames. By the time Mapleson got to the Haymarket most of the building was ablaze and he was unable to save anything. His sets and costumes were uninsured and his losses were said to be in the region of £10,000 to £12,000 – well over a million pounds in modern values.[49] He realised that, if he were not to be wiped out financially as an opera impresario, he had to secure another theatre as quickly as possible, so he went to the house of Henry Jarrett, his business manager, and told him to go to Chatterton's house in Kennington as early in the morning as possible and get a contract for Drury Lane's summer season, preferably before Chatterton knew about the fire.

According to the account Mapleson gives in his memoirs, when Jarrett arrived at Chatterton's house he saw *The Times* on the table in the hall, carrying a report of the fire, so he laid his coat over it and sat quietly until Chatterton was able to receive him. He carried out his negotiations calmly, so as not to raise suspicions, and at 9.30 a.m. he was able to hand Mapleson the signed agreement. An hour later, Gye turned up at Chatterton's house to offer him £200 a week *not* to let Drury Lane to Mapleson.[50]

This colourful story is typical of the sort of legends that impresarios weave around their careers, but it is only partly true. Theatrical leases are complicated affairs, not cobbled together in half-an-hour. Three months later, Chatterton wrote to *The Morning Post* announcing that he had been negotiating the terms of a sub-lease of Drury Lane to Mapleson since the day after the fire and that the details were almost finalised.[51] Clearly, Henry Jarrett had not left Chatterton's house early in the morning on 7 December with a signed lease in his pocket, and it also seems unlikely that Chatterton would have been unaware of the destruction of a major West End theatre by a fire that had lit up the London sky. A more probable explanation is that Chatterton and Jarrett reached an outline agreement and that Chatterton, being a man of honour, would have resisted subsequent inducements from Gye to renege on it.[52]

'Engaging Children for the Christmas Pantomime at Drury Lane'. The 1867/68 pantomime was *Jack the Giant Killer*. A poster advertising Samuel Phelps in *The Doge of Venice* can be seen on the wall.

The Drury Lane pantomime in 1867/68 was *Jack the Giant Killer*, with Master Percy Roselle as a sort of Cornish Puck called Pigwiggin. This was a small part compared with his previous leading roles, and a review in *The Athenaeum* suggested that he had been intended for Jack but his voice had broken.[53] A more probable explanation is that knowledge of his real age was becoming too general. Kate Terry (Ellen Terry's sister) had told Lewis Carroll during the run of *Little King Pippin* that Percy was really eighteen or nineteen, which would have made him twenty or twenty-one by this stage.[54] After *Jack the Giant Killer* he went to America, then returned to appear in the pantomime at the Surrey Theatre in Lambeth in 1870/71 and at the Pavilion Theatre, Mile End, in 1871/72. He then disappears from the record altogether. One writer mocked those infant prodigies who 'clung pertinaciously on to childhood, till they were proved to be thirty, and were only driven away by a combined assault of baptismal registers'.[55] In Percy's case there are no registers, baptismal or otherwise, to enlighten us, so we will probably never know the truth. If he was a fraud, he was a very successful one, and certainly clever enough to find a new identity for himself when his days as a child star came to an end.

The pantomime was preceded by a farce called *Honeydove's Troubles* until the end of January, after which it became the afterpiece to a series of performances by Samuel Phelps in his 'legitimate' repertoire.

Barry Sullivan rejoined the company to appear as Richard III at the end of February, after which he and Phelps appeared in *Othello*, *The School for Scandal* and *The Merchant of Venice*, which now included the magnificent Venetian carnival created for *The Doge of Venice*. The pantomime closed on 2 March, after which a series of Shakespearean plays plus a revival of *Rob Roy* were followed by a new play called *The Prisoner of Toulon*,[56] which flopped. The season closed with Chatterton's benefit on Saturday 21 March 1868. This consisted of scenes from *The Great City, Henry IV Part 2, King Lear, Hamlet, As You Like It, Belphegor* and the carnival scene from *The Doge of Venice*. It went on until nearly midnight and the demand for seats was so great that Chatterton filled the orchestra pit with stalls and moved the orchestra backstage. His transformation of Drury Lane from a place that could only be filled by circuses and masked balls to a home for serious plays was appreciated by those who followed the fortunes of London theatre.[57] He made a speech from the stage explaining that he been planning another dramatic attraction like *The Great City* for the summer months but he had been persuaded by the fire at Her Majesty's to allow Italian opera to replace English drama 'in this our National Theatre' for one season only.[58] A week later, James Mapleson opened 'Her Majesty's Opera at Drury Lane'. For Mapleson, it was a sort of homecoming as he had an association with the Lane that was literally lifelong: on 21 May 1830, as a seventeen-day-old baby, he had appeared on the stage there to be christened as 'Princess Elizabeth' in a production of Shakespeare's *Henry VIII*.[59]

The financial backbone of an opera season was the subscription list. People paid a large sum of money that entitled them to attend all performances on the subscription list – forty in this case. This money was paid up front and provided the manager with the operating capital he needed to mount the season. In order to attract subscriptions, Mapleson produced a pamphlet explaining to opera-lovers that, while he regrets not being able to entertain his public at Her Majesty's, with its long tradition of Italian opera, 'pending the reconstruction of "the old house", he deems himself fortunate that… he has been enabled to secure, as a temporary substitute, so advantageous a locale as the Theatre Royal, Drury Lane, admirably adapted as it is by its dimensions and the general convenience of its structure, for the accommodation of a large and fashionable audience and the requirements of Grand Italian Opera'.[60]

There was a good deal of work to do, however. Opera pricing was much higher than theatre pricing. Stalls cost one guinea (three times the normal price), seats in boxes cost 10*s*. 6*d*., and even the gallery cost 2s. 6d. (compared with 6d. and 1s.) There was no pit, no cheap seats, and most opera patrons wanted their own private boxes. This meant that the auditorium of Drury Lane had to be altered to make it look more like the auditorium of Her Majesty's. Mapleson cut back the forestage to enlarge the orchestra pit and removed the pit seating altogether. Where the pit had extended underneath the dress circle, a new set of private boxes was created around luxurious armchairs in the stalls. The dress circle and the tier above were completely partitioned to create private boxes with 'amphitheatre stalls' in the centre of the tier above that, also flanked by boxes. Paintwork and gilding were renovated and the front of house area was recarpeted. The walls were lined with grey chintz and the boxes hung with amber satin curtains that Mapleson claimed (somewhat improbably) to have rescued from the burnt-out ruins of Her Majesty's. A team of architects, builders, painters, gilders and upholsterers carried out these major alterations to the auditorium in the astonishingly short time of six days, and it would all have to be put back as it was before, ready for the start of Chatterton's autumn season.[61] Mapleson claimed this work cost him between £3,000 and £4,000[62] – over £400,000 in modern values – which was a lot of money, but then the prices he was charging were pretty eye-watering as well:

The Subscriptions will consist of forty nights	
Two Pair	115 guineas
One Pair	200 guineas
Grand Tier	250 guineas
Pit Boxes	225 guineas
Orchestra Stalls	35 guineas
Dress Circle	17 guineas

Although these prices represented a saving compared with the cost of buying a ticket for individual performances, in modern terms Mapleson was asking nearly £30,000 in advance for a box to see forty operas, with a single seat in the stalls costing over £4,000 for the season.

The season was a success and ran for over three months until 1 August with four performances in most weeks (Wednesday and Friday nights were normally not performance nights). Chatterton had found a valuable source of additional revenue to support his management and he didn't keep his promise to allow opera to replace drama for one season only: Italian opera would occupy Drury Lane for the summer months of each of the next eight years bar one.

6

Success

1868 – 1869: Swerving from the legitimate course

Chatterton knew that he couldn't afford another season like the last one. The revival of *Faust* had made no money, the loss on *The Doge of Venice* had been unprecedented and the 'legitimate' dramas that followed the pantomime had all lost money, leaving *Jack the Giant Killer* as the only successful production in the season.[1] There was a limit to the extent to which the pantomime could be relied upon to cover the losses on everything else.

Whilst keen to avoid bankruptcy, Chatterton didn't want to betray what he saw as the trust invested in him as the manager of the National Theatre. He needed some compromise between 'the classical drama, which had proved so provokingly insufficient to sustain the fortunes of the theatre, and a downright and unreserved adoption of the modern sensational drama'.[2] It was Andrew Halliday, author *The Great City*, who came up with the answer. He suggested producing stage versions of the novels of Sir Walter Scott as 'a hybrid between pure legitimacy and thoroughbred sensationalism'.[3] Scott was a classic author whose novels featured action-packed plots offering the scope for scenic spectacle. High drama and spectacle, seasoned with a suggestion of 'legitimacy', might be enough to fill those thousands of seats with 'the miscellaneous public who patronise the national theatre'.[4]

Stage versions of Scott's novels were by no means a new idea. They had been appearing from the early years of the century within weeks, or even days, of the publication of the novels.[5] What was new in the sequence that Chatterton and Halliday were about to launch was the skilfulness of Halliday's scripts coupled with the magnificence of Beverley's scenery. Halliday had a genius for being able to select the essential scenes and characters from vast three-volume novels and make them work on the stage. His first attempt for Chatterton was *The Fortunes of Nigel* which he refocused on the character of King James VI of Scotland and I of England and called *King o' Scots*. Samuel Phelps (known for his convincing Scottish accent) doubled as the King and as the character of Trapbois the Miser.

The rising of the apprentices in Fleet Street from Andrew Halliday's King o' Scots

Instead of easing himself into the new season with revivals of previous productions, Chatterton decided to open cold with *King o' Scots* on 26 September. It received excellent reviews, especially for Halliday's skilful adaptation, for Phelps's acting of the two parts (reminiscent of his doubling of Henry IV and Justice Shallow in *Henry IV Part 2*) and, of course, for Beverley's magnificent sets. These included a huge set of Old London Bridge 'in which Mr William Beverley has shown again his complete mastery over the resources of this fine stage',[6] a royal hunt in Greenwich Park with real horses and hounds, and a riot of apprentices in Fleet Street. The spectacle was so splendid that it had one critic worrying about Chatterton's bottom line: 'we trust that it receives the abundant patronage without which it is impossible that the costly outlay incurred can be returned to the treasury'.[7]

He needn't have worried. *King o' Scots* was a great success and ran for seventy-three continuous performances until it had to be taken off for the pantomime prior to a tour of Edinburgh, Liverpool, Glasgow and Manchester.[8] Chatterton boasted that it had been seen by more people than any other show at Drury Lane,[9] but it had high running costs, so the profits were not large. Nevertheless, the important thing from Chatterton's point of view was that it didn't make a loss. For the first time since taking over Drury Lane, Chatterton didn't have to anticipate the profits of the pantomime to cover losses on the autumn season: he arrived at Boxing Day in the black.[10] Furthermore, he could live with his choice. As Oxenford put it in *The Times* review:

> The manager of Drury Lane, by having recourse to a standard novel, written by an author of such high repute as Sir Walter Scott, is able to swerve from the legitimate course without too great a sacrifice of the dignity necessary to be preserved at a theatre which owes much of its success to the popular conviction that it is, in some sort, national.[11]

The pantomime which opened thus unmortgaged was *Puss in Boots*. It included a sequence on the deck of a man of war 'manned by 300 children'. After inspection by a miniature Duke of Edinburgh, there were several songs and a hornpipe danced by 'sixty able-bodied young British tars'. After engaging with the enemy, the audience witnessed the 'success of the flag that's braved a thousand years the battle and the breeze'.[12] Drury Lane pantomimes were always intensely patriotic.

The pantomime ran, with Wednesday and Saturday matinees, until 20 February, always following a one-act farce called *My Wife's Out*. The times were announced as: *My Wife's Out* 7.00 p.m.; *Puss in Boots* 7.45 p.m.; performance ends at 11.00 p.m. The increasing number of patrons travelling by overground and underground railways (the underground had opened in 1863) meant that the finishing time was important. Managers whose shows went on until midnight could expect to see a lot of people leaving early to catch their last trains. This was the first year in which the opening farce was not replaced by full-length plays towards the end of the pantomime's run. Both *My Wife's Out* and *Puss in Boots* ended together on 20 February.

In the previous year, Chatterton had only a few weeks to fill between the close of the pantomime and the opening of the Italian opera season. This year there was no opera because James Mapleson had entered into a partnership with Frederick Gye at Covent Garden to present a 'coalition season' which would give them a monopoly over Italian opera in London – a potentially highly profitable arrangement. They were anxious to keep their plans secret as, had they been known, a rival impresario could have taken Drury Lane and competed against them. They were so successful that by the time their plans became known, it was too late for a rival impresario to take Drury Lane for opera, which left Chatterton to find other ways of keeping his theatre open.

The Easter holidays were good for business at theatres and many managers launched their new productions on Easter Monday, which fell on 29 March that year. Chatterton planned a stage version of

Victor Hugo's *Les Misérables* called *A Man of Two Lives*, starring Charles Dillon as Jean Valjean. He filled the gap between the end of the pantomime and the opening of *A Man of Two Lives* with what one critic called 'the legitimate month',[13] four weeks of the plays of Shakespeare, Sheridan and other 'legitimate' authors in repertory. Samuel Phelps and Dillon took it in turns to play Macbeth and alternated as Falstaff and Hotspur in *Henry IV Part 1*. Phelps gave his last performance of the season on 19 March, as he wasn't in the cast for *A Man of Two Lives*, leaving Dillon as the leading man in the company.

The fact that Chatterton employed Dillon at all at this stage of his career was an indication of the struggle he was having to maintain the calibre of his company. The last time Dillon had acted for him was at the St James's Theatre in 1860. Dillon had spent most of the intervening years in Australasia, North and South America, where his acting deteriorated. His voice had been affected by drinking and his style coarsened.[14]

Drury Lane closed for Passion Week and re-opened on Easter Monday with *A Man of Two Lives*. To back it up, Chatterton revived *Puss in Boots*, which had closed five weeks before, as an afterpiece, ending with the transformation scene. The meant that the harlequinade was scrapped, which was unfortunate as it contained the pantomime's big scene on the deck of a man of war. However, Chatterton decided to put on Saturday matinees during this revival, consisting of the Christy Minstrels, then *Puss in Boots* up to the transformation scene, concluding with the deck of the man of war and its crew of 300 children. The matinees started at 2.00 p.m. and ended at 5.15 p.m. April was very late in the year to be doing matinees of the pantomime, and after two-and-a-half weeks Chatterton abandoned the whole programme. *A Man of Two Lives* had not been a success and even the friendly critic John Oxenford had commented on the 'peculiarities' of Dillon's acting.[15]

The season staggered on for another nine days of 'legitimate drama' with Thomas King (always billed as T. C. King) appearing as Hamlet and as Iago to Dillon's Othello. Aged fifty-one, King was new to Drury Lane but had many years of provincial experience behind him. His acting was described as reflecting 'the formal style of former days'.[16] Chatterton was very optimistic to think that he could carry *Hamlet* at Drury Lane.

Meanwhile Chatterton had been engaged in his first attempt at provincial management since the short and disastrous season at Rochester in 1860/61. In May 1868 he took over the lease of the Theatre Royal, Hull from John Coleman. The theatre was only three years old, having been rebuilt after a fire, and the first manager had been William Brough. Neither Brough nor Coleman had made a success of it, but Chatterton may have seen it as a satellite to which he could transfer his stars and productions from Drury Lane. He aimed for a grand opening with an autumn season and advertised for a tenant until then, but without success. He put in some touring companies, none of which did good business. The autumn season opened on 31 August 1868 with Samuel Phelps as Bottom in *A Midsummer Night's Dream*, followed by a week of T. C. King as Macbeth. The local paper warned him that tastes in Hull were not so refined, but he had more success with a revival of *The Great City*. He put on a series of what Victorian audiences regarded as 'legitimate' plays – *Masks and Faces* by Tom Taylor and Charles Reade, *The Hunchback* by Sheridan Knowles, *The School for Scandal* by Richard Brinsley Sheridan – and he managed to get some West End stars to make the journey to Hull. On Boxing Day he opened 'the very best pantomime ever seen in this town',[17] *Robinson Crusoe or Harlequin Hull Sailor Boy*, with a scene of Hull in 1659 and lots of topical local jokes. Just when things were looking more promising, the theatre burnt down again on 5 February 1869. Chatterton made Drury Lane available for a charity matinee on 11 March which raised £153 3*s*. 6*d*. for the relief fund.[18] The theatre was rebuilt and reopened in November, but without Chatterton: he never ventured outside the West End again.

However the idea of maximising the takings from his productions by transferring them to other theatres still appealed to Chatterton, so he began what would turn out to be a regular series of transfers to the National Standard Theatre in Shoreditch with *Manfred*, still starring Samuel Phelps and opening there in May. The Standard had recently been rebuilt on an enormous scale after a fire and was said to be the largest theatre in London after Her Majesty's. It was often described as the Drury Lane of the East End owing to its size and magnificence, and had one of the few stages capable of taking scenery built for the cavernous stage of Drury Lane. In spite of this, the scenery for Chatterton's transfers was almost always repainted by Richard Douglass, the son of the proprietor John Douglass, who was trying to establish himself as a scene painter. The transfer of *Manfred* therefore had scenery painted by Douglass from the designs made for the original 1863 Drury Lane production. Whilst it may seem odd that large shows could profitably be transferred between theatres that were only a few miles apart, the inhabitants of the West End and the East End tended to keep to their own districts, so a transfer to the Standard opened up the possibility of access to a large potential new audience. The experiment was a success and set a precedent: 'The majority of

Drury Lane successes are sure to find their way to the Standard,' said *The Era*, a few years later.[19]

The 1868/69 Drury Lane season had not been a disaster for Chatterton, but nor had it been a triumph. The modest profits of *King o' Scots* had been eaten away by losses on *A Man of Two Lives*, and the 'legitimate month' failed because West End audiences were unenthusiastic about actors going through their paces in roles they had been playing for years, supported by under-rehearsed companies and using scenery out of stock. Standards were rising and this old-style repertory system was no longer attractive. Chatterton needed another big success, so he went to the man who could be relied upon to provide one: Dion Boucicault.

1869 – 1870: The tawny siren of Hyde Park

The Drury Lane season for 1869/70 opened on the astonishingly early date of 5 August with Dion Boucicault's play *Formosa or the Railroad to Ruin*. To open the autumn season in summer seemed eccentric, but Boucicault had no time for outmoded traditions and said that London was full of people at any time of year and those people wanted to be entertained. He was right.

Formosa was a rare thing: a new play for the London stage that was not based on a French original. Nor was it one of Boucicault's Irish dramas. It was 'a new drama of modern life' which told the story of Jenny, the seemingly virtuous daughter of Sam Boker, landlord of The Old Swan on the river at Oxford and coach to the Oxford Boat Race crew. When she is not helping her parents to run the inn, Jenny spends a lot of time in London as the companion to a rich and indulgent old lady who showers her with gifts – or so she claims. In fact, Jenny is leading a double life as Formosa – Latin for beautiful – 'the tawny siren of Hyde Park' and one of London's leading courtesans. The villain of the piece, Compton Kerr, wishes to marry the sister of Tom Burroughs, the Oxford stroke, to get his hands on her fortune, but Tom opposes the match as Kerr had a bad reputation at Eton. Kerr is facing ruin as a result of borrowing money on the strength of this marriage, so he decides to get Tom out of the way and to fix the Oxford and Cambridge Boat Race in the process so that Oxford will lose. This will be achieved by debauching Tom and getting him thrown into prison before the race. Kerr recognises Jenny when he visits The Old Swan and tells her that, unless she assists him in this scheme, he will reveal the truth about her double life to her parents. In the next act, set in Formosa's luxurious villa in Fulham where a crowd of more-or-less repulsive demi-mondaines are drinking, gambling and swindling, we see how successfully Tom has been debauched. He is thrown into prison for gambling debts and I.O.U.s amounting to £20,000, but a suddenly reformed Formosa persuades one of her admirers to sell all her ill-gotten spoils and redeem him. The admirer duly arrives at the prison on the very morning of the Boat Race with the money, but the sheriff's officer says he cannot release Tom until the sheriff arrives, which will be after the race. At this point the entire Oxford crew storm the prison and release Tom, assisted by the entire Cambridge crew who refuse to win the race under a dishonourable advantage. The final scene shows the boat race viewed from the foot of Barnes Bridge. Oxford wins.

This was just the sort of copper-bottomed sure-fire hit that only Boucicault could deliver, but the nature of the subject matter was obviously going to be controversial. Although the words 'prostitute' and 'prostitution' are never used, it is quite clear how Formosa is earning her living. There were going to be objections to the depiction of a life of sin on the stage – and not just any stage, but the stage of the National Theatre. There was also the related question of whether Drury Lane should be presenting crowd-pleasing melodramas of the sort more associated with the Adelphi Theatre and other 'minor' houses. Boucicault, who as a young man had met Phineas T. Barnum and thoroughly internalised his maxim that all publicity is good publicity, relished the prospect of controversy. He didn't have long to wait.

On 19 August *The Times* published a long letter from 'An Amateur Critic' who found himself in 'a hopeless state of bewilderment'. Having visited Drury Lane to see *Formosa*, a play praised by the critics and talked up by the town, he finds it to be 'one of the most impudent and... most mischievous attempts that have ever been made to corrupt the English stage... the heroine, who gives the play its name... is, in plain English, a harlot... And not only is a harlot the heroine of the piece, but her harlotry is made one of its most prominent features... To assist the effect... three or four subordinate harlots... are artistically thrown in, and the British public has... exhibited before it a faithful picture... of life in the *demi-monde*'. As the peppery old gentleman warmed to his theme, he cast the net of his outrage wider. Not only is a harlot the heroine, but she is shown to prosper from her evil-doing. When she decides to give it all up and go back to pulling pints in Oxford, her parents instantly forgive her and a wealthy gentleman, who has long been one of her ardent admirers, proposes marriage.[20] 'Imagine... the moral conveyed by such a history as this to all the servant girls and milliners who fill the pit and galleries of Drury Lane Theatre, to say nothing of the tradesmen's daughters in the dress circle, or the underpaid governesses at the back of the boxes.' The Amateur Critic had no confidence in the ability of the 'very ornamental but not very useful champion of decency, the Lord Chamberlain' to sort this out, so he appeals to Mr Boucicault to print a warning on his posters that no unmarried women or minors will be permitted to enter Drury Lane while *Formosa* is playing.[21]

Boucicault must have been hugging himself when he read this – assuming he hadn't written it. It was not unknown for him to stir up publicity by writing pseudonymously to the papers to attack his own plays, and the Amateur Critic certainly had a good grasp of English prose style. The reply, signed by Chatterton, was published five days later.

Chatterton began by saying that he didn't want to discuss the morality of *Formosa*, beyond saying that if he had felt it had any corrupting influence he would not have staged it in the first place. As for banning unmarried ladies, the ladies had settled that question themselves. His boxes and stalls were bursting with 'ladies the highest and the most respectable in London... do you think that this overwhelming majority of ladies would be found in my audience if the play were as indelicate a picture as he represents it to be? If he sees indecency where they do not, am I not permitted to suspect that he brings the excitement of an unchaste mind to the subject?' Having disposed of the moral question, Chatterton goes on to confront the charge that he has degraded the National Theatre:

> Now, Sir, it is time the public were put in possession of some statistics, by the help of which they may judge what I have done for what is called the legitimate drama, and if I may be justly accused of deserting it or turning it out of doors. For seven years I have been the manager of this house, and this is my experience. I have produced the best plays of Shakespeare, Byron, Milton and Goethe. To illustrate these works I engaged Miss Helen Faucit, Mr Phelps, Mr Barry Sullivan, Mr Anderson, Mr Montgomery, and all the tragic talent to be obtained. I employed Mr Beverley and numerous assistants to paint the scenery, sparing no expense to render the representations perfect. My enterprise was supported cheerfully by the pit and galleries, but my boxes and stalls were sadly deserted. I lost money. Had not the pantomime and Christmas come to my rescue I could not have stood my ground at all. I was stubborn, and pursued this policy for pride's sake during six years. But, Sir, I am neither a literary missionary nor a martyr; I am simply the manager of a theatre, a vendor of intellectual entertainment to the London public, and I found that Shakespeare spelt ruin and Byron bankruptcy.

The amount taken daily at my box-office before the doors open for securing stalls and private boxes alone to see *Formosa* exceeds the gross contents of my theatre to witness *Macbeth*. Five years ago I produced *Comus* in the most splendid manner. The public would not come to see it. They praised it and kept away. At the same time Mr Boucicault's drama *The Streets of London* was produced at the Princess's Theatre, and for 200 nights that theatre was crammed nightly with those who deserted Milton.

The public have been a good deal abused, managers have been called mercenary, and we have been led to understand that there is an intellectual and refined class somewhere, who only want the opportunity to come out and support the higher class of dramatic entertainment. Where are they? Mr Macready, my predecessor in management here, tried to discover their existence, but retreated from the search with very sore pockets, just as I did. No such customers exist. There is, however, a class of literary men and dilettanti that profess to deplore the degradation of our times. I have remarked, however, that when I produce Shakespeare these gentlemen, who are entitled by courtesy to admission to the theatre, rarely ask for orders, but since I have produced *Formosa* I have been overwhelmed with applications from this quarter for private boxes for their wives and families. I state facts; I allow others to comment upon them.

Yours obediently

F. B. Chatterton, Theatre Royal, Drury Lane, Aug. 21.[22]

This letter would come to define Chatterton in the eyes of his contemporaries and of posterity as a philistine who should never have been left in charge of the National Theatre. He would be forever known as the man who thought Shakespeare spelt ruin and Byron bankruptcy. The epigram would stick to him to the end of his life and beyond the grave, which was unfortunate as he didn't write it.

The protestations of unfairness, of being criticised for not being 'legitimate' by people who didn't come to the theatre to see the legitimate drama when it was produced, of complimentary seats that were left empty for the legitimate drama but filled for 'sensation', were Chatterton's, probably mediated through Charles Lamb Kenney.[23] However, aphorisms were not Chatterton's style, and the offending words had actually been written by Boucicault. Chatterton soon regretted putting his name to Boucicault's 'now historical platitude',[24] which damaged his reputation and was not even literally true at the time.

The Doge of Venice had lost money, but Byron's *Manfred* had been a success. Samuel Phelps and Helen Faucit had been popular both jointly and severally in their Shakespearean productions of 1864 and 1865: the big Shakespearean losses were still in the future.

The same issue of *The Times* carried a long leader dismissing Chatterton's justification of *Formosa* as specious and irrelevant. He had begun his letter by saying that he didn't intend to discuss the morality of the play, but that was the whole point of the debate. His excuse, that presenting the legitimate drama at Drury Lane had left him out of pocket and he had to put on shows the public wanted to see, was unanswerable. However, to say that he was forced to present sensation drama was no excuse for presenting an *immoral* sensation drama.[25]

Two days later, Boucicault pitched in to stoke the flames of controversy even higher. He assumed that 'An Amateur Critic' must be the father of a large brood. He wondered if, when the Amateur Critic went to his club, he left his copy of *The Times* lying around for his daughters to read. If so, they would be exposed to lurid accounts of adultery in the proceedings of the divorce courts. And did he ever allow these young ladies to attend the opera, where the most popular operas of the day would regale them with spicy tales of lust and murder? Did he ever allow these charming young ladies to accompany themselves on the pianoforte at home whilst warbling the plaintive confessions of female frailty depicted in *La Traviata*? If so, Boucicault could not see why the drama should be forbidden to treat subjects that were unobjectionable in opera. He ended his letter with the provocative statement that he aimed at nothing less than a revolution in the English stage. 'I have proclaimed a literary thoroughfare and… I intend to keep it open.'[26]

This time the Thunderer replied with a leader that was even longer and sterner than the last one, and clearly designed to head off the revolution Boucicault was threatening. It began by congratulating him on at least engaging with the issue, unlike Chatterton, but pointed out that his approach was not to say that his play was good, but that lots of others things were as bad. With regard to the proceedings of the divorce courts reported in *The Times*, everyone knew that in any well-regulated household young girls would be forbidden to read this section of the paper. On the comparison with opera, *The Times* was on weaker ground. There was certainly a double standard operating, as had been proved when E. T. Smith was refused a licence for Alexandre Dumas's play *The Lady of the Camelias* at Drury Lane in 1853 on grounds of indecency, only to see Verdi's operatic version of the same story, *La Traviata*, granted a licence by the Lord Chamberlain three years later.[27]

However, *The Times* took the view that no one could confuse opera with real life and that therefore people would not be influenced by it. 'The mere fact that all the sinning is done to tune, and that one class of crime is usually assigned to the bass and another to the tenor, would alone suffice to destroy all resemblance between it and our unmusical matter-of-fact world.' Opera takes place in a sort of Utopia or Fairyland, while Formosa, on the other hand, lives not in Fairyland but in Fulham. The Thunderer concluded by stating that Boucicault's notion that the best way to preserve the innocence of girls was to expose them to the seamy side of life was too disgusting for debate.[28]

The Times allocated very little space to the theatre, which John Thadeus Delane, its legendary editor, regarded as being 'of very little consequence to the great body of our readers'.[29] In spite of this, it had now devoted several long columns to letters and leaders discussing the morality of the current play at Drury Lane. Whilst Chatterton, a devout Christian and family man, would have been made uneasy by accusations of immorality, for Boucicault they represented the sort of publicity money can't buy. It certainly had the desired effect on business.[30] *Formosa* ran continuously until it had to make way for the pantomime on 18 December, notching up 117 performances and overtaking *The Great City* as the longest continuous run at Drury Lane. It made a profit of £10,000[31] which was divided between Boucicault and Chatterton. (Boucicault was sufficiently aware of his worth to managers to permit his plays to be produced only on a profit-sharing basis.[32])

The controversy about the morality of the play had not escaped Lord Sydney, the Lord Chamberlain, especially after one paper called for the abolition of his office if he couldn't stop Boucicault from demoralising society with plays of this sort.[33] Lord Sydney asked his Examiner of Plays, William Donne, why he had issued a licence for *Formosa* without referring the matter up to him, as was customary with potentially controversial pieces. Donne replied that the play was 'vulgar, foolish and improbable' but Formosa repented for her evil-doing and 'vice was throughout represented under a repulsive aspect'. Donne offered to issue a statement to the effect that the Lord Chamberlain would never have issued a licence had he known the contents of the play, but Lord Sydney decided to let the matter rest.[34]

The curtain-raiser to *Formosa* was a ballet-farce called *Belles of the Kitchen* in which all the parts were played by members (or pretended members) of the Vokes family: Fred, his sisters Jessie, Victoria and Rosina, and 'Fawdon Vokes' who was really Walter Fawdon but changed his name to join the troupe. They specialised in comic dancing, involving contortions and acrobatics, and were said to have rubbery limbs with no bones 'except perhaps the "funny bone".'[35] They were the children of a theatrical costumier called Frederick Vokes who had worked on costumes for a number of Chatterton's shows, including *Formosa*, and most had made their first appearances as child performers. They made their first London appearance as a troupe in pantomime at the Lyceum in 1868/69, but after appearing in *Belles of the Kitchen* they would work for Chatterton almost continuously for the next ten years.

The Vokes family depicted in 1874 when they were appearing in *Aladdin*

The pantomime was *Beauty and the Beast*, with 'the extensive use of the Vokes family'[36] in both the 'opening' (the fairy-tale part of the programme) and the harlequinade. 'Too many Vokes for some folks' was one rather sour observation on their ubiquity.[37] The curtain-raiser was a one-act farce called *I'm Not Myself At All*, which started at 7.00 p.m., with the pantomime starting at 7.45 p.m. and finishing by 11.00 p.m. This continued until 12 February, after which the pantomime became the afterpiece to two full-length plays by Sheridan Knowles, now forgotten but at the time a pillar of the 'legitimate' drama: *William Tell* and *The Wife*, for one week each. *William Tell*, which began at 7.00 p.m., was cut from five acts to three to allow the pantomime to start at 9.00 p.m. The performance ended at 11.00 p.m., so an hour-and-a-quarter had been shaved off the pantomime, while the drastic cuts to *William Tell*, which involved the deletion of whole scenes and characters, made it almost unintelligible, according to one critic.[38] This was Chatterton's last attempt to produce 'legitimate' plays towards the end of the pantomime season. For the next five years he would use shortened versions of melodramas[39] to precede the shortened pantomime as it reached the end of its run, and from 1875/76 onwards he left the pantomime at its full length until it closed.

Boucicault had wanted to revive *Formosa* after the pantomime but Chatterton was against it. It had been taking over £1,600 a week at its peak but before Christmas this had dropped to £600, so Chatterton favoured a change of programme.[40] Boucicault exercised his right as co-producer of the play to mount other productions of *Formosa* at the Princess's and the Standard Theatres.[41] Meanwhile Chatterton decided that the time was right for another revival of *Peep o' Day*, of which the rights had reverted to him after Falconer's bankruptcy. Although the 1863 revival at Drury Lane had flopped, the state of Ireland was highly topical in 1869 as a result of Gladstone's act of parliament to disestablish the Church of Ireland. Chatterton produced the show himself on a large scale, with 300 extras employed for the 'faction fight', which must have looked more like a battle scene from one of Shakespeare's history plays than a punch-up at a village fair. The Vokes family joined the cast, with Fawdon Vokes playing 'Billy o' the Bowl' and Fred 'Tim with the Wooden Leg', parts which offered obvious scope for their 'grotesque dancing'. The Vokes family were also starring in the farce *Phobus' Fix* which was the curtain-raiser for the production. They were referred to in the advertisements as 'the celebrated Vokes family', an epithet that would stick to them. They lived opposite the stage door of Drury Lane and, when they went to worship in St Paul's Church, Covent Garden, people would come just to stare at them.[42]

Peep o' Day made a profit of £2,000 in five weeks. 'Think of that!' Chatterton told John Coleman, 'A profit of £2,000 in Lent!'[43] He had to curtail the run to make way for the summer opera season so he transferred the production to Astley's Amphitheatre in Lambeth, then the Standard Theatre in Shoreditch.

The 1869/70 season at Drury Lane had been a long (201 nights) and a profitable one. However the success of Bouicault's drama led to a serious falling out between Chatterton and Samuel Phelps that ended in court. Phelps had not been in the cast of *Formosa*, so his services were not required at Drury Lane for several months. He was still on the Drury Lane payroll, but Chatterton released him to make a tour of the provinces while *Formosa* was playing. All went well until Phelps booked himself into Sadler's Wells for a week. Chatterton objected to this on the grounds that Phelps was not meant to be appearing at any theatre in London other than Drury Lane, and he began placing advertisements stating that all enquiries about booking Phelps must come to him.[44] Phelps was already annoyed by the 'Shakespeare spelt ruin' epigram, which he took as an insult both to Shakespeare and to himself as the man for whom Shakespeare had certainly *not* spelt ruin at Sadler's Wells for eighteen years. After appearing as Othello on the Saturday night, 'Mr Phelps came forward and addressed the audience, complaining of the conduct of Mr Chatterton towards him'. He told the audience that 'these crowded houses are the best answer to Boucicault's insolent and mendacious epigram – an epigram which is an impudent advertising trade gag, worthy of a quack at a country fair'.[45] Chatterton sued Phelps for breach of contract and Phelps issued a counter-claim. Both cases were heard by Mr Justice Wills who decided that both claimants were in the right and also in the wrong. He did not award costs to either party, so the whole affair was a waste of time and money for both men.

In the summer of 1870 there was once again an opera season at Drury Lane, but it was not under the management of James Mapleson. Mapleson and Gye were again running a 'coalition season' at Covent Garden, but now that their plan was known, the reason for its initial secrecy became apparent. With the two leading opera impresarios engaged in a joint and profitable venture at Covent Garden, there was a gap in the market. It was filled by Henry Jarrett, Mapleson's former business manager, who went into partnership with the impresario George Wood to take the summer lease on Drury Lane and launch an Italian opera season in competition. It ran from 16 April to 30 July and, in spite of featuring the first British performance of Wagner's *The Flying Dutchman*, was a financial failure, forcing Wood to sell and mortgage all of his assets to stay afloat. According to Mapleson (who was gloating of course): 'anyone but a man of Mr Wood's indomitable energy and courage would have been ruined beyond hope of recovery'.[46]

1870 – 1871: The people's theatre

In October 1870, as the new London theatre season was getting underway, *The Illustrated London News* announced an expansion of Chatterton's sphere of influence in the West End:

> In these days, when united kingdoms are political facts... we ought not to be surprised that, with the increase of theatres, some of them should be, in like manner, united under one management. Mr Webster and Mr Chatterton have combined their forces, and the Princess's and Adelphi houses are now under their joint management.[47]

What the paper didn't say, but what everyone in the theatre community knew, was that Chatterton had entered into this partnership to save Benjamin Webster from financial ruin.

Benjamin Webster, known as the Nestor of the Stage, was by this time seventy-two with a distinguished career in the theatre going back over half a century. He had appeared at Drury Lane under Elliston and Bunn in the 1820s and 1830s before he went into management on his own account, taking the lease of the Theatre Royal, Haymarket in 1837. During his sixteen-year tenure there, he made it the home of high-quality drama, in spite of the patents which, until 1843, made it a 'summer theatre' only, restricted in its opening to avoid competition with Drury Lane and Covent Garden. The Haymarket couldn't compete with the patent houses in terms of spectacle, but Webster turned that to his advantage: his theatre was small enough for the audience to be able to see and hear the actors clearly. Webster put together a good company of actors and put on good plays, including many new works. In the winter, when the Haymarket was forced to close, he took the company out on tour, making the Haymarket the first theatre to tour its complete company and productions. In 1844 Webster acquired the lease of the Adelphi Theatre, installing his long-term partner Madame Céleste, the French dancer and actress, to run it. In 1852 he acquired the freehold of the Adelphi, becoming 'proprietor' instead of lessee,[48] and in 1853 he gave up the lease of the Haymarket to concentrate on the Adelphi. In 1856 he acquired the freehold of the property next door to the Adelphi in the Strand and rebuilt the theatre on a larger scale, financed by the sale of debentures which he described as possessing 'unapproachable' security in view of the fact that the Adelphi was the only freehold theatre in London.[49] In October 1869 George Vining's management at the Princess's Theatre in Oxford Street collapsed and Webster took over the lease, so he was running two theatres. This appears to be the point at which things started to go seriously wrong. By 1870 it was known within the profession that Webster was in trouble. In April he had been forced to deny a rumour that he had sold his interest in the Adelphi and the Princess's to Dion Boucicault by claiming that he had no intention of disposing of the theatres.[50] Nevertheless, the vultures were circling, and Chatterton was asked if he could help the old man out.

The request came at a time when Chatterton's relationship with the proprietors of Drury Lane was going through a rocky patch. Under the terms of his lease, he should have completely redecorated the theatre between June and September 1869. Because *Formosa* opened on 5 August, it had been impossible to complete the work and, according to the theatre's architect Marsh Nelson, the work carried out was done to a very poor standard. Nelson served Chatterton with a schedule of work still to be carried out that was estimated to cost £3,250 – about £380,000 in modern values. No more work could be done until the week before Christmas, when the theatre was closed for the get-in of the pantomime, but once again only a small amount of work was carried out, also to a low standard. Nelson estimated that there was still work left undone to the value of £2,250 and Chatterton agreed to pay the committee £1,200 in earnest of his good intentions. The annual meeting of the proprietors on 7 February 1870 was a stormy one as Chatterton had packed it with his friends who objected to his subjection to frivolous and vexatious demands by Marsh Nelson. Chatterton then sued Nelson for slander.

The action was heard on 16 June 1870. Chatterton alleged that, at a stormy meeting involving Nelson, Chatterton and Chatterton's contractor, Nelson had told the contractor he wasn't going to be paid and threatened Chatterton with eviction for infringing the terms of the lease. Nelson said that he had not used the words attributed to him, had never meant to insult Chatterton, and wished only for the restoration of the friendly relations that used to exist between them. By this time tempers had cooled and, after a short consultation between counsel and the judge, the case was dropped. The judge made it clear that Chatterton left the court without the slightest stain on his character, which was exactly what Chatterton wanted to hear.[51]

Friendly relations with Marsh Nelson must have quickly been restored because Chatterton agreed to a complete redecoration of the theatre, obliterating work that was less than a year old.[52]

Nevertheless, the idea of escaping this sort of interference by the Drury Lane proprietors and their architect by taking on two more London theatres must have appealed to Chatterton, especially as the Adelphi was a freehold with no annoying ground-landlord to make demands. Chatterton understood that Webster was being pressed by creditors to the extent of £6,000, and that there were a few liabilities on top of that. He himself was making between £15,000 and £16,000 a year at the time (around £1.8 million in current values), so he told his bankers to credit Webster with £6,000 while he sorted out the management of the two theatres. It was a step that would ultimately lead to his ruin.

Meanwhile, the Drury Lane season had opened with *Amy Robsart*, an adaptation of Sir Walter Scott's *Kenilworth*. The script was by Andrew Halliday, who was the obvious choice after the success of *King o' Scots*, but it was not his first stage version of the novel. Halliday's very first attempt at dramatic writing had been a burlesque for the Strand Theatre called *Kenilworth or Ye Queene, Ye Earle and Ye Maydenne* which opened on Boxing Night 1858 and ran for over one hundred nights. It was a spoof of Scott's novel and had the Earl of Leicester saying to Elizabeth I: 'And so, your majesty, mind what you're arter/ And don't be violating Magna Charta'.[53] *Amy Robsart* was a far more serious affair. John Oxenford explained to readers of *The Times* the rationale behind the production:

> Constructed with a view to spectacular effect, and surrounded as it were by a historical halo, this is exactly the sort of piece that, according to modern notions, is suitable to a large theatre. The days when it was universally believed that a genteel comedy could be properly performed on the spacious area of the old patent stage has [sic] long passed away, and yet there is a feeling that Drury Lane is to some extent desecrated when employed for the production of mere melodrama.[54]

The last sentence recalled *Formosa*, tainted by accusations of immorality, but no one could make that charge against *Amy Robsart*. Indeed, the only serious departure from Sir Walter's story was the ending in which, instead of having Amy fall to her death, the villainous Varney falls victim to his own trap. It was a theatrical truism that London audiences, especially working-class audiences, would not tolerate the destruction of a virtuous heroine, and James Anderson, who saw *Amy Robsart* a few days into the run, wrote that, when Amy was saved: 'the righteous gods shouted until they were hoarse. It is curious to see how the gallery and pit people enjoy the triumph of virtue over vice, while the stalls scarcely give a hand.'[55]

Visually, *Amy Robsart* was stunning. The first of Beverley's big sets was the old Palace of Greenwich, from which Elizabeth I departed in her state barge 'which floats magnificently on the mimic Thames'.[56] This was followed by the big set-piece of the show: the revels at Kenilworth to celebrate the arrival of Good Queen Bess. For this Chatterton hired 300 extras, drilled in a series of tableaux involving circus acts, musicians, a Pyrrhic dance of Amazons and a procession of 'ancient Britons, Saxons, Romans, Normans etc., and ending with the floating pageants on the lake'.[57] As *The Observer* put it: 'Ballet succeeds ballet, procession follows procession; music and dancing, limelight and glitter, spectacle and show, are all combined.'[58] Chatterton ran nine separate classified advertisements containing extracts from reviews, most of them praising the spectacle.

Samuel Phelps was no longer at Drury Lane as a result of his legal spat with Chatterton, but the company had acquired a new star in the person of Adelaide Neilson, a beautiful twenty-two-year-old who had made her London debut five years before and established a reputation in both Shakespeare and melodrama. Her performance as Amy was highly praised. The Vokes family were in the cast, with Fred Vokes playing Flibbertigibbet as 'a creature of supernal acrobatic power'.[59] (It was a busy time for the Vokes as their ballet-farce *Phobus' Fix* was also in the programme.)[60]

Amy Robsart ran for seventy-three continuous performances until it had to make way for the pantomime, generating a profit of nearly £10,000 – over £1.1m today.[61] The demand for tickets was so great that on 9 and 23 November there were matinee performances 'in answer to numerous applications from parties residing in the suburbs'. Children and schools were admitted at reduced prices. Matinees had been pioneered by E. T. Smith at Drury Lane for the pantomime in 1853 and had quickly become customary at other theatres for their Christmas shows. Their rationale was that shows aimed at children should be put on before their bedtime. However, matinee performances of anything other than children's shows were extremely unusual, apart from charity fundraisers or attempts to stage a play that could only be expected to have a very limited appeal, either because it was too old-fashioned or too avant-garde. This was the first experiment at Drury Lane with a matinee of the play that was being staged in the evening. Adelaide

Neilson felt unwell after the matinee on 9 November so Victoria Vokes took over as Amy at the evening performance[62] and was asked to play the part again for the matinee on 23 November. The last night of the autumn season was 19 December which was Adelaide Neilson's benefit. Keen to burnish her Shakespearean credentials, she chose to appear as Shakespeare's Juliet, after which she recited *The Charge of the Light Brigade*.

The pantomime, *The Dragon of Wantley*, featured so many Vokes it 'might very appropriately be called an evening with the Vokes family, and an enlarged and amplified edition of the "Belles of the Kitchen"' according to one critic, who was less than enchanted by their acrobatic dancing.[63] John Oxenford began his annual review of the Christmas shows for *Times* readers by observing that pantomime was dying out in central London, as managers preferred to keep successful productions running throughout the holiday period. Covent Garden and Drury Lane kept up the tradition, but theatregoers seeking a pantomime anywhere else would be obliged to 'cross the water [i.e. go south of the Thames] or penetrate the remote suburbs'. In fact, Sadler's Wells was presenting a pantomime, and Islington is not exactly a remote suburb, but the boundaries of the West End have always been defined by more than geography.

In Oxenford's view, nothing could approach the status of the pantomime at Drury Lane, 'which is still really the people's theatre… though high tragedy and genuine comedy have disappeared from boards once consecrated to "legitimacy", the truly national drama, the Christmas pantomime, survives in full vigour, and this, in many minds, is associated with the theatre that, in spite of many vicissitudes, remains an exceptionally national institution.'[64]

Chatterton announced that he had banned 'advertisement scenes' – we would say product placement – whereby actual London shopfronts would be painted onto the scenery and brand names were promoted in the harlequinade. Although this was a source of additional revenue for the manager, audiences were irritated by it and had booed a scene in the previous year's pantomime that was introduced solely to demonstrate the superiority of a particular brand of sewing machines.[65] The new policy was appreciated and Chatterton was compared favourably with other managers who 'would have stuck a puffing placard on the tail of the dear old Dragon of Wantley himself, if a few pounds could have been gained by the exhibition'.[66]

The Dragon of Wantley ran for fifty-three performances with a one-act farce called *Rule Britannia* as the curtain-raiser, then, on 27 February, *Amy Robsart* came back, with Victoria Vokes in the title role as Adelaide

Neilson was in Liverpool with the touring production. It started at 7.00 p.m. and was followed by *The Dragon of Wantley* as an afterpiece; *Amy Robsart* was cut by half-an-hour and the pantomime was cut by half to run for one-and-a-half hours, allowing the programme to end at 11.30 p.m. This programme ran for five weeks and the season closed on 1 April with Chatterton's benefit. This was a mammoth event, starting with the Vokes family in *Belles of the Kitchen*, followed by Act II of *Hamlet*, followed by Benjamin Webster's play (in which he also acted) *One Touch of Nature*, followed by a poem about Mary Queen of Scots, followed by a concert with Chatterton's sister Kate on the pianoforte and Uncle Frederick on the harp, followed by the last two acts of *Amy Robsart*.

Amy Robsart was the first play to run from the beginning to the end of the season at Drury Lane, with the exception of the nine weeks when the pantomime was running as the mainpiece – a total of 105 performances. *The Dragon of Wantley* was advertised as 'the most successful pantomime ever produced'[67] and became the first to reach one hundred performances.

The summer of 1871 saw James Mapleson and his Italian opera back at Drury Lane. This was meant to have been the third of the coalition seasons at Covent Garden but, to the delight of operagoers who, like true Victorians, relied on competition to drive up standards,[68] Mapleson and Gye had fallen out in an atmosphere of poisonous mutual mistrust.[69] Rather confusingly, Mapleson was still calling his season Her Majesty's Opera at Drury Lane, even though Her Majesty's Theatre, rebuilt after the fire, had been standing empty for nearly two years.[70] Once again, the auditorium was magnificently transformed, with the stage cut back by seven feet to enlarge the orchestra pit and the floor of the pit sunk to accommodate a tier of boxes around stalls upholstered in crimson damask. Amazingly, this work was carried out in eight days.[71] The season ran from 15 April to 5 August, and Mapleson was delighted when the Prince of Wales took a box, 'as well as all the leading supporters from the old house'.[72]

1871 – 1872: Scott is synonymous with success

In September Chatterton was once again setting up his colossal bust of 'the Ariosto of the North' (Sir Walter Scott) in the foyer of Drury Lane. The success of *Amy Robsart*, coupled with the celebration in 1871 of the centenary of Walter Scott's birth, made it almost inevitable that Chatterton would 'seek for the next subject in the rich and bounteous storehouse of Sir Walter Scott'.[73]

What he produced from the storehouse was *Ivanhoe*, transformed into *Rebecca* by Andrew Halliday, whose success with *Amy Robsart* had given him the extraordinary privilege of having his name on the publicity in letters as large as those used for William Beverley, and much larger than those used for Sir Walter Scott. 'How nice it must be to be an original dramatic author', one critic sarcastically observed of the discrepancy.[74] Adelaide Neilson returned to the Lane as the beautiful Jewess with Samuel Phelps as her father, Isaac of York. The spectacle was reliably eye-popping, with a grand masque under the greenwood tree, Torquilstone Castle destroyed by fire in a battle between Saxons and Normans, and the tournament at which Ivanhoe and Brian de Bois Guilbert joust for the life of Rebecca, tied to a stake. There were real horses, glittering armour and 300 extras creating what *The Daily Telegraph* hailed as 'a stage picture which probably stands unrivalled in the bright history of stage tableaux... If Shakespeare spells ruin and Byron bankruptcy, surely Mr F. B. Chatterton must complete the lame alliteration by declaring that Scott is synonymous with success'.[75]

John Oxenford, in his now familiar role as apologist for Chatterton's management, used his *Times* review to discuss the position of Drury Lane in the changing ecology of London theatre. Covent Garden and Drury Lane, once considered suitable for the presentation of all sorts of dramatic entertainments, were now no longer regarded as appropriate for serious plays or comedies that dealt with modern life. Smaller theatres were more suitable for plays like Tom Robertson's 'cup-and-saucer' comedies that had made the fortune of the Bancrofts at their tiny Prince of Wales Theatre on Tottenham Street, and which would have been completely lost on the vast stage of Drury Lane. So, given that Covent Garden had become an opera house, that left the question of what to put on at Drury Lane.

> Mr F. B. Chatterton, evidently aware that his appeal must be made not to an exceptional, but to a general public, uses his stage exactly for the purpose for which... it is fitted. His pieces... completely fill it, and could not be brought out to equal effect on one of smaller dimensions. On Saturday night... there was a correspondence between the crowd of mailed warriors beyond the range of lamps and the enthusiastic throng occupying stalls, pit, boxes and gallery which gratified one's sense of the fitness of things. Indeed, such a shout as that which arose when the curtain fell on the rescue of the fair Jewess could scarcely have been produced elsewhere than at Drury Lane.[76]

Rebecca ran for seventy-five performances (including a charity matinee that raised £250 for the victims of the great fire of Chicago) and made a profit of £6,000.[77]

The pantomime was *Tom Thumb* with Fred Vokes as King Arthur and Tom Thumb as one of the Knights of the Round Table who leads a child army to repel the Anglo-Saxons. It had become a Drury Lane tradition that the overture to the pantomime would contain popular and patriotic songs with which the gallery would sing along, and this year the band played *God Bless the Prince of Wales* to mark Prince Edward's recovery from a serious illness. The gallery demanded three encores, with the singing becoming louder and more raucous each time.[78]

At the end of February Chatterton revived *Amy Robsart* (with Mrs Hermann Vezin in the title part) followed by a shortened version of the pantomime for three weeks. The season closed on Saturday 23 March with a benefit performance for Chatterton – or rather with two, because there was another one on Monday afternoon. The official reason for this was that 'not one half of the admirers of this gentleman's managerial sagacity' could get into Drury Lane on the Saturday, but this was disingenuous as they had always been planned as separate events with different programmes.[79]

Andrew Halliday, Chatterton and E. L. Blanchard are shown grinding money out of Drury Lane with their pantomimes and Walter Scott adaptations.

The Saturday night performance was the standard affair, with members of Chatterton's company performing extracts from shows in the current Drury Lane repertoire, but the Monday matinee was very different. It involved performances by leading actors from other theatres in their most popular parts: Benjamin Webster in *One Touch of Nature*, Samuel Phelps in *The Man of the World*, Charles Fechter doing an act of *Hamlet*, J. L. Toole in *The Spitalfields Weaver*, and even the Christy Minstrels. It was a marathon, starting at one and ending after six o' clock,[80] and the scale of this benefit indicated Chatterton's status in the London theatre world at the time. 'This gentleman's management of the theatres under his control has been singularly satisfactory,' one paper reported. 'His business tact is indisputable, and his constant urbanity attaches to him many sincere friends.'[81] The last remark suggests that the journalist did not know the famously bad-tempered Chatterton very well.

James Mapleson was back at Drury Lane for another opera season in 1872, as the rebuilt Her Majesty's had still not been fitted out. Mapleson managed to secure the services of the Swedish soprano Christine Nilsson once again after a two-year gap at the enormous salary of £200 per performance. To his unconcealed delight, this caused problems at Covent Garden for Frederick Gye who was paying his prima donna Adelina Patti £80 a night. When Patti heard about Nilsson's demands she refused to go on for less, but even when Gye offered her £200 she said it was not enough. She insisted on receiving more than Nilsson, so Gye had to up the offer to 200 guineas.[82]

The Adelphi and the Princess's Theatres 1870 – 1872

Since the beginning of the 1870/71 season, Chatterton's name had been appearing on the management billing for three theatres. At Drury Lane he was still 'Sole Lessee and Manager'. At the Adelphi, where Webster held the freehold, the billing was: 'Sole Proprietor Mr Benjamin Webster; Managers Mr B. Webster and Mr F. B. Chatterton'. At the Princess's it was: 'Sole Lessee Mr B. Webster; Managers Mr Webster and Mr Chatterton'.[83] Chatterton was confident that he could run the three theatres successfully. In fact, as he later confessed: 'I might as well have attempted to drive the horses of the sun.'[84]

Of the two, the Adelphi was the easier theatre to manage. First, it had an enviable West End location in the Strand; secondly, it had a strong house identity as the home of high-class melodrama. Benjamin Webster had taken over the lease in 1844 but, as he was already running the Theatre Royal, Haymarket, he passed the management of the Adelphi to his long-term partner Madame Céleste. Céline Céleste was a French dancer, mime and actor who arrived in Britain in 1831 where she appeared successfully at Covent Garden, Drury Lane and the Haymarket. During her engagement at the latter she became Webster's mistress and, although they were never married, they were widely accepted as a couple in Victorian London. Together they would turn the Adelphi into one of the most profitable theatres in town.

Madame Céleste's most popular part was Miami in John Buckstone's *The Green Bushes*, a fiery half-native American/ half-French huntress of the Mississippi who kills her Irish lover in a fit of passion when she finds he has been unfaithful to her. The play opened at the Adelphi in 1845, to be followed by other melodramatic triumphs for Céleste like Cynthia the Gypsy Queen in *The Flowers of the Forest* (1847) and the title role in Boucicault's *Janet Pride* (1855). In 1853 Webster handed over the lease of the Haymarket to John Buckstone and went to work with Céleste at the Adelphi. They had a serious falling-out in 1859 after which she set up in management on her own account, first at the Lyceum, then at the Olympic. After some highly successful tours of the USA and Australia, she made what was supposed to be her farewell appearance at the St James's Theatre in 1868. It was no such thing, and in October 1870, having made up her differences with Webster, she returned to the Adelphi for what was meant to be a two-week season, although it turned into two months. Almost all of her appearances were as Miami in *The Green Bushes*, the part she had created twenty-five years before and for which she was now, at fifty-five, rather too old. Her final 'farewell performance' on 17 December was in fact nothing of the kind: there would be many more.[85]

The Christmas attraction was a 'balladic burlesque' called *A Mistletoe Bough*, followed by a new drama by F. C. Burnand called *Deadman's Point*. That closed after six weeks and the theatre remained dark until Easter Monday, when *Notre Dame*, Andrew Halliday's stage version of Victor Hugo's *The Hunchback of Notre Dame*, opened. Halliday's skill in selecting the essential elements of a long book resulted in a tense drama, culminating in a scene set amidst the topmost turrets of the Cathedral of Notre Dame de Paris – an enormous set that filled most of the stage. The audience went wild as Quasimodo hurled the villainous Frollo ('the goblin monk') to his death in the Seine far below. Once again, Halliday saved the life of his heroine. In the book Esmeralda is hanged on a false charge of attempted murder, but Halliday produced a last-minute royal pardon. It would achieve 197 continuous performances over seven months, giving it the longest first run of any of the of Halliday/ Chatterton collaborations, and was then revived almost immediately when other shows proved less successful. By the time it closed, on 2 March 1872, it had achieved 255 performances.

Chatterton then put Charles Fechter into the Adelphi for four weeks performing *Ruy Blas* – one of his most popular parts – which in turn made way for a new drama called *Hilda the Miser's Daughter* on 1 April 1872. This was yet another of Andrew Halliday's adaptations, this time of a historical romance by Harrison Ainsworth set at the time of the 1745 rebellion led by Bonnie Prince Charlie. The scenes included Vauxhall Gardens, the cloisters of Westminster Abbey, an escape across the rooftops and a 'floating pleasure palace on the Thames'. It became another of Halliday's hits, with a continuous run of 97 nights.

The Princess's was always more of a challenge for Chatterton, as it was for all those who took it on. It had never really established a clear identify for itself, apart from the period of Charles Kean's management (1850 – 1859) when it was known for lavish and historically accurate Shakespearean productions. The problem was its location: it was in Oxford Street, too far from the main theatre district. Whether he wanted to play it safe, or just didn't have time to think of anything original, Chatterton pursued a policy of reviving old successes at the Princess's. He put on a big production of *Peep o' Day* involving 200 men, women and children in the jig and faction fight, supported by a shortened version of *The Great City*. The latter was taken off after four weeks and *Peep o' Day* only lasted for another three. The Christmas programme was a stage version of *A Christmas Carol* followed by an extravaganza called *Little Gil Blas*. Then, in January 1871, Samuel Phelps and Chatterton made up the differences that had led to their farcical appearance in court the previous year and Phelps joined the Princess's company. He did two weeks as Sir Archibald McSycophant in *The Man of the World* by Charles Macklin (one of his most popular parts) followed by a revival of *King o' Scots* in which he repeated his double act as King James I and Trapbois the Miser. Chatterton alternated the two plays for six weeks, after which the Princess's closed for three weeks, re-opening on Easter Monday with a production of *Faust and Marguerite* starring Samuel Phelps as Mephistopheles. This was not Bayle Bernard's *Faust*, seen at Drury Lane in 1866. Chatterton had obtained from Charles Kean's widow the script of his 1854 production at the Princess's of a French version of Goethe's play, adapted by Boucicault. Kean's scenery was no longer in the stock at the Princess's but it was recreated from the original designs.[86] This was, in all respects, a close copy of Kean's highly successful production, but Chatterton, remembering his own comparatively unsuccessful *Faust* of five years before, was taking no chances. He put it into a strong programme, starting with the ever popular Vokes family in a farce called *The Wrong Man in the Right Place* and finishing with a new piece by E. L. Blanchard called *The Man in the Moon*. This featured a ballet with Telbin's panorama of the Lakes of Killarney that had been so popular at the Lyceum as an afterpiece to *Peep o' Day* in 1862. Nevertheless, *Faust and Marguerite* lasted only four weeks, making way for seven weeks of Phelps in a range of other parts.

Thus far, Chatterton's policy for the Princess's had been revivals of productions that had been hits at other theatres, which was clearly not the way to forge a strong identity for the theatre. His next production, on 29 June 1871, was more surprising: a new play by his alcoholic ex-partner Edmund Falconer.

When Falconer arrived in America in 1866, having fled his creditors after the sudden closure of *Oonagh*, he found that *Peep o' Day* was extremely popular. It brought him celebrity but no profits as there was no copyright law to protect British plays in the USA. He enjoyed some success as an actor and wrote more plays in America, but when he came back to England in 1870 he wanted to recapture the glory days of *Peep o' Day* which had made him the most successful playwright in London for a brief period. He took the lease of the Lyceum and opened on 17 September 1870 with his play *Innisfallen* which was described as the biggest disaster since Falconer's last big disaster and so ineptly constructed that it was hard to believe it was the work of an experienced playwright.[87] Oblivious to it all, Falconer thanked the audience that had spent the evening jeering at him and promised them more of the same. *Innisfallen*, and Falconer's management of the Lyceum ended two weeks later.

The resemblance between elements of *Innisfallen* and *Peep o' Day* had been noted, but Falconer now took the much bolder step of simply recycling the whole plot of *Peep o' Day* using different names for the characters and giving it a new title: *Eileen Oge*. This contained all of the same plot elements: the upright young farmer forced to leave Ireland and his beloved fiancée by false charges of treason; his fiancée pursued by the wicked landlord who has falsified the evidence and who is threatening to evict her father unless she agrees to marry him; a dance of haymakers followed by a fight with the police (instead of a jig followed by a faction fight); a sensation scene (in a haunted mill rather than a disused quarry) in which the sister of the now-returned farmer is to be ruined; and even a loveable Irish rogue (played by Falconer) who saves the day by shooting the villain and saving the sister. As John Oxenford pointed out, with considerable understatement: 'The materials of which this drama is composed are not remarkable for novelty.'[88] Even the title was an echo of the earlier play: 'Eileen Oge' was a traditional Irish air from which Falconer had used one verse in all of the publicity material for *Peep o' Day*. There is no character with this name in either play, but it is supposed to be the nickname of Ellen Moriarty, the fiancée of the young farmer in *Eileen Oge*. Chatterton must have had a strong sense of *déja vu* when he saw the script, but he would have realised what Falconer was up to. Chatterton already owned the rights to *Peep o' Day*, which meant that Falconer received no author's payment when it was revived, but he would be paid if *Eileen Oge* were treated as a new play.

By one of those peculiar flukes that make theatre so interesting, this obvious knock-off turned out to be Falconer's first successful play in London since *Peep o' Day*, running for 117 performances. It might seem strange that Chatterton would be prepared to produce a play by his former partner who had swindled him out of thousands of pounds from the Lyceum profits and then left Chatterton to pay his debts at Drury Lane, but Chatterton's famous temper was a volcano that soon cooled. Even when his disputes ended up in court (which they often did), Chatterton was always willing to forgive and forget afterwards. Besides, he felt sorry for Falconer, who had thrown away what could have been a successful career by his drinking, and whom he regarded as 'a victim to his surroundings'.[89]

Eileen Oge closed on 11 November and went out on tour. It was followed at the Princess's by *On The Jury*, a drama by Watts Phillips which starred Samuel Phelps and Benjamin Webster, two veterans of the stage who were appearing together for the first time. This ran for eighty-three performances, then, after remaining closed for Passion Week in accordance with Chatterton's custom, the Princess's opened on 1 April 1872 – Easter Monday – with a melodrama by H. J. Byron called *Haunted Houses* which ran for ninety-three performances. Its popularity was due to a 'sensation scene' in which the villain lures the heroine to a supposedly haunted house which he intends to bring down over her head. The hero arrives in the nick of time and gets the heroine out of an upper window and onto the bowsprit of a passing boat on the Thames, while the house collapses on the villain.

Chatterton would later tell Coleman that his profits at Drury Lane had been eaten up by the losses at the Adelphi and Princess's,[90] but there was no sign of this at the end of the first two years. Both theatres had produced a high proportion of successes, and there were certain economies of scale that Chatterton could invoke as the manager of three theatres. He could move theatrical properties of which he possessed the rights, like *Peep o' Day*, *The Great City* and *King o' Scots*, from one theatre to another. He could also move around the talent. When the Vokes family finished their stint in the Drury Lane pantomime *The Dragon of Wantley*, he put them into the Princess's in a short piece called *The Wrong Man in the Right Place*. They followed this with a revival of *Belles of the Kitchen* that had been a hit for them at Drury Lane two years earlier. After this the Vokes could take *The Wrong Man in the Right Place* into Drury Lane in the autumn of 1871 as the curtain-raiser for *Rebecca*, which lasted until the Vokes were required for the next Drury Lane pantomime. They were working for Chatterton full-time and he could put them wherever they were most needed.

'F. B. Chatterton Esq. A shrewd demonstration of "The Rule of Three"'. Chatterton tries to produce a novelty from one of his three theatres.

Chatterton also told Coleman that his problems as the manager of three theatres were partly owing to the fact that he spent so much time in hansom cabs travelling from Drury Lane to the Strand to Oxford Street.[91] In fact Drury Lane and the Adelphi were within easy walking distance of each other, but he did need someone to put into the Princess's to take over the day-to-day management, and he found that person in James Guiver his treasurer (we would say finance director) at Drury Lane since 1864. At the beginning of August 1872 the management billing at the Princess's changed to: *Lessee Benjamin Webster; Manager Mr James Guiver.* This billing was used for the next five weeks, at the end of which Chatterton gave Guiver the extraordinary favour of a double benefit performance, matinee and evening, on Saturday 7 September. Chatterton had pioneered what one journalist sarcastically dubbed the 'double-barrelled benefit'[92] for himself and never granted it to anyone else, except on this occasion. The fact that Guiver's name would have been unknown to most of the theatregoing public just makes it more surprising. Guiver must have made himself very useful indeed to Chatterton to be thus rewarded, and it looks as if he had somehow found the funds to take over the lease of the Princess's and get Webster out of it altogether. Webster's name never appeared again in the management billing of the Princess's. Either Chatterton or Guiver would be named as manager (except during the seasons of French plays when Messrs Valnay and Pitron were joint managers) until Chatterton was finally able to describe himself as Sole Lessee in 1874.

7

The Cracks Begin to Show

1872 – 1873: The best lessee ever

During the course of 1872, Chatterton moved house. The family had been living in the Kennington Oval, but Chatterton now moved them into much grander accommodation at The Hawthorns, 193 Clapham Road. This area was still on the edge of London, where there had been little housebuilding before the last years of the eighteenth century. By the time Chatterton moved in, Clapham Road was lined with the dwellings of prosperous middle-class families. The oldest houses, built before the coming of the railways, were substantial properties with carriage entrances and coach-houses. The Hawthorns was one of these, with extensive grounds which would provide ample space for Chatterton, his wife Mary and their five children: Mary (fifteen), Annie (fourteen), Frederick junior (twelve), Edmund (ten) and Florence (five). The establishment was handsomely furnished, with a collection of paintings and musical instruments including, of course, the harp which was almost the family crest. Chatterton took great pleasure in sitting beside his daughter Mary as she practised on the instrument, coaching her in the finer points of light and shade. The Hawthorns was a house that required a staff of servants and reflected Chatterton's status as the manager of three West End theatres. Unfortunately his luck was about to change.

The Drury Lane season opened on 21 September with yet another Walter Scott adaptation: *The Lady of the Lake.* True to form, Chatterton put out a flyer to announce his new season, but this time the policy backfired. The flyer was written by Andrew Halliday who managed to irritate the critics by telling them in advance that his new piece would be a hit, co-opting the bon-mot of the previous year's review of *Rebecca* in *The Daily Telegraph* that 'Scott is synonymous with success'.[1] Critics – and audiences – like to make that judgment for themselves, and Halliday didn't help matters with his absurd claim that Scott's poem led to Queen Victoria building Balmoral.[2]

In his account of Chatterton's first ten years as lessee, Charles Lamb Kenney quotes the old saying that the pitcher goes once too often to the well, and it proved to be the case this time. In spite of its title, *The Lady of the Lake* had nothing to do with the Arthurian legend, and it wasn't even a novel. Scott had written it as a long narrative poem about the struggles between Highlanders and Lowlanders, with the clansman Roderick Dhu leading a rebel uprising against James V of Scotland. The poem, with its long descriptions of the Scottish landscape and the colourful life of the Highland clans, was credited with inspiring the Highland revival, but, as a drama, it presented problems. The story, in which the King in disguise is offered hospitality whilst out hunting by a beautiful young woman and her rebel father, was not especially dramatic. The verse had to be turned into prose, as rhyming verse was by this stage only associated with pantomime and burlesque, so even the admirers of Sir Walter's poetry were to be disappointed. To a greater extent than with any of the previous adaptations, the fortunes of *The Lady of the Lake* were going to depend on the spectacle, and Beverley certainly didn't disappoint. His panorama of the lakeside of Loch Katrine which scrolled across the back of the stage while a boat followed the shore was greeted with great applause. There was also a fantasy sequence involving elves, kelpies and witches, with nymphs rising from the lake and celestial maidens descending from above, and the last act presented a magnificent pageant in the park of Stirling Castle that was an attempt to replicate the revels at Kenilworth which had been the most popular feature of *Amy Robsart*. 'Beverley's scenery very good, the rest very bad' was Blanchard's verdict, which was more or less what the critics said about it.[3]

Although Chatterton kept it running for seventy-seven performances, *The Lady of the Lake* was losing money. With thin houses and mounting losses, but nothing else ready to put on, there was nothing for it but to wait for Boxing Day and the pantomime, when 'the arrival of Clown, Harlequin and Pantaloon was hailed as a detachment of surgeons would be on the field of battle after a severe engagement'.[4]

Fortunately for Chatterton, *The Children in the Wood* would prove his most successful pantomime ever, achieving 105 performances. It ran as the mainpiece until 1 March, after which it was shortened to follow Chatterton's big new production: a revival of a melodrama about the abolition of female infanticide in India by the British called *The Cataract of the Ganges*. Written by W. T. Moncrieff and now updated by E. L. Blanchard, this had first been seen at Drury Lane almost exactly fifty years before and had never been revived since. 'Believing in the judgement of my predecessor, Mr Robert William Elliston, who produced this drama with an unexampled success fifty years ago,' Chatterton announced, 'I have been induced to revive *The Cataract of the Ganges* in order to test whether what proved so vastly attractive to a past generation may now have an equal popularity.'[5] The test came back negative. It seems strange that Chatterton should have failed to understand that public taste in entertainment changes so rapidly that the likelihood of a fifty-year-old hit being successfully revived is very low. According to Kenney, it wasn't so much a revival as a disinterment, and the fact that it was directed by the seventy-four-year-old Benjamin Webster, who had been in the original production, didn't help.[6] In spite of Blanchard's revisions to the text, it was hopelessly old-fashioned with an absurd plot leading up to the 'sensation scene' in which the hero, to save the heroine from being burnt alive, sweeps her onto his white charger and gallops the horse up the eponymous cataract. Or rather, as *The Pall Mall Gazette* put it, 'canters gently with her up a flight of stairs down which a moderate shower-bath is musically tinkling'. There had been so many horses and so many water-effects since 1823 that no one was going to be overwhelmed by this 'one-horse show',[7] but the production was certainly 'a brilliant living picture of Oriental magnificence' with a 'Grand Hindoo ballet and Brahmin Festival' in gorgeous costumes made by Mr Vokes. It ran at a loss for less than four weeks and then transferred to the National Standard Theatre in East London for a further three weeks.[8]

The season came to an end with another of Chatterton's double benefits for himself, on Saturday 29 and Monday 31 March. The programme was identical on both nights: the Vokes family in *Fun in a Fog* (the season's new vehicle for their talents that they would use for many years) followed by Mr and Mrs Rousby making their first London appearance in *King Lear* (described in *The Athenaeum* as 'the last degradation of which tragic art is susceptible'[9]) followed by the last act of *The Cataract of the Ganges*. At the end of the Monday night's performance, Chatterton announced from the stage that his lease of Drury Lane was soon to expire, but the proprietors had been happy to issue him with a new five-year lease in view of the fact that he had doubled the shareholders' dividends over the period of his management.[10] *The Times* told its readers that: 'Those who recollect to what a depth "Old Drury" had sunk not very many years ago, and who… see what it has become under Mr Chatterton's direction, will acknowledge that that fact communicated was really of public interest.'[11]

Chatterton's claim was almost literally true. The last dividend payable from E. T. Smith's time in charge of Drury Lane had been £4 15s. In 1873, it was £8 5s, and the renters knew whom they had to thank. They passed a vote of thanks to Chatterton 'because he had made the theatre so prosperous and was the best lessee they had ever had'.[12] Compliments to Chatterton became a fixture at AGMs, especially after he introduced Mapleson's summer seasons of Italian opera in 1868. The renters had the right of free admission to any performance and this right was tradeable. They could sell the right to admission each September for the coming season, and the value of these transactions rose when people found they could have three months of opera included. Saleable admissions went up from £1 for a year under the previous management to between £5 and £6 by 1873.[13] What Chatterton didn't share with his audience was the fact that he had been the victim of his own success: Drury Lane was now so successful that the rent had gone up by thirty per cent to £6,500 a year, with additional payments of £5 for each night over 200 in the season.[14]

Mapleson returned once again to Drury Lane for a summer season of Italian opera into which, for the first time, he introduced some dramatic performances between the operas. He presented operas on only three or four nights a week, so the theatre was available for the other two or three nights. The Italian tragedian Adelaide Ristori was returning from one of her many tours of America and wanted to do some performances in London, so Mapleson offered her two nights a week at Drury Lane for five weeks.[15] She performed with her own company, always in Italian. Booklets of the text were sold in the auditorium to help the audience to follow the play.[16]

Chatterton had mixed fortunes at his other two theatres in the 1872/73 season. At the Adelphi, where he was now billed as 'Sole Manager', the season had begun with yet more farewell performances from Madame Céleste in *The Green Bushes*. Chatterton then brought in an American performer called J. K. Emmett in *Fritz or the Adventures of Our Cousin German*, which was no more than an excuse for Emmett to appear as different characters, all representing national stereotypes through singing and dancing. It was popular and ran for eighty-two performances. On Easter Monday 1873 Chatterton opened *The Wandering Jew*, Leopold Lewis's version of the ever-popular legend. Benjamin Webster played Rodin, a wily Jesuit priest and the last new character he would create. The play was a success and ran until October, clocking up 152 performances.

The Princess's, where Chatterton was also 'Sole Manager', was more of a problem. He seems to have decided to treat his smallest theatre as a 'legitimate' house, where he could run the sort of repertoire he had staged at Drury Lane until Shakespeare was edged out by Sir Walter Scott. He hired Samuel Phelps for a season of classics in repertory: *Macbeth*, *The Merchant of Venice*, *Othello*, *Hamlet* and Phelps's ever popular Sir Pertinax Macsycophant in *The Man of the World*. This was a risky policy for a West End theatre, where audiences expected something more than a venerable old-timer going through his paces in performances that went back decades and seemed stale.[17] Now aged sixty-eight and in failing health, Phelps collapsed during a performance of *The Man of the World* on 23 November 1872 and had to be carried off. For the remaining weeks of the autumn season Chatterton was announcing his imminent return, but Phelps didn't come back. His health problems may have been more serious than had been thought, but Phelps and Chatterton subsequently had another of their massive rows (we don't know the cause of this one) and Phelps never worked for Chatterton again.[18]

Chatterton tried to fill the gap left by Phelps at the Princess's by putting on *The School for Scandal* with Benjamin Webster as Sir Peter Teazle. It was one of Webster's most famous roles, but once again it was a museum piece. It ran for forty-four performances, to be replaced by a German couple, Herr and Frau Bandmann, doing *Hamlet* and *Macbeth*. Whoever the Bandmanns might have been, they were going to have problems attracting audiences to Oxford Street with Shakespeare. They lasted for six weeks, probably working in some sort of partnership arrangement with Chatterton. On Easter Monday 1873, he at last found someone who was willing to take the Princess's off his hands temporarily: he let the theatre to Messrs Valnay and Pitron for a three-month season of French plays. There was a well-established tradition of a summer season of French plays in London, although they usually took place at the St James's. Chatterton must have been deeply relieved to be able to let someone else worry about filling the Princess's for a while.

1873 – 1874: The judicious few looked coldly on

In spite of the fact that the previous season at Drury Lane had not been Chatterton's most successful, he had nevertheless been awarded a new lease in respect of the value he had added to the property. This may have caused him to reflect on what he really wanted to do with it. The early aspirations towards legitimacy has been pushed aside as he raked in the profits from *Formosa, Amy Robsart* and *Rebecca*. In the previous four seasons there had been no Shakespearean productions at all, beyond a handful of benefit performances.[19] At his benefit performance in March he had boasted to the audience about the great authors he had staged in his time as lessee – Shakespeare, Sheridan, Goethe, Byron. To commence his new lease, he decided to return to his original plan of making Drury Lane the home of the poetic drama by mounting a spectacular revival of Shakespeare's *Antony and Cleopatra*.

Antony and Cleopatra had a patchy stage history. There is no record of any performance in Shakespeare's lifetime or before the English Civil War. Following the restoration of the monarchy and the re-opening of the theatres in 1660, Shakespeare was not highly regarded. He appeared to be ignorant of the rules of the drama as laid down by Aristotle, which were supposed to include the unities of time, place and action. In the eighteenth century a strong nationalist reaction set it towards what was seen as French-inspired carping and Shakespeare was elevated to the status of national poet and epitome of everything English. His very departures from classical precedents were praised as examples of the true-born Englishman's love of liberty. He may not have been to university, but his wisdom was deeper than anything to be found there. As Dryden said, he 'needed not the spectacles of books to read nature; he looked inwards and found her there'.[20] This insight didn't stop Dryden from rewriting *Antony and Cleopatra* as a classically correct tragedy called *All For Love* which observed the unities of time, place and action, while Shakespeare's text went unperformed. Even the Bard's doughtiest champions, with hearts of English oak, found it difficult to defend *Antony and Cleopatra*'s ramshackle plot, spread across three continents over a decade. Dr Johnson described it as 'produced without any art of connection or care of disposition' and even A. C. Bradley, one of the greatest twentieth-century Shakespearean critics, called the play 'the most faultily constructed of all the tragedies' which makes the audience take 'frequent and fatiguing journeys over thousands of miles'.[21] Even modern audiences, used to the fluid style of contemporary Shakespeare productions, can still find it hard to follow. Unless you have a fairly good grasp of ancient history, there is a big problem with the backstory.

The first production of *Antony and Cleopatra* of which we have a record was mounted by David Garrick at Drury Lane in 1759, and that was so unsuccessful he only gave it six performances. John Philip Kemble produced it at Covent Garden in 1813 in a version that mixed Shakespeare with Dryden, but that only lasted for nine performances. The first person to make a success of Shakespeare's unadulterated text was Samuel Phelps, who put it on at Sadler's Wells in 1849, with himself as Antony and Isabella Glyn as Cleopatra. However, even Phelps, who reverenced Shakespeare's words as holy writ, cut ten scenes entirely and sections of three others. It played to good houses for twenty-two nights, attracting audiences from all over London to see such a theatrical curiosity.[22] Chatterton badly needed Phelps's advice for his Drury Lane production but the two men were not on speaking terms since their falling out of the year before, so Chatterton went ahead with his own ideas. He asked Andrew Halliday to put together a version of *Antony and Cleopatra* that would provide opportunities for the sort of scenic splendour associated with Drury Lane.

Chatterton put out the usual manifesto for his new term as lessee, saying that seven years' experience at Drury Lane had convinced him that 'to be acceptable to all classes in a large theatre like that of Drury Lane [a play] must appeal to the eye and the senses as well as to the understanding'. He cleverly cited Coleridge (in a quote no doubt dredged up for him by Charles Kenney) who believed *Antony and Cleopatra* was 'too vast, too gorgeous, to be approached without some prostration of the understanding'.[23] He therefore set William Beverley to work on one of the most spectacular collections of sets ever seen at Drury Lane before which he hoped the audience would prostrate their understanding. Cleopatra's barge (copied from William Etty's painting *The Triumph of Cleopatra*) sailed across the stage; there was a huge Roman wedding feast for Antony and Octavia with four processions and a ballet; Cleopatra was bitten by the asp in a recreation of the Temple of Isis; and the Battle of Actium was fought between full-sized galleys on a canvas sea amidst a hail of arrows. This was the real show-stopper, after which Chatterton was called before the curtain to take a bow. Even *The Builder* was impressed, concluding an article on the replacement of the lavatories at Drury Lane with praise of the Battle of Actium: 'Nothing better of its kind... has ever been done on the stage'.[24] It must have been really spectacular to get the *Builder's* correspondent out of the lavatory and into the auditorium.

The Battle of Actium from *Antony and Cleopatra*, 1873

The price for the spectacle was cuts in the text. Andrew Halliday reduced Shakespeare's five acts to four and his thirty-three scenes to twelve. Characters and plotlines disappeared, including Pompey, the death of Enobarbus, Antony's second defeat and the scene between Caesar and Cleopatra in the last act. Because of the time required to change the enormous sets, the running order had to be radically altered, with all Roman scenes in Act II and the remaining three acts in Egypt. Even at a time when it was accepted that Shakespeare had to be re-arranged to suit the Victorian stage, it was felt that Halliday had gone very far indeed. 'We… hope that… the shade of the Bard of Avon was not present to witness these proceedings,' wrote one critic.[25] Halliday's defence was that textual purists were responsible for keeping some of Shakespeare's plays off the stage altogether, as managers were frightened by the potential criticism that would result from producing acting versions. 'If half a loaf be better than no bread, surely it is better to have a little of Shakespeare than none at all.'[26]

In the absence of Samuel Phelps (who was acting Shakespeare in Manchester), James Anderson had been brought back to Drury Lane to play Antony. According to John Oxenford, he was welcomed as a survivor of Macready's legendary company of thirty years before, as well as a manager who had tried to revive the poetic drama at Drury Lane, but 'he does not exactly correspond to the notion of the love-stricken triumvir'.[27] Anderson disliked the part, which he had never played before, and it showed: *The Pall Mall Gazette* described him as 'torpid'.[28] Anderson admitted that he hadn't been good in the part but claimed he was 'stunned and cowed' by the thunderous noise of large sets being erected behind him.[29]

The more surprising casting was Ellen Wallis as Cleopatra. Chatterton had wanted Helen Faucit to play the part, but she became far too grand for Drury Lane, or anywhere else, when her husband was commissioned to write the official biography of Prince Albert and the couple became intimates of Her Majesty.[30] Aged twenty and extremely beautiful, Ellen Wallis was absurdly young and inexperienced[31] for Shakespeare's greatest older-woman part, but, in spite of these drawbacks, she garnered a set of rave reviews along the lines of 'a star is born'. Just in case her professional colleagues might not have seen them all, she paid to have the best bits inserted into the columns of the theatrical paper *The Era* throughout the run of the play, and Chatterton was so impressed he had them transcribed into a leather-bound album as a present for her.[32] 'After playing Cleopatra thus, there is nothing that Miss Wallis may not safely attempt in the whole range of our best and choicest drama,' gushed one critic. 'We are convinced she could act

Lady Macbeth as no one else has recently done.'[33] Two months later, the opportunity to demonstrate the truth of this claim occurred when James Anderson chose *Macbeth* for his benefit performance, but Miss Wallis, perhaps having a more accurate notion of her abilities than some of her fans, declined to appear. Anderson had to bring in his Lady Macbeth from outside the company and he blamed the failure of the performance on this.[34]

Amongst those who were less enthusiastic about Ellen Wallis's Cleopatra, and everything else to do with the production, was the tragedy queen Isabella Glyn, the Cleopatra to Samuel Phelps's Antony at Sadler's Wells in 1849. She had been highly praised for her performance and had ever since taken a proprietorial attitude towards the play. This led her to write a scathing letter to *The Athenaeum* denouncing the 'desecration of Shakespeare upon the boards of Drury Lane Theatre' by a production that treated the lines written by 'the greatest dramatist in the world' simply as pegs on which to hang spectacular scenes 'too vulgar for the vulgarest pantomime'. 'I would not have performed Cleopatra in that production,' Miss Glyn told *The Athenaeum's* readers, 'for one thousand pounds a minute.'

This sparked off a spirited three-way correspondence between herself, Ellen Wallis and Andrew Halliday that entertained readers of *The Athenaeum* for the next two months. According to Andrew Halliday, far from despising Chatterton's production, she had been desperate to appear in it. As soon as she heard that the play was to be staged at Drury Lane, she made a nuisance of herself to Chatterton, insisting that she was the only actress capable of playing Cleopatra. Chatterton found himself able, as Halliday rather archly put it, to resist Miss Glyn's charms, which probably wasn't difficult as she was now fifty and somewhat portly, while Ellen Wallis was twenty and gorgeous. Miss Glyn furiously denied this, claiming that she had been offered the part but refused to appear in such a degraded production, telling Chatterton: 'I will not perform in this production for one thousand pounds a minute. I will sooner take a broom and sweep the crossing opposite Drury Lane Theatre, dressed in the costume of Cleopatra, and you shall put a placard on my back to this effect: "This *was* the Cleopatra, but she will not be Cleopatra *now*."' In that case, Halliday countered, it was hard to understand why, when Ellen Wallis had fallen ill during the run, Isabella Glyn had leapt at the chance to take over the part at a modest salary – nowhere near a thousand pounds a minute – her only condition being that she would play the part for the rest of the run. Chatterton didn't care for this idea and told Ellen Wallis to pull herself together and get back onstage.[35]

A packed house responded enthusiastically to the first night of *Antony and Cleopatra* but business fell off after that. Anderson has left a telling account of audience reaction: 'The spectacle (it could not be called a tragedy, being all made up of scenery, processions, ballet, gaud and glitter) was accepted by a maddening demonstration of approval by the pit and galleries; but the "judicious few" looked coldly on.'[36] These 'judicious few' were the people who sat in the stalls and dress circle – the most expensive seats that had to be occupied if a large-scale production like this were to stand any chance of making a profit. As the losses mounted, an ominous announcement was made in the *Times* classifieds:

> *Important Notice.* This grand spectacular play will not be performed this season after Thursday December 18th, on which occasion Mr Chatterton will address the audience and either withdraw or substantiate the declaration he made some four years since, namely that Shakespeare spells ruin and Byron bankruptcy.[37]

It is easy to sense the frustration behind this threat. For four years Chatterton had been criticised for saying that Shakespeare spelt ruin at Drury Lane. Now, when he had pulled out all the stops to do a big production of a rarely-seen poetic masterpiece, the judicious few – the very people who had called him a philistine – 'looked coldly on' and stayed away. In his notorious letter to *The Times* of four years before, he had justified his decision to produce *Formosa* by pointing to the low level of support he received from the educated classes whenever he staged the legitimate drama: 'My enterprise was supported cheerfully by the pit and galleries, but my boxes and stalls were sadly deserted.'[38] As Dion Boucicault said: 'The dilettanti are more fond of praising the legitimate drama than of paying to see it.'[39]

For once in his life, however, Chatterton allowed his judgement to rule his temper, and there was no such speech on 18 December. 'There was by no means a good house for the finish,' James Anderson wrote in his memoirs, 'no enthusiasm, no call for the manager; consequently Mr. Chatterton made no farewell speech. "All was stale, flat, and unprofitable."'[40] From a business point of view, this was the right decision, on the basis that you don't draw attention to your failures, but it is hard not to regret missing whatever variant of 'I told you so' the irascible manager would have delivered. The losses by this stage were between £4,000 and £5,000 (over half-a-million pounds in modern terms).[41]

Antony and Cleopatra ran for seventy-five nights plus two matinees. There were reduced prices for children and school parties, not just at the matinees but for all performances. This was one of Chatterton's innovations, as schools had not previously been offered discounts to encourage them to bring their pupils to Shakespeare.

Once again, Chatterton found himself relying on the profits of the pantomime, *Jack in the Box*, to cover the losses on the autumn drama, but there was a special cause for anxiety this year. The Vokes family, who had been the mainstay of Drury Lane pantomimes for the last four years, had gone on a tour of America. Chatterton needed someone who could imitate their special skills in comic dancing, and he found a candidate in Kate Vaughan. Aged twenty-one, she had made her London debut in the previous year in a burlesque of his own production of *Rebecca* called *In re: Becca* at the Court Theatre, after which she played the Spirit of Darkness in *Orpheus in the Underworld*. She introduced the 'skirt dance' which was a more respectable version of the can-can involving much swirling of fabric without actually displaying any underwear.

On 15 November Chatterton introduced 'Kate Vaughan and her celebrated ballet troupe' to the Drury Lane public. Appearing in the afterpiece to *Antony and Cleopatra*, she certainly made an impression. When Gladstone went to see the performance on 1 December he recorded in his diary: 'Miss K. Vaughan in the ballet, dressed in black and gold, danced marvellously.'[42] (He was less complimentary about *Antony and Cleopatra* – 'How low our stage has fallen.') In the pantomime she once again displayed 'her grotesque talent'[43] (this was meant as a compliment) as the Dark Fairy. It was another mammoth production, with a set of the Fairies' Fancy Fair occupying the entire depth of the vast Drury Lane stage, a chorus of one hundred ballet girls and the usual large troupe of children.

Jack in the Box has become one of the most famous Victorian pantomimes in academic circles as it was analysed by the greatest of all Victorian cultural commentators: John Ruskin. Ruskin's standing as a cultural and social critic is hard to appreciate today as his work went out of fashion after his death in 1900, but in the last half of the nineteenth century he was regarded as a sort of secular prophet and the conscience of the age. He moved from writing about great art to writing about the kind of society that produces great art. He was the champion of the Pre-Raphaelites, the pioneer of the Gothic Revival and the fiercest critic of the industrial capitalist system that had made the British economy the largest in the world – at the expense, he argued, of the quality of life of those who produced the wealth. His most famous aphorism was: 'There is no wealth but life.' Ruskin was a man of towering intellect and passionately held moral convictions, so it is perhaps surprising to find that he was so fond of pantomimes that he would visit his favourite ones over and over again.

In 1871, Ruskin had begun publishing a series of letters addressed 'to the workmen and labourers of Great Britain' called *Fors Clavigera*, in which he shared his views on life, art and everything else. The March 1874 letter described how he had spent most of his leisure-time during three weeks in the New Year going between performances of *Jack in the Box* at Drury Lane and *Cinderella* at Hengler's Circus (now the site of the London Palladium). As he walked between the two theatres through the streets of Soho he was struck by the contrast between the children in the pantomimes – beautifully dressed, well-behaved, a delight to look at – and the children in the street – 'ill-dressed and ill-taught, and ill-behaved, and nobody cares to look at them'.[44] If only life could be more like a pantomime:

> At Drury Lane there's just everything I want people to have always, got for them for a little while... Mushroom Common, with its lovely mushrooms, white and grey,[45] so finely set off by the incognita fairy's scarlet cloak; the golden land of plenty with furrow and sheath... they can't have enough, any more than I can, of the loving duet between Tommy Tucker and Little Bo Peep... and yet contentedly return to what they call the necessary state of things outside, where their corn is reaped by machinery, and the only duets are between steam whistles... they return to their underground railroad, and say, 'This, behold – this is the right way to move and live in the real world.'[46]

E. L. Blanchard would been flattered by these profound reflections on his pantomime by one of the greatest thinkers of the age as he took care to embed a moral in all of his pantomimes, and the moral message of *Jack in the Box* was that girls should learn the wifely virtues of patience, economy, industriousness and humility.[47] This is a message that would have resonated with Ruskin, whose own marriage had been annulled in humiliating circumstances.

Jack in the Box ran for five weeks as the mainpiece until, at the beginning of February, it became the afterpiece to a revival of *Amy Robsart* with Ellen Wallis in the title part. Kate Vaughan, 'the dancing wonder of the pantomime',[48] was playing Flibbertigibbet, the part created in the original production by Fred Vokes. Chatterton may have been trying to impress upon the Vokes family, during their American tour, that he could manage without them.

He ran the *Amy Robsart/Jack in the Box* programme for four weeks, then brought the season to an early close with the biggest benefit ever seen.

On 2 March 1874 there was a matinee performance of *The School for Scandal* to raise money for Benjamin Webster who was now seventy-five and long overdue for retirement. It featured an all-star cast, with Phelps as Sir Peter Teazle and Helen Faucit coming out of retirement to play Lady Teazle. Even the servants were well known 'names'. It was organised by John Hollingshead who never took a benefit for himself, which he said gave him time to organise them for other people. He certainly threw himself into the task, claiming that: 'The amount I got... by manipulating private boxes, interviewing and swindling friends, and selling programmes which contained a few autographs at a guinea apiece, would have convicted me at any police court of obtaining money under false pretences.'[49] Seat prices were high, the pit was turned into stalls, and hundreds were turned away. At the end of the performance Andrew Halliday, honorary secretary of the organising committee, announced that the proceeds came to £2,000 – the largest amount ever raised at a Drury Lane benefit. Charles Mathews, who had been playing Charles Surface, then came in front of the curtain to say that co-incidentally the combined age of the cast came to the same figure. Chatterton led Webster on to the stage to hear an address, written by John Oxenford, that acclaimed him as: 'The drama's pillar in a wav'ring age/ The pride and honour of the British stage.' The address praised his work in the legitimate drama at the Haymarket and melodrama at the Adelphi, but made no mention of the Princess's. His failure there had been so complete as to bring him to the verge of bankruptcy, and it was no doubt felt that the less said the better. When his great-granddaughter Margaret Webster wrote the history of her famous theatrical dynasty in 1969 she also omitted any reference to her ancestor's involvement with the Princess's. It was known in the business as 'a proverbially unlucky house'[50] and when it was demolished in 1931, after many years as a furniture warehouse, it was not much lamented.

Webster's benefit was not to mark his retirement from the stage – he was acting again at the Princess's in August in one of his old melodramas – but his retirement from *management*. Chatterton had been emphasising this in the many advertisements he placed in the weeks running up to the benefit performance, and the reason is not hard to guess. Chatterton found himself being drawn deeper and deeper into the mess Webster had created at the Adelphi and the Princess's, where the financial situation was far worse than he had been told, and he was coming under great strain as he struggled to run three theatres. The original arrangement had been that Chatterton would take over the management of the two theatres, leaving Webster to concentrate on his acting,[51] but Webster didn't want to let go, as the frequent changes in the management billing made plain. As recently as the previous September, the billing at the Adelphi had suddenly changed from *Sole Proprietor B. Webster, Manager F. B. Chatterton* to *Sole Proprietor and Manager B. Webster*. For Chatterton, who never found it easy to work in harness, this was intolerable. If he was going to be responsible for paying the bills, he had to be in complete control. As it became clear that Webster would never be able to pay back the money Chatterton had put into the partnership, and that more would be required, he told Webster that he must take over the leases himself. Transferring the lease of the Princess's was relatively straightforward,[52] and the management billing simply became *Sole Lessee: F. B. Chatterton*. However, Webster owned the freehold of the Adelphi which meant that he would continue to be Chatterton's ground landlord, creating problems in years to come. He wanted £3,550 a year for the lease, but Chatterton offered him £2,550 a year for a twenty-one-year lease in return for writing off all Webster's debts to him.[53] This was agreed and, from March 1874, the management billing at the Adelphi became *Proprietor B. Webster, Sole Lessee and Manager F. B. Chatterton*.

The 1873/74 season at the Adelphi was an unusually successful one. When *The Wandering Jew* ended its long run in October, it was followed by yet another revival of *Peep o' Day*, directed by Edmund Falconer who also appeared in his original part. This revival had a long run of eighty-three performances and was even more successful when Chatterton added the ever-popular ballet of *Killarney*, with Telbin's famous panorama of the Lakes, as an afterpiece. Chatterton made doubly sure of success of the ballet by casting his new dancing talent Kate Vaughan, even though she was still appearing in *Jack in the Box* at Drury Lane. She must have had some quick dashes down the Strand to make her entrance on cue.

Peep o' Day was followed by a revival of an old melodrama by Frederick Reynolds called *Elizabeth or the Exiles of Siberia* which was staged to mark the marriage of Queen Victoria's second son, the Duke of Edinburgh, to a Russian princess. It failed and had to be taken off after three weeks. Something was needed at short notice, so it was decided to revive *The Prayer in the Storm* which Webster had written for the Adelphi twenty years before.[54] Webster directed the revival himself and it starred an actress new to London audiences called Geneviève Ward. Although she was making her acting début, the American performer had been known only a few years earlier as an opera singer at both Covent Garden and Her Majesty's until vocal strain, coupled with diphtheria, put an end to her singing career. She retrained as an actress and scored a great success in this story of a captain whose crew mutiny and cast him adrift with his wife and small daughter. They land on an ice-flow but realise they will perish as the ice melts. One by one they drop through the thinning ice, and at the climax of the scene the little girl is washed into view riding on a block of ice and singing 'The Prayer of the Shipwrecked'. The remaining acts of the play, set years later, show her as a beautiful young woman who meets and marries the man responsible for the mutiny. She ensures that he is convicted and executed for the deaths of her parents. Geneviève Ward played both the mother in the ice-flow scene and the grown-up daughter. *The Prayer in the Storm*, intended as a two-week stop-gap, ran for six months and closed in September 1874 after being seen by 296,000 people.

At the Princess's, where he had once again installed James Guiver as the manager, Chatterton seemed determined to pursue his policy of presenting the 'legitimate' drama he had been forced to abandon at Drury Lane. On 18 August 1873 he opened a revival of the Drury Lane production of *Manfred* from ten years before, this time starring Charles Dillon, with the 1863 set designs repainted for the smaller stage of the Princess's. Henry Bishop's music was re-used and there was a choir of fifty voices. It lasted for fifty-four performances.

There was a three-week revival of Tom Taylor's historical drama *Twixt Axe and Crown*, about the young Queen Elizabeth, leading up to the main dramatic offering of the season: a new play called *Griselda or the Patient Wife* by Mary Elizabeth Braddon. Miss Braddon was already famous as the author of *Lady Audley's Secret*, a sensational novel which made the fortune of William Tinsley, her publisher. The stage version of *Lady Audley's Secret* became one of the most popular Victorian melodramas, but the play was not written by Mary Braddon so she received no royalties from it. She therefore decided, after writing other successful novels, to set up as a playwright. Given that her novels were known for their dramatic situations, it is strange that she chose as her story the tale of Patient Griselda from Chaucer's *Canterbury Tales* (taken in turn from Boccaccio) in which a wife demonstrates her virtue by allowing her husband to treat her in the most abominable way. Although Braddon altered the story to try to make Griselda less nauseating and her husband less evil, the result was an undramatic plot with unbelievable characters. Nevertheless, the name of Miss M. E. Braddon was sufficient to keep it running for seventy-four performances.

This was followed, on 23 February 1874, by W. G. Wills's play *Mary Queen of Scots*. Wills was an eccentric Irish painter and writer whose absent-mindedness and poor personal hygiene were sometimes taken for signs of other-wordly genius, but this was a misleading impression.

His plays were ponderous and poorly structured, although *Charles I* had been a success at the Lyceum in 1872, largely owing to Henry Irving's popularity, and his adaptation of Oliver Goldsmith's *The Vicar of Wakefield* had also been a success for Ellen Terry. Nevertheless, Wills viewed himself primarily as a painter and didn't normally attend his own first nights. In *Mary Queen of Scots* he managed to make a play about one of the most colourful characters in history extremely dull by concentrating on the early years of Mary's life, before the appearance of Darnley and the falling-out with Elizabeth I, focusing on the Queen's relationship with the Protestant reformer John Knox. This was essentially undramatic, and Wills's High-Tory approach to history, which had caused offence with his depiction of Cromwell as a wholly evil character in *Charles I*, was in evidence once again in his portrait of John Knox as a buffoon. The play closed after only thirty performances and must have lost a good deal of money, given that the production had been mounted with some splendour. However, it would not have been able to continue longer at the Princess's in any case as the theatre had been booked for another season of French plays, produced for the second year running by Messrs Valnay and Pitron from Paris.

The French producers had taken the Princess's for three months from 6 April 1874. Chatterton was no doubt relieved to be receiving rent without having to worry about putting on shows, but this second season turned out to be a controversial one as Valnay and Pitron seemed determined to push the boundaries of what was permissible on the London stage. William Donne, the Examiner of Plays, had told the Lord Chamberlain in 1873 that they were 'slippery to deal with' and that having 'made loud protestations of a desire to raise… the moral character of the Anglo-French theatre… they seem to me to do all in their power to keep it at a low standard'. Donne made many cuts to their plays that year, but in 1874 he refused a licence outright for several plays that he considered 'thoroughly indecent and unfit'. A certain amount of leeway was allowed in French plays, which were expected to trade on their Parisian naughtiness, and of course the lower classes would not be corrupted by dialogue spoken in French. Nevertheless, there were lines that could not be crossed, and Valnay and Pitron crossed one of them when they advertised a performance of *Le Demi-Monde* by Alexandre Dumas. Like *La Dame Aux Camelias*, by the same author, this play had come to symbolise the sort of foreign filth that could never be permitted to pollute the London stage. Valnay and Pitron took advertisements to say that they had brought one of the leading actresses from Paris to appear in this play, but she would not be seen because the Lord Chamberlain refused to reconsider an earlier ban, even though the play had been performed all over Europe and they were willing to make any cuts required.[55] Challenging the censor has often been good for the box office, but not in this case. When the season closed, the French actors were in such financial distress that they didn't have their fares home. Richard D'Oyly Carte gave them a benefit matinee at the Opéra Comique to raise funds, but it seems unlikely that Chatterton got all of his rent paid.

Mapleson's 1874 Italian opera season at Drury Lane opened earlier than ever – on 17 March – and ran for longer than ever – four months. This was good news for Chatterton, who received £3,000 in rent;[56] it was good news for the Drury Lane proprietors, who received additional rent from Chatterton of £5 per night for every night over 200 in the season; and it was very good news indeed for the Drury Lane renters who had free admission to four months' worth of opera.

The most interesting production of the opera season was the posthumous premiere of Michael Balfe's last opera. At the time of his death in 1870, Balfe had almost completed an opera based on Sir Walter Scott's novel *The Talisman* which he called *The Knight of the Leopard*. Balfe's widow was keen to have it staged so she approached his old friend, the conductor and composer Sir Michael Costa, who had been musical director for many years at both Her Majesty's and Covent Garden. Although Balfe had no particular theatre or company in mind when he wrote it, he had offered the leading female role to Swedish soprano Christine Nilsson, who, as one of the stars of Mapleson's Italian opera seasons at Drury Lane, was able to bring some pressure to bear on him to produce it. As Mapleson presented only Italian opera, this meant that the original English libretto had to be translated into Italian and the opera became *Il Talismano*. There was a certain irony in this as Balfe had been one of the leading figures in the movement for opera in English.[57] Of his twenty-eight operas, nineteen (including *The Talisman*) were composed to English *libretti*. *The Bohemian Girl*, written for Alfred Bunn's Drury Lane management in 1843, was the only nineteenth-century opera in English to become an international success, being translated into French, Italian and German and performed throughout Europe, America, Canada, Australia, New Zealand and South Africa. The Paris production of *La Bohémienne* in 1869 had been such a success that Balfe was awarded the *Légion d'Honneur*.[58] His last opera, which Balfe thought his best, did not disappoint his admirers. *Il Talismano* was well received but its production had not been without problems, having originally been announced for the previous year, and the Prince of Wales, who wished to support it, was not available on Thursday 11 June 1874 for the premiere. As a result, he sat in an almost empty auditorium together with 'the elite of the musical and critical world' to watch the final dress rehearsal on the Tuesday, after which he sent for Mrs Balfe to congratulate her on her late husband's work and to say that he would be pleased to accept the dedication.[59]

Some idea of the importance attached to the production can be gauged from the fact that it had entirely new scenery designed by William Beverley. Beverley had been under exclusive contract to Drury Lane since 1866, and when Mapleson rented Drury Lane he was entitled to Beverley's services in the scenic department, but the operas were not normally designed from scratch. Most of the scenery came out of stock, with occasional new scenes being painted or touched up as required. According to the terms of his lease, Mapleson was able to commission new scenery and costumes on condition that he left them in the theatre when his season came to an end, which was an obvious disincentive to paying for anything new.[60] However, a dramatic version of *The Talisman*, entitled *Richard Coeur de Lion*, was to be the autumn drama at Drury Lane, and Chatterton may have arranged to share the cost of sets he anticipated being able to re-use.

Il Talismano was acclaimed as one of the composer's greatest works. It provoked a resurgence of interest in Balfe and his music, so his widow decided that it was time for a biography. Charles Lamb Kenney seemed the obvious candidate to write it, owing to his long association with both Drury Lane and with the world of opera as a librettist. Mrs Balfe gave Kenney a handsome advance on the understanding that he would start work immediately. She handed over to him the family papers, which he was to combine with his own recollections and research. Unfortunately Mrs Balfe failed to take into account Kenney's congenital idleness. He soon spent his advance and then asked for more, which he was given, but still the book made no progress. When William Tinsley, the publisher, tried to hurry him along, Kenney demanded an advance on his royalties which Tinsley refused. Kenney eventually submitted a very thin piece of work which Tinsley had to bulk up with thick paper and a large font. It pleased neither Madam Balfe nor the publisher, who described it as 'a failure in book writing almost lamentable'.[61]

A more satisfactory tribute to the man who was known as the 'English Rossini' (although he was Irish) was the colossal statue in the rotunda of Drury Lane. The driving force behind this was fellow Dubliner Dion Boucicault who wanted a memorial in Westminster Abbey. The Dean refused, saying there was no space, so Boucicault formed a committee to raise funds for a statue to stand in Drury Lane.

Both of Balfe's daughters had married rich husbands who made generous contributions, together with the Rothschilds, Christine Nilsson, the conductor and composer Julius Benedict, Boucicault himself, the music publisher Thomas Chappell and many others.[62] On 25 September 1874 the seven-foot statue in white Carrara marble, by Belgian sculptor Louis-Auguste Malempré, joined those of Shakespeare, David Garrick and Edmund Kean in the rotunda. Kenney felt that there was something 'minor or second-rate'[63] about the siting of the statue in Drury Lane instead of Westminster Abbey, but it now seems completely appropriate as Balfe's connection with Drury Lane went back a long way. When he arrived in London as an ambitious fifteen-year-old, he had joined the Drury Lane orchestra as a violinist; his first opera in English had been *The Siege of Rochelle*, which enjoyed a huge success at Drury Lane in 1835; the popularity of *The Bohemian Girl* was legendary; and his last work had been posthumously staged there as well, making it the twelfth of his operas to be premiered at Drury Lane. Old Drury book-ended the career of the most successful British operatic composer of the nineteenth century and was a far more fitting place for his statue than Westminster Abbey,[64] given that Balfe was not a religious man and composed no sacred music. His fame has faded since his death, and theatregoers passing through the rotunda today must wonder why this statue is there. Nevertheless, Balfe wrote operas that gave enormous pleasure and generated enormous profits when Drury Lane's patrons were circulating in the same space nearly two centuries ago.

1874 – 1875: The meretricious aid of dogs and horses

The day after the unveiling of the statue, *Richard Coeur de Lion*, Andrew Halliday's adaptation of *The Talisman*, opened at Drury Lane. Chatterton was hoping to capitalise on the success of *Il Talismano* but he was taking a big risk. *The Talisman* is one of Walter Scott's weaker novels, and, fatally from the point of view of the stage, it lacks love interest. The haughty Edith Plantagenet is an unappealing character, and although Halliday wrote some love scenes for her that weren't in the book, putting the focus of the drama on Richard the Lionheart just made the problem worse. Beverley made sure that it was a magnificent spectacle, with another tournament and an 'Arabian Night's Entertainment' in the square of Damascus, but Chatterton had already discovered with *The Lady of the Lake* that spectacle needs to be grounded in a strong narrative to be a success.

Chatterton hired his two leads from last year's autumn drama. Ellen Wallis played Edith Plantagenet and the title role of the Lionheart was taken by James Anderson. As he had a few weeks free before the start of rehearsals, Anderson went to Brighton for a holiday. The weather was bad, so he decided to pass the time by writing his own stage version of *The Talisman*. He read the novel carefully and produced a five-act play in which all of the important elements of the plot were dramatised 'without the meretricious aid of dogs and horses'. This was purely for his own amusement: he knew that Andrew Halliday had already written the script, but he wanted to prove, if only to himself, that it was possible to put a major work of fiction on the stage without swamping it with spectacle. Needless to say, when he was given his copy of Halliday's version he thought it compared poorly with his own and took pleasure in pointing out a number of errors.[65]

The production was given only fifteen days of rehearsal ('chiefly for horses, dogs, and supers') which seems astonishing given the scale of the scenic effects, crowd scenes and live animals. In spite of this, the first night went off well and Anderson records that it 'was received with uproarious applause and favour by the "gods", who sustained it for about seventy consecutive nights to more or less paying houses'. Once again, Anderson was confusing the reaction of people in the cheaper seats with the profitability of the show. *Richard Coeur de Lion* was a ranting melodrama that didn't appeal to the educated theatregoers who sat in the stalls:

> Mr Halliday may get a few cheers from the gallery when he makes his hero talk about the unsullied honour of England, the supremacy of the British lion, and the utter inferiority of humanity not born within the boundaries of this tight little island; but this will hardly satisfy those persons who would prefer a work of art to a preponderant expression of blatant rhodomontade.[66]

The losses on *Richard Coeur de Lion* were on the same scale as those for *Antony and Cleopatra* and, according to Charles Kenney, if Chatterton hadn't found a good troupe of jugglers for the scene in the market of Damascus, 'backed up by the wild and grotesque dancing of Miss Kate Vaughan', the results would have been worse still.[67]

In spite of the losses, Chatterton kept the show running until it was time for the pantomime. On 14 December 1874, Anderson played Falstaff (his first time in the part) in *The Merry Wives of Windsor* for his benefit performance. The next night William Creswick played *Hamlet* for his benefit, and the next night Ellen Wallis chose *Romeo and Juliet* for hers. It wasn't worth reviving *Richard Coeur de Lion* so close to the end of the autumn season, so Chatterton put on one more

Hamlet and, on Friday 18 December, one more *Romeo and Juliet*. Anderson was playing Mercutio, a part he much preferred to Romeo (for which he was in any case rather old at sixty-three), and he decided to make it his last appearance on any stage. He told nobody, so there was no announcement and no final farewell performance; he just decided to stop acting. He had given up hope for the 'legitimate' drama, and his experience of Chatterton's two blockbusters had been so depressing that Drury Lane reminded him of the inscription over the gate of Dante's Hell: 'Abandon hope, all ye who enter here'. Anderson had no grudge against Chatterton. He understood all too well the pressures on the manager of Drury Lane who tries to be 'legitimate' when the economics are against him, but he felt the struggle had become pointless. 'The heroic actors, together with the poetic and legitimate drama, have gone into the realms of endless night.'[68]

He must have been reading the reviews. Joseph Knight, the influential dramatic critic of *The Athenaeum*, devoted a whole page to explaining why the enthusiastic reception given to *Richard Coeur de Lion* by the first-night audience was the last nail in the coffin of Drury Lane as the home of serious drama. 'The public has gradually shown that it will accept Drury Lane as a species of amphitheatre, and an amphitheatre it has become. It is impossible to pronounce upon the play or the actors, except as participators in a pageant or circus entertainment.' For Knight, Drury Lane was the most superb mausoleum imaginable for the drama, and the glittering spectacle of *Richard Coeur de Lion* gave it the most imposing funeral procession that devotees of the defunct art-form could desire.[69]

Anderson's memoirs were not published until after Chatterton's death, so Chatterton probably knew nothing of the decision to retire. Had he learnt of it, he might have seen it as an omen, because his triumphs at Drury Lane were at an end. Apart from the pantomimes, Chatterton would have only one more hit show, and that was of such a nature that he felt he had to apologise for it.

Six months earlier, a nasty piece had appeared in *The Times* which showed how little respect people had for his attempts to restore Old Drury as the home of the poetic drama. It was a review of a one-off performance of *Romeo and Juliet* at the Queen's, of which the aim was to introduce a new actress to the London public. It was extremely unusual for *The Times* even to notice such a minor event, but the point of the article was its observation on the position of Shakespeare in the London theatres. 'At the present day the theatrical tendency of London is decidedly not Shakespearean,' the anonymous critic began, stating that only the Crystal Palace was putting on occasional performances.

What was needed was 'a series of Shakespearean dramas, conscientiously put upon the stage and acted as well as present resources will allow [which] might even now attract a numerous public'.[70] Suggesting that nobody was producing Shakespeare adequately, only six months after Chatterton's *Antony and Cleopatra* had closed, was a pointed insult. It can't have been written by John Oxenford, who was still hailing every production by Chatterton as a sign of the restored prestige of Old Drury. However, Oxenford was in poor health and this review may have been written by the man who would soon replace him, and who would savage Chatterton's productions in a way he had never experienced.

The Drury Lane pantomime for 1874/75 was *Aladdin*, featuring the welcome return of the Vokes family after their tour of America. It ran as the mainpiece until the middle of February, when it became the afterpiece to a four-week revival of *Rebecca* with Geneviève Ward in the title role. ('Not the *début* of my dreams for Drury Lane', wrote the rather grand actress in her memoirs.)[71] The season ended on 12 March, leaving just over two weeks to get the theatre ready for what James Mapleson was promising would be his last season of Italian opera at Drury Lane. In an advertisement that occupied a whole column of *The Times*,

E. L. Blanchard depicted as *Aladdin* in his own 1874/1875 pantomime for Drury Lane

Mapleson made the startling announcement that he had undertaken to build a new opera house in London: his Grand National Opera House would soon start rising on the newly-built Victoria Embankment. The Embankment, officially opened in 1870, was the work of Sir Joseph Bazalgette, engineer to the Metropolitan Board of Works. It was one of three embankments of the Thames, the other two being the Albert and Chelsea Embankments, but it was the biggest and the most important. It played a critical role in the scheme to get sewage out of London without dumping it in the Thames, and it also enclosed the new District Line of the underground railway system. Its construction had created many acres of new land in the centre of London, and many opportunities for property developers.

Mapleson was convinced that London would support a new and magnificent opera house to rival the recently completed *Palais Garnier* in Paris. Frederick Gye was still running the Royal Italian Opera at Covent Garden, but the rebuilt Her Majesty's was standing empty. Mapleson therefore took a site of almost two acres on the Embankment, close to the corner with Westminster Bridge Road, and set about finding investors for his new opera house. His architect was Francis Fowler and the conception was certainly magnificent. An iron frame was to support a lavish beaux-arts style structure with columns, balustrades and a dome. It was to contain a concert room and art gallery, and would be connected to the underground station and to the Houses of Parliament (with a division bell). There would be billiard rooms and two Turkish baths for the principal performers, to deal with the eternal threat to music impresarios of sore throats.[72]

Mapleson wanted his last season at Drury Lane to be a memorable one so he announced the first British production of Wagner's *Lohengrin*, plus more performances of Balfe's *Il Talismano*, which had opened so late in the previous season it was still a comparative novelty. Finally, he could not allow this opportunity to pass 'without thanking Mr F. B. Chatterton, who so readily placed the magnificent theatre at his disposal on the destruction of Her Majesty's Theatre, notwithstanding the many advantageous offers he received from other quarters'.[73]

Unfortunately Mapleson's warm relationship with his benefactor was about to be poisoned by another innovation he was introducing this season, which he may or may not have mentioned to Chatterton when they were negotiating the lease. Right at the bottom of the column in *The Times*, occupying the only two lines not taken up by the announcement of the opera season, was another advertisement: 'Salvini as Othello, Thursday April 1st and Saturday April 3rd, Theatre Royal, Drury Lane.'

Mapleson had entered into a contract with an Italian actor called Tommaso Salvini to present him in London. Salvini had made a name for himself by playing Shakespearean leads, especially Othello, on international tours of France, Spain, Portugal, South America and the USA. His style of acting was so powerfully naturalistic that it was said he carried in his pocket a free pardon, signed by Italian King Victor Emmanuel, in case he might really smother Desdemona one night. Salvini travelled with his own troupe of Italian actors, rehearsed in Italy, who performed entirely in Italian. It may seem strange that audiences were prepared to sit through plays of which they understood little, if anything, of what was being said, but the age of the international superstar had been pioneered by the French tragedian Mademoiselle Rachel (1821 – 1858), and consolidated by the great success of Salvini's compatriot Adelaide Ristori (1822 – 1906), whose Italian Lady Macbeth had been received with applause in London, the USA, South America and Eastern Europe.

Mapleson's opera company had never done six shows a week at Drury Lane, and usually no more than four, so his idea was to present Salvini on the nights that would have been 'dark', plus a matinee. This meant that Mapleson had the receipts from seven shows a week instead of three or four, making it potentially a very profitable season for him, especially as the ticket prices for Salvini were lower than the opera prices but substantially above the usual Drury Lane prices for a play.[74]

He opened with Salvini as Othello on Thursday 1 April, repeated on Saturday, Monday, Wednesday and Friday. The first opera – *Fidelio* – was performed on Saturday 10 April, after which the season settled into a routine of Salvini on Wednesday and Friday evenings plus a Monday matinee, with opera on the other nights. Salvini's interpretation of the jealous Moor – a part for which hot-blooded Italians were regarded as especially suited – was already famous, having been described by Robert Browning (who saw it in Florence) as: 'absolutely the finest effort of art' he had ever seen, and by Henry James as 'the finest piece of tragic acting that I know'.[75] By the time he reached London, the atmosphere was bordering on hysterical. 'The historical boards of Drury Lane must have felt proud to have been trodden by such an actor as Salvini,' wrote one hyperventilating critic.[76] In the theatre listings of *The Times*, the line immediately underneath 'Theatre Royal, Drury Lane', which was normally occupied by the name of the lessee or manager, read 'Salvini

Tommaso Salvini as Othello

as Othello', while his name in the cast lists was in bolder and bigger letters than the names of his fellow-actors. This star treatment was unprecedented in living memory. Of the forty-seven performances that Salvini gave at Drury Lane in the summer of 1875, thirty-four were of Othello, nine of Hamlet (in which he was judged to be good but not quite as good) and four of a melodrama about Spartacus by Alexandre Soumet called *The Gladiator*. William Poel, whose crusade for 'original practices' in the staging of Shakespearean drama had a profound effect on the way in which Shakespeare was presented in the twentieth century, said that seeing these performances by Salvini at Drury Lane made him want to dedicate his life to the theatre.[77] According to *The Times*: 'The interest excited in every direction by Signor Salvini's performances at Drury Lane Theatre is one of the most extraordinary phenomena to be mentioned in the record of the modern London stage',[78] and when 400 actors petitioned him to give a matinee performance as Othello to enable actors in other London theatres to be inspired by his genius, he gladly agreed and offered free admission to members of the profession. The house was packed, with many frustrated Thespians turned away.

Chatterton was furious. This was not the first time that Mapleson had presented drama mixed in with his operas, since he had included some appearances by Madame Ristori in his 1873 season, but she gave only eleven performances, none of them in plays by Shakespeare.[79] Chatterton took the view that, if anyone was making money out of Shakespeare at Drury Lane, it should have been him, especially after the enormous loss he had sustained on *Antony and Cleopatra*.[80] His anger over this affair would cloud his judgement in all future dealings with James Mapleson, very much to his own disadvantage.

Edmund Falconer as Danny Mann and Agnes Robertson (Mrs Dion Boucicault) as Eily O' Connor in *The Colleen Bawn*, Adelphi Theatre, 1861. Watercolour by Egron Sellif Lundgren. Royal Collection Trust/© HM Queen Elizabeth II 2019

Dundag Bay with the Royal Family in the foreground, one of six scenes in the panorama of the Lakes of Killarney, *Little Red Riding Hood*, Lyceum Theatre 1861. Watercolour by William Telbin © Victoria and Albert Museum, London

The auditorium of Drury Lane as it was in the 1860s and 1870s. The forestage was cut back to allow for an enlarged orchestra pit during the summer seasons of Italian opera, then re-instated at the end of each season. Houghton Library, Harvard Library, Harvard University

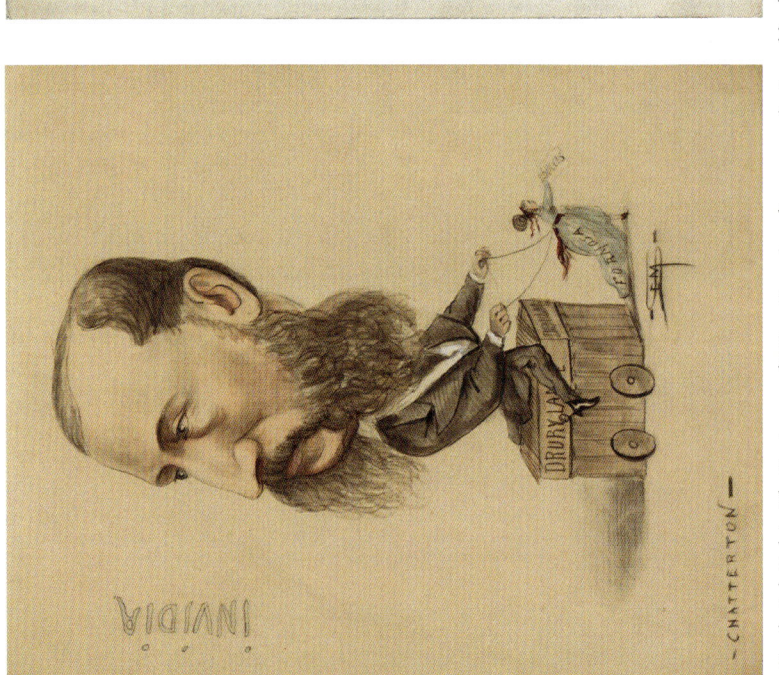

Frederick Balsir Chatterton and Dion Boucicault were caricatured by 'Sem' in connection with the production of *Formosa* at Drury Lane in 1869. The heroine of Boucicault's melodrama is pulling the weight of Drury Lane and holding a scroll inscribed 'Success'. *Formosa* is the Latin for beautiful and Invidia means envy or jealousy. © National Portrait Gallery, London

8

Indian Summer

1875 – 1876: Apollo, Pan and paying the piper

With the exception of the pantomimes, the big shows at Drury Lane had been losing money for several years. The last real hit had been *Rebecca* in 1871, so Chatterton needed to produce something successful now. The last two excursions into Walter Scott country had failed, as had the overblown Shakespeare. Chatterton needed a sure-fire hit, with or without pretensions to National Theatre status, so he went to the biggest hitmaker of the nineteenth-century stage who had packed out Drury Lane six years before: Dion Boucicault.

Boucicault's latest play, *The Shaughraun* (*The Vagabond*), had opened in New York in November 1874 where it broke all records and grossed nearly a quarter-of-a-million dollars. It enjoyed the same sell-out success in Boston, San Francisco and across America, earning Boucicault a personal fortune of half-a-million dollars. It gave him his greatest success, not only as a playwright but as an actor, since he played Conn the Shaughraun himself. Aged fifty-five, he had no difficulty in charming the audience as a young rogue who was 'the soul of every fair, the life of every funeral, the first fiddle at all weddings and patterns'.

Chatterton was only too delighted to have the prospect of presenting the London premiere of such a sure-fire hit, but there was a problem. His last Boucicault play at Drury Lane had been *Formosa* in 1869, when he had been roundly condemned for promoting immorality and degrading the National Theatre. Attempting to defend himself, he had put his name to Boucicault's epigram about Shakespeare and Byron that had stuck to him and damaged his reputation. There were no moral issues with *The Shaughraun* – no prostitutes, no high-class brothels – but the question of degrading the National Theatre with melodrama still arose. Chatterton decided to get his defence in first.

He commissioned Charles Lamb Kenney to write an account of his management of Drury Lane since 1866, when he became sole lessee, which would show his detractors that a course of 'pure legitimacy' at Drury Lane would ruin any manager, and that it was necessary to balance 'legitimacy and high art that will not pay with sensational drama and realism that will'.[1] The resulting pamphlet, *Poets and Profits at Drury Lane Theatre*, was the most extended of all the pieces of ephemera that Kenney produced for Chatterton, running to fifty-eight pages and giving us a unique insight into the problems confronting whoever found himself in charge of a National Theatre with no state subsidy.

The pamphlet begins with a letter from Chatterton to Kenney, dated 3 August 1875, asking Kenney to write an account of the profits and losses of his Drury Lane seasons with a view to justifying the claim that 'Shakespeare spelt ruin and Byron bankruptcy'. Chatterton promises to place in his hands all the papers and accounts relating to his management so as not 'to compromise your reputation as a critic and dramatist of thirty years' standing'. Of course, the idea that Kenney was to play the part of a 'purely impartial historian'[2] was a fiction. He had been on Chatterton's payroll as 'literary advisor' for years and it was obvious that nothing would be published without his boss's approval, but that just makes the pamphlet more valuable. Chatterton's lack of formal education made him uncomfortable about writing for publication, but he is speaking directly to us through his publicist.

The bulk of the pamphlet is taken up with an account of Chatterton's nine seasons as sole lessee, describing the failures and successes. He says nothing about the previous four seasons of the partnership with Falconer, when Chatterton was for the most part determining policy even though Falconer held the lease. This may be because Chatterton wanted to emphasise how difficult his position was by avoiding any mention of the 1863/64 and 1864/65 seasons when his policy of making Drury Lane the home of the poetic drama had been successful, in spite of carrying Falconer's dead-weight.

Kenney concludes his account of 1866/1875 period by summing up Chatterton's position. He fully accepts that Drury Lane is a national institution, and that its manager is obliged to respect 'its high intellectual and artistic associations'.[3] However, unlike similar theatres in other European countries, Drury Lane receives no government grant. Patrons must therefore allow the manager to make compromises. 'If Apollo's lute is to be heard at Drury Lane, Pan with his less elegant but more popular instrument must be allowed his turn, or else there will be no one to "pay the piper".'[4] Apart from the fact that Apollo played the lyre, this is one of Kenney's happier classical allusions, but it masks Chatterton's morbid sensitivity to the charge that he had failed in his responsibility 'to uphold the cause of the higher drama'.[5] Ever since putting his name to Boucicault's 'Shakespeare spelt ruin' epigram, he had felt 'the air poisoned... by the breath of insidious calumny whispering its malignant aspersions in the well-tiled coteries of obscure clubs, or drawing its slimy trail of false insinuations across the columns of obscurer prints'.[6] Even allowing for Kenney's tendency to hyperbole, there is an element of paranoia about this.

The purpose of *Poets and Profits* was to deflect criticism of the forthcoming production at Drury Lane of *The Shaughraun* 'which in the strict sense is not termed legitimate'.[7] The irony of this is that it should not have been necessary to defend *The Shaughraun* at all. Not only was it Boucicault's best play, it is almost the only British nineteenth-century play before those of Wilde and Shaw in 1890s that is still produced today. To debate whether or not it is legitimate 'in the strict sense' seems absurd.

The Shaughraun opened on Saturday 4 September 1875 and received a glowing review in the following Monday's *Times*. Although, as usual, it was unsigned, the review bears all the hallmarks of John Oxenford's style. He begins by describing the opening night of the Drury Lane autumn drama and the opening of the pantomime on Boxing Night as two of the great nights of the year for theatregoers – a point he frequently made. He describes the packed house and atmosphere of goodwill in the audience towards whatever the manager had prepared for them. He pointed out that the stage Irishman was a well-established stock type in English drama, but the Irish peasant seen in his own country, with the whiff of rebellion in the background, was the invention of Boucicault. Not, he hastened to point out, that there was

The Shaughraun at Drury Lane

any overt Fenianism in the play: the most conservative opponent of Home Rule could watch it unperturbed. Conn, the Shaughraun, is 'endowed with a sort of disreputable virtue, whereof ethical writers treat scantily, but [which] always appeals to popular sympathy'. He can lie, steal and break his promises, but he is good-hearted and funny. 'No doubt we have here a success.'[8]

Oxenford was right about that. *The Shaughraun* packed Drury Lane from the expensive seats in the stalls to the sixpenny seats in the upper gallery. It took enormous sums at the box office and Boucicault, true to his custom, was on a profit-sharing arrangement, receiving between sixty and seventy pounds a night – or more than £45,000 a *week* in modern terms.[9] During its run, Chatterton had Andrew Halliday's stage version of Charles Dickens's *Nicholas Nickleby* at the Adelphi. It opened on 20 March 1875 and ran for 191 nights until 29 October, making it one of Chatterton's most successful productions. At the Princess's he had the American actor Joseph Jefferson starring in *Rip Van Winkle*. This version of Washington Irving's story had been written for Jefferson ten years before by Dion Boucicault and performed with great success at the Adelphi.[10] The revival was also very successful, opening on 1 November 1875 and running for 154 performances until the end of April 1876.

That autumn of 1875 was Chatterton's Indian summer. He had the three most popular shows in London and claimed to have cleared a profit of £20,000 (more than £2.25m today) in six months.[11] However, *The Shaughraun* would be his last successful show at Drury Lane, apart from the pantomimes, and he faced the future without key members of his support group. In 1875 his father and trusted advisor Edward died; John Oxenford retired as dramatic critic of *The Times*; and Andrew Halliday had a stroke that brought his writing career to an end. As if he needed another bad omen, Chatterton lost a case he had been pursuing through the courts for two years, relating to the Drury Lane renters' rights to free admission.

At the beginning of the nineteenth century, theatre auditoriums were divided into boxes, pit and gallery, as they had been since the re-opening of the theatres in 1660. The most expensive seats were in the boxes, which were not, for the most part, private boxes, but simply sections of seating in the tiers surrounding the pit that were divided by partitions. The best boxes were called dress boxes, on the first tier, which eventually became the dress circle, where patrons wore evening dress. The second price range was the pit and the cheapest seats were in the gallery. Managers eventually realised that the seats at the front of the pit gave the best view in the house so there was no need to let them go for the second price, which led to the removal of the first few rows of benches and their replacement by comfortable chairs that were known as orchestra stalls, since they were up against the orchestra pit. The first stalls seem to have been created at the King's Theatre in the Haymarket (now Her Majesty's) in 1802 when a single rows of chairs was placed in front of the orchestra pit.[12] They spread throughout the West End and were created at Drury Lane in 1844 when Alfred Bunn held the lease.

The creation of stalls raised an issue at Drury Lane that had not arisen anywhere else. When Sheridan pulled down the old Drury Lane in 1791 and replaced it with his new and much more magnificent theatre, he had financed the construction by selling 300 shares at £500 each. These shareholders, known as the new renters, were entitled to a payment of 2s. 6d. for every night the theatre was open plus free admission to all performances. By the time Sheridan's Drury Lane burnt down in 1809, the renters had received virtually nothing by way of dividends and the arrears amounted to nearly £44,000 – over £3.4m in modern values. The project to rebuild Drury Lane could not proceed without reaching an agreement with these renters, who were willing to forfeit their arears in return for a payment of 1s. 3d. per performance from that point on, coupled with the continuation of their right of free admission.[13]

The Act of Parliament that guaranteed the rights of the renters specified that they were entitled to free admission 'into the usual audience part of the theatre', which meant everywhere except the private boxes. When this Act was passed there were no stalls in Drury Lane, but after the introduction of stalls in 1844 it was tacitly accepted by renters that their freedom did not extend to the stalls, and that if they wished to sit there, they had to pay the difference between the price of a seat in the dress circle (where they were entitled to sit free) and the price of a seat in the stalls. When Chatterton took on the lease in 1866 he asked for, and received, an assurance that he was not obliged to admit renters free to the stalls. This was important for two reasons. First, although there were only 120 stalls, their high price meant that they represented a significant part of the total value of a house; second, orchestra stalls were an important tool for encouraging 'the educated classes' to come to the theatre because stalls could be reserved for the whole evening, whereas seats in the dress circle (the only other part of the house that could be reserved in advance) were only held until the end of the first act. One of the reasons for the absence of middle-class theatregoers was said to be the lateness of the dinner hour, which had moved from 3.00 p.m. in the eighteenth century to 6.00 p.m. by the early part of the nineteenth. By the time middle-class people had finished their dinner and travelled to the theatre, they would be arriving between 8.00 and 9.00 p.m., when the play was half over. They wanted to be sure that their seats were guaranteed and that they would not be scrambling for whatever places were still vacant. There was also the class issue. Nineteenth-century theatre auditoriums were carefully constructed to segregate the different classes, and not just rich and poor: there were several categories of rich. 'The regular patrons of the stalls cannot be induced to occupy the dress circle,' said Andrew Halliday, 'though the seats are quite as comfortable as the stalls, and the price is less.'[14] When the great and the good went to the theatre, they sat in the stalls, which is why Chatterton wanted to keep those seats available for them.

All went well until 21 March 1873 when a renter called Alexander Dauney, who was a barrister, turned up for a performance of *The Cataract of the Ganges* and decided to test the legality of this restriction. Having identified himself as a renter, he was shown to a seat in the dress circle from which he claimed he could neither see nor hear the performance. He said that he wanted to sit in the stalls and was given a token which he had to show. When he was asked to pay the 2s. difference, he refused, saying that he was a renter. He was denied admission to the stalls but barged in anyway. He was removed by two policemen and he consequently brought an action against Chatterton for assault.

The case turned on whether the words 'the usual audience part of the theatre' could include the stalls, when there were no stalls at the time the Act had been passed. Three judges in the Court of Common Pleas took the view that they did and found for Dauney, but Chatterton refused to accept defeat and went to appeal. The appeal was heard on 10 December 1875 when three appeal court judges ruled that the stalls must be considered as part of the usual audience part of the theatre, and therefore renters were entitled to sit in them. However, renters were not entitled to sit in one part of the theatre and then move to another part, as Dauney had done. Judgement was therefore entered for the defendant – Chatterton – but with each party paying their own costs.

It was a Pyrrhic victory because the main point had been lost: in future, renters would simply go straight to the stalls. *The Era*, the theatrical newspaper, had been following the case with interest,[15] and on the delivery of the appeal court verdict published a leader expressing outrage over the way in which Chatterton had been treated:

> Mr Chatterton, above all managers in London, deserves to be treated with consideration. For years he has striven hard to

maintain the reputation of the National Theatre… he has catered well and liberally for the playgoing public… and proprietors have not had to mourn the sight of a magnificent house lying idle and unremunerative. This, then, is not the manager who should be worried and vexed and disgusted by the conduct of the very men whose interests he is labouring so assiduously to promote… We hope that the decision, so far as it was in his favour, will encourage him… to continue his managerial career, and to provide Her Majesty's lieges with renewed opportunities of applauding the histrionic efforts of 'Her Majesty's servants'.[16]

The generosity of the tribute must have gone some way towards consoling Chatterton for his defeat in court, but the ruling was a serious setback. He had warned that if Dauney carried his point, it would mean 'little short of ruin' for him.[17] This was an exaggeration, but as Chatterton entered into the final and most difficult phase of his management of Drury Lane, it can't have helped to feel that the theatre's own shareholders were working against him.

Boucicault wanted to continue the run of *The Shaughraun* at Drury Lane over the Christmas period but Chatterton had no intention of interfering with the pantomime, so it was agreed that the production would transfer to the Adelphi for six months, opening there on Boxing Day. In theory this should have been an easy transfer of an established hit from one theatre to another, requiring the repainting of some of the scenery to make it fit the smaller stage but no more than that. In reality, Boucicault made himself as obnoxious as possible in his characteristic fashion. First of all he declared that the sets by William Beverley – a universally acknowledged master of his art – were not good enough and commissioned new ones. He then recast the play, saying that 'he thought he was going to be supported by artistes, not by barn-stormers'. He created a poisonous atmosphere backstage, just as he had done during the run of *The Colleen Bawn* in 1861. Chatterton, who was busy with the Drury Lane pantomime, was constantly hearing 'news of wars and rumours of wars' from his dissatisfied crew at the Adelphi, and on Boxing Night, while he was supervising the transformation scene of the pantomime, an unknown American approached him backstage at the Lane and asked for an interview. He told Chatterton that Boucicault was unhappy with arrangements both before and behind the scenes at the Adelphi and wished to cancel their six-month contract. Chatterton said he would be only too happy to do so and that the arrangement would end one month from that date.

After that there was no communication between the two men, but Chatterton began to suspect that Boucicault was planning a demonstration in favour of Irish republicanism on the last night of the run. Unlike *Peep o' Day*, *The Shaughraun* was set in the present day and contained references to recent events like the Fenian bombing of Clerkenwell prison that killed twelve people. The plot was carefully constructed so that audiences could enjoy the play without feeling they were being asked to support treason against the crown, but during his six-month stay in London Boucicault had become involved with the campaigners for home rule in Ireland and adopted a much more overt political stance. He wrote an open letter to Benjamin Disraeli, the Prime Minister, requesting the release of Irish political prisoners in the name of the thousands who had seen *The Shaughraun* and who would, according to Boucicault, feel that it was time to show mercy to men who had been in prison since the abortive Fenian uprising of 1866.[18] Disraeli ignored the letter but it generated enormous publicity and debate, mainly hostile in the English and favourable in the Irish press.[19] The letter was published in newspapers on 10 January, by which time *The Shaughraun* was running at the Adelphi, but Boucicault had used 'Theatre Royal, Drury Lane' as his address, drawing Chatterton into a political controversy against his will.[20]

'One word for the Fenian prisoners and how many for *The Shaughraun*?' Alfred Bryan's cartoon mocked Boucicault's letter to Disraeli as a publicity stunt.

Chatterton's fears of a political demonstration against the government were confirmed when one of his staff at the Adelphi told him that Boucicault had purchased blocks of fifty tickets in the pit, gallery and upper circle for the last night, obviously intending to pack it with his supporters who would cheer a seditious speech by Boucicault, allowing him 'to make his exit to America amidst a blaze of fireworks'.

Chatterton responded by hiring 250 heavies of his own (one hundred from Jack the Packer, one hundred from P. the builder and fifty Lillie Bridge athletes) who would jump on Boucicault's men as soon as they made their attempt. 'Heads were to be punched, as gently as possible... not too much punching but just punching enough.'[21]

Chatterton decided that he would replace *The Shaughraun* at the Adelphi with a further revival of *Peep o' Day*, another play about Irish peasants set against the background of rebellion against the British. He began placing advertisements for *Peep o' Day* that drew comparisons between the two plays that were unfavourable to *The Shaughraun*, like this one:

> *Peep o' Day*, written by Edmund Falconer, originally produced on the 9th November, 1861, and played during 400 consecutive nights [actually 346] before an aggregate audience of 600,000 people, will be revived... founded on an episode of the Irish rebellion of 1798, but depending for its success, not on its treasonable propensities, but on its literary merits and on the sympathy excited for a victim falsely accused of political conspiracy.[22]

The clear implication of this is that *The Shaughraun* lacked literary merit and *was* founded on treasonable propensities, a theme Chatterton developed in an increasingly weird advertising campaign against a show he was presenting in one of his own theatres. On 22 January 1876, the last night of the run, there were no fewer than ten classified advertisements, one above the other, in *The Times*, headed either *Peep o' Day* or *The Shaughraun*, drawing comparisons that were always unfavourable to the latter and describing plot elements in a way that suggested Boucicault had plagiarised Falconer's play:

> *The Shaughraun* A patriotic Irish drama written by Dion Boucicault; originally produced in America in 1874, afterwards at Drury Lane in 1875
>
> *Peep o' Day* A patriotic Irish drama written by Edmund Falconer; originally produced in London in 1861, and performed for 400 consecutive nights, revived at Drury Lane Theatre in 1863 and again in 1869
>
> *The Shaughraun* A drama of stirring incidents. 'As a literary effort, it has no pretensions', *vide* the author's letter to the Rt. Hon B. Disraeli
>
> *Peep o' Day* 'A drama of stirring incidents, and depending on its literary merits' *vide* public opinion[23]

And so on. To imply that Boucicault had plagiarised Falconer was ironic, considering that, when *Peep o' Day* had first appeared, people pointed out its similarities to *The Colleen Bawn*, in which Falconer had acted. Such was the strange vibe that had been created by the time the curtain went up on the last performance of *The Shaughraun* at the Adelphi on 22 January 1876.

Although he had laid on his gang of heavies, Chatterton's aim was to prevent Boucicault from making an inflammatory speech from the stage at all. He arrived at the Adelphi around 9.00 p.m. and was almost immediately approached by a police inspector who had come to tell Boucicault that his son William, known as Dot, had been killed in a railway accident at Huntingdon. Chatterton knew that Dot was the only person in the world whom Boucicault really cared for, beside himself, and he was determined that Dot's parents, who were both acting in the play, should not hear of their son's death until they got home after the performance. He told the inspector that he would deliver the bad news himself, which left him with two things to worry about, of which the prospect of Boucicault's anti-British speech was not the worst.

At the end of the performance Boucicault's claque set up a cry for a speech from the author, to which Chatterton's men responded by shouting 'No! Chatterton!' Chatterton positioned himself in the wings to block Boucicault's passage to the front of the curtain and when Boucicault came down from his dressing room saying 'Don't you think I'd better go on?' he replied that Boucicault would have to walk over his body first, and then the stage carpenters would grab him. Boucicault glared at him for a moment then said: 'Very well, come to my room, have a glass of wine, and let us shake hands anyhow.' Boucicault was jolly and his wife was charming, but it was agonising for Chatterton to have to make small talk, knowing that their beloved son was lying in a morgue. When he left the dressing room he discovered that his own family doctor and Boucicault's brother William were both in the theatre. William Boucicault undertook to get Dion home, Chatterton got Mrs Boucicault out through the royal entrance to a waiting cab in Maiden Lane, and the doctor went straight to their home to break the news. The ghastly evening had been more like a scene from one of Boucicault's melodramas than real life.[24]

The production of *Peep o' Day* that followed *The Shaughraun* was another big show, with two hundred extras and Falconer once again in his original role as Barney O'Toole. It ran for eleven weeks until the theatre closed for Passion Week, after which Chatterton had arranged a season of plays featuring James Williamson (always styled J. C. Williamson) and his wife Maggie Moore. They were American actors who had scored a great success in Australia with a play called *Struck Oil* which bore more than a passing resemblance to the version of *Rip van Winkle* that Boucicault had written for Joseph Jefferson. Williamson knew Boucicault, having been in the original cast of *The Octoroon* in New York, and had appeared in several of his other plays. Chatterton offered him and his wife a share in the profits to appear at the Adelphi until the following March in plays which he (Chatterton) would select, mostly by Boucicault. They opened with *Struck Oil*, followed by *The Colleen Bawn*, followed by Bouciault's *Arrah-na-Pogue*. The next play was meant to be Boucicault's *The Streets of London*, but Chatterton changed his mind and announced *The Shaughraun* for Saturday 18 November. Boucicault was acting in America, but as soon as he heard about this he applied for an injunction to prevent Chatterton from staging the play. He didn't object to the staging of his other plays which were 'worn out', but '*The Shaughraun* is a new play in the freshness of its popularity', and he was intending to appear himself as Conn on his return to London. When Williamson heard of the dispute he told Chatterton that he and his wife would not appear if Boucicault objected, so Chatterton sued him for breach of contract.[25]

The application for an injunction was heard on the Wednesday before the show was due to open. The judge announced that, with great regret, he had to rule against Boucicault as there was no agreement respecting literary copyright between Britain and the USA. A work first published in the USA was not protected by British copyright laws, and *The Shaughraun* had first been performed in New York.[26] (For a play, performance counted as publication.) Boucicault appealed the decision and the appeal was heard a month later. All the judges found against Boucicault and awarded costs against him as he had been involved in a similar case thirteen years earlier in connection with *The Colleen Bawn* so he should have known the law.[27]

On Christmas Day 1875 a classified advertisement in *The Times* informed readers that Mr James Mapleson would be presenting an opera season at Drury Lane next year after all as his hope of opening the National Opera House in time had been disappointed. Mapleson's plans for a magnificent new opera house on the Thames Embankment had run into serious problems. The first brick had been laid by his leading soprano Thérèse Tietjens on 7 September 1875, followed by a rather grander ceremony in December when the Duke of Edinburgh laid the foundation stone. Constructing the foundations had been extremely difficult as the builders had to go down fifty feet through underground springs, quicksand and the rubbish of centuries to find the London clay, while water was pouring in from the Thames.

Pumps had to be kept running night and day to allow the work to proceed and massive concrete foundations were created to withstand the pressure from the river. By the time the work reached ground level, the foundations, which should have cost £5,000, had actually cost £33,000, and the finances of the whole project were endangered. Mapleson realised that if he wanted an opera season in 1876, he had to deal with Chatterton again.

Chatterton had neither forgotten nor forgiven Mapleson's Shakespearean exploits in 1875, so he drew up a lease for the 1876 summer season that made it impossible for Mapleson to present any more Shakespeare plays during his opera season. Chatterton had wanted to present Salvini himself but Mapleson already had the Italian under contract for a further London season and refused to give way to Chatterton, so he needed another theatre quickly.[28] He had originally planned to put Salvini into his new opera house on the Embankment, but that wasn't ready.

Fortunately for Mapleson, John Coleman was about to fulfil his ambition of running a London theatre season after a lifetime spent in the provinces, and he had taken the lease of the now-vanished Queen's Theatre in Longacre. In order to get the lease, Coleman had to commit from the spring, although he didn't want to begin performances until the autumn, so he was paying rent for a theatre to stand empty for several months. He was therefore glad to hear from Mapleson, and the two of them agreed to be co-producers of Salvini's second season in London, opening in May 1876. Salvini, who had been contracted to appear at either Drury Lane or the new opera house, agreed to the far less prestigious venue of the Queen's to enable the season to go ahead.[29]

Chatterton had no objection in principle to mixing Italian opera with Italian Shakespeare, as long as he was the one making money out of Shakespeare. If the public wanted to hear the Bard's immortal lines spoken in the language of Dante, he, Chatterton, would arrange that. In May 1875, therefore, when Salvini's Othello was packing them in at the Lane, Chatterton had already arranged for Salvini's closest rival, Ernesto Rossi, to act Shakespeare in Italian on Chatterton's behalf for the 1876 summer season.[30] He would co-present with John Hollingshead of the Gaiety Theatre. Mapleson's operas would still be at Drury Lane, as Chatterton wanted the rent, but his contract limited him to four nights of opera per week, with Chatterton retaining Wednesdays and Fridays plus Saturday matinees for his own use. Mapleson complained that he was paying as much rent for these four nights as he had paid for six nights the year before,[31] but this probably means that Chatterton has not *raised* the rent in 1875 above what he usually charged

Mapleson, as he didn't know that Shakespearean performances were planned when the 1875 lease was drawn up. He wasn't going to be caught out twice.

By entering into an agreement with Mapleson to present Salvini at the Queen's, Coleman was putting himself in direct competition with Chatterton's season of Rossi at Drury Lane, thus incurring the resentment of a man known for his readiness to take offence. It was by no means obvious that London would support two Italian Shakespeareans acting against each other. In the event, there wasn't the demand for one.

Chatterton was first in the field, opening with Rossi as Hamlet on Wednesday 19 April. The first night didn't go well, largely because Rossi was losing his voice and the next scheduled performance, on the Friday, was cancelled. There was a further problem in that, although Salvini and Rossi were exactly the same age and their careers followed very similar paths, Rossi did everything just after Salvini and tended to be regarded as the second best. Furthermore, Chatterton had been undermined before the season even opened by a bad review of Rossi, written when his company was appearing in Paris the previous autumn and published in *The Times*. The reviewer said that Rossi's supporting company of Italian actors was as bad as those who had supported Salvini at Drury Lane and represented 'one of the worst vices of the starring system... He is announced to appear at Drury-lane next Easter under the joint direction of Messrs Hollingshead and Chatterton, and those experienced gentlemen will doubtless see that Madame Ristori and other eminent "artistes" are engaged to play with him.' The reviewer further suggested that Rossi should not appear as Othello in London as he would draw unfavourable comparisons with Salvini, and that Ristori, Rossi and Salvini should be persuaded to appear together in *Macbeth*.[32] This last suggestion was wildly improbable. Although Ristori, Salvini and Rossi had appeared together in Florence in 1865 for the Dante Festival,[33] this was at a time when Salvini's international reputation was in its infancy and Rossi's hadn't begun. The idea that the two rivals would agree to appear in the same production to allow London audiences to compare them was absurd, especially as they hated each other 'with a fervour known only to fratricidal foreign tragedians'.[34]

Nineteenth-century reviews were anonymous, but the author of this one is known. It was none other than John Hollingshead, who was already committed (as he mentioned in the review) to presenting Rossi with Chatterton at Drury Lane. Hollingshead had been a journalist before he became a theatre manager, and on this occasion he allowed the journalistic instinct to triumph over his own self-interest. When he returned to London, Hollingshead went to see Chatterton who asked for his opinion of Rossi. It was so lukewarm that Chatterton offered, 'with a little warmth', to release him from his share of the bargain. 'This I declined, although I knew we were in for a loss, but I could not withdraw with honour.'[35] Chatterton's warmth may have been owing to a feeling that Hollingshead should not have holed their joint enterprise below the waterline before it had even been launched.

Three weeks after Rossi's opening at Drury Lane, Salvini made his first appearance at the Queen's. The classified advertisements boasted of extra rows of stalls that had been inserted to accommodate the expected demand, but those extra stalls proved surplus to requirements. According to Coleman, Salvini opened to a house worth £103, dropping to £18 by the third performance.[36] After that it was downhill. The experience of playing to empty rows was so humiliating for Salvini that after two weeks he cancelled all further performances, pleading ill health. Although he insisted in his autobiography that he really had been unwell, this was seen as an excuse to save face.[37] Rossi soldiered on at Drury Lane for two months, playing to houses worth as little as £12.[38] 'Before dwindling audiences [he] attempted many Italianised Shakespearean parts, and, to English eyes, failed in all,' was one damning verdict.[39]

Unlike Chatterton, John Hollingshead had a sense of humour and could not resist tweaking the tail of his famously irascible partner. Hollingshead was at the time managing the tiny Charing Cross Theatre, where he was presenting two farces and a burlesque every night. The receipts for this modest programme were a good deal larger than Rossi's at Drury Lane, so he told his box office manager to send the figure to Chatterton every night, without comment. 'The expected outburst was not long in coming. "I don't care a damn," said Chatterton; "he's a thundering good actor! There!"'[40]

Chatterton harboured a grudge against Coleman and Mapleson for going head-to-head with him, even though the 1877 Italian seasons at Drury Lane and the Queen's were financially disastrous for all four producers. It would be years before either of the Italian Shakespeareans ventured into London again.

9

Drury Lane in Decline

1876 – 1877: The most repulsive Richard III

Chatterton's future biographer, John Coleman, had spent the previous thirty years barnstorming the provinces and decided that now, at the age of forty-six, he would display his talent to the more discerning public of the metropolis in one of Shakespeare's most heroic characters: Henry V. Samuel Phelps, who knew he was approaching the end of his own career, took a kindly interest in Coleman's attempts to break through in the West End (always difficult for 'provincial' actors) and offered to play the dying Henry IV in some of the later scenes from *Henry IV Part 2* which could be tacked on to the front of the play. Coleman's career as an actor-manager in the provinces had been successful and he spent his savings on *Henry V*, which cost £6,000 and involved considerable spectacle. Coleman borrowed the costume designs from Charles Kean's 1859 production at the Princess's Theatre; photographs were taken of Westminster Abbey and the Jerusalem Chamber for exact recreation on the stage; replicas were made of the coronation chair and the Stone of Scone; real horses appeared together with real soldiers, lent by the army. 'Shakespeare was illustrated by a display of appropriate scenery, real armour, real horses, and hundreds of supers, banners, and ballets, but no actors', was James Anderson's withering verdict.[1] *Henry V* was a failure, partly because of metropolitan snobbery ('Mr Coleman… is understood to be a provincial manager of some standing') but mainly because all of the effort had gone into the spectacle and not into the acting ('the play can hardly have been so badly acted on any former occasion').[2] Coleman kept it going for two months until his savings were exhausted; he was then declared a bankrupt.[3] 'Mr John Coleman… has learnt to spell Shakespeare according to the Chatterton method,' was the spiteful observation of one theatrical newspaper.[4]

The production would have failed under any circumstances, but Chatterton, whose motto was 'never hurt a man a little',[5] had decided to damage Coleman's management by going head to head with him over Shakespeare, just as Coleman had gone head to head with him over the Italian tragedians. Chatterton therefore mounted an extravagant production of *Richard III*, with Barry Sullivan in the title part, to open at Drury Lane a week after Coleman's *Henry V*. The feud between the two men became so notorious that one newspaper reported (probably facetiously) that the pavements of Longacre (site of the Queen's Theatre) had become unsafe for pedestrians since the sandwich-board men advertising *Richard III* were scrapping with those advertising *Henry V*, 'inspired, maybe, by the warlike tendencies of the plays they proclaim'.[6]

The spectacle of Chatterton's *Richard III* was, as usual, magnificent. The problem was the acting, described as 'worse than I ever beheld in town or country' by James Anderson, who judged Barry Sullivan's Richard III 'the most original and repulsive reading of the part I ever witnessed'.[7] *The Spectator* critic thought Sullivan looked more like Quasimodo than Richard III, but pitied him for having to appear with actors as bad as his Catesby and Buckingham, 'and still more for a Lady Anne who talks like a dull schoolgirl blundering over a "piece" on a breaking-up day'.[8]

Richard III gave Chatterton his first experience of a full-scale onslaught against a Drury Lane production by Mowbray Morris, John Oxenford's successor as dramatic critic of *The Times*. Oxenford had been eased out of his position during the course of 1875 following a relentless critical onslaught from the popular weekly paper *The World*. *The World* had been launched by the journalist Edmund Yates in the previous year, specialising in society gossip, arts coverage and exposés of corruption. It had notched up an impressive number of scalps in its first few months and Yates published a table of these triumphs over fraud and conspiracy in his November and December issues of 1874. One of them had been Marmaduke Sampson, the *Times's* city editor, who was fired after the exposure of his collusion with Albert Grant (the original for Trollope's appalling fraudster Augustus Melmotte in *The Way We Live Now*). It seems that, having disposed of the *Times's* city editor, Edmund Yates thought he could use his influence to change the dramatic critic as well.

On 2 December 1874, *The World* published an article entitled 'The Degradation of the Stage' that accused John Oxenford of dereliction of duty. 'The criticism of the drama in the *Times* newspaper,' *The World* told its readers, 'is in the hands of a gentleman who has conducted it for over a quarter of a century [actually thirty-five years], and who is at once marvellously erudite, singularly appreciative, and hopelessly weak.' In the opinion of the writer, the London stage had been overwhelmed by filthy comedians and near-naked girls. 'If we are asked to what we owe the presence of these persons on the stage... we say unhesitatingly to the *Times* newspaper.' The reasoning behind this startling assertion was that the critic of *The Times* occupied a position of such influence that a few stern reviews could have nipped these decadent tendencies in the bud, but Oxenford had declined to use his influence. Not that he was entirely to blame: he was under the control of his editor and proprietor who regarded the stage as simply too unimportant to be taken seriously.[9] Nothing was said about the more blatant forms of critical corruption, but just in case readers might have missed the point, there was a letter in a subsequent edition of *The World* (signed 'The Ghost That Walks') pointing out that critics who send their own plays to managers are in a position to damage those managers who decline to produce them; that lavish hospitality offered to critics must affect their judgements; and that providing boxes on first nights (Oxenford was the only critic to be given his own box) suggests an attitude of cringing subservience. Although John Oxenford (the only critic mentioned by name) was specifically exonerated from the charge of corruption, and described as 'a ripe scholar [whose] remarks are usually worthy of perusal', it was well known that he was guilty of all of these crimes against the spirit of independent criticism.[10]

There was an irate response to The Ghost That Walks from W. S. Gilbert and another from 'A Dramatic Critic'. Gilbert insisted that the leading dramatic critics were honourable gentlemen who could not be accused of anything worse than letting a friend down gently. He pointed out the anomaly of the Ghost's position, accusing critics who wrote plays of corruption but exempting John Oxenford from the criticism, when Oxenford was one of only two practising critics who was also a dramatist. The other was E. L. Blanchard who was dramatic critic of *The Daily Telegraph* as well as writing the Drury Lane pantomimes. The Dramatic Critic made the same point about Oxenford and Blanchard, and angrily refuted the charge that managers got good reviews by pouring wine down critics' throats.[11]

Two weeks later The Ghost walked again, refuting the whitewash of the London critics by A Dramatic Critic and making some severe observations on W. S. Gilbert's dealings with theatre managers.[12] Gilbert wrote an angry reply and elicited the probably unwelcome information that the Ghost had observed his (Gilbert's) methods at first hand and didn't like them.[13] The identity of the Ghost was never revealed, but this phantom certainly knew a great deal about what was going on in the London theatres. Yates brought the correspondence to a close by delivering an Olympian judgement that there was no doubt much in the charges that had been brought against dramatic critics, but on the whole they weren't too bad a bunch and nothing much could be done anyway.[14]

John Oxenford was in an uncomfortable position, having been named repeatedly in a newspaper correspondence about critical corruption stretching over two months. It can have come as no surprise that in November 1875 *The World* was able to claim another scalp, announcing that Mr Oxenford had been replaced by a gentleman who had let managers know that he would be buying his own seats, so that 'managers may hope to be gradually freed from the tax levied on them in the shape of gratuitous boxes and stalls for journalists on first nights'.[15] This sea-green incorruptible gentleman was Mowbray Morris.

Morris's father, also called Mowbray Morris, had been manager of *The Times* for twenty-six years and a member of the triumvirate who took the paper to the height of its prestige and influence. The other two members were John Walter III, the proprietor, and John Thadeus Delane, the editor. Mowbray Morris senior married Delane's sister and his own sister married John Thadeus Delane's brother, so the great editor was uncle by marriage twice over to the incoming dramatic critic.[16] Having thus grown up in the purple of the *Times* aristocracy, Mowbray Morris junior was unlikely to be worried by the theatre managers' usual threat to cancel advertising in response to hostile reviews. Morris had a low opinion of the theatre of his time and an even lower one of its critics. He believed that dramatic criticism had fallen into 'its present state of bondage'[17] as the result of a relationship between critics, actors and theatre managers that was far too cosy, involving banquets of chicken and champagne which clouded critical judgement. (As a result the book which Mowbray published at the end of his seven-year stint at *The Times*, 'chicken and champagne' immediately became a shorthand term for the corruption of criticism.)[18] He was even more contemptuous of 'those Januses of criticism' who run with the hare and hunt with the hounds, writing 'plays... with one hand and "criticism" with the other'.[19] His readers could have been in no doubt that he was referring to his immediate predecessor at *The Times*. Morris was determined to lead dramatic criticism out of this condition of bondage, and Chatterton would suffer because of it.

Although reviews were unsigned, *Times* readers must have noticed the change in tone. Edmund Yates, who believed that dramatic criticism suffered from a lack of 'emphatic straight-speaking', admitted that Morris delivered 'a distinct judgment on plays and players such as in former times would not have been gathered from the same source'.[20]

That was putting it mildly. John Oxenford had represented the old school of dramatic criticism in which 'the exceeding good nature of our critics' had led them to praise everything that could be praised and 'to let the rest down very easily'.[21] By the 1870s, readers were no longer prepared to accept reviews of this sort. They wanted 'a fair and honest endeavour to tell the truth, in a kindly spirit, without fear or favour',[22] and Mowbray Morris was the man to give it to them. 'He seems to approach the consideration of a play without any foregone conclusions, and with the intention to praise or to blame plays and players according to their merits and demerits.'[23] This novel approach would come as a shock to managers of Chatterton's generation.

Chatterton had his first experience of Morris's frank reviewing style at the two other theatres under his control.[24] In April 1876 Morris had given a bad review to *Struck Oil* at the Adelphi ('not worth even the very slightest consideration'), in which James Williamson's wife Maggie Moore played the daughter of his character. Morris advised that she 'might perhaps be seen to better advantage in a less youthful character', betraying a lack of gallantry of which John Oxenford would never have been guilty.[25] In May he gave a worse review to *Abel Drake* at the Princess's, which Morris thought was so bad it 'reflects but little credit on the management of the Princess's Theatre'.[26] Now it was Drury Lane's turn.

He began his review of *Richard III* by saying that if Shakespeare spelt ruin, it was the fault of the managers who made a hash of his work. Chatterton had been running press advertisements claiming that there was a revival of interest in Shakespeare, but then he produced Colley Cibber's 'formless and purposeless jumble of several plays of Shakespeare'. Morris strongly implied that Barry Sullivan, 'an actor high in favour in America and on our own provincial stages', was not good enough for London – a widespread view. 'He has certain tricks of voice which are curiously unlike the ordinary inflections of that organ and which appear to be mostly independent of the meaning of the words spoken.' He ended by saying that while *Richard III* was not quite as bad as Coleman's *Henry V* at the Queen's Theatre, 'we do not wish to believe that "the whole performance has reached the full level of dramatic excellence attainable at the present day"'. This was a sarcastic quotation from Chatterton's advertisements.[27]

Chatterton was so angry that he replaced the Rimmel's perfume advertisement on the back page of the Drury Lane programme with his response to Morris, entitled: 'Past and Present Critics of *The Times*'. He compares 'the present youthful critic of *The Times*' unfavourably with his illustrious predecessor Oxenford who was recognised throughout Europe as an expert on dramatic literature. Chatterton says that he would never object to fair criticism, however unfavourable, but he did feel that 'as manager of Drury Lane, a position of no slight embarrassment, difficulty and anxiety, which I have held for a longer period than any of my predecessors' that he should at least be able to expect 'that judgment should lean to the side of kindness, and that praise where deserved should be bestowed at least as ungrudgingly as censure'. Morris, on the other hand, damns with faint praise and emphasises all the negatives, because he is prejudiced: 'the present critic of *The Times* has seemingly conceived so violent a dislike to my system of management that he is unable to believe that there can be any good in what is produced at a theatre under my control'.

Chatterton claimed that he had been inspired to put on *Richard III* by an excellent review which Oxenford had given to Barry Sullivan's performance as Richard at Drury Lane in 1868. Oxenford had praised Sullivan's performance in the highest terms and only regretted that the production was not as lavish or as archaeologically accurate as the public taste was by then demanding.[28] Chatterton had borne this in mind and waited for the opportunity to do Richard on a larger scale. It was his misfortune that he had waited so long that his efforts were reviewed, not by the kindly Oxenford, but by his young firebrand of a successor. He complained that Morris has filed his review late (the production opened on Saturday 23 September but Morris's review didn't appear until the following Wednesday) then spent half of it attacking Chatterton for using Colley Cibber's version of the play. Chatterton had already justified his decision on this point in the pre-publicity, 'if any justification be needed', by citing the example of illustrious predecessors including Garrick, Kean and Macready. Chatterton allows for the fact that Morris's critical stance maybe 'the result rather of youthful inexperience than of malice', but he describes it as 'aimless abuse' rather than criticism, and he asks 'Is it fair? Is it even honest?'[29] Just to ram his point home, Chatterton placed two classified advertisements in *The Times*:

> MR BARRY SULLIVAN – RICHARD III – 'When we take into consideration this performance it is scarcely too much to augur that he will soon be acknowledged as the leading legitimate actor of the British stage' Morning Paper February 20th 1868
>
> RICHARD III – 'It must honestly be admitted that with the style in which this particular play has now been produced no fault is to be found' Morning Paper September 27th 1876[30]

Everyone knew that 'Morning Paper' meant *The Times* but, as these advertisements were set in a very small font, only eagle-eyed readers would have noticed the discrepancy between the two dates. The first quotation was from Oxenford's old review; the second represented the only sentence Chatterton could have used from Mowbray Morris's review in which he praised the scenery and costumes.

Was Morris's review unfair or dishonest? With regard to the acting, there is reason to believe that it was as bad as he claimed, but to take Chatterton to task for using Colley Cibber's *Richard III* was perhaps unfair, when he was following a path trodden by actors and managers for 177 years. It was his misfortune to be staging the play just at the time when critical opinion was shifting towards the view that Cibber's changes to Shakespeare were no longer unacceptable and that it was 'time... that this state of affairs should come to an end'.[31] 'Mr Chatterton's education is progressing,' sneered Edmund Yates in *The World*. 'Having mastered the fact that Shakespeare spells "ruin" and Byron "bankruptcy", he seems likely to learn next that Colley Cibber spells "collapse".'[32]

Of all the attempts to 'improve' Shakespeare that followed the re-opening of the theatres in 1660, Cibber's *Richard III* was by far the most successful. First acted at Drury Lane in 1699, it represented an attempt to fill in the backstory by interpolating scenes from other Shakespeare history plays; slashing Shakespeare's text by removing characters and plotlines; and then inserting many lines by Cibber himself. Some of these were so successful – 'Off with his head – so much for Buckingham' and 'Richard's himself again' – that they still crop up, most famously in Laurence Olivier's 1955 film version in which Cibber received a writer's credit. Actors and audiences felt that Cibber's *Richard III* worked better on the stage than Shakespeare's original, which depends upon a fairly detailed knowledge of the Wars of the Roses that was becoming more inaccessible as the centuries passed. Macready tried to restore Shakespeare's text in a Covent Garden production of 1821, but it only lasted for two performances. When Samuel Phelps was running Sadler's Wells he used Shakespeare's version in a production of 1845, revived in 1849, but when it was revived a second time in 1862 he went back to Cibber. Even Charles Kean, who made a great thing of only using the original texts during his management of the Princess's in the 1850s, made an exception for *Richard III*.[33] Chatterton could legitimately claim a long and distinguished line of precedents for his choice, but it made no difference: Mowbray Morris was determined to make an example of him in order to drive Colley Cibber from the stage.

Chatterton was no scholar and his interest in textual issues would have been limited. He was still working in the old tradition in which managers hired actors who were already known for their portrayal of certain parts and left them to get on with it. Barry Sullivan had been playing Richard III for nearly twenty years, always in Cibber's version. It seems unlikely that he would have responded positively to a suggestion that he should learn the whole thing again from scratch. And if not Sullivan, who? Chatterton had fallen out again with Phelps, who was appearing for Coleman at the Queen's Theatre. The dramatic critic of *The Illustrated London News* said that, when Chatterton first announced *Richard III*, he had been hoping for Shakespeare's version, but in the end he resigned himself to Cibber's. He believed that the stage was in such a decadent condition that it would be unrealistic to expect Shakespeare's Richard until such time as the drama was led out of bondage into the promised land in which the poet was king.[34] Coincidentally, the patriarch who would lead this exodus was acting just around the corner from Drury Lane.

In 1871 the American impresario Colonel Bateman had taken the lease of the Lyceum Theatre in order to promote the careers of his three actress daughters, Kate, Isabel and Virginia. He needed a leading man and Henry Irving, who had scored a great success at the Vaudeville Theatre in James Albery's play *Two Roses*, was taken on to play opposite the Bateman girls, especially the pretty but hopelessly untalented Isabel. The first two productions failed and it looked as if the management might have to close, so Irving persuaded Bateman to allow him to produce an English translation of a French melodrama called *Le Juif Polonais*. It opened as *The Bells* in November 1871 and, as Mathias the innkeeper, whose prosperity derives from the murder of a wealthy Jewish traveller years before, Irving became an overnight sensation, saving Bateman's management. Although Bateman was still the lessee, Irving's star-status allowed him to play a greater part in choosing the repertoire and in 1874 he told Bateman he wanted to play Hamlet. Bateman was opposed to the idea because, as Irving later told his biographer, 'there was a motto among managers – Shakespeare spells ruin'. The relevance of the motto had been only recently re-enforced by its supposed author's enormous losses on *Antony and Cleopatra* at Drury Lane, but in the end Bateman had to give in, although he gave Irving a budget of only £100 for the production.[35] Irving's *Hamlet* was a sensational success, running for an unprecedented 200 continuous performances. On the day after a banquet to celebrate the 100th, Bateman died, and the management of the Lyceum passed to his widow.

Mrs Bateman was heavily dependent on Irving, who was now effectively artistic director. He added Othello and Macbeth to his Shakespearean repertoire and then, in January 1877, just a month after the close of Barry Sullivan's *Richard III* at Drury Lane, Irving appeared as 'SHAKESPEARE'S KING RICHARD III, first time since the days of the author on the London stage according to the best obtainable information. Strictly the original text.'[36] This was an exaggeration, as it ignored Phelps's efforts plus the fact that Irving had cut 1,600 of Shakespeare's lines so it was scarcely 'the original text', but Irving could justifiably draw attention to his boldness. He showed that Shakespeare's text could work and he triumphed as Richard. The production was a commercial and critical success, with Morris's review in *The Times* headed 'Shakespeare's Richard the Third' instead of the more normal 'The Lyceum Theatre'. Morris gave it nearly two columns, rejoicing that Cibber's version would now be consigned to oblivion together with Nahum Tate's *King Lear* and Garrick's *Hamlet*. He criticised the acting of some of the cast but praised Irving, his one reservation being that he felt Irving should not attempt the part every night as it was beyond the energy levels of any actor.[37] In fact, Irving kept it up for eighty-three continuous performances to packed houses. Chatterton's production had achieved sixty-two performances, alternating with Sullivan as Macbeth for the last two weeks, and lost nearly £6,000 (about £680,000 today).[38] It represented Colley Cibber's last gasp at Drury Lane and almost his last in London: after Irving, Shakespeare's text became the default option.[39]

The Drury Lane pantomime for 1876/77 was *The Forty Thieves*, starring the Vokes family, which ran until 5 March. It was less successful than usual and Chatterton needed another good play to boost the season's takings. Unfortunately he put on *Haska*, written by Henry Spicer. Spicer was the now very elderly author of *The Lords of Ellingham* which had fired the teenage Chatterton with enthusiasm for theatre management a quarter of a century before. His plays hadn't been seen in London during the intervening years, but Spicer decided that he wanted to appear before the public one last time, so he offered Chatterton £1,000 (about £114,000 today) to stage Haska. It was a ripe old melodrama that reminded one critic of the excesses of the 'Penny Plain, Tuppence Coloured' melodramas that were performed in the toy theatres of an earlier generation. The eponymous heroine is a virtuous peasant girl who is spotted by a lustful Transylvanian count on the day of her wedding. He exercises his rights as lord of the manor and forces her to come to his castle that very night. When she looks out of the window she sees her husband dangling from a gallows.

She locks her tormentor in a torture chair with which the room is conveniently furnished and threatens to kill him, but when he is rescued by his servants she jumps out of the window and then leads a peasants' revolt. The wicked nobleman turns out to be her brother and her husband turns out not to be dead at all. Chatterton admitted that he should never have allowed himself to be influenced by sentiment, but he couldn't help remembering that in a sense he owed his managerial career to Spicer, which influenced his decision to stage this awful potboiler.

The fact that Spicer was subsidising the production became known and one critic said that it was inconceivable that Chatterton would have staged such nonsense without the inducement. Another said that, although *Haska* was in one sense a joke, it also reflected badly on Chatterton that he was allowing such rubbish to be staged at Drury Lane. It attracted a certain amount of publicity because Spicer had already placed *Haska* in the hands of an agent who had sold a three-year option to an aspiring actress called Miss Campbell in 1875, but she had done nothing with it. Miss Campbell suddenly announced on the Wednesday before the opening that she was planning to stage it, and brought an injunction against Chatterton on Thursday. The injunction was granted on Friday morning; on Friday afternoon Chatterton obtained leave to appeal; on Saturday the appeal was heard and the injunction dissolved. The play opened at Drury Lane that night.[40] This was just the sort of thing Chatterton enjoyed and the court case proved to be the most successful thing about the play, which was 'likely to owe its celebrity to the litigation it has provoked rather than to any merit it possesses'.[41]

The first night did not go well. The acting was so bad the audience could scarcely hear what was being said and, as was often the case, critics found nothing to praise except Beverley's scenes. 'The entire performance was discreditable to English art,' according to *The Athenaeum*, and suggested to the dramatic critic of *The World* that 'some lack of capacity or of judgement characterises Mr Chatterton's proceedings as a manager'.[42] As the curtain came down, the white-haired author appeared on the stage to jeering from the pit.[43] Chatterton was so desperate to save the play that he kept Drury Lane open during Passion Week for the first time (with the exception of those years when the Italian opera season had already begun). He tried to strengthen the bill by pruning *Haska* and putting in into a double-bill with a revival of *The Corsican Brothers*, then *The Colleen Bawn*, but business was still bad and *Haska* came off after four weeks, with Spicer losing his £1,000 and Chatterton losing £1,500 on top of that.

Chatterton's financial problems were compounded by the fact that in 1877 there was no summer season at Drury Lane. During the 1876 opera season, James Mapleson's patrons had been able to see in the foyer of Drury Lane a model of the 'New Grand Opera House' where he still confidently expected that he would be holding his 1877 season. However, by the beginning of 1877 it was clear that the new opera house would not be ready, which left Mapleson to negotiate with Chatterton, at very short notice, for another season. He claimed in his memoirs that Chatterton had tried to take advantage of him by imposing new restrictive clauses obliging Mapleson to pay the full rent but to occupy the theatre for only three days a week, handing over the keys to Chatterton on midnight of each day. This meant that he would have been unable to rehearse on his 'dark' days, and he found 'nothing but impossible clauses and conditions in the contract now offered'. Chatterton denied these claims and said he had simply asked for the same rent as before – £3,000 for sixteen weeks – but Mapleson wanted to reduce this to £2,500, which is understandable given his precarious position with the new opera house.[44] Chatterton refused, even though he was at the same time negotiating with the Drury Lane proprietors for a £500 reduction in his rent for the period of the next lease. Mapleson felt he was being badly treated by Chatterton after paying him thousands of pounds in rent over seven opera seasons at Drury Lane, 'in addition to cleaning and carpeting his theatre every year, which was very much required after the pantomime',[45] so he called Chatterton's bluff and announced that he was opening at Her Majesty's in the Haymarket.[46] Her Majesty's Theatre had been rebuilt immediately after the fire of 1867 but, apart from some meetings held by the American revivalists Moody and Sankey, it had been standing empty – 'a disgrace to London' according to one irate theatregoer.[47] Mapleson took over a bare shell which had to be fitted out at his own expense, but by spending £6,000 at Mr Maple's furniture emporium in Tottenham Court Road on four miles of carpet, thousands of feet of specially woven drapes, chairs, looking glasses and wallpaper, he was able to open on 28 April.[48] He still confidently expected to be able to move into his own opera house for the following season, but by the end of 1877 these plans were, almost literally, in ruins. By the time the magnificent new structure reached roof level, Mapleson had spent £80,000, but then the money ran out owing to the overspend on the foundations. He needed £40,000 to put the roof on, after which he was confident that he could raise a mortgage to fit the building out.[49] Unfortunately no one would lend him the £40,000, as the money men took the view that the whole project was now financially unsound.

Mapleson complained that if he had wanted the money to back a horse, or to start a sports club, it would have been found in a few hours. Exposed to the elements, the building began to decay and Mapleson was forced to sell the shell to speculators for only £29,000. They, in their turn, were forced to dispose of it to a contractor for £500, who then spent £3,000 to demolish it and sell the materials. The site was then acquired for New Scotland Yard, home of the Metropolitan Police Force. Mapleson joked that his massive foundations would ensure that occupants of the cells might not be comfortable but they would at least be dry.[50] The structures on the site are now part of the parliamentary estate, known as Norman Shaw North and Norman Shaw South. A lesser man would have been crushed by this disaster, but Mapleson expanded his activities to the USA where he achieved greater success than ever before. He later ran opera seasons at Covent Garden but he never went back to Drury Lane.

When negotiations with Mapleson for a summer opera season fell through, Chatterton advertised for another tenant, but without success.[51] As a result, for the first time in eight years, Drury Lane was closed for the summer. The proprietors were dismayed to see their theatre shut at the height of the social season when other London theatres were open; the renters were furious to miss out on three months of free opera; and Chatterton was deprived of the £3,000 in rent that he had been receiving[52] which covered nearly half of the full annual rent he was paying to the proprietors. His famous obstinacy and bad temper were now propelling him towards ruin.

During this disastrous season at Drury Lane, Chatterton had virtually turned the Adelphi and the Princess's into Dion Boucicault houses. At the Adelphi, the controversial production of *The Shaughraun*, staged in defiance of Boucicault's attempted injunction, ended in March 1877, to be followed by a revival of the previous year's production of *The Colleen Bawn*. Chatterton then put on a play called *True to the Core* by Angiolo Slous which lasted for four weeks, followed by another revival of Falconer's *Peep o' Day*, still with Falconer as Barney O'Toole, for another four. Then came Boucicault's *The Streets of London* which ran from May to August. At the Princess's, there was a return of Joseph Jefferson in Boucicault's version of *Rip van Winkle* on Easter Monday, which was followed by a revival of *After Dark*, a Boucicault drama that had first been seen in the same theatre nine years earlier. *After Dark* ran at the Princess's until 24 August 1877, which was Chatterton's last night as lessee, having finally managed to dispose of the lease of the Princess's to the actor-manager Walter Gooch. *After Dark* then transferred to the Adelphi where it ran until

October, to be replaced by a revival of *Formosa* that ran until the following February. Chatterton's repeated staging of plays written by Boucicault, a man he detested and had only recently been fighting in court, shows the extent to which London theatre managers were dependent on Boucicault for the product to keep their doors open. Although not well known today, he was by far the most successful playwright of the nineteenth century.[53]

The 1876/77 season had been Chatterton's worst so far, but in the midst of his various failures, he still managed to come up with a successful and innovative idea: a pantomime for children performed entirely by children. It was called *Little Goody Two Shoes* and opened at the Adelphi on 23 December 1876. It was not initially part of the evening programme but ran every day as a matinee performance until 7 February. After that it became the curtain raiser for *The Shaughraun*, starting at 6.45 p.m. and running for two hours. It remained as part of the evening programme, either as curtain-raiser or afterpiece until 18 May – an astonishingly late date for a pantomime. There had been matinee performances on Wednesdays and Saturdays until 7 April, after which there were Wednesday matinees until the end of the run. With a total of 151 performances, it was Chatterton's most successful pantomime in terms of number of performances. Realising that he had discovered a winning formula, Chatterton opened another children's pantomime, *Little Red Riding Hood*, at the Adelphi on 4 August. It ran as the afterpiece or curtain-raiser of the evening programme until the end of October, with regular Wednesday matinees that continued until the middle of November. Chatterton's innovation of all-child pantomime companies had enabled him to run pantomimes at the Adelphi throughout the whole year apart from June and July, with an extraordinarily high number of matinee performances. Both *Little Goody Two Shoes* and *Little Red Riding Hood* had regular midweek matinees throughout their runs, which was a novelty. It was customary to have matinees of pantomimes during January and February, but for the rest of the year managements only rarely ventured to put on matinees, and then almost always on Saturdays. These two children's pantomimes introduced regular midweek matinees as a viable part of a theatre's programme.

1877 – 1878: The estimation in which Mr Chatterton is held

As Chatterton prepared for the opening of the 1877/78 season, he was distracted by a pointless and time-consuming feud with Edward Ledger, editor of the theatrical newspaper *The Era*, over the Royal Dramatic College.

The feud was exacerbated by the fact that, since April, Chatterton had owned his own newspaper which he used to promote his shows and pursue his current obsessions.

Frustrated by bad reviews, especially in *The Times*, Chatterton launched a theatrical weekly called *Touchstone or The New Era*. The first issue appeared on 7 April and almost immediately ran into controversy as Edward Ledger, proprietor of *The Era*, applied for an injunction to stop Chatterton from using 'The New Era' as his sub-title, on the grounds that people would think they were buying *The Era* or its successor. The injunction was granted but overturned on appeal five days later.[54] Chatterton's name was never mentioned in court because the nominal proprietor of *Touchstone* was Edgar Ray, the editor. Presumably Chatterton thought that glowing reviews for his shows would carry less weight if people knew he owned the paper. However, Edgar Ray was a man of straw: Chatterton decided on the policy, and this expert navigation of the court system to get an injunction overturned within days certainly had his fingerprints all over it.

The reviews of Chatterton's productions were the main point of the paper. Like *The Era*, *Touchstone* reviewed all West End productions that had opened during the week. Reviews were for the most part generous, but any production at Chatterton's three theatres would receive unqualified praise in reviews that were substantially longer than those for other managers' productions. This still left a lot of space to fill as *Touchstone* ran to twenty-four pages compared with twenty in *The Era*. Chatterton was therefore able to use *Touchstone* to promote those he wanted to promote, like his daughter Mary making her first appearances as a harpist, and to undermine those who challenged him, like Henry Irving, whose 'authentic' *Richard III* was supposedly so far superior to Chatterton's production of the previous year.[55] He was also able to use *Touchstone* to wage a fierce and increasingly bitter campaign to save the Royal Dramatic College.

This theatrical charity had been set up in 1858 by Charles Kean, not as an educational institution (as its name might suggest) but as a set of almshouses for old and destitute actors. Prince Albert became the patron and in 1860 laid the foundation stone for twelve almshouses to accommodate twenty-four pensioners in Maybury, outside Woking. Kean had anticipated that the theatrical profession would support the College by benefits and donations but this didn't happen to the extent he hoped. There were already several well established theatrical charities, notably the Royal General Theatrical Fund, but whereas the RGTF was a friendly society, to which members contributed and from which they were entitled to draw benefits, the Royal Dramatic College catered for those who had never been able to contribute to any fund. It depended entirely on charitable donations and fundraising activities, which were insufficient to support what one paper described as 'this tomfoolery of a grand College, with a noble hall, and gardens'.[56] There was also a feeling that it was in the wrong place. John Hollingshead lamented that 'a few needy actors – the most town-loving creatures on earth – should be transported to a Tudoresque prison near a Surrey cemetery'.[57]

Chatterton was asked to join the committee, probably by Benjamin Webster who took on responsibility for it after the death of Kean in 1868, and he accepted the challenge of turning the situation around. In spite of the fact that he was in serious financial difficulties himself, he put money into the College to keep it afloat but, in February 1877, the council were told that there were no funds to pay the pensions for the next month. In May, Chatterton chaired a meeting of the Council at which it was decided to close the College formally at a meeting of subscribers to be held at the Adelphi Theatre on 5 June. Determined to keep it open, Chatterton took a full page in *Touchstone* for an open letter attacking those who were undermining the College's position and insisting that, although there had been mismanagement in the past, it was still possible to fulfil the original objectives by good management and tight control of costs. He urged those attending the meeting in June to vote against the proposal.

He got his way by effectively highjacking the meeting. Edgar Ray, editor of *Touchstone*, attended the meeting and proposed an amendment to the motion to close the College to the effect that it should be kept open. The amendment was passed, but in its report of the meeting *The Era* revealed that Ray had become a subscriber to the College only twenty-four hours before the meeting. The clear implication was that Ray had been Chatterton's stooge to subvert the decision of the Council. The situation deteriorated even further when it was discovered that a small sub-group on the Council, led by Chatterton and Webster, had raided a trust fund established under the terms of the will of the actor T. P. Cooke to provide prize-money for a playwriting competition and then used the money for running costs. Several members of the Council, including Edward Ledger, editor of *The Era*, resigned in protest.

Chatterton was furious. On 17 July an extraordinary open meeting was held on the stage of Drury Lane to discuss the affairs of the College, but when Chatterton spotted the representative of *The Era* in the audience he roundly abused him and expelled him from the meeting. The unfortunate journalist then received a letter from Chatterton's solicitor (his younger brother Horace) threatening him with prosecution for intrusion, while Edward Ledger also received a letter asking him for the address at which papers could be served on him in respect of 'various statements made… reflecting upon my client Mr F. B. Chatterton'. Chatterton cancelled all advertising in *The Era* for theatres under his control and kept this ban in place until the end of the year.[58] On 5 August *The Era* published a letter signed by members of the profession opposing the use of 'discreditable means' to raise funds (meaning the raiding of the Cooke trust fund) and saying that it was time to close the Royal Dramatic College. A note to the letter, which carried 111 signatures, explained that these had been gathered in a few days from members of the profession in London: those in the provinces were asked to send in their names if they supported the views expressed. On 12 August the letter was reprinted with 214 signatures and again on 9 September with 432. These signatories included many 'star' names and leading managers. The impression was created that Chatterton had set himself up in defiance of virtually the entire profession ('with the exception of those owing allegiance to Mr Chatterton'[59]) by adopting a stubborn and violently confrontational position on a failed charity.[60]

Chatterton gave up and on 12 November 1877 another meeting was held at the Adelphi which voted unanimously for the dissolution of the College. Chatterton had failed in his objective, but more importantly he had been devoting time and energy to this charitable lost cause when he should have been thinking about the forthcoming season at Drury Lane. He had been planning to open the new season with a 'grand realistic drama of London life', presumably along the lines of *The Great City*, but towards the end of July he suddenly changed his mind and announced another stage version of a novel by Sir Walter Scott: *Peveril of the Peak*, to be adapted as *England in the Days of Charles the Second*.[61] (There were so many objections to the length of the title, it was soon contracted to *England*.) The lateness of the decision left only two months to prepare a large-scale production, and the result was a mess, starting with the script.

Andrew Halliday had died earlier in the year,[62] so Chatterton entrusted the task to W. G. Wills. This was risky, given Wills's track record as a dramatist. He had a long line of flops to his name, but his association with Henry Irving and Ellen Terry enveloped him in an aura of 'legitimacy' which persuaded managers to go back to him. As one critic archly observed: 'Little success has hitherto attended Mr Wills's ventures as a dramatist, but he has been so far fortunate that many opportunities of failing have been afforded him.'[63]

The challenge Wills faced in adapting *Peveril of the Peak* was daunting. It was Scott's longest novel, with a complicated plot concerning Julian Peveril, the son of a cavalier, who falls in love with Alice Bridgenorth, the daughter of a Puritan army officer. The story contains a great deal about the political and religious disputes of England following the restoration of the monarchy in 1660 but not much love interest, so it was going to be difficult to transform it into a Drury Lane drama. Wills decided that the material was so intractable that he would have to make up a story of his own, using only a few of the situations from the book. In spite of this, the resulting play was so confusing that 'after the first act, no one could possibly tell what the play was about… To say that Mr Wills… does not possess the late Mr Halliday's skill in stage carpentry is to give the very feeblest suggestion of his… weakness.'[64] Each scene had little to do with the scene before and didn't lead to the scene after. One critic said it was like reading Sir Walter Scott through a glass, darkly.[65] The first night went so badly that scenes were subsequently cut and transposed, then Chatterton cut the play from four acts to three, but that didn't solve the problem.

The reviews varied from lukewarm to awful, with one striking exception. *Touchstone* carried a long and enthusiastic review which consisted of nothing but praise for the clever plot, the noble language, the excellent acting and the beautiful scenery. The usefulness of this rave review was undercut by the fact that by this time everyone in the business knew that *Touchstone* was owned by Chatterton. Secrets are difficult to keep in the gossipy world of the theatre, so Chatterton abandoned the pretence and started using the *Touchstone* office as his contact address, as well as advertising it in Drury Lane programmes.

The most eagerly awaited critical assessment was, of course, Mowbray Morris's review for *The Times*. Having been publicly castigated by Chatterton the year before, he was not likely to be in an indulgent mood, and he certainly didn't hold back. The production opened on Saturday 22 September, but Morris didn't bother to attend the first night. He went to see the performance on Monday and his review didn't appear until Thursday – even later than his review for *Richard III*.[66]

He wasted no time on complimenting and encouraging the lessee of the National Theatre, as Oxenford would have done, but started as he meant to continue: 'An historical drama at this house has long ceased to mean anything more than a succession of more or less effective pageants… in which the principal figures are labelled with historical names.' It was a waste of time to discuss Wills's views of history – 'he has his own opinions on historical matters' – but, for the sake of his reputation as a dramatist, Morris hoped he wasn't really responsible for what was being acted on the stage. None of it made sense and a knowledge of the book would not help as the play 'has no likeness to *Peveril of the Peak*, nor to anything else in the world of fact or fiction'. You don't expect much by way of acting in plays of this sort, but in this production the acting was well below even the usual low level. Morris had never seen anything as bad as the actors playing Charles II and the Duke of Buckingham. Beverley's scenery was good but Morris criticised the 'dingy finery' of the costumes which looked as if they had already done service in many a pantomime and opera. The only really spectacular scene was a recreation of Ben Jonson's 'Masque of the Golden Age' (in reality performed for Charles I, not Charles II, sixty years before the action of the play) in the Banqueting House on Whitehall. Morris said that it bore as little relation to Ben Jonson's masque, or any masque, as the Charles II of the play bore to the Charles II of history.[67]

Two days later, *The Times* reported a complaint from Edward Stirling, Chatterton's stage manager, about the reference to 'dingy finery'. He insisted that the costumes were brand new and very expensive.[68] Five days later the paper printed a furious letter from Wills, writing as 'the well-abused author... having sustained the broadside of nearly the entire press'. He argued that *Peveril of the Peak* was essentially undramatic and that he had been obliged to come up with his own story. He cared little for historical accuracy as a play is not a history lesson. He argued that there must be something to say in favour of a play that has a large audience sitting in silence 'without a stir or a cough' for three hours to listen to blank verse.[69]

Answering back to critics is always a risky business and Wills exposed himself to the mocking humour of *The World*, which ran a letter written in illiterate schoolboy (or skoolboi) English by 'C. J. Yellowplush, jewnior' calling into question some of the irate author's claims. Mr Yellowplush jr. thought that it might have been unwise for Mr Wills to compare himself to Shakespeare, and as for the claim that large audiences were sitting in rapt silence every night, with no coughing, to listen to three hours of blank verse – well, Mr Yellowplush, for one, could scarcely believe it. When he saw the play, coughing wasn't the noise he heard. (Presumably it was booing.) Mr Wills should leave the critics to get on with their job, while he concentrated on his, and tried to write a good play. If he could only do that, there would be no shortage of praise, starting with yours truly.[70]

Stretched over two long columns, the humour of Master Yellowplush's letter became somewhat strained, but two weeks later the editor of *The World* was crowing over the fate of playwrights who take on critics. 'But a week or two has elapsed since the author… wrote to the papers to say that his play was a very good play, and was listened to nightly by large audiences who never stirred nor coughed… I do not think he mentioned whether they slept. What do I see now as I gaze at the theatrical advertisements? Exit from the stage of Drury Lane Mr Wills's "cough no more" play.'[71]

The production had lasted only four weeks, making it Chatterton's biggest disaster. In previous seasons he had been able to keep the big autumn drama running until Christmas, even if it was running at a loss. The only exception had been Barry Sullivan's *Richard III*, which he had alternated with Sullivan's *Macbeth* for the last three weeks of the run, but that didn't look like a major climb-down. *England* had to be scrapped completely and replaced by the trusty old war-horse *Amy Robsart*, Chatterton's most successful show, now experiencing its fourth revival. The swapping of one Walter Scott adaptation for another emphasised the scale of *England's* failure: 'Mr Wills failed completely… where Mr Halliday had enjoyed thorough success.'[72]

Mowbray Morris reviewed this revival of *Amy Robsart* for *The Times*, which was unusual, as revivals were not normally considered important enough to notice. However the purpose of the review was to heap further abuse on *England* as well as to denigrate the whole class of such dramas. Morris said that *Amy Robsart* was more successful than *England*, not because it was better artistically, but because Halliday knew his place as author. He realised that the playwright can't compete with the scenery and the dancers, and that his job was to get the audience from one piece of spectacle to the next as quickly as possible. Halliday had no literary aspirations: 'He never falls because he never tried to rise.' As far as the acting is concerned, all that actors are required to do in a show like this is to be heard and to stand in the right place. The Drury Lane cast were able to cope with these not very extravagant demands.[73]

Admittedly *Amy Robsart* was now seven years old and may not have been looking its best, but the sneering tone of Morris's review gives a clue as to why he may not have been the ideal person to become a theatre critic: he didn't seem to like the theatre. The amount of theatre coverage fell when he took over from Oxenford: he reviewed fewer productions and did not include the snippets of theatre news that Oxenford fed to his readers. His habit of avoiding what he called the 'vapid noise and adulation'[74] of first nights and filing his reviews later than other critics was peculiar. There is a buzz about first nights that energises people who work in, or just go to, the theatre. Second nights, on the other hand, are often flat. Morris's smart put-downs were funny, but it is hard to escape the conclusion that he preferred reading plays in his study to seeing them on the stage – a common prejudice amongst literary men at the time. Chatterton was not the only manager who complained about the unhelpfulness of his savage reviews.[75]

The autumn season closed early, leaving Drury Lane dark for two-and-a-half weeks before the opening of the pantomime. This was *The White Cat*, announced as E. L. Blanchard's twenty-eighth consecutive Drury Lane pantomime. In fact it was the twenty-sixth, but there must have been a mistake on the list kept at Drury Lane because the ordinal numbers of Blanchard's pantomimes, given in the publicity, were always two years out. Once again, *The White Cat* starred the Vokes family, and there was a Fairy Ballet Chorus which danced to a new waltz called *The New Grand Ballet 'FBC'*. The ballet shared its initials with the lessee, to whom the Fairy Queen gave a knowing nod: '**Chatter ton**ight you may of work before us/ In "F. B. C.", our "Fairy Ballet Chorus".' *The White Cat* ran until 2 March after which Chatterton had nothing to follow it, and once again there was no opera season. Chatterton had been advertising for a tenant to take the theatre for the summer but without success, so Drury Lane closed for six months. Things were looking bad for Chatterton's management after two very poor seasons, and to make things worse his five-year lease, signed in 1873, was just about to expire. It seemed doubtful if he would be able to continue.

At this low point in Chatterton's career, his supporters decided to remind people of just how successful he had been in raising the status of Drury Lane. Chatterton had always been happy to give himself benefits, but this year John Hollingshead got together a group of titled people and theatrical luminaries to organise a benefit for Chatterton that would be something out of the ordinary. Towards the end of February a meeting was held in the Grand Saloon of Drury Lane to consider some way of 'professionally and publicly marking the estimation in which Mr Chatterton is held' with 'a fitting testimony to one who had managed a most difficult property for over twelve years'.[76] Lord William Lennox said that he felt a benefit on its own would not be sufficient; there should be a banquet in Chatterton's honour. This was seconded by Sir Mordaunt Wells who referred to the great increase in the dividends paid to the renters under Chatterton's stewardship of Drury Lane. An executive committee was formed, under John Hollingshead's chairmanship, including Henry Irving and Ellen Terry.

The benefit, which took place on the afternoon of 4 March, represented an impressive show of support, including Henry Irving in the first act of *Richard III* and Adelaide Neilson in the balcony scene from *Romeo and Juliet,* together with a scene from the biggest hit of the moment, H. J. Byron's comedy *Our Boys,* which had just become the first play to pass one thousand consecutive performances. The benefit raised £1,000 (£117,000 today) for Chatterton.[77] He made an emotional speech from the stage acknowledging the generous tribute of his professional colleagues and giving a brief overview of his tenancy of Old Drury. He had started with the aim of restoring the fortunes of the theatre of Betterton, Garrick and Kean. He had staged works by the great authors – Shakespeare, Byron, Goethe – but his 'legitimate successes' had been Pyrrhic victories, too costly to be repeated. He therefore produced realistic and spectacular dramas – *The Great City, Formosa,* the Walter Scott adaptations – with great success. He could boast of three things: first, he had run Drury Lane for longer than anyone else since David Garrick (he was forgetting Sheridan); second, he had banned patrons from coming backstage, a practice degrading to the theatre; third, no actor in his company had ever gone unpaid. He thanked his team: E. L. Blanchard for his pantomimes, William Beverley for his scenery, the Vokes family for their performances and the late Andrew Halliday, whose talent he would always admire and whose friendship he would ever miss, for his dramas.[78]

The banquet took place a week later, when over a hundred ladies and gentlemen gathered at Willis's Rooms, with Lord William Lennox, chairman of the Drury Lane Company of Proprietors, presiding. In proposing the toast to 'a man possessed of an honest, manly, English heart', Lord William spoke of the onerous task imposed upon the lessee of Drury Lane. In former times, Drury Lane and Covent Garden had been the only theatres in London, but now the lessee had to compete with over twenty other theatres. Whereas formerly the best actors all congregated at the patent theatres, they were now spread around town and did not think it beneath their dignity to act in the suburbs. The late dinner hour made it difficult to attract the upper classes to the theatre, and there was the added problem of attacks on the morality of the theatre by sanctimonious hypocrites. Productions were expensive to mount, tempting managers to stage cheap, low-class trash, but Chatterton had always maintained the highest literary standards, producing Shakespeare's greatest plays and the works of Sir Walter Scott. Chatterton's private character was unimpeachable: he was kind, honourable and charitable. Lord William hoped that Chatterton's life would long be spared to uphold the past glories of Drury Lane Theatre. In reply, Chatterton said that he felt keenly the responsibility of upholding the great traditions of Drury Lane, 'whose very name he cherished as it if were a living thing'. He would never forget the great compliment that his friends had paid him that night.[79]

It seems strange that the leading lights of the profession should have paid this compliment at the end of his most unsuccessful season. *England* had been a disaster; the season had closed early as Chatterton had nothing to put on after the pantomime; and there was nothing booked in for the summer season.[80] In retrospect, it is easy to see this as a very heavy hint to Chatterton that it was time to retire. Everyone who works in theatre knows that both hits and flops are unpredictable. Sometimes the most surprising shows catch the mood of the moment; conversely, those with all the ingredients of sure-fire hits can fail. There is a great deal of luck involved, which is why theatre people are often superstitious. However, the catastrophic failure of *England* looked more like incompetence than bad luck, suggesting that Chatterton was not on top of things. *England* had been fundamentally misconceived, which Chatterton might have noticed had he not been busy conducting a feud over the Royal Dramatic College through the columns of *Touchstone*. 'Drury Lane has… forfeited the regard of playgoers,' said *The World's* dramatic critic, 'it contributes so insignificantly to the records of the stage.'[81] It was well known that Chatterton's lease was about to expire,[82] and that the proprietors would soon be starting the process of awarding a new one. John Hollingshead, who knew Chatterton as well as anyone and who liked him in spite of their occasional spats, must have felt that now was a good time to conclude his lesseeship of Drury Lane, while he could still depart with honour. Chatterton had other ideas. He had been the most powerful manager in the West End for a long time, and inevitably he was surrounded by flatterers who told him what he wanted to hear. 'These toadies appear to believe that their chance of occupation depends upon the amount of favour they enjoy from the Colossus who at present wields the sway at three theatres, and under whose legs they are ready to crawl at any moment.'[83]

With more bravado than prudence, Chatterton decided to carry on at the Lane. Within a year he would be bankrupt and fighting a legal battle with the proprietors that would bring his management to an ignominious close.

10

The Collapse

1878 – 1879: Cold and wintry enough in all conscience

Chatterton's lease expired in August. There was a rumour that Baroness Burdett Coutts was going to take the lease and put Henry Irving in charge, but this proved to be false,[1] so in April the committee started advertising for offers for a seven-year lease. They ran the bidding process three times and many people visited their solicitor's office to inspect the terms, but there were only two bids. One of them was from 'a gentleman totally unknown to them, and who stated that he had a sort of syndicate of his bank to support him'. No evidence could be found of the syndicate, so, 'the man being a stranger to them', they declined.[2] This man would not be a stranger for much longer: he was Augustus Harris and would take over the lease in the following year.[3] There was another offer that was too low and it was known that Chatterton wanted to continue as lessee but wasn't prepared to go on paying £6,500 a year. On 9 July, the day before the third bidding process expired, Chatterton offered £6,000 per annum and the proprietors took the view that, after trying to find a tenant for three months, it was the best offer they were going to get. Chatterton was therefore awarded the lease, but for five years, rather than the seven originally offered. As a sweetener for the £500 reduction in rent, he offered

'When Mr F. B. Chatterton heard that the proprietors of Drury Lane Theatre had decided to again entrust the fortunes of their establishment to his keeping, did he make any unbecoming show of exultation? Perish the thought!' Alfred Bryan's cartoon suggests that even Chatterton was surprised by the renewal of his lease.

to pay £10 per night for every night in the season over 200, whereas he had been paying £5, but with no summer season of opera it was extremely unlikely that he would ever go over 200 nights. Not everyone looked forward to another five years of Chatterton at the Lane: 'Closed for six months in the year, it presents simply a melodrama in the autumn and a pantomime at Christmas… Change in [Chatterton's] method of direction is not to be looked for, nor any brightening of the prospects of Drury Lane.'[4]

The fact that the proprietors took three months to come to an agreement with Chatterton, with whom they had been dealing very successfully for twelve years, suggests that they had reservations about extending his tenure. They probably knew that he was experiencing severe financial problems which put a question mark over how much longer he would be able to operate. In October 1877 Chatterton had borrowed £2,000 from his bank to pay for that year's pantomime, with Benjamin Webster standing as guarantor. The loan was not repaid so the bank pursued Webster. He got off on a technicality, but in the course of the hearing the bank revealed that Chatterton had two accounts with them, both of which had been overdrawn since January of 1878.[5] By March of that year, Chatterton was so desperate for funds that he was forced to borrow £10,000 from Thomas Clarke, who held the catering concession at the Adelphi, and the brothers Stefano and Agostino Gatti, nephews of the Swiss-Italian entrepreneur Carlo Gatti whose family fortune was based on manufacturing Italian ice-cream for the mass market. The three of them gave Chatterton a mortgage for the amount, with the lease of the Adelphi as collateral. He was to make repayments at seven per cent interest, which he did in April and May. He was unable to make the repayments in June and July, at which point the mortgagors foreclosed and took possession of the lease.[6]

However, the transfer of the lease was not straightforward. Benjamin Webster, as freeholder, went to court to stop it and to demand what he regarded as unpaid rent on the Adelphi going back to the time at which Chatterton took out a lease from him in 1874. Webster maintained that Chatterton had taken advantage of his poor health and the fact that he did not have independent legal representation to get a lease for a longer period and at a lower rent than he had realised. He thought he was giving a lease for five years at £3,550, not twenty-one years at £2,550. He also exercised his right to block any transfer of the lease without his agreement. His son, a solicitor, had instructed counsel to instigate proceedings for the appointment of a receiver to collect the back-rent. Chatterton and the solicitor who had handled the transfer in 1874 presented sworn affidavits to the effect that Webster had fully understood the terms, had been allowed to peruse the documents and made corrections, and that the rental and the length of the lease reflected the fact that Chatterton was writing off the debt of over £16,000 that Webster owed him as a result of Chatterton becoming involved with the management of the Adelphi and the Princess's in 1870. At this point Webster's counsel said that if he had been aware of this he would never have brought the case before the court. The judge criticised Webster's solicitor (his son) in very strong terms for instructing counsel when there was no evidence whatsoever to support charges which could only have the effect of damaging the reputation of Mr Chatterton in the eyes of the public at the very time when he was negotiating for a fresh lease of Drury Lane. 'Some sinister and undisclosed motive must have prompted the plaintiff to make such charges.' Under the circumstances, the charges of fraud were utterly inexcusable and the case was dismissed with costs against Webster.[7] The transfer went ahead and the Gatti brothers then bought out Clarke's interest, leaving them as joint lessees of the Adelphi.[8] They certainly got a bargain. There were seventeen years left on the lease and £2,550 per annum was an extremely low rent for such a prestigious West End theatre. It reflected the fact that Chatterton had written off debts from Webster amounting to over £1.7 million in current values, but he didn't begrudge the brothers their good fortune, describing it as: 'a stroke of business, and I'm glad to find it has turned out a good stroke for them'.[9]

As he had disposed of the Princess's Theatre the year before, this meant that Chatterton was finally free to concentrate his energies on Drury Lane. He prepared for what would be his last big opening night in the usual way: he had the theatre redecorated and got Charles Lamb Kenney to write a grandiloquent prospectus. Kenney's fanfare for the season was longer than usual and was published in pamphlet form, with the words *The public are respectfully requested to circulate this pamphlet* at the bottom. It was, as ever, much more than a puff for a few plays: it was a statement of Chatterton's mission to turn Drury Lane into 'a National Theatre, devoted to the highest order of drama'. Kenney compares Chatterton, thrice lessee of Drury Lane, to Dick Whittington, thrice Lord Mayor of London, and describes the challenges facing the lessee of Old Drury, 'an heirloom from the old masters', at a time when the theatregoing public was showing little interest in 'the purest and best types of the dramatist's art'. Chatterton had never shirked his responsibilities and continued to present the poetic drama even when it was losing money, on the principle of *noblesse oblige*. How different things might be could the government only see its way to establishing 'a National Theatre subsidised by the state', but that was not likely to happen. Nothing daunted, Chatterton was once more setting sail 'bound for El Dorado with a cargo of Shakespearean wares'.[10]

In spite of the flowery hyperbole, there is something touching about Kenney's passionate plea for 'my old friend, Mr Chatterton (he was, when I began, my young friend, being then the youngest of managers)'. Kenney had been with Chatterton since the start of his Drury Lane management, but now he was ill and impoverished, dependent on charity since the health problems that would end his life two years later prevented him from working.[11] Brilliantly witty and the best of company, Kenney never lived up to his early promise: 'Of him great things were once predicted,' said one obituary, 'but the expectations were never fulfilled.'[12] The prospectus was the last thing he would write for publication[13] and he certainly pulled out all the stops. Alas, the cargo of Shakespearean wares with which Chatterton was setting sail included a production of Shakespeare's *The Winter's Tale* that would sink this last voyage to El Dorado.

The Winter's Tale has never been one of Shakespeare's most popular plays. Even by his own standards, the geography and chronology are all over the place, mixing up references to the Delphic Oracle, Christian burial and the Italian Renaissance painter Giulio Romano. Bohemia sports a coastline and there is a sixteen-year gap in the middle of the play to allow Perdita to grow up. Garrick produced a version called *Florizel and Perdita* in 1756 which chopped out the first three acts to eliminate the time-lapse; John Philip Kemble restored the Shakespeare text in a production at Drury Lane in 1802, and there were later productions by Macready and Phelps. However the most strikingly successful version of the play was produced at the Princess's Theatre in 1856 by Charles Kean. Kean did not get himself elected a fellow of the Royal Society of Antiquaries by countenancing historical inaccuracies, so he trimmed the text a little and set it firmly in Syracuse in 330 B.C. when Sicily was at the height of its prosperity. Bohemia became Bithynia, which does have a coastline and which is conveniently near to the supposed site of Troy, allowing Kean to stage '*tableaux vivants* of the private and public life of the ancient Greeks at a time when the arts flourished to a perfection'.[14] Kean added a 'Pyrrhic Dance' of three dozen beautiful ballet girls that had nothing to do with Shakespeare, plus an enormous festival of Dionysus that involved three hundred men, women and children, some dressed as satyrs. Astonishingly, given the relative unpopularity of the play, this production became one of the first 'long runs', notching up 103 continuous performances.

Chatterton's production was copied from Charles Kean's version, scaled up for the Drury Lane stage, but without the bear.[15] Kean's Pyrrhic dance was repeated and the big set was a recreation of a Greek-style amphitheatre in which the trial of Hermione took place, while the festival of Dionysus became a wild throng of shrieking Maenads and Sileni. The actors were dressed to look like the characters painted on Greek vases in the British Museum. No one complained about the spectacle; the problem, as ever with Chatterton's productions, was the acting 'by a wholly incompetent troupe of players'.[16]

The statue scene from *The Winter's Tale*

For years, Chatterton had been trying to manage without stars. He seemed to feel that, if he had Beverley's sets, gorgeous costumes and big dance numbers, the public would be content. He had parted company with Phelps in 1872; Helen Faucit had turned her back on the 'degraded' London stage as she began to style herself Mrs Theodore Martin and eventually Lady Martin;[17] Adelaide Neilson had been a success in *Amy Robsart* (1870) and *Rebecca* (1871) but then moved on; James Anderson was respected for his efforts on behalf of 'the legitimate drama' but was old-fashioned – 'an actor of the old time and school' who ranted and roared, and he gave up acting after

Richard Coeur de Lion in 1874;[18] Barry Sullivan had been a disaster in *Richard III* in 1876 and Chatterton's next big production of *England* was a starless black hole. In 1878, however, Chatterton finally patched things up with Phelps, and it was agreed that Phelps would appear as Leontes in *The Winter's Tale*, then do a series of farewell performances concluding in the following March. It was not to be. Phelps was now seventy-four, suffering from poor health and declining powers. In February 1878 he was acting at the Aquarium Theatre in Westminster, alternating the Cardinals Wolsey and Richelieu. He caught a cold but insisted on continuing until, on 1 March, he had to be carried offstage. It was obvious that he would not be well enough for a September opening at Drury Lane, but he was still being announced for a series of farewell performances commencing on 18 November. Phelps died on 6 November.

Needing a Leontes at very short notice, Chatterton hired Charles Dillon, which proved to be a serious error of judgement. Dillon's glory days were now twenty years in the past and whatever talent he then possessed had been undermined by a lifetime of drinking and improvidence. He hadn't been seen in London since Chatterton presented him in *Manfred* at the Princess's in 1873, and he was now too decayed to be attempting a Shakespearean lead anywhere, least of all at Drury Lane. 'He is what is termed "an actor of the old school", one paper told its readers, 'which seems to be a school of emphasis, exaggeration, and laboured mediocrity'.[19] This was typical of the critical mauling he received. He couldn't remember his lines, was often inaudible, and appeared in such an absurd make-up that the audience laughed. With a performance as bad as this at the centre of the play, the rest of the cast would have had to be very good indeed to save it. Unfortunately they were, for the most part, as bad or even worse. 'It is a lamentable thing', wrote Joseph Knight in *The Athenaeum*, 'to see a performance of *The Winter's Tale* in which the Hermione displays no poetry, the Leontes no passion, and the Autolycus no fun,'[20] but, in a sense, it should have come as no surprise. As the novelist Henry James pointed out, Paris had its House of Moliere in the Comédie Française, but London had no House of Shakespeare, and after decades during which its stage had been dominated by French translations, burlesque and melodrama, there were not enough actors who could speak blank verse to cast a play by Shakespeare, who can't be acted 'by players who have been interpreting vulgarity the day before, and who are to return to vulgarity on the morrow'.[21]

James Anderson, who made his London debut as Florizel in Macready's 1837 production of *The Winter's Tale*, found the whole thing 'cold and wintry enough in all conscience'.[22] He thought the present generation of actors were so bad that the public no longer knew what good acting looked like. The shining exception in this heap of dross was the Paulina of Mrs Hermann Vezin who 'redeemed the entire performance from intellectual sterility'.[23] 'The main personages of the drama are... completely overshadowed by Mrs Hermann Vezin', said the critic of *The Theatre*, while The *Figaro* called her 'the greatest actress that we have now upon the stage'.[24] It is a sign of Chatterton's poor judgement of acting that he failed to recognise the talent of Mrs Vezin, who had been appearing for him at Drury Lane since 1864, and cast her in a secondary part, whilst the female lead was given to the pretty but untalented Ellen Wallis, described by critics as 'most unsatisfactory... stagey without being artistic... as ignorant of the meaning of what she is saying as a poll-parrot... a worse Hermione it is difficult to conceive'. The best part of her performance was said to be her impersonation of the statue – no need to speak.[25] One publication held itself aloof from this critical bloodbath, describing Miss Wallis's performance as a complete triumph, 'such as might have been anticipated from a lady so highly gifted and so thoroughly mistress of the mechanism of her art', and heaping praise on every aspect of the production, especially the excellent acting. As the publication in question was *Touchstone*, which Chatterton owned and which had been plugging the production relentlessly for weeks, its endorsement was worthless. Chatterton sold *Touchstone* after this issue and it closed a few months later.[26]

No amount of spectacle could compensate for performances like these. It is not enough, warned one critic, 'to produce some Shakespearean play with correct archaeological accessories... when blank verse is mouthed and ranted by some, mumbled inaudibly by others, and by others uttered without rhythm or measure.'[27] Reeling from the critical onslaught, Chatterton wrote to *The Times* complaining that, 'as the manager of what has been popularly styled our National Theatre,' his pursuit of 'art for art's sake' was being made more difficult by critical hostility and nit-picking, and that if people wanted him to continue his 'Shakespearean campaign' at Drury Lane, he needed 'a more charitable and discriminating criticism on the part of a certain section of the press'.[28] However, one interesting thing about the reviews was the way in which, whilst excoriating this particular production, several acknowledged the effort Chatterton had made to maintain artistic standards in a notoriously difficult house. 'It has been the fashion of some persons to sneer at Mr Chatterton's management,' wrote the *Figaro* critic (William Archer), who was having none of it.

Chatterton had always tried to maintain high artistic standards and Archer hoped that *The Winter's Tale* could still be saved by some judicious changes. If not, and Chatterton was forced to abandon 'the glorious poetry' of Shakespeare for 'realism and spectacular sensationalism, let us not deny that he has bravely done his best to elevate the taste of the masses for whom he caters'.[29] Even *The Builder*, a publication that normally showed little interest in theatres beyond their bricks and mortar, took the unusual step of publishing a full-scale review of *The Winter's Tale* that was highly critical but concluded by praising Chatterton's good intentions and hoping that 'the public will fully support him in the course he has entered upon'.[30]

Chatterton must have been glad to receive even such qualified support as this, because he was now fighting for his professional life. *The Winter's Tale* was losing so much money that Chatterton resorted to a most extraordinary classified advertisement in *The Times* to drum up support, not so much for the production as for the principle it represented:

> In once more calling the attention of the public to the fact that a classical play has been produced at what has always been regarded as the home of the legitimate drama, the manager appeals for the support not only of those members of the general playgoing public who prefer a performance which is as elevating as it is instructive and amusing, but also to those who, recognising the necessity for an immediate attempt to stay the tendency of the taste of a certain section of the public to degenerate more and more into a love of what is frivolous, if not depraved, are willing to lend their assistance and personal influence to what cannot but be regarded as an educational work, and to the removal of what threatens to become a national stigma. The attention of the public is particularly called to the opinions of the press on this production, which, whilst acknowledging the merits of the artists engaged in expounding this work of our great poet, are of one mind as to the desirability of encouraging an effort to bring home to the public a knowledge of the works which are an ornament to our national literature.[31]

This appeal seems to be asking the public to see *The Winter's Tale*, whether or not they think it is a good production, in order to support Chatterton's efforts to hold back the rising tide of frivolity and depravity that threatens to overwhelm the London stage. Chatterton ran the advertisement for a week and then gave up. After only four weeks of continuous performances, Chatterton began to alternate

The Winter's Tale with *Macbeth* and *Othello*, also starring Charles Dillon. Of his Macbeth, Joseph Knight wrote in *The Athenaeum* that: 'Mr Dillon has not only no adequate grasp of the character, he has, so far as can be ascertained, no conception of it whatever.' On 15 November, Chatterton admitted defeat and withdrew *The Winter's Tale* altogether after only thirty-three performances.

The situation was now extremely serious. 'The news of my losses got buzzed about,' Chatterton told John Coleman, 'and my credit was seriously impaired. The rats began to desert the sinking ship, and we were drifting on the rocks.'[32] He needed to put on something – anything – that would make some money. Another revival of *Amy Robsart* might have done the trick, or almost anything written by Dion Boucicault. Instead, he doggedly continued to present Charles Dillon in the 'legitimate' drama: *Othello, Cymbeline, The Merchant of Venice, Belphegor* (Dillon's old hit) and Colman's eighteenth-century comedy *The Jealous Wife*. Inevitably, things went from bad to worse or, as one critic put it, from an unsatisfactory Leontes to an unintelligent Macbeth and an Othello so grotesque it was laughable: 'A worse Shakespearean performance than this…it has rarely been our lot to witness.'[33]

It was madness, little short of professional suicide, to continue with this, but Chatterton needed to burnish his Shakespearean credentials as he had been asked to produce the first season of plays in the new Shakespeare Memorial Theatre at Stratford-upon-Avon, due to open in April of the following year.[34] The building of this theatre resulted from the longstanding enthusiasm for the Bard manifested by the Flower family of Stratford-upon-Avon, brewers of Flowers Ale. Edward Fordham Flower, founder of the brewery and four times mayor of Stratford, had been the driving force behind the 1864 tercentenary celebration of Shakespeare's birth, and when his son Charles Flower took over the brewery, he also inherited the commitment to performing Shakespeare in Stratford. A temporary theatre had been built for the celebration in 1864, and the success of the plays produced there suggested to the Flower family that there should be a permanent structure in the town where the works of its most famous son could be adequately staged. The Shakespeare Memorial Theatre owed its somewhat lugubrious name (which it retained until it became the Royal Shakespeare Theatre in 1961) to the fact that both the London and Stratford committees for the 1864 Shakespeare tercentenary celebrations had as their stated aim the erection of a memorial or monument to Shakespeare. This had been understood to mean a statue, but no statue appeared in either town. Charles Flower took the enlightened view that the best way to honour

Shakespeare's genius was to perform his plays – the view put forward by Chatterton in his 1864 pamphlet 'The Shakespeare Tercentenary' – and for this you need a theatre.

Chatterton had not been involved with the 1864 celebration, largely because his star Samuel Phelps got into a dispute with the committee, but he was keen to become involved with the Memorial Theatre. On 23 April 1875 (Shakespeare's birthday), Chatterton mounted a performance of *As You Like It* at Drury Lane, with Helen Faucit as Rosalind, which raised £173 for the Shakespeare Memorial Theatre Fund.[35] That day's edition of *The Times* carried a list of those who had already contributed towards the fund for a theatre, library, art gallery and, eventually, a dramatic training school in Stratford-upon-Avon. Those contributing £100 or more would become governors and managers of the project, and Chatterton was one of them.[36] The foundation stone of the theatre was laid on 23 April 1877 and by the autumn of 1878 preparations were in hand for the opening performances, to start on 23 April 1879. Directing this festival would have been the crowning achievement of Chatterton's long career as a producer of Shakespeare and it goes some way towards explaining why he was so determined to make the 1878/79 season at Drury Lane Shakespearean, whatever it cost.

By December Chatterton had lost £3,200 (over £370,000 in modern values) on the season and everything depended on the pantomime being a greater success than ever before.[37] For the first time, it flopped. The story chosen was that of Cinderella, which is now the most successful pantomime story but was relatively new at the time. This was Drury Lane's first *Cinderella* but it wasn't a new script. Blanchard adapted a *Cinderella* he had written for the Crystal Palace in 1874/75, omitting the spectacular bits like the Butterfly Ball and a Grand Fairy Wedding which Chatterton couldn't afford to stage. 'In former time Mr Chatterton spent money on the spectacular portion of his pantomime,' said *The World* in a post-mortem on the season, 'this year he had it not to spend.'[38] The production was accused of 'dinginess and meanness';[39] it didn't look like a Drury Lane pantomime and the whole thing seemed dull compared with previous efforts. Victoria Vokes made things worse by playing Cinderella as a burlesque character and spoiling the romance of the story.

In the first five weeks of the run, takings were £4,280 (more than half-a-million pounds today) below the same period in the previous year. On Saturday 1 February the whole company were paid in cash, apart from the Vokes family and Fred Evans (one of the clowns in the harlequinade) who were paid by cheque. The takings for both performances on that day were so poor that James Guiver, the treasurer, realised that the cheques would bounce, and had to ask Fred Vokes to wait until Thursday before banking the cheque for his family. On Monday evening a notice was put up in the Green Room calling all members of the acting company to a meeting the following day at noon. The musicians and technical crew were to meet at one. Chatterton didn't come to the meeting himself, but Edward Stirling, the stage manager, explained the financial situation and asked everyone to agree to a reduction in salaries for three weeks, allowing the pantomime to close in an orderly fashion. Those receiving more than £2 per week were to accept half-pay; those on less, a one-third reduction. Stirling explained that he needed agreement immediately, otherwise bills would be posted announcing the closure of the theatre that night. Fred and Fawdon Vokes were present but Victoria and Jessie were not. Everyone agreed apart from Charles Lauri, one of the clowns, and Fred Vokes, who said that he needed to consult his sisters. He was given until two o' clock, but the answer was no. As Victoria was playing Cinderella, Jessie the Prince, Fred Baron Pumpernickel and Fawdon the Buttons character, it was impossible to go ahead without them. Bills were posted announcing that:

> Owing to a combination of unforeseen circumstances, this theatre is unavoidably closed for the present.
> F. B. Chatterton, Sole Lessee and Manager,
> Tuesday 4th February 1879

The entire cast and crew, numbering 676, were out of work.[40] William Beverley wrote to *The Daily News* saying that, in a long career, he had often been involved with managements that got into difficulties. In such circumstances, the members of the company invariably rally round and do whatever is necessary to get the sinking ship off the rocks. This was the first time he had known the stars of the show to refuse to cooperate to save the jobs of their colleagues.[41] In response, and continuing the nautical metaphor, Fred Vokes justified his family's behaviour by saying that when the passengers were invited to take their berths, they should have been warned that the hold was leaking.[42] *The Theatre* published an account of the affair called 'The Drury Lane Disaster' that censured Vokes for behaving ungenerously, but observed that, if Shakespeare hadn't spelt ruin in the autumn, the pantomimists wouldn't have been asked to take a pay cut in the winter. 'It is rather hard upon the exponents of… the illegitimate drama to ask them to suffer for the shortcomings of the legitimate drama.'[43]

A week later Chatterton petitioned for bankruptcy, with liabilities of £38,690 (over £4.7m today) and assets of about £1,500.[44] For James Anderson, there was a horrible sense of déjà vu about the whole affair. 'This same "Old Drury" has been the ruin of many a better manager. It is a fascinating and treacherous property, "the guiled shore to a most dangerous sea" – in short a quicksand, where whoever builds his hopes of fortune is sure to sink.'[45]

The process of Chatterton's discharge lasted for several weeks during which his creditors disputed with each other and with the proprietors of Drury Lane. It must have been a painful process for Chatterton, who had never, in the whole course of his career, failed to pay a debt, honour a contract or treat everyone who worked for him justly. Bad-tempered he might have been, but he was scrupulously honest. Even at this stage, he did not regard himself as a spent force, and he still had dreams of restoring the lost glories of Drury Lane. He applied to the proprietors for another lease, but the trustee of his bankruptcy had threatened legal action against the proprietors for the return of the £1,500 deposit he had paid on the issuing of his last lease. Chatterton claimed that he owed no rent at the time of his collapse, so this sum should have counted amongst his assets. The proprietors disputed this and claimed that they retained the deposit to cover arrears of rent, as well as paying for repairs that Chatterton had failed to carry out under the terms of the previous lease that expired in 1878.[46] When Chatterton approached the proprietors about obtaining a new lease, they told him that no negotiations were possible while he was pursuing legal action against them. He therefore persuaded the trustee to drop the claim.

This matter had still not been resolved in July when the Drury Lane renters had their annual meeting. They wanted to know why the theatre was standing empty after five months, and accused the committee of not trying hard enough to find a new tenant. Sir Mordaunt Wells said that, while he admitted the situation was not good, he would only sanction a 'substantial tenant' who could commit to a rental for five years that would yield a good dividend.[47] Such potential tenants were in short supply as Drury Lane had acquired a reputation for blighting the careers of anyone who went near it. In James Anderson's words, 'the royal property was a vampire and sucked the life-blood out of everyone'.[48]

Apart from Chatterton, there was one other person who was chasing the lease of Drury Lane, although he was far from being the 'substantial tenant' the committee were looking for. Augustus Harris was twenty-seven, with a modest career as an actor behind him and a slightly more impressive one as a stage manager. He had been James Mapleson's stage manager for three years during the Drury Lane opera seasons and, never one to underestimate his own abilities, took the view that he could have run Drury Lane more efficiently than his boss. Although he had no direct managerial experience himself, his father – also Augustus Harris – had been manager of the Princess's Theatre and then, for twenty-seven years, stage manager of the Italian opera at Covent Garden. His grandfather had built the Coburg Theatre (which we know as the Old Vic) so theatre was certainly in the genes.

August Harris junior had applied for the lease of Drury Lane in 1878, when Chatterton's second term as sole lessee came to an end, but the committee were unimpressed by his meagre financial assets and lack of managerial experience. Less than a year later he was walking past the theatre when he saw the notices of closure, so he renewed his attack. The committee still had reservations about this inexperienced young man, but he probably seemed better than the alternative. Amongst those seriously interested in theatre, Drury Lane looked like an anachronism that should be abolished:

> Drury Lane Theatre, with its enormous rent, its 'committee', its 'secretary' – a worthy old gentleman but a kind of dramatic dodo – its 'architect', its 'renters', and all the rest of its cumbrous machinery, is as much behind the age as a flint-and-steel tinder-box or a farthing rushlight.[49]

This damning verdict was delivered by *The World*, which recommended conversion of the building to retail or other use.[50] The upmarket monthly *The Theatre* wondered where 'the hungry proprietors and renters' would find a tenant prepared to pay the 'ridiculously high rent' for their 'old-fashioned and over-rated theatre… during the rest of the short period for which it exists as a theatre'.[51] *Truth* described Drury Lane as 'a white elephant…The best thing that could be done with the "National Theatre" would be to convert it into a "National Circus"'.[52]

Faced with these bleak prospects, the Drury Lane committee swallowed whatever reservations they might have had about Augustus Harris and awarded him the lease, subject to a £1,000 deposit (£122,000 today). At the time his total resources amounted to £3 15s, but he managed to borrow the funds from several sources just in time to complete the deal.[53]

There used to be a pub on Russell Street, across the road from Drury Lane, called the Albion. It was popular with theatre people, attracting a clientele of actors, managers, critics and fans. Chatterton, Falconer, Webster and Halliday were all regulars, as was William Tinsley, the theatre-loving publisher. One day in September 1879, Tinsley passed a few anxious hours in the Albion with Chatterton and other friends, some of whom had been trying to use their influence with members of the Drury Lane committee to give Chatterton another chance. They were waiting for the committee's decision, and when Augustus Harris rushed in, excitedly announcing that he had the lease, some of them laughed. It seemed incredible that an inexperienced young person could be put in charge of the most historic theatre in the country. Chatterton got up and sadly walked away.[54] He resented the way in which the committee had favoured Harris, 'entirely unknown as a manager and [who] had no moral claim whatever on the proprietors, whereas I had been associated with the theatre for a space of sixteen years, during which I had paid for rent alone a sum of something like £80,000... yet, thanks to the magnanimity of this irresponsible proprietary body... I was left high and dry without a shilling!'[55] Lord William Lennox, chairman of the proprietors, had described Chatterton to the guests at his testimonial banquet the year before as one of the best tenants they had ever had and denied rumours to the effect that the committee was negotiating with someone else for renewal of the lease: 'he hoped not to lose so good a tenant'.[56] If Chatterton remembered the words, they must have sounded hollow.

As if 1879 had not been bad enough for Chatterton, in November Benjamin Webster was allowed to resurrect his charge of fraud over the terms of the Adelphi lease. He wanted the lease to be set aside – in spite of the fact that it had been transferred to the Gatti brothers the year before – and the books of the partnership to be examined. Considering the very strong language used by the judge to dismiss the case the year

MASTER GUSSY HARRIS.
"WHAT WILL HE DO WITH IT?"
The young Augustus Harris was a surprising choice for the proprietors of Drury Lane

before as being utterly groundless and a disgraceful attempt to blacken Chatterton's reputation, it seems astonishing that Webster was allowed into court with the same charges a second time. Once again, his case proved to be without foundation. He admitted that he was over eighty (he was eighty-one) and had a very imperfect recollection of events. The next witness was the person in charge of the finances of the Adelphi at the time who testified that Webster had been kept fully informed of the financial situation on a weekly basis so it was not the case that he had been misled as to the true financial position. At the end of his examination, Webster's counsel announced that he would not be proceeding with the case. Webster was senile by this stage,[57] but Chatterton was furious that his good name had been called into question not once but twice over the same unfounded allegations and that he had not even been given the opportunity to go into the witness box to clear himself. He had his solicitor write to *The Times* protesting that their coverage gave the impression that there might have been a case to answer, but there was in fact no case at all.[58]

It was the worst possible end to the worst year of his life. His attempt in 1870 to save Webster from ruin had played a major part in his own downfall.[59] Three theatres had proved to be two too many: 'I ought to have been content with one, that one, too, the first, the finest and the cheapest in the world.'[60] He claimed that profits from Drury Lane were being eaten up by losses at the other two theatres, but this is hard to credit given the number of long-running shows at both.[61] The real problems were at Drury Lane, where Chatterton seems to have been too distracted to stay on top of things. He kept producing Walter Scott adaptations long after the format had been exhausted and his Shakespearean productions, without the aid of Samuel Phelps, were overblown and unintelligent. It was the failure of three successive autumn dramas at Drury Lane – *Richard III* (1876), *England* (1877) and *The Winter's Tale* (1878) – that led him into the bankruptcy courts, not losses at the Adelphi and the Princess's. After all this, his reward for helping Webster had been to find himself hauled into court twice on the same charge of fraud, while Webster was telling everyone who would listen that Chatterton's 'ingratitude' towards him was the cause of his ruin.[62] The view that Chatterton swindled Webster went down in Webster family legend. When his great-granddaughter Margaret Webster wrote the history of her theatrical dynasty in 1969, she claimed that Webster 'took in Chatterton as a partner, but it proved disastrous… Ben emerged in print from time to time to protest furiously against the unauthorised debts contracted in his name.'[63] Truly, no good deed shall go unpunished.

11

The Last Years

'Mr F. B. Chatterton, so long the intelligent and enterprising lessee of the Theatre Royal, Drury Lane, has fallen upon evil days,' George Augustus Sala told the readers of his column in *The Illustrated London News*. 'I am very sorry for it.'[1] Sala praised William Beverley for calling on people to support the ruined manager, and the extent to which the profession got behind Chatterton in his hour of need was indeed remarkable, especially considering how many people he must have offended with outbursts of his famously bad temper.

Within days of the closure of Drury Lane, a committee had been formed to organise a benefit performance. The Gatti brothers were producing the pantomime at Covent Garden and offered the free use of the theatre, but the pantomime season was coming to a close so time was short. They also set up a subscription fund, chaired by the Earl of Londesborough and Lord William Lennox, and got the ball rolling with a donation of fifty guineas. The benefit, which took place on 3 March, was packed, in spite of the shortness of time and dreadful weather conditions. It raised £500, plus £400 in subscriptions – the modern equivalent would be nearly £110,000.[2]

In the following month the Shakespeare Memorial Theatre opened in Stratford-upon-Avon. Chatterton had been hoping to direct the opening festival of plays but his situation made this impossible. Charles Flower contacted Barry Sullivan who undertook to organise the festival and star in all the plays without remuneration. Nevertheless, the programme announced that: 'The general dramatic portion of the Festival is under the direction of Mr F. B. Chatterton', which was a generous compliment to a ruined man. Only days after the closure of Drury Lane, *The Era* printed a letter from Charles Lowndes, secretary to the Stratford committee, insisting that: 'In the notice you gave of the Shakespeare Memorial last week it should have been stated that the dramatic arrangements will be under the management of Mr F. B. Chatterton of the Theatre Royal, Drury Lane.' There was a determination on the part of many who knew Chatterton not to allow his achievements to be forgotten, in spite of his fate.[3]

In the midst of several court appearances, Chatterton managed to get to Stratford-upon-Avon for the opening of the theatre on 23 April 1879, Shakespeare's 315th birthday, with a production of *Much Ado About Nothing* starring Helen Faucit and Barry Sullivan as Beatrice and Benedick. In spite of the somewhat elderly lovers (Faucit and Sullivan were aged sixty-four and fifty-seven respectively) the performance was a great success. It had been preceded by a lunch in the Town Hall for local dignitaries, nobility and gentry, as well as representatives of the arts. Chatterton was asked to respond to the toast to 'the drama' and he rose to the occasion with a favourite theme. He described the theatre as one of the noblest of all institutions, on a par with the church in terms of teaching right conduct and morality. The purpose of a play, in the words of Stratford's most famous son, was nothing less than to 'hold the mirror up to nature; to show virtue her own feature, scorn her own image, and the very age and body of the time his form and pressure'. He just wished that the universities of Oxford and Cambridge would be more mindful of the theatrical profession when handing out their honorary degrees.[4]

Being asked to reply to the toast, at this awful point in his life, would have meant a lot to Chatterton. He had taught himself Shakespeare from the penny-editions he carried in his pocket as a boy; he had staged Shakespeare's plays to the very best of his abilities at Drury Lane, which he made available for benefit performances to raise funds for the new theatre in Stratford. He had been forced to distance himself from the tercentenary celebrations in 1864 owing to the dispute between Phelps and the organisers, and he had joined in the chorus of metropolitan scorn for Warwickshire yokels who thought they could honour the Bard. Now it was different. He could see the point of performing Shakespeare's plays in a properly designed theatre in Stratford and he was honoured to be associated with the project. The continuing opposition to the pretensions of Stratford on the part of the London media was perhaps best summed up by *The World*, which, in a long and bilious account of the opening festival, described 'the idea of erecting a theatre capable of holding one thousand people [actually 700] in a tiny Warwickshire town' as 'so plainly preposterous that only a mind devoid of any trace of humour could have conceived it… The new theatre at Stratford-on-Avon will be given up to the rats and the moths.'

Edmund Yates, owner and editor of *The World*, regarded himself as an expert on theatrical affairs. He was the son of two highly-regarded actors and had grown up in the manager's flat over the entrance to the Adelphi Theatre, which his father ran. He had always despised Chatterton's style of management and, from its launch in 1874,

The World repeatedly belittled his efforts. Now that the man was down, it was just too tempting to give him one last kicking, and the author of *The World's* article (almost certainly Yates himself) couldn't resist a poisonous reflection on the inappropriateness of giving the response to the toast to Chatterton:

> A theatrical speculator, who, as the lessee of what he likes to call the national theatre, signalises himself by producing Mr Boucicault's disgraceful play of *Formosa*, and nonsensical tailorings by the late Mr Halliday from Shakespeare and Dickens; who boldly declares that 'Shakespeare spells bankruptcy'; and who so faithfully illustrates the truth of his remark that he winds up as a hopeless insolvent to the tune of £40,000 – such a one as this it is who is selected as the representative of the art... which Shakespeare adorned.[5]

Others were more generous in their response to Chatterton's plight. On 23 February 1880 there was another benefit performance at Covent Garden. A packed house saw Henry Irving and Ellen Terry in the fourth act of *The Merchant of Venice*, Barry Sullivan and Mrs Hermann Vezin in the screen scene from *The School for Scandal*, and the trial scene from a stage version of *Pickwick Papers* with the popular comic actor J. L. Toole as Sergeant Buzfuz.[6]

Towards the end of the year, the Gatti brothers came to Chatterton's rescue once again, hiring him to produce their next pantomime, *Valentine and Orson*, at Covent Garden. He behaved as if he was back at Drury Lane, engaging John Cormack as choreographer and Beverley for the sets. (Beverley was available because he tore up his exclusive contract with Drury Lane when Augustus Harris took over. He couldn't take the bumptious young tyro seriously.)[7] More surprisingly, he hired the Vokes family who had closed his last Drury Lane pantomime by refusing to take half-pay. They had been in Augustus Harris's first Drury Lane pantomime the year before, but Harris then decided to rid himself of what he described as their 'tyranny'.[8] Why Chatterton decided to subject himself to this tyranny again is a mystery, unless he was so terrified of failure that he wanted to use the same formula that had worked at Drury Lane for so many years.

Another Chatterton trademark that travelled with him to Bow Street was the combative use of the classified columns. One bewildering outburst informed readers of *The Times* that: 'The Directors deprecate all comparisons between this *chef d'oeuvre* and other Christmas productions, their aim having been to delight and amuse the public, and not, by the sumptuousness with which they have mounted and produced their pantomime, to crush or discourage the efforts of would-be rivals, who offer them in so many ways the flattery of imitation.' This was followed by a separate advertisement consisting of the gnomic observation: *Palmam qui meruit ferat* ('Let he who has earned the palm bear it', but not translated in the advertisement). A further advertisement contained a puff for the pantomime from an Italian newspaper, in Italian.[9] The Gatti brothers would have understood it, but they must have been wondering about the way in which Chatterton was spending their money.

Valentine and Orson closed early on 19 February. Officially this was because the theatre was required for the preparation of the Italian opera, but the opera didn't open until 14 April. Chatterton blamed the failure of the show on the heavy snow which caused 'half a dozen West End theatres [to be] closed at a moment's notice in consequence of the streets being impassable'.[10] In fact, no other theatres closed and the Drury Lane pantomime, *Mother Goose*, ran until 12 March.

Chatterton had failed publicly and noisily, thanks to his aggressive advertising, and he had let his two staunchest supporters down. Unforgivably, he then turned on the Gattis in a row over his benefit. Presumably he had been promised a benefit at the end of the season, but as the show closed early, no doubt with losses, there was no benefit. Chatterton's graceless behaviour shows him in his worst light. He regretted it later.[11]

In fact, he had just been given yet another huge and prestigious benefit by the profession at the Lyceum, made available by Henry Irving, on 17 February 1881. Irving and Ellen Terry appeared in the first act of *Richard III*; Edwin Booth appeared in the fourth act of *Richelieu*; J. L. Toole did *The Spitalfields Weaver* and John Hollingshead sent his Gaiety company in *The Forty Thieves*. The highlight was, for the second year running, the trial scene from *Pickwick Papers* in which the jury comprised some familiar faces: Charles Lamb Kenney, William Beverley, and playwrights Leopold Lewis, H. J. Byron and F. C. Burnand.

Chatterton had now been the recipient of what were known as 'monster benefits' from the profession for the last four years. No one else was treated so well, but there was a feeling that Chatterton was entitled to special consideration in respect of his efforts to run Drury Lane as the National Theatre. Raising between £500 and £1,000 each (between £60,000 and £120,000 today), these benefits represented a solid source of income for Chatterton that would have enabled him to live in reasonable comfort. Unfortunately, it wasn't enough. Chatterton needed to be in charge of a theatre, so towards the end of 1881 he scraped together whatever he had been able to save for one last reckless throw of the dice: he took the lease of Sadler's Wells.

Chatterton announced his appearance as 'Sole Lessee and Manager' with the usual flourishes in the classified columns. He had arranged for a new border to be painted around the proscenium with medallion portraits of the Queen and the Prince of Wales to mark Her Majesty's resumed patronage of the drama. (The Queen, who refused to go to theatres after the death of Prince Albert, had been persuaded by the Prince of Wales to watch a private performance of F. C. Burnand's play *The Colonel* in the coach-house of his Scottish estate.) The familiar aggressive note then crept in: 'Mr William Beverley has been specially engaged to illustrate the scenery for the Christmas pantomime, which will be produced showing experience, delicacy and refinement as a contrast to the common-place vulgarity and daring audacity which some people indulge in.'[12]

In fact, Beverley would not design the pantomime, and it would be the newspaper advertising columns, in which Chatterton has made himself such a familiar presence, that would flag up the fatal flaw in his management: he was desperately under-capitalised from the start. After opening on 8 October with a melodrama by Leopold Lewis called *The Foundlings*, Sadler's Wells would appear in the theatre listings and classified columns for one or two nights, then disappear for a week. Performances were taking place, but Chatterton didn't have enough money to insert even basic details in the listings. For a pioneer of the use of newspaper advertising in theatre marketing, this was a bad sign.

Chatterton tried a revival of *Peep o' Day*, then a shortened version of *Amy Robsart*. This preceded the pantomime which was *The Forty Thieves*. The ballet girls representing the thieves were dressed as lawyers, which has been taken as a sign of Chatterton's disillusion with the legal profession after a busy lifetime of litigation. Against this, it should be remembered that he died in the house of his solicitor and his eldest son became a solicitor's clerk. Also, he was going to need serious legal representation very soon to keep himself out of prison.

Business for the pantomime was so bad that takings very seldom rose to £30 and were often below £10.[13] John Coleman went to see the show and described it as 'the saddest sight I have ever witnessed. An empty house, and a shabby, tawdry show which would have disgraced a respectable barn.'[14]

Chatterton had borrowed money to keep his management afloat, promising to pay the lenders £5 out of the receipts of every performance. The payments were not kept up so a receiver was appointed. He arrived at the theatre on Monday 9 January demanding immediate payment of £5 out of the night's takings but the treasurer refused to hand it over, saying that the takings for the night were only £15 9s., the actors were already on half-pay and there were pressing bills to settle. He was soon found to be telling the truth, as a man arrived from the gas company the next day to turn off the supply and bring the season to a premature close. Chatterton and his treasurer were then prosecuted for obstructing an officer of the court and threatened with imprisonment, but the judge found the action heavy-handed and threw it out.[15]

It was a lucky escape, but Chatterton's management of Sadler's Wells had already collapsed. When the bailiff arrived, demanding the keys to the building, the porter went to Chatterton in the manager's office. 'Am I to part with them, sir?' he asked. Chatterton had his head in his hands as he said: 'Yes, old man.'[16]

The Sadler's Wells débâcle was described by John Coleman as 'absolutely ruinous to his reputation',[17] and even Chatterton now had to accept that his career in theatre management was over. He set up as a teacher of elocution and acting skills, but only attracted a few clergymen and MPs as clients. He briefly tried to earn a living by giving public recitals, mainly of the novels of Charles Dickens, but his voice was too weak to be successful.[18] He suffered from chronic rheumatism and his eyesight was failing, although he was not yet fifty. Financially he was in a bad way as there were no benefits in 1882, 1883 or 1884, and in 1884 John Coleman found Chatterton living in modest rooms in the Strand. Coleman noted that his pride prevented him from living with his brother Horace, now a prosperous solicitor who would have given him a comfortable home,[19] but ignores the more obvious point that Chatterton could have been living with his wife Mary at 24 Kennington Oval, their home since moving out of The Hawthorns after the bankruptcy in 1879. Chatterton was living there until 1883, but he then moved into lodgings over a tea merchant in the Strand where he spent the rest of his days. Mrs Chatterton remained at the Oval, either alone or with her spinster daughter Mary, until the end of the century.

Coleman realised that something had to be done urgently, so he approached Augustus Harris who agreed to make Drury Lane available for a benefit on 5 March 1885. This one certainly lived up to the *soubriquet* of a 'monster benefit'. It featured the Moore & Burgess Minstrels; Wilson Barrett as the doomed boy-poet in *Chatterton* (no relation); the Adelphi company in the first act of *In The Ranks*; the Drury Lane company in a selection of scenes from the current pantomime *Aladdin*; plus songs, poems and impressions. The audience had been in their seats for five hours by the time the highlight of the show started: the ever-popular trial scene from *Pickwick*, with a celebrity jury including Stefano Gatti, with whom Chatterton had made up after their row over the missed benefit at Covent Garden, and E. L. Blanchard who had written all of his Drury Lane pantomimes. The jury foreman was Augustus Harris. The greatest novelty, however, was the appearance of Chatterton himself, for the first time ever as an actor on the boards of Drury Lane, in the character of Serjeant Buzfuz. The audience loved it. 'Mr Chatterton, whether addressing a British jury composed of authors, managers and others, or in examining, or cross-examining, the witnesses, was very distinct and emphatic and was fully entitled to the splendid fee represented by the day's receipts.' The receipts came to nearly £500.[20]

It was Chatterton's last benefit and his last public appearance. His health declined rapidly and he was reported to be seriously ill, wandering 'ghostlike round the scenes of former triumphs'.[21] Chatterton tried to organise another benefit, but this time he encountered resistance. There seemed to be a feeling that he had been given quite a lot of benefits already, and some people might have wondered what he was doing with the money, especially after the fiasco of the Sadler's Wells management. On 6 February 1886 he had dinner with John Coleman, feeling depressed and suffering from severe laryngitis. Two days later he wrote to say that he was giving up the idea of a spring benefit as he was too ill to organise it, and it would have to wait until the autumn. On 11 February his mother died, and Chatterton, who was a devoted son, was unable to attend her funeral in Brompton Cemetery two days later. A week after that, he died at the house of his solicitor Frederick Moojen in Dalston. The cause of death was given as bronchitis with carcinoma of the glands in his neck. A tracheotomy had been considered but abandoned, given his extreme frailty. He was fifty-one.

His body was removed to his wife's house in Kennington Oval, from which he was buried on Tuesday 23 February 1886 in the tomb in Brompton Cemetery that he had prepared for his parents. The tomb comprises a handsome slab of pink Italian marble, purchased by Chatterton when his father died in 1875 and when he himself was still prosperous. The marble is inscribed with the name and dates of his father, but there is no mention of his mother or of Frederick Balsir Chatterton. There was no money left to pay for cutting inscriptions.

The chief mourners at the funeral were members of Chatterton's family supported by Frederick Moojen and John Coleman. There was a group of members of the Savage Club, of which Chatterton was a member, but, as Coleman sadly noted, only half a dozen of the thousands of members of the theatrical profession to whom Chatterton had given employment over the years, and not one of his fellow managers.[22] As George Augustus Sala said after the funeral of E. T. Smith, Chatterton's predecessor at Drury Lane, no one cares much about theatre managers 'when they can take no more theatres and pay no more salaries'.[23] Towards the end of his life, Chatterton had been haunted by the fear that his failure would wipe from people's minds all recollection of his great achievements. 'I feel that I am almost forgotten already, and the knowledge is hard to bear.'[24] The fact that his remains still lie in an unmarked grave would suggest that he was right.

12

Man and Manager

The man

As a man, Chatterton's best known characteristics were his stubbornness and his volcanic temper, closely allied to his litigiousness. His temper caused him to fall out with people then pursue them through the courts. The fact that he had paid for his younger brother Horace's training as a lawyer just made this worse, as he had free legal advice always available within the family. Chatterton denied that this was the case, and pointed out that he usually won his cases, because Horace would warn him off those that looked uncertain. Nevertheless, the frequency with which Chatterton appeared in court was remarkable, and, at a time when he was pursuing three separate actions (against Dion Boucicault over the rights to *The Shaughraun*, against the actor James Williamson for breach of contract and against a rival manager for plagiarism), one journalist wondered how he found the time to run three theatres: 'and I can assure him that if my brother were a solicitor instead of a parson, the wrongs I have suffered would have cried out in a court of law long ere this'.[1] It is difficult to avoid the suspicion that Chatterton was a man who compensated for feelings of inferiority, especially with regard to his education, by seeking validation in court.

Chatterton was aware of his reputation and didn't deny the bad temper. However, he felt that people's assessment of his character changed when he fell from grace. 'My overflow of bile had been attributed to the eccentricities of genius. Now… my outbursts of temper [were due] to my ungovernable brutality. I had been a rough diamond; I was [now] an untutored savage.'[2]

In spite of the temper, Chatterton was a sentimental man and capable of great kindness. When he discovered that William Aspull, his boyhood music tutor, had fallen on hard times, he hired him as his private secretary. The post was a sinecure, as there was a clerk to do most of the work, but when Aspull became incapable of even these light duties, Chatterton took him into his own home and looked after him until his death.

Chatterton wasn't one to bear a grudge, and when the temper had cooled he was willing to shake hands and make up, as the on/off relationship with Samuel Phelps shows. Although he had to go to law to get out of the partnership with Falconer, whose drinking and incompetence cost him thousands of pounds, Chatterton did everything he could to help his former partner when he was struggling financially. He revived *Peep o' Day* three times at the Adelphi with Falconer in his original part.[3] Chatterton owned the play, so Falconer received no author's royalties but had his actor's salary. He staged Falconer's play *Eileen Oge* at the Princess's in 1871, even though it was a carbon copy of *Peep o' Day*, and in 1875 he chaired a committee to organise a benefit for Falconer. This took the form of matinee of *The Colleen Bawn* at Drury Lane with Dion Boucicault, his wife and most of the original cast, including Falconer in his original part of the wicked boatman Danny Mann. There was a lot of goodwill towards Falconer, even though his downfall resulted from his drinking, and the committee was delighted to raise over £500. When Falconer was presented with the cheque, he was silent for a moment and then blurted out: 'Sure, is this all?' He wasn't the easiest person to help.[4]

Chatterton was a family man, devoted to his parents and to his children. He had an especially close relationship with his father Edward who supported him throughout his managerial career. Edmund Yates described them as 'the Chatterton dynasty'.[5] Chatterton had great respect for his father's opinion and freely admitted that his ruinous decision to join Benjamin Webster in the management of the Adelphi and the Princess's was contrary to paternal advice. Chatterton's career began its steep downward spiral after his father's death in 1875. He adored his mother and always supported her, even when money was tight. After her death, a note was found amongst her papers:

> Mr dear Mother
> The idea of your being without money makes me unhappy, so please accept this ten-pound note, with best love, from
> Your little boy[6]

Chatterton took his duties as a father seriously. When his children were growing up, he was a prosperous man and they lived in some style. However, he impressed upon them the uncertainty of the source of his income and urged them to take their education seriously so that they would be able to support themselves in case of a change of fortune. In the last years of his life Chatterton lived apart from his wife Mary, but this was not because he was living with anyone else. He was never associated with scandal of any sort and was never known to use the casting couch, which would have been very easily available to him.

Chatterton was a devout Christian who took his children to church every Sunday or, if weather prevented that, read them the church service in his dining room. His religion was far from being a Sundays-only affair: he was prepared to lose money for his beliefs. The law requiring theatres to remain closed throughout Passion Week was rescinded in 1862 (with the exception of Good Friday) but Chatterton kept Drury Lane closed when other theatres were open. The only years when Drury Lane was open in Passion Week were those when Chatterton had sub-let the theatre.[7] After 1862 the only days in the year on which theatres in London were forbidden to open, apart from Sundays, were Ash Wednesday, Good Friday and Christmas Day. When John Hollingshead began to agitate for the abolition of Ash Wednesday closure, Chatterton opposed him. He particularly objected to Hollingshead's suggestion that actors didn't even know why they weren't working that night.[8] Chatterton wanted to heal the breach between churchgoers and theatregoers and felt that such statements were unhelpful. His very last public pronouncement was a letter to *The Times*, published on 5 October 1878, entitled 'The Church and the Stage'. 'It must not be presumed,' he insisted, 'that there does not exist on the part of a very large section of the dramatic profession a desire to co-operate with the Church in the work of kindling the sympathies and evoking the best emotions of those who come under its influence.'[9]

There was a change in Chatterton's personality towards the end of his life. John Coleman records that he was surprised, when he got to know Chatterton well in his last few months, to discover how completely different he was from his reputation. Instead of being 'strong-headed and wrong-headed, frequently ill-tempered', he 'had a heart as impressionable as that of a child, as tender as that of a woman'.[10] The actor Geneviève Ward also noted the change that came over Chatterton in adversity:

> After his fall his overbearing manner entirely vanished, and he reverted to the obsequiousness of the box office. To many who could hardly get a word from him in his prosperous days he appeared almost unduly humble.[11]

The snobbish reference to the box office is characteristic of Ward, but the change in Chatterton's manner may have had a medical cause. Although this can be no more than speculation now, Chatterton's bankruptcy may have precipitated a nervous breakdown. For a man who made it one of his proudest boasts that 'no one has ever until this year left the treasury on a Saturday with even a farthing less than was his due',[12] to see his company out of work and his suppliers out of pocket would have been a terrible thing. John Coleman described 'the breakup of his nervous system'[13] that followed his downfall, and which might explain the chaotic nature of the Sadler's Wells management in 1881/82, so uncharacteristic of the well-organised Chatterton. A breakdown would account for the slightly crazy tone of his classified advertising for both the Sadler's Wells and the Covent Garden pantomimes, as well as the inexplicable way in which he turned on the Gatti brothers, who had shown him nothing but kindness. It might also explain the separation from his wife.

The manager

Chatterton was not an actor-manager, like Samuel Phelps and Henry Irving, nor was he a playwright-manager like Edmund Falconer. Theatre management was not a means to an end but a discipline that fascinated him from the first time he made a profit by staging amateur productions in his teenage years. So what sort of a manager was he?

Edmund Yates recalled in his memoirs 'the advent of Mr Augustus Harris... after the "marvellous boy" had "perished in his pride"'.[14] The reference to the 'marvellous boy' was a facetious attempt to associate Chatterton with his famous but unrelated namesake, the forger Thomas Chatterton, who committed suicide at the age of seventeen when his 'medieval' manuscripts were exposed as fakes. Henry Wallis's painting *The Death of Chatterton* (1856) had made the boy-poet a Pre-Raphaelite icon, but there was no similarity between the two men. FBC might have been wilful and bad-tempered, but there was nothing fraudulent about him. If he had been asked which characteristics defined his management style, he would probably have said honesty and integrity. He was a man of his word, he honoured his contracts and he paid his bills on time. Chatterton was described by Henry Labouchere, the editor of *Truth*, as: 'the best type of a good business manager now directing a London theatre... He neither affects to be a fine gentleman nor a literary man. He is a manager who looks to make money out of the public, and who, as he does make it, pays his way. In private life he is a most liberal and charitable man; but in his relations to his *employés*, great and small, he is neither liberal nor illiberal, he is just.'[15]

Chatterton would have been gratified by this tribute, but had the shareholders of Drury Lane been asked to name the defining characteristic of his managerial style, they would probably have said profitability.

Chatterton lasted longer as lessee of Drury Lane than any of his predecessors. With the exception of E. T. Smith, all of these earlier lessees had been bankrupted or suffered catastrophic losses or both. There had been many years when the rent had not been paid, or not paid in full, and as Drury Lane acquired white-elephant status, the rent which the Company of Proprietors could demand fell dramatically.

Rent charged for the lease by the Drury Lane Company of Proprietors (selected years)

YEAR	LESSEE	RENT PER ANNUM
1819	Robert Elliston	£10,200
1826	Stephen Price	£10,600
1830	Captain Polehill/ Alexander Lee	£9,000
1833	Captain Polehill	£8,000
1835	Alfred Bunn	£6,500
1836	Alfred Bunn	£6,000
1839	William Hammond	£5,000
1841	William Charles Macready	£3,400
1843	Alfred Bunn	£4,000
1847	Louis Jullien	£3,500
1853	E. T. Smith	£4,000
1859	E. T. Smith	£4,500
1862	Edmund Falconer	£4,500
1866	F. B. Chatterton	£5,000
1873	F. B. Chatterton	£6,500
1878	F. B. Chatterton	£6,000
1879	Augustus Harris	£6,000
1894	The lease issued by the Duke of Bedford to the Drury Lane Company of Proprietors in 1812 expires. A new lease is issued to Augustus Harris, the tenant in occupation, and the Company of Proprietors is dissolved.	

By the time E. T. Smith took over in 1852, he was paying only forty per cent of the rent paid by the first lessees, but Chatterton took the rent on an upwards trajectory. Furthermore, the rent was for a season of 200 nights. When Chatterton's seasons ran for longer than that, which they always did when there was a summer season of Italian opera, he paid an additional £5 per night. The regular payment of these higher rental amounts meant higher dividends for the shareholders.

Dividends paid to the debenture holders of the Theatre Royal, Drury Lane

YEAR	DIVIDEND	IN 2018 VALUES	LESSEE
1852	NIL	NIL	Jullien and Gye
1853	£?	£?	E. T. Smith
1854	£3	£327	E. T. Smith
1855	£2	£212	E. T. Smith
1856	NIL	NIL	E. T. Smith
1857	£2	£222	E. T. Smith
1858	£3	£366	E. T. Smith
1859	£3 10s	£432	E. T. Smith
1860	£3	£358	E. T. Smith
1861	£3 10s	£409.24	E. T. Smith
1862	£3 15s	£448	E. T. Smith
1863	£4 15s	£586.25	E. T. Smith
1864	£6	£749	Edmund Falconer
1865	£6 6s	£777.55	Edmund Falconer
1866	£7	£818	Edmund Falconer
1867	£7 6s 8d	£807	F. B. Chatterton
1868	£7 10s	£833.10	F. B. Chatterton
1869	£8	£935	F. B. Chatterton
1870	£8 5s	£964.64	F. B. Chatterton
1871	£8 5s	£954.59	F. B. Chatterton
1872	£8 5s	£916.41	F. B. Chatterton
1873	£8 5s	£881.16	F. B. Chatterton
1874	£8 15s	£971.95	F. B. Chatterton
1875	£9 2s 6d	£1,034.28	F. B. Chatterton
1876	£11	£1,247	F. B. Chatterton
1877	£12 10s	£1,431.44	F. B. Chatterton
1878	£11 17s 6d	£1,388.50	F. B. Chatterton
1879	£7	£854	No lessee appointed
1880	£5	£591	Augustus Harris

Source: Newspaper reports of the annual meetings of the renters and proprietors of the Theatre Royal, Drury Lane plus classified advertisement announcements of the dividend. Various years. For details of sources see www.jacobtonson.com/dividends

After years of receiving only £2 or £3 per share – and sometimes nothing – renters found themselves receiving annual increases that took the payments above £10. The dividend for 1877 was the highest for over forty years.[16] Not surprisingly, there were grateful votes of thanks to the lessee at these meetings for 'the manner in which he had conducted the theatre, by which not only the property itself but the value of the renters' shares had been greatly increased'.[17] The renters were able to sell their rights of free admission each September for the coming season, and the value of these rights grew from about £1 per season under E. T. Smith to as much as £8.[18] These values fell again in Chatterton's last seasons when he didn't have the Italian opera, but it is noticeable that, even as he was losing money and heading towards bankruptcy, the dividends held steady at record levels.

Chatterton was proud of his reputation for integrity and he was proud of his business skills that increased the value of Drury Lane's shares, but it wasn't all about the money for him. He had a genuine passion for Drury Lane, its history and its traditions, and he felt keenly the responsibility of inheriting the mantle of Garrick and Sheridan. He wanted to restore Old Drury's reputation as a temple of the drama that had been become degraded throughout the nineteenth century, and especially under his predecessor E. T. Smith. Chatterton was largely self-educated, and he had to employ others to write his public pronouncements because he lacked the formal education to make those classical allusions that distinguished an educated man, but his love of what was called 'the higher drama', and especially his idol Shakespeare, was absolutely genuine. He wanted to make Drury Lane as culturally important as it had been under Garrick, when it was described as the Fourth Estate – 'King, Lords, Commons and Drury Lane playhouse'.[19] Unfortunately he was trying to do this when changes in theatrical ecology, over which he had no control, had made the task impossible.

Throughout the nineteenth century there was a growing conviction that the theatre was in a decadent state and that the country which had produced Shakespeare and the greatest corpus of dramatic literature in the world was failing to live up to its traditions. This reached a peak during the 1870s, when the novelist Henry James wrote that: 'The English stage has probably never been so bad as it is at present' and Matthew Arnold described it as 'perhaps the most contemptible in Europe'.[20]

The journalist and MP Henry Labouchere provided a sort of running commentary on the awfulness of the English stage in his weekly paper *Truth*, founded in 1877. He made a name for himself as a journalist by exposing City frauds in Edmund Yates's paper *The World*, which owed at least part of its meteoric success to these scandalous exposés. Eventually Labouchere decided that, if anyone was making money out of his nose for fraud, it should be him, so he set up his own publication. He imitated the format of *The World* in many ways, especially by having a scandalous gossip column which he called 'Entre Nous' to rival *The World's* 'What the World Says', and he also included a considerable amount of arts coverage. The dramatic critic of *Truth* wrote under the pen-name of 'Scrutator', but it soon became clear to readers that Scrutator was the editor himself. It might seem strange that the editor, who was writing the gossip column and sniffing out City frauds, would find the time to be the paper's dramatic critic as well, but Labouchere had a great interest in theatre and was full of theories about how to rescue it from its decadent state. For the first year of the paper's publication, Scrutator devoted more space to these matters than to actual reviews of shows.

Labouchere wrote about every conceivable aspect of theatre in his time: the managers, the actors, the actor-managers, the actresses set up as managers by rich lovers, the dramatists, the financial rewards for dramatists, the effect of censorship by the Lord Chamberlain. He was at pains to demonstrate the catholicity of his taste: he liked a good play, a good melodrama, a good comic opera and a good burlesque. His views were always interesting, although he sometimes allowed his personal obsessions too free a rein, as with his incessant campaign of abuse against W. S. Gilbert. Gilbert was a bully, especially towards women, and was engaged in a feud with an actress called Henrietta Hodson who, unfortunately for him, was Labouchere's mistress.

Labouchere's theories were all the more interesting because he was in a position to put them into practice: he owned the Queen's Theatre in Longacre. However, he was frank enough to tell his readers that he preferred to let his theatre to someone else who could innovate at his own risk. One of Labouchere's obsessions was what were known as 'orders' – we would say comps, or paper, meaning free seats. He recognised that managers wanted full houses, as half-empty houses create a bad atmosphere, but he believed that the system of orders had got out of hand and that fully a third of the theatre audience in London was composed of people who had scrounged their tickets. Labouchere was particularly critical of Chatterton for scattering orders 'broadcast' whenever a play was failing. He thought that it would be preferable to ban orders altogether and lower the seat prices, as it is better to have one thousand people in the pit paying one shilling than three hundred paying two shillings.[22]

In October 1877 Labouchere sublet the Queen's Theatre to Alexander Henderson who was prepared to put this theory into practice by offering 'popular prices' (pit one shilling, dress circle three shillings). With a hubris that was soon to be punished, Henderson renamed it The National Theatre and opened his management on 27 October with a melodrama called *Russia*. It was so bad that people couldn't be persuaded to sit through it at any price and it closed after four weeks, so Labouchere's theory didn't get a proper test, especially as Henderson had been desperately giving away a thousand free seats for every performance.[23] Henderson left, the name reverted to the Queen's, and Labouchere had to take over the running of the theatre, describing himself as 'An Impresario Malgré Lui'.[24] What would he put on there? Wait and see, he teased his readers. Five months later, the Queen's Theatre closed for good.

The fact that Labouchere, an intelligent and successful man with a passionate interest in the theatre, could not keep the doors of his own theatre open, had a sort of symbolic significance. There was almost universal agreement amongst those who interested themselves in the theatre that the London stage was as debased as Labouchere said, but there was no agreement about the solution to the problem, partly because there were so many possible causes. Some of these related to social and religious factors that were beyond the control of theatre managers, such as the late dinner hour which meant that middle-class families would arrive in the middle of a play, and the feeling amongst evangelical Christians that the theatres were places of temptation.

Ironically, perhaps, this supposed decadence of the drama was taking place against a background of increasing prosperity. More theatres were being built, managers made fortunes, star actors could command large sums and were increasingly accepted in 'society'. The problem lay in what was happening on the stage, dominated by girls showing their legs in burlesque, translations of the latest hits from Paris and melodrama. Labouchere was unusual amongst cultural commentators in refusing to condemn melodrama, which he described as 'a good honest English dish' and 'essentially our national form of dramatic art',[25] but most people who were seriously interested in theatre felt that we should have been able to do better than that. Chatterton advertised Drury Lane as being 'open for the performance of legitimate drama', but this begged the question of what the legitimate drama should look like for Victorian audiences. For many, it meant getting as close to Shakespeare as possible with blank-verse dramas about historical characters. There were a small number of successful plays that fitted this template and which were held up throughout the century as the pinnacles of legitimacy, such as Sheridan Knowles's *Virginius* (1820) and Bulwer Lytton's *Richelieu* (1839), but by the 1860s people were tiring of stories about Roman senators and Renaissance cardinals: they wanted to see plays about people like themselves, confronting the issues of modern life.

Marie and Squire Bancroft struck gold when they mined this seam with the plays of Tom Robertson at their tiny Prince of Wales's Theatre in Tottenham Street from 1865 onwards. These were small-scale domestic dramas of modern life which had dramatic one-word titles like *Caste* and *Society*, but which never offended against the middle-class proprieties. They were exquisitely produced, with long rehearsals, solid furniture, real crystal and tailored suits. Their popularity was such that the Bancrofts became the first managers in the West End who could charge 10*s*. for a seat in the stalls, when a stall at Drury Lane cost 7*s*.

These small-scale 'cup-and-saucer' comedies would have died from exposure on the vast stage of Drury Lane, but Chatterton didn't want to produce plays of this sort. For him, the legitimate drama meant Shakespeare, Byron, Milton and Goethe – the work of the greatest authors who had ever written for the stage. This brought him up against another major problem in the Victoria theatre, which was the shortage of good actors. It had become a truism to observe that there weren't enough actors in London who could handle blank verse to cast a Shakespeare play.

By the second half of the nineteenth century the provincial circuits of theatres, where actors had traditionally learnt their craft by playing different parts every night in different towns every week, had collapsed. The big regional theatres were, for the most part, no longer producing managements but receiving houses for the touring productions of the latest West End hits. The replacement of the old repertory system with long runs made the problem worse because actors who had been appearing in London for years might have played only half-a-dozen parts, when actors of previous generations would have played hundreds by that stage of their career.[26] The Shakespeare Memorial Theatre in Stratford-upon-Avon was originally intended to have its own acting school, but that was never a practical proposition. As one journalist pointed out, Stratford was not Bayreuth: how could actors and their teachers be persuaded to go to such a remote place? 'They would wilt… at that great distance from Drury Lane.'[27] There was no formal training school for actors until the founding of the Royal Academy of Dramatic Art in 1904, so they had somehow to learn on the job. During his eighteen-year management of Sadler's Wells, Samuel Phelps had coached many actors in the interpretation of their parts and Sadler's Wells was described by critics as a school of acting,[28] but even when Chatterton made Phelps artistic director at Drury Lane, he never had the same degree of authority he had been able to exercise in Islington. One reason was that his Sadler's Wells company contained many young and inexperienced actors, new to London, who would not object to being guided in their parts. Chatterton, on the other hand, wanted 'names' like Helen Faucit who would never have taken direction from Phelps or anyone else. Phelps played his last Shakespearean roles at Drury Lane in the 'legitimate month' following the pantomime in 1869, but by that time he was exerting little control over the rest of the company and was handing over roles to the bibulous Charles Dillon.

At the same time, Joseph Knight became dramatic critic of *The Athenaeum*, a position he would occupy for nearly forty years until his death. One of the first reviews Knight wrote in his new role was a notice of the production of *Macbeth* in which Phelps was alternating with Dillon. Knight was no admirer of Phelps – 'a hard, dry declaimer' – but Dillon was infinitely worse: 'jerky, inelegant and inexpressive... void of dignity and even of intelligence'. As for the rest of the cast: 'Actor after actor, each more incompetent than his predecessor, appears upon the stage and struts, rants, or declaims... Not one man now upon the boards of Drury Lane has shown the ability to speak blank verse.'[29]

The bad acting at Drury Lane would become a *leitmotif* of Knight's reviews. He sometimes tried to find something to say in favour of the principals, but left no doubt that the 'list of obscurities' by whom the other characters were represented were 'nameless incompetents... void of distinction... feeble when they were not offensive....' In particular, he blamed 'the failure of Shakespeare at Drury Lane [on] the fact that, while competent actors were secured for the leading characters, subordinate parts were allotted to people fitted for little more than to carry a flag in a procession... Men who do not know the rudiments of verse... are thrust upon the stage to enact characters every one of which demands high intelligence and prolonged study.'[30]

Chatterton was loyal to his actors, employing many of them for season after season, so we have to wonder why he didn't try to address the problem with some sort of training programme, such as Phelps had developed at Sadler's Wells. Perhaps, as he was not an actor himself, he felt unequipped to solve a problem that wasn't of his making, and just used spectacle to compensate. 'One cannot help being depressed,' the *Spectator* critic wrote of *King o' Scots* in 1868, 'at seeing how much is done to make a play do without acting, as if the attempt to get actors was hopeless.'[31] Geneviève Ward paid Chatterton the backhanded compliment of attributing some of the bad acting to his kind-heartedness: 'He often kept old actors on his staff out of pure kindness. "Why do you do it?" he was once asked. "Well, if I don't employ them, who will? What are they to do?"'[32] For the sake of his audiences, it might have been kinder if Chatterton had installed them as pensioners of the Royal Dramatic College in Woking.

Perhaps Chatterton's biggest problem was the fact that Drury Lane had been built at a time when the theatrical landscape looked different. For 180 years it had benefitted from the 'patent privileges' that gave Drury Lane and Covent Garden the exclusive right to put on plays. There were few other theatres operating in London, and few alternatives to going to the theatre for an evening's entertainment. After the passing of the 1843 Theatres Regulation Act, Drury Lane had to compete with the new theatres that were built, most of them seating far fewer people than its own vast auditorium. These smaller theatres could specialise, with light comedy at the Vaudeville, burlesque at the Gaiety and comic opera at the Opéra Comique, where Gilbert and Sullivan's operettas made enough money to build the Savoy Theatre for them to move into. They could create an exclusive atmosphere by targeting a particular class of patron, like the Bancrofts at the Prince of Wales's where white lace antimacassars on the armchairs in the stalls made the upper-class patrons feel as if they might well be in their own drawing-rooms.

Exclusivity wasn't an option at Drury Lane, which had been built when, as Leigh Hunt put it, 'the various classes of society felt a greater concern in the same amusements',[33] with aristocrats in the boxes, middle classes in the pit and working classes in the gallery, forming a sort of symbolic community as they watched the same play. Chatterton had to pull in 4,000 punters a night to get a full house, so he couldn't afford to be exclusive, but his problem was that the different classes no longer wanted to see the same show. The aristocrats had long since deserted plays for the opera and the working-class audience had been eaten into by the music halls. That left the middle class.

Today we are used to hearing theatre audiences described as almost exclusively middle-class, which is supposed to be a problem. One justification for public subsidy through the Arts Council has been that it allows theatres to hold their prices below a commercial level, in the hope of encouraging less well-off patrons to attend. 'Inclusion' is the buzzword for everyone involved with the arts and heritage sectors, and organisations in receipt of public funding are expected to demonstrate their efforts to attract members of low-income and ethnic minority groups. It can come as a surprise, therefore, to find that in the nineteenth century people were concerned that the middle classes *weren't* going to the theatre. The absence of what were described as the 'educated class' made life difficult for anyone who wanted to write, produce or act in serious plays that required an audience to sit and listen to the words, without talking and flirting until the next appearance of the dancing girls. 'The great want of the stage in our day is an educated public,' wrote Henry Morley, drama critic of *The Examiner*, in 1866, just as Chatterton became sole lessee of Drury Lane. In the absence of such a public, Morley feared that the fate of plays rested with loungers and louts who preferred shows that were 'all leg and no brains, in which… the actress shows plenty of thigh'.[34] Getting the educated classes back into the theatre became the holy grail for theatre managers. 'If the managers can make it a habit with that class to attend the theatre regularly instead of exceptionally,' *The Illustrated London News* told its readers in 1869, 'the good old days will come back.'[35]

This was Chatterton's aim, as he had no intention of staging burlesques in which the girls showed plenty of thigh. He needed those educated people in his theatre if his policy were to work, and in the early years he was praised for attracting them with his classical bill of fare.[36] With Samuel Phelps as his star and artistic director, he managed to keep this going for several years, but it was a high-risk strategy. He had to abandon the 'legitimate month' after the pantomime, when Phelps appeared in what were regarded as the supreme examples of 'legitimate' drama by Richard Brinsley Sheridan, George Colman, Sheridan Knowles and Bulwer Lytton, because it lost too much money.[37] Chatterton could claim, with perfect truth, that these plays had filled Drury Lane in the past, but audience expectations had changed. Edmund Yates said that Drury Lane would have been perfect for acting if every actor had a megaphone and every audience-member a telescope. The Lane was 'a great big rambling barn, where… facial play and delicate intonation are… lost'.[38]

This left Chatterton with Shakespeare, whose histories and tragedies are full of battles and pageants that can fill a large stage, and once again he was successful in the early years, with Phelps. After Phelps's departure, the Shakespeare productions became overblown, the poetry crushed by spectacle and massacred by actors who couldn't speak blank verse, turning 'what should be a national theatre into something not widely different from a circus'.[39]

However, even before the final rupture between Phelps and Chatterton in 1872, Phelps had been marginalised at Drury Lane and the original high cultural tone of Chatterton's management compromised. Commercial pressures forced him to inaugurate the series of crowd-pleasing Walter Scott adaptations and even out-and-out melodrama like *Formosa*. The populist policy allowed Henry Labouchere to mock Chatterton's 'mania' for claiming 'that Drury Lane is a national theatre, whereas it is a theatre precisely like any other theatre in the metropolis',[40] but Chatterton made one last, desperate attempt to regain the cultural high ground with his Shakespearean season of 1878/79. In an article written just six months before the opening of that calamitous final season, Henry Labouchere had warned that the reason it had become so difficult to raise standards in the theatre was that the people who deplored the condition of the stage registered their protest by staying away, instead of 'supporting those managers, who are quite ready to aid in the task, if only they are supported'.[41] Chatterton experienced the bitter truth of that, but there was one manager who did succeed in getting those armchair critics to come to his theatre and take their seats in the stalls.

In the last half of the 1870s, Henry Irving created exactly the sort of cultured, socially prestigious ambience at the Lyceum that Chatterton had wanted for Drury Lane, and this came into full flower in 1878, when Irving took over the lease of the Lyceum just as Chatterton's lesseeship at Drury Lane was collapsing. Henry Irving had been directing the artistic policy of the Lyceum since the death of Colonel Bateman in 1875, but Mrs Bateman had inherited the lease from her husband and was still determined to promote the careers of her daughters, particularly the youngest, Isabel. In 1878 Irving decided to revive *Hamlet* but he told Mrs Bateman that he must be free to choose his own cast and that he was not prepared to have Isabel as his Ophelia. The protective mother refused to agree to demoting Isabel: what would become of her if she could not pursue her career on the stage, Mrs Bateman asked? (She became a nun.) Mrs Bateman preferred to withdraw completely, allowing Irving to take over the remainder of the lease.[42] From this point on, he was in sole charge and within a few years William Archer was congratulating Irving on bringing 'the world of letters, art and fashion' into the theatre, while another critic saw 'men and women... in the Lyceum to-day who, a few years ago, would have been shocked at the thought of being seen in a theatre'.[43]

As soon as he had control of casting, Irving hired Ellen Terry as his leading lady and inaugurated one of the great stage partnerships that would make his Lyceum management legendary. They opened in *Hamlet* on 30 December 1878, when the memory of the disastrous Drury Lane *Winter's Tale* was still fresh in people's minds, and there could scarcely have been a greater contrast between Irving's method and Chatterton's. Irving was everything we expect a director to be. He had an intellectual conception of the play and he expected the actors, the set designer, the costume designer, the composer and the man in charge of the gas fittings to understand that. In contrast, Chatterton's Shakespearean productions during the 1870s were scarcely directed, as we would understand the term, at all. *Antony and Cleopatra* (1873) was produced by Chatterton and Andrew Halliday; the programme for *Richard III* (1876) made no mention of a director so presumably it was left to stage manager James Johnstone who was playing two small parts; while *The Winter's Tale* (1878) (criticised for being 'gravely deficient in intellectuality'[44]) was directed by Edward Stirling, also stage manager. Under these conditions, the stage manager's job was to get the scenery in place at the right time and make sure the actors knew where to enter and exit. Actors like James Anderson, Barry Sullivan and Charles Dillon would neither have expected nor appreciated discussions about their interpretation of parts. They would show up for rehearsals knowing what they were going to do and expecting everyone else to work around them. As Chatterton usually allowed only two weeks for rehearsals of even the biggest productions, and that was 'chiefly for horses, dogs and supers' according to Anderson, there was in any case little time to devise any coherent artistic approach.[45] Irving's method went so far beyond this that, even had Chatterton not been forced into bankruptcy, it is difficult to see how he could have continued to produce Shakespeare. The public expected something far better than his, by now, outmoded approach.

It was obvious that Henry Irving had succeeded where Chatterton had failed. A review of the 1878/79 theatre season in *The World* observed with a somewhat brutal cheerfulness that: 'If the season has shown the door to an old impresario, it has by way of compensation ushered in a new one,'[46] while *The Theatre* told its readers that:

> Mr Chatterton… will probably be remembered… chiefly by the epigram… that 'Shakespeare spelt ruin'… But, by the instrumentality of the Lyceum… the leaven of brains, and taste, and culture, has been obtained to lighten the lump of playgoers… A new audience is attracted by a new school of dramatic performance… [Irving] may aim as high as he likes now… How will he continue to satisfy those whom he has convinced of the real resuscitation of the poetic drama upon the London stage?[47]

It must have been doubly galling to Chatterton to have the unwelcome comparison illustrated by the hated epigram that was clearly going to be his epitaph. As if he needed reminding of what posterity would make of his legacy, the Christmas 1878 edition of *Truth* carried a pastiche of Dante's *Inferno* in which the theatrical characters are confined to the 'Dramatic Circle' of Hell. The managers are forced to carry sandwich boards advertising their most hated rival's productions: Chatterton is advertising the Lyceum.[48] During the last quarter of the nineteenth century, if any theatre could have been described as the National Theatre, it was Irving's Lyceum.

> Mr Irving has only to go on as he has begun to make the Lyceum Theatre a national institution, not by a vote granted by Act of Parliament, but by the consensus of opinion amongst those who take most interest in our acted drama as it is, and who have most faith in its future development.[49]

Chatterton's management of Drury Lane was a failure, and not only because it ended in bankruptcy; his vision of Drury Lane as the home of the poetic drama had been fading for years before that. 'Drury Lane has in truth so forfeited the regard of playgoers' said one critic just before the start of Chatterton's last season, 'that the once famous establishment has fallen in general estimation to the level of the Surrey, the Britannia, or the Standard' – all populist theatres in working-class areas.[50] It was a noble failure, nevertheless, and Chatterton respected noble failures, as he showed at an event that took place shortly before the collapse of his management.

One day a carriage drew up at the entrance to Drury Lane from which an elderly lady descended, wearing an old-fashioned black silk dress, bonnet and shawl. Fanny Kelly (always referred to, even after her death, as Miss Kelly) had been a star at the Lane sixty years before, appearing in Shakespeare, melodrama, comedy and opera. She was the niece of Michael Kelly, Sheridan's musical director at Drury Lane, and played Ophelia in the production of *Hamlet* that opened the new theatre in 1812. Although not beautiful, she was intelligent, talented and charming, a familiar figure in literary and artistic circles. Charles Lamb had proposed marriage to her, but she remained single, concentrating on her career and hoping to be able to raise standards in the theatre, especially with regard to the training of actors. By the time she retired from the stage in 1835 she had saved £20,000 (nearly £2.5m today) and she decided to spend this on the creation of a small but well-planned 'model' theatre, using the latest technology, in the garden behind her house in Dean Street, Soho, where she would train students for the stage and put on occasional performances. The theatre was called Kelly's Theatre but became known as the Royalty. (An office block called Royalty House stands on the site today.) The opening night in 1840 was a disaster as she had installed new and untried machinery to change the scenery which was so noisy it drowned out the actors, so the stage had to be rebuilt. The theatre continued to lose money and Fanny Kelly's health broke down. Her students left her, she ran through her savings and in 1849 the bailiffs seized the theatre. She moved to Feltham in Middlesex where she lived in such straitened circumstances that Henry Irving organised a petition to the Prime Minster for a Civil List pension.

As her ninetieth birthday approached, Miss Kelly decided that she wanted to see Drury Lane for one last time. When she arrived she found a reception committee waiting for her; the men shook hands and the ladies curtsied. Miss Kelly was still a star at Drury Lane, although many members of the company had been born after her retirement from the stage. As her biographer described it: 'When it is realised that F. B. Chatterton, that most kindly and sympathetic manager, was in control of affairs at Drury Lane, the pleasant gesture of the reception will be readily understood… but that which pleased her most was the sight of so many young people in the theatre, well cared-for and happy in their chosen profession. Perhaps, after all, her work and sacrifices had been worthwhile.'[51]

Chatterton must have been hoping the same thing, with bankruptcy looming and all of his dreams turning to dust and ashes. He would soon be joining Miss Kelly in Brompton Cemetery, but there we shall leave them, enjoying the satisfaction which comes from knowing that, whatever happens, you have done your very best. Drury Lane was their magical place, their Hundred Acre Wood with painted trees, and it frames a fitting tableau upon which to bring down the curtain on our story about a man for whom Shakespeare spelt ruin, but who kept on producing him just the same.

Epilogue

Drury Lane as the National Theatre

The novelist Henry James was born in the USA but spent most of his writing career in England. He was an Anglophile in almost every respect except that, as an ardent theatregoer, his heart lay in Paris. He believed that the French valued theatre more highly than the English and that the standard of acting and playwriting was incomparably higher in Paris than it was in London. In particular, nothing, in James's view, could approach the perfection of the Comédie Française, 'not only the most amiable but the most characteristic of French institutions'.[1] He was therefore delighted when, in the summer of 1879, while Drury Lane stood dark and tenantless, 'the children of Molière'[2] came to London to appear at the Gaiety Theatre under the auspices of John Hollingshead.

Hollingshead had conceived the idea of a London season for the most famous theatre company in the world towards the end of 1878 when an unusual set of circumstances in Paris provided the opportunity. The company was normally forbidden to leave Paris as a condition of its grant from the French government, but in 1879 there were to be building works in their theatre which would entail several months of closure. Hollingsworth negotiated for a six-week season in June and July 1879, but he found the French actors were hard bargainers. He offered them £148 per night plus two-thirds of any takings over £200. They refused to accept any share-of-the-profits deal and insisted upon £1,600 per week for six evening performances and a matinee. As the value of a full house at the Gaiety was normally £200, Hollingsworth was worried about the financial viability of such a scheme and asked Henry Irving to become joint producer with him. Irving replied that 'if the "first company in Europe" would not come to England on more moderate terms, they ought to remain at home'.[3] Hollingshead realised that the only way to make this arrangement pay was to use the business model of an opera season: high prices and subscriptions paid in advance. Orchestra stalls were to cost one guinea and pit stalls (rear stalls, normally the pit) 10s. Subscribers to the whole season would receive a fifteen per cent discount. He delayed signing the contract until he had a chance to see how the subscription offer was taken up, but the response was so encouraging (£12,000 in nineteen days) that Hollingshead decided to go ahead. The season was a great success, financially and critically, and it gave him some satisfaction to reflect that the French actors would have gained another £4,000 had they taken the profit-sharing deal.[4]

Sitting in the audience for many of those performances was the cultural commentator Matthew Arnold, and the August 1879 issue of *The Nineteenth Century* carried an article in which he reflected on the lessons that might be learnt from the success of the Comédie Française in London. Arnold's starting point was the assumption that theatre is an important part of the culture. People like going to the theatre, and will go, whether the dramatic entertainment on offer is of high or low quality. Given the formative influence of theatre on citizens, it becomes a concern of the state that they should be seeing good plays rather than bad plays. Arnold summed up this point of view in a phrase that would become the rallying cry of campaigners for a national theatre for the next century: 'The theatre is irresistible; *organise the theatre!*'[5]

But how was the theatre to be organised? The Comédie Française had been formed in the reign of Louis XIV – 'France's great century'[6] – as a state-protected and subsidised company that would present the classics of French drama to the highest possible standard. In England, we did things differently. In the 1660s Charles II awarded patents to Thomas Killigrew and Sir William Davenant, giving them the exclusive right to present plays in London – but no subsidy. The rationale for the patents was that, by eliminating competition, the two theatres operating under these patents (Drury Lane and eventually Covent Garden) would be able to put on high-quality plays without pandering to the lowest public taste. They never worked like that, and by the beginning of the nineteenth century it was notorious that neither Covent Garden nor Drury Lane, both of which had been rebuilt on a gigantic scale, was interested in, or suitable for, serious plays. In 1843 the patent privileges were abolished by Act of Parliament. Arnold admits that there were failings in the old system, but he regrets that it was replaced by no system at all. Instead of trying to think of a better way to organise the theatre, 'we gladly took refuge in our favourite doctrines of the mischief of state interference… We left the English theatre to takes its chance. Its present impotence is the result.'[7] Arnold imagines what advice the French actors might give us as they head back to Paris. 'Form a company out of the materials ready to your hand in your many good actors and actors of promise. Give them Drury Lane Theatre. Let them have a grant from your Science and Art Department.' Arnold took it as a matter of course that the state-subsidised company he was proposing would find its home in Drury Lane. As Old Drury had been called the National Theatre for as long as anyone could remember, it was the obvious site for a more formal arrangement. Only the year before, the journalist George Augustus Sala had prophesied that in twenty-five years' time (1903) Drury Lane would be: 'a National Theatre... supported and endowed by the State to an extent which shall secure the Lessee against pecuniary loss... the manager of which shall be bound... to produce in the course of every year a certain number of what are terms legitimate dramas, old and new'.[8]

Three years after its publication in *The Nineteenth Century*, Arnold's article was reprinted in book-form as one of a collection of essays, but with one small change. 'Give them Drury Lane Theatre' had become: 'Give them a theatre at the West End.'[9] The alteration would have surprised no one who followed the fortunes of London's theatres because, when Arnold was writing his article in the summer of 1879, Drury Lane's days as the National Theatre had just come to a close.

As Drury Lane stood empty throughout the spring and summer of 1879, many people wondered if it would ever open again, at least as a theatre. Chatterton was only the most recent in a long line of Drury Lane bankrupts; the theatre seemed to be jinxed, blighting the careers of anyone who took it on. One commentator said that the wonder was not that Chatterton's management had collapsed, but rather that it had lasted so long. He had certainly long since passed the record set by E. T. Smith of ten years; prior to Smith, most lessees had lasted for only a few years, or even a few weeks in the most disastrous cases. Chatterton had not pandered to the lowest level of taste, like Smith; he had done his best for the legitimate drama and the art of the stage, but where had it got him? The enormous expense and the peculiar difficulties involved in running Drury Lane had ruined him, as they had ruined his predecessors. In the opinion of this anonymous commentator, the time had come to make the vague talk about a National Theatre into a concrete reality.

> For a long time a subsidised theatre has been wanted, and if we are to have a real 'national theatre', where the performances are to be... up to a certain art standard, there can be no better time than the present for founding it. It is quite unlikely that in the face of F. B. Chatterton's ill-luck any single speculator will be found bold enough to take it [Drury Lane], and it would be a national

disgrace to allow such a time-honoured temple of the drama either to lie idle or to be put to baser uses. Now is the time, therefore, for the country to take the theatre in hand, and to give representations of the standard drama with the best available means.[10]

For the writer, these truths were self-evident: the nation needed a National Theatre; Drury Lane was the place for it; and Chatterton was the person to run it. However, there was no realistic possibility at the time of any British government agreeing to subsidise a theatre, and the Drury Lane proprietors were not inclined to wait for a change in the political climate. They needed a tenant who would pay them rent, and late in the summer they found one in the person of Augustus Harris.

Harris was determined from the start that he was not going to join the line of ruined managers of Old Drury that was threatening to stretch, like Banquo's posterity, to the crack of doom. To this end, he threw overboard all of the cultural baggage associated with National Theatre status and treated Drury Lane as a purely commercial speculation. Harris's plan was to depend on a mixture of pantomime and melodrama; Drury Lane pantomimes would be the biggest and best ever seen and the melodramas would be on a scale never before witnessed. His first production was the 1879/80 pantomime *Bluebeard*, but he had nothing to put on before that so he sub-let the theatre to the actor-manager George Rignold who wanted a London showcase for his spectacular production of *Henry V*. He had toured this extensively in the USA, Australia and New Zealand before trying it on London audiences at Drury Lane where his reception by the critics was so unfriendly that he returned to Australia for the rest of his career.

The Era congratulated Harris on opening his management with Shakespeare and hoped 'to see old Drury itself once again and flourishing with worthy fare'.[11] This hope was to be disappointed. Harris didn't mind sub-letting the theatre for what was essentially a vanity project, but he had no intention of committing financial suicide by dedicating his Drury Lane to the Swan of Avon. There would be no in-house production of a Shakespeare play at Drury Lane for more than forty years.

Henry V did what he was supposed to do: he got Harris safely to the opening of the pantomime. It was *Bluebeard*, with a script by E. L. Blanchard and yet another outing for the Vokes family, who played most of the leading roles. Harris produced it himself, as he would do every pantomime under his management, and, without being anything particularly out of the ordinary, it was well done. On the first night,

Harris appeared before the curtain at the end, in evening dress and Inverness cloak, and asked the audience: 'Well, are you satisfied?' They shouted 'Yes!' This would become a tradition of Harris's management, and as the years went by, the roars of assent from the audience got louder and louder.

Bluebeard provided Harris with the working capital he needed for his next venture, a melodrama of modern life that would define his management. While it was in preparation, he needed something to keep the doors open, so he put on a production of a comic opera called *La Fille de Madame Angot,* paid for by a man who presumably had his girlfriend in it.[12] Harris followed this by bringing in Marie Litton's company for a few weeks. Marie Litton was an actor-manager who had run the Court Theatre (now the Royal Court) in Sloane Square, then the Imperial Theatre in Westminster (where Methodist Central Hall now stands). She excelled in high comedy roles such as Lady Teazle in *The School for Scandal* and Kate Hardcastle in *She Stoops to Conquer*, but her biggest success was as Rosalind in *As You Like It.* Once again, Harris was happy to have Shakespeare at the Lane as long as he wasn't producing it.

Marie Litton's run at Drury Lane ended on 10 July 1880, leaving Harris three weeks to stage *The World*, which opened on 31 July. To describe *The World*, of which Harris was co-author, as a melodrama doesn't really sum it up. Melodramas were nothing new at Drury Lane: they had been around for the best part of a century. What was new was the professionalism and the scale of it. Harris understood that if you do something well enough, even people who would normally be sniffy about that sort of thing will come to see it. His melodramas were unlike any previous melodramas at Drury Lane: they had strong scripts and amazing spectacle. The plot of *The World* involved an explosion on a ship at sea, a scene in which the survivors cling to a raft on the billows of the ocean, and – another nascent Harris tradition – a scene in a well known London location, in this case the aquarium at Westminster. As if writing and producing weren't enough, Harris appeared as one of the villains (there were seven of them) who met a satisfying end by plunging down a lift-shaft. When he came before the curtain at the end and asked: 'Are you satisfied?' the response was thunderous.

Harris would follow this pattern of autumn melodrama followed by pantomime for his entire management, and indeed it survived his death by nearly thirty years. Those who regarded Drury Lane as a temple of the national drama realised that the cause was lost under his management, and the grumbling began. Increasingly irritated by criticism, Harris responded with an article for *The Fortnightly Review* in which he tackled claims about the National Theatre status of Drury Lane and the obligation of the manager to support them:

> The fact that Drury Lane has been known from time immemorial as the National Theatre seems to have given a section of the public a prescriptive right to interfere in its management, and even to dictate to its proprietors and lessees the bill of fare which they should provide for its gratification. This benevolent intervention has usually taken the form of a more or less imperious demand for the exclusive performance at all risks of what its patrons are pleased to designate the legitimate drama, and a vigorous attempt to declare the intrusion of all other classes of entertainment little less than the wanton desecration of a time-honoured shrine.[13]

The note of irritation that Harris felt towards dramatic theorists who expect other people to risk their money for the sake of 'the legitimate drama' is audible. Harris maintained that his successful policy of pantomime and melodrama had been devised before he even got hold of the lease, and that any deviation towards 'high art' had lost money: George Rignold's *Henry V* and Marie Litton's *As You Like It* both resulted in deficits.[14] Harris was unapologetic about taking 'the taste of those I endeavour to please' as his guiding star, and he was very clear in his own mind about what would and wouldn't work at Drury Lane. Small-scale 'cup-and-saucer' dramas were no good: Drury Lane demanded 'strong situations and striking spectacle... a performance which must be... dramatic, full of life, novelty and movement; treating, as a rule, of the age in which we live'. 'Literati and antiquarians' might pine for Shakespeare at Drury Lane, 'but the practical and prudent theatrical manager will ever learn a lesson from the eventful history of Drury Lane and carefully frame his programme in accordance with the tastes of the majority of his paying patrons and the old law of supply and demand'. Of course, if the 'literati and antiquarians' were prepared to put their hands in their pockets and offer a subsidy, Harris would take a different view – 'or perhaps they might be influential enough to secure the realisation of their hobby at the expense of the State'.[15]

Harris mentions the possibility of a state subsidy for the theatre as something almost incredible, which it was at the time. However, the essence of the growing campaign for a National Theatre was not necessarily subsidy from the state, but protection from market forces and the tyranny of the box office. Supporters argued that there should be at least one theatre where plays could be produced to a high standard without always worrying about whether or not the takings would cover the wage bill on Saturday. This could be achieved by a state subsidy from taxation, by a local government subsidy taken out of the rates or by private philanthropy. The notion had been gaining traction since the purchase of Shakespeare's birthplace for the nation in 1847, when a London publisher called Effingham Wilson proposed that preserving Shakespeare's house was all very well, but what was needed was a National Theatre in which Shakespeare's plays could be constantly performed to a high standard and at prices within the reach of all.[16] The idea was discussed intermittently by theatre professionals and theatregoers for the rest of the century, with increasing passion.

In 1876, when Samuel Phelps was appearing in John Coleman's disastrous production of *Henry V* at the Queen's Theatre, he was invited to attend a banquet being given by the Lord Mayor of London for members of the theatrical profession. Phelps was a very private man who disliked any sort of public appearance or speech-making, other than on stage and in character, so he intended to decline the invitation. Coleman persuaded him that his position in the profession entailed certain duties, and that he should be prepared to speak on behalf of his colleagues on such an occasion. Phelps agreed, and found himself responding to the Lord Mayor's toast to the drama.

He spoke of his eighteen-year management of Sadler's Wells, spent principally on producing the works of Shakespeare, which had not made him rich, but had at least covered its costs and supported him whilst raising a large family. He spoke of the power of Shakespeare's words and their effect upon people's minds. He spoke of the letters he had received from people who dated the start of their education from the first time they heard Shakespeare's words at this modest theatre in Islington. 'Well, if that could be done by me as a humble individual, why could it not be done by the government of this country? Why could not a subsidised theatre, upon a moderate scale of expense, be added to the late educational scheme, by which children are forced somehow or other into school?'[17] Phelps said that if any member of parliament were willing to take up the cause, he would willingly devote the rest of his life to working for it.

No member of parliament came forward, and twenty-five years later John Coleman was appealing to the London County Council.[18] Coleman, who had a somewhat fanciful view of his own standing in the profession, claimed that the role of advocate for a National Theatre had passed from Macready to Phelps and from Phelps to himself.[19] He argued that the patent houses had been, nominally at least, the home of the 'higher drama', but since the abolition of the patents in 1843: 'Covent Garden has been turned into an Italian opera-house; whilst at Drury Lane the national drama has ceased to exist ever since the retirement of Chatterton'.[20] Coleman admitted that there had been a great improvement in the standard of theatre buildings in the previous twenty years, but 'the theatre of the future, the National Theatre, has yet to be built'.[21] He then went into some detail about the building required for the theatre of the future. It should be a new structure of some architectural magnificence with spacious foyers, dressing rooms and offices, serving 'three complete stages, fully equipped with every modern scenic appliance'.[22] The building would cost £150,000, the site £50,000, and there should be a subsidy of £15,000 per year. Coleman thought it could all be paid for by one-fifth of a penny on the London rates.[23]

Coleman's article for *The Nineteenth Century* became the final chapter of his autobiography, published in May 1904. 'In the name of my dead masters and comrades,' he told his readers, 'in the name of my living brothers and sisters… I appeal to you… to remember the noble saying of the wise Greeks, "Take care of the beautiful – the useful will take care of itself".'[24] The appeal gained a certain poignancy from the fact that Coleman had left the ranks of his living brothers and sisters and joined those of his dead masters the month before the book was published, leaving others to carry the battle forward.

Later in that year, William Archer and Harley Granville Barker published *Scheme and Estimates for a National Theatre*, which is usually taken as the foundational document of the movement that eventually resulted in the opening of the purpose-built National Theatre on the South Bank in 1976. Archer and Granville Barker went into great detail about the sort of theatre they envisaged, in terms of what it would contain and how it would operate. They discussed the governance, staffing, casting, wages, repertoire and finances, and they made it clear that they wanted a new building. They didn't follow Coleman in requiring more than one auditorium, although in 1922 Granville Barker would publish a revised proposal called *The Exemplary Theatre* requiring two. An architectural competition was launched for a National Theatre with a large auditorium to seat 1,800 and a smaller one for 600.[25]

Even at this late stage, there was still one champion of the idea of making Drury Lane the National Theatre. In 1924 Basil Dean was appointed as joint managing director of Drury Lane. In reality he was what we would describe as artistic director, responsible for the productions, but he had no real power as he reported to a board dominated by the forceful figure of Sir Alfred Butt, a powerful impresario with interests in many theatres and music halls. At the time, Drury Lane was regarded as a dinosaur that had somehow survived the Ice Age: everything exciting in theatre was happening at smaller, newer venues. However, Dean was aware of the Lane's great historical legacy and was tempted by the opportunity to make it, once again, the home of great drama 'by presenting some of our leading actors in Shakespeare and the English classics'.[26] He planned an 'original practices' production of *The School for Scandal*; a big drama about the French Revolution by Hilaire Belloc; and a spectacular *Midsummer Night's Dream* with Mendelssohn's score. Unfortunately he failed to realise that Alfred Butt had no intention of risking shareholders' dividends on anything other than sure-fire commercial hits. Relations between the two men deteriorated until Butt told Dean that he could put on his *Dream* as long as he wrote his letter of resignation first.

When *A Midsummer Night's Dream* opened on Boxing Day 1924, it was an historic occasion, as it was the first in-house Shakespearean production since Chatterton's disastrous *Winter's Tale* of 1878. The production looked magnificent and had a strong cast with Edith Evans, Athene Seyler and Gwen Frangçon-Davies. There was the Mendelssohn music, ballets by Fokine and a splendid final effect as the walls and columns of Theseus's palace became transparent to reveal a tableau of the fairies, hoisted aloft on the stage's largest hydraulic lift. It was well received by the critics and public alike, but the American musical *Rose Marie* had already been booked to follow it into Drury Lane in March 1925. *Rose Marie* would be the first of a long line of American musicals to occupy the Lane in the years ahead, and Drury Lane has been the home of musical theatre ever since.

As late as 1956, Basil Dean still believed that Drury Lane would make the ideal National Theatre, and that the whole National Theatre movement, which had failed to build its theatre after more than half a century, had been bedevilled by 'cranks and enthusiasts', most notably George Bernard Shaw who 'never understood the theatre in the professional sense'.[27] As an experienced actor, playwright, director and producer, Dean believed that Drury Lane was just as well qualified to be the state-subsided theatre as Covent Garden was to be the state-subsidised opera house.

Dean argued that, now that state aid for the arts had been accepted in principle with the founding of the Arts Council in 1946, this must be extended to the theatre. (Maynard Keynes, first chairman of the Arts Council, kept funding closely focused on his own particular interests of opera and ballet.) 'The cornerstone of state aid for the drama should be a National Theatre,' Dean wrote, and where better than at Drury Lane? He called upon the government to do for Drury Lane what it had already done for the Royal Opera House: set up a trust to acquire the freehold of the theatre. Alternatively, if that were regarded as going too far, the Old Vic and Stratford-upon-Avon companies could be presented there from time to time under the auspices of the trust. 'One immediate effect of the scheme... would be to break the stranglehold of American musical comedy over what is still regarded as the national shrine of our theatrical tradition.'[28]

Dean tells of a meeting he had with a member of the Royal Academy committee set up by Sir Edwin Lutyens to report on the future development of London. Dean was asked what he would recommend for the Covent Garden area and he suggested what we would now call a cultural hub, based on the Royal Opera House and Drury Lane. He wanted to clear away the market, introduce smart restaurants and academies for drama, opera and ballet, with a central booking hall. He envisaged a new approach to Drury Lane from Waterloo Bridge: a sweeping avenue adorned with fountains and statuary leading to the National Theatre. Dean was delighted to learn that Lutyens had incorporated his ideas in the grand plan.[29]

Many of Dean's wishes have come true: the market has gone and Covent Garden is a smart area of retail and restaurants, with much improved public access to the Royal Opera House through the Floral Hall. But there are no statues or fountains in front of Drury Lane because, when the National Theatre finally opened in 1963, it was on the other side of the Thames at the Old Vic.

Appendix 1

Chatterton's Drury Lane Seasons

A more detailed version of this table can be accessed on www.jacobtonson.com/seasons

	1862/63	1863/64	1864/65	1865/66	1866/67
First night	26 December	12 September	24 September	23 September	22 September
Last night	25 April	21 May	20 May	24 March	13 April
Number of nights (excl. summer season)	103	205	194	151	169
Total performances of Shakespeare's plays as mainpieces	1	48	123	87	34
Total performances of non-Shakespeare plays as mainpieces	98	146	40	39	113
Shakespeare mainpieces as % of all nights	1%	23%	63%	58%	20%
Total performances of pantomime	75	70	98	94	87
Summer Season	NONE	NONE	NONE	NONE	*The Great City* by Andrew Halliday

	1867/68	1868/69	1869/70	1870/71	1871/72	1872/73
First night	21 September	26 September	5 August	24 September	23 September	21 September
Last night	21 March	24 April	2 April	1 April	25 March	31 March
Number of nights (excl. summer season)	152	170	201	157	151	158
Total performances of Shakespeare's plays as mainpieces	35	25	0	1	1	2
Total performances of non-Shakespeare plays as mainpieces	100	96	157	105	99	100
Shakespeare mainpieces as % of all nights	23%	15%	0%	0.6%	0.7%	1.3%
Total performances of pantomime	73	83	72	100	94	105
Summer Season	Mapleson's Italian opera	NONE	Wood's Italian opera	Mapleson's Italian opera	Mapleson's Italian opera	Mapleson's Italian opera & *Madame Ristori*

Appendix 1: Chatterton's Drury Lane Seasons

	1873/74	1874/75	1875/76	1876/77	1877/78	1878/79
First night	20 September	29 August	4 September	23 September	22 September	28 September
Last night	2 March	13 March	4 March	11 April	6 March	3 February
Number of nights (excl. summer season)	133	162	153	157	127	101
Total performances of Shakespeare's plays as mainpieces	79	5	1	73	0	53
Total performances of non-Shakespeare plays as mainpieces	24	93	94	42	67	31
Shakespeare mainpieces as % of all nights	59%	3%	0.6%	46%	0%	51%
Total performances of pantomime	77	92	87	85	85	50
Summer Season	Mapleson's Italian opera	Mapleson's Italian opera and *Salvini*	Mapleson's Italian opera and Chatterton/Hollingshead presenting Rossi	NONE	NONE	NONE

Appendix 2

Cast of Characters

James Anderson (1811 – 1895) was an actor in Macready's legendary companies at Covent Garden (1837 – 1839) and Drury Lane (1841 – 1843). In 1849 he entered into an arrangement to take the lease of Drury Lane for six months of each year, with Louis Jullien holding the lease for the other six months and using the theatre for promenade concerts. Anderson's six months began on Boxing Day, to allow him to stage a pantomime. He opened his first season with *The Merchant of Venice* on 26 December 1849 and closed it on 4 May 1850 with *The Beggar's Opera*. His second season opened on Boxing Day 1850 with *The Winter's Tale* and closed on 24 June 1851 with *Ingomar*. At this point his management, which should have continued until 1853, collapsed with the loss of his life's savings. He was briefly imprisoned for debt. He continued to act at Drury Lane from time to time and his popularity in the USA and Australia enabled him to recover his financial position. In 1863 he took over the Surrey Theatre which burnt down in January 1865, at which point Chatterton hired him for the Drury Lane company for the rest of the year. Anderson returned to Drury Lane to play the male leads in *Antony and Cleopatra* (1873) and *Richard Coeur de Lion* (1874). At the end of the run of the latter he decided to stop acting, disillusioned with the stage in general and Drury Lane in particular.

William Roxby Beverley (1810? – 1889) was the youngest son of an actor-manager called William Beverley who had changed his name from Roxby to avoid embarrassing his family when he went into the theatre. William Beverley junior learnt his craft as a scene painter working for his father, who managed the Durham circuit of theatres. His work was seen in London at the Victoria (Old Vic) and Princess's Theatres, but his great fame began when he worked at the Lyceum Theatre under Madame Vestris and her husband Charles Mathews. He created scenery for a series of extravaganzas of which the most famous was *The Island of Jewels* (1849). He devised the transformation scene, the highpoint of Victorian pantomime splendour, in which moving canvas cloths and gauzes, together with changes in lighting, would create breath-taking visions of fairyland. In 1853 he was put in charge of the scenery for the Italian opera at Covent Garden and in 1854 he designed the pantomime for E. T. Smith at Drury Lane, beginning an association with the Lane that would last almost continuously until his death. When Augustus Harris took over Drury Lane in 1879, Beverley didn't take the young pretender seriously and resigned. When it became clear that Harris's management was a success, Beverley returned to work on the pantomimes, but only as one of a team of designers, until failing eyesight forced him to retire.

E. L. (Edward Leman) Blanchard (1820 – 1889) wrote the Drury Lane pantomimes from 1852 to 1888, as well as pantomimes for other theatres, so he sometimes had several running concurrently. He had an encyclopaedic knowledge of theatre and was much in demand to write historical articles and obituaries for the theatrical newspaper *The Era* and its annual Almanack, as well as other publications. He was chief dramatic critic of *The Daily Telegraph* from 1863 to 1878, when he handed over to his assistant Clement Scott. Blanchard looked older than his years and the fact that he knew the details of theatrical productions that had taken place before he was born made people think he was very old indeed, although he was only sixty-eight when he died. After his death Clement Scott edited his diaries which were published in a two-volume edition in 1891. Exploiting the trope, familiar since the days of Grimaldi, of the funny man who is crying inside, Scott depicted Blanchard as a tragic figure grappling with 'despair such as would have crushed the strongest of us' and his diary as 'the record of some extraordinary martyrdom'. In fact, there was nothing tragic about Blanchard's life. He had a long and successful career doing what he loved and, although he sometimes struggled financially, he managed to support himself, his mother and his improvident brother's family. He waited a long time to marry the woman he loved (she had first married someone else) but they were blissfully happy together. He may have suffered from depression, but the downbeat note of some of the diary entries could be caused by no more than exhaustion at the end of a long day when he was writing his diary in the early hours. He was a kind, gentle man who was loved and respected by all who knew him.

Dion Boucicault (1820 – 1890) was born in Dublin and educated in London at various schools including University College School where one of his fellow pupils was Charles Lamb Kenney. Kenney's father, James Kenney, was a successful playwright who was able to obtain free admission for the boys to the London theatres. When he was still only twenty, Charles Mathews and Madame Vestris produced his comedy *London Assurance* at Covent Garden, where it enjoyed great success. He began writing plays for Benjamin Webster at the Theatre Royal, Haymarket, then worked for Charles Kean during his management of the Princess's Theatre, making successful adaptations of the French plays *The Corsican Brothers* (1852) and *Louis XI* (1855). To Kean's fury, he married Agnes Robertson, a young actress in the company towards whom Kean acted as guardian. They went to America where Boucicault wrote *The Colleen Bawn* which opened in New York in March 1860, giving Boucicault his greatest success so far as both playwright and actor, playing the loveable rogue Myles-na-Coppaleen. He opened the London production at the Adelphi Theatre, managed by Benjamin Webster, later in the same year and insisted on a profit-sharing arrangement with Webster. *The Colleen Bawn* became London's first 'long run', with continuous performances for ten months, bar the month when Boucicault forced Webster to close the Adelphi while he took the play to Dublin. Boucicault then demanded, in addition to profit-sharing, a royalty of one pound per act for every night one of his plays was performed. This was the first time a playwright had received royalties instead of a flat fee. In mid-1862 Boucicault broke his agreement with Webster and took a four-month sub-lease on Drury Lane where he presented *The Colleen Bawn, The Siege of Lucknow* and *The Octoroon*. His melodrama *Formosa* opened at Drury Lane in August 1869 and had the longest continuous run of any play in the theatre until then. *The Shaughraun* opened in New York in 1874 and in London at Drury Lane in 1875. He spent most of the rest of his career in America where he died. He was a ruthless and dishonourable man who fell out with everyone he worked with and even with his own family when he bigamously married a twenty-one year old actress and claimed his first marriage was invalid. He had a low opinion of his own plays, describing them as 'guano', but he transformed the position of playwrights by making it possible for them to become rich on their royalties. He was the first playwright to get away from the stereotypical Irish clown and create Irish peasant characters who were admirable and even heroic.

John Coleman (1830? – 1904) spent most of his career as an actor-manager in the provinces, taking charge of theatres in Stockport, Oldham, Sheffield, Lincoln and the Worcester/Shrewsbury/Coventry circuit. He was also a playwright whose most successful production was a spectacular adaptation of *Uncle Tom's Cabin*, revived several times. In 1876 he decided to set up as a manager in the West End and took the lease of the Queen's Theatre (now demolished) in Longacre. He co-presented there (with James Mapleson) the Italian tragedian Salvini in an attempt to repeat the triumphs of the previous year at Drury Lane, but the season failed so badly that Salvini withdrew. Coleman then produced a spectacular version of *Henry V*, starring himself, on which he lost his life's savings. In 1896, when Augustus Harris died, Coleman tried to get the lease of Drury Lane. He hurriedly mounted a melodrama there called *The Duchess of Coolgardie*, under the impression that he was a favoured candidate for the lease, but it was awarded to Arthur Collins, who was stage-managing the show. He wrote several books, including biographies of Samuel Phelps (1886) and Charles Reade (1903), as well as his collection of brief lives *Players and Playwrights I Have Known* (1888) which included Chatterton among its subjects. Coleman's autobiography *Fifty Years of an Actor's Life* (1904) was published a month after his death. He had an exaggerated view of his own importance in the profession, and the theatre historian J. C. Trewin described him as being 'like every old-actor joke, collected, indexed and in a leather binding', but Coleman was a kind man with a genuine passion for the theatre. His memoirs provide a fascinating last glimpse of the world of the old provincial circuits which had disappeared by the time he was writing about them.

Edmund Falconer (Edmund O' Rourke) (1814 – 1879) was born in Dublin and spent many years acting on English provincial theatre circuits. In 1856 he was hired by Charles Dillon, who had taken over the Lyceum Theatre, where Falconer's play *The Cagot* was produced. His next play, *Extremes*, was in rehearsal when Dillon's management collapsed in March 1858. Chatterton, who was Dillon's acting manager, went into partnership with Falconer to take over the Lyceum and mount the production themselves. *Extremes* opened in August and ran until October when the theatre was booked for a season of promenade concerts, but Falconer and Chatterton were back at the Lyceum on Boxing Day for another season in management. They staged a pantomime that failed and they struggled to pay the wages. Falconer found other partners and Chatterton withdrew. After further failures, Falconer sold the remainder of his lease. He wrote the libretti for two operas composed by Michael Balfe (*The Rose of Castille* [1857] and *Satanella* [1858]) and for *Victorine*, composed by Alfred Mellon, in 1859. In September 1860 Falconer appeared as the villainous boatman Danny Mann in the original London production of Dion Boucicault's *The Colleen Bawn*. In August 1861 Falconer and Chatterton again went into partnership, taking the Lyceum to produce Falconer's new play *Woman or Love Against the World*. This was a failure but Falconer followed it with *Peep o' Day* which became the first play in London to run continuously for a year. It generated profits of £16,000 (over £1.9m in modern terms), of which Chatterton should have received one-third, but Falconer spent the money on his own lavish lifestyle and began to drink heavily. The lease on the Lyceum expired in December 1862 and was not renewed. Falconer and Chatterton took on the lease of Drury Lane from E. T. Smith and Chatterton agreed to allow the money owed to him by Falconer to be treated as his investment in the partnership. Falconer became lessee and Chatterton was acting manager, still entitled to one-third of the profits. Falconer rapidly descended into full-blown alcoholism and became a liability, leaving Chatterton to run Drury Lane unaided. In February 1866 Falconer was imprisoned for debt and declared bankrupt, so his lease fell in. Chatterton took on the lease together with £10,000 of debts incurred by Falconer. In November 1866 Falconer took Her Majesty's Theatre for his new play *Oonagh*. This ran for ten performances, at the end of which Falconer fled to the USA to escape his creditors. In 1870 Falconer returned to London and took the lease of the Lyceum Theatre to present his new play *Innisfallen*. It ran for two weeks. In October 1870 Falconer had a stroke and was not expected to survive. He recovered and wrote *Eileen Oge* which was a reworking of *Peep o' Day* with different names for the characters. Chatterton staged *Eileen Oge* at the Princess's Theatre where it had a successful run.

Augustus Harris (1852 – 1896) was the son of another Augustus Harris who was involved with the management of Covent Garden for twenty-seven years. Augustus Harris junior made his debut as an actor and then became stage manager for James Mapleson's opera company, including the Drury Lane summer seasons. Harris harboured managerial ambitions and, when Chatterton's lease on Drury Lane came up for renewal in 1878, he applied to the Company of Proprietors. The proprietors doubted that he had the financial backing, so they offered a new five-year lease to Chatterton. In 1879 Harris renewed his application following Chatterton's bankruptcy and this time he was successful. The proprietors granted a lease to Harris, even though he was still only twenty-seven years old and had no experience of running a theatre, if he could pay £1,000 down for the lease. Harris estimated that he needed another £2,000 on top of that to mount his first season, but his assets came to only £3 15s. He borrowed the money from several people, most of it from the property developer William Edgecombe Rendle, whose daughter he married. Harris had no intention of running Drury Lane as the National Theatre and was only interested in staging shows the public would pay to see. He established a routine of gigantic autumn melodramas followed by even more gigantic pantomimes, followed by a few weeks of 'high culture' (which had to be subsidised out of the profits of the pantomime) to fill the time until the close of the season. His policy was successful and, for the first time since the days of David Garrick, Drury Lane consistently generated large profits. In 1888 he took over Covent Garden with the support of a wealthy group of opera-lovers and made it a world-class opera house. He became sheriff of London and was knighted. In 1894 the lease issued by the Duke of Bedford in 1812 to the Drury Lane Company of Proprietors fell in and the Duke issued a new lease to Augustus Harris, as the tenant in residence. Harris died in 1896 from a combination of exhaustion, diabetes and cancer. The drinking fountain erected against the front wall of the theatre in his memory is still there.

Charles Lamb Kenney (1821 – 1881) was the son of Irish playwright James Kenney. He became an author and playwright, but most of his works were translations, usually from French. He translated the libretto of Offenbach's *La Grande-Duchesse de Gérolstein* for a production at Covent Garden in 1867. This was the first full-scale production in London of one of Offenbach's opera bouffes and its success led to commissions for Kenney to translate the same composer's *Barbe-Bleue*, *La Princesse de Trébizond* and *La Belle Hélène*. Kenney first worked with Chatterton in 1859 when Chatterton was managing the St James's Theatre. When Chatterton moved to Drury Lane he employed

Kenney as his literary advisor, although 'publicist' would have been a more accurate term. Kenney was Chatterton's favourite ghost-writer, producing programme notes, prospectuses, letters to the editor and any other print vehicle Chatterton wanted to deploy. Kenney remained with Chatterton until the very end of his Drury Lane management, having developed the knack of reproducing in prose his employer's mixture of high principles and extreme combativeness. Kenney's style was full of flowery circumlocutions and classical allusions that must have represented the way in which Chatterton wished to present himself to the public. Kenney wrote several dramatic pieces that were performed at theatres under Chatterton's management, including the English translation of the operetta *Six demoiselles à marier* by Léo Delibes that appeared as *Wanted Husbands for Six* at Drury Lane in 1867, and the musical farce *Autumn Manoeuvres* at the Adelphi in 1871. Kenney had a reputation for idleness and struggled to support his family, particularly as his health declined. He was popular in literary circles but he failed to live up to his early promise.

William Charles Macready (1793 – 1873) was regarded as the greatest exponent of Shakespeare of his generation and the leader of the profession, although he despised his profession and longed to be free of it. His father was an actor-manager who was sufficiently prosperous at one point to send his son to Harrow where he was to be prepared for a career in the church or the law. However, at the age of fifteen Macready was withdrawn from Harrow as his father's financial situation deteriorated. He had to save his father's company from ruin and for several years he played the juvenile leads until he struck out on his own. He joined the Drury Lane company in 1823 where he appeared intermittently for the next thirteen years. When Alfred Bunn was running Drury Lane, relations between the lessee and his leading tragedian were difficult as Macready regarded Bunn as a vulgarian. Things reached a climax when Macready was made to appear in the first three acts only of *Richard III*, which was curtailed to make way for a musical extravaganza. Returning to his dressing room, Macready passed the open door of Bunn's office and saw his hated manager engaged on the accounts. Macready attacked him and a struggle ensued. Bunn brought an action for assault, which he won, and Macready departed for Covent Garden. He took on the lease of Covent Garden in 1837 and attempted to run it as a national theatre, persuading many of the leading actors of the day to join him at less than their normal salaries. At the end of two years he gave up the lease, saying that it was costing him too much, even though his management had been successful artistically. In 1841 he took on the lease of Drury Lane where he spent another two years. His problems here were more severe as Drury Lane was in poor condition, and he claimed to have lost a great deal of money. These two periods of management acquired legendary status and fed into the debate about the need for a real national theatre. Although it is impossible to quantify Macready's losses at Covent Garden and Drury Lane, it is certain that he was able to make much more money by starring in other people's productions. He concentrated on earning enough money to achieve his highest goal as an actor, which was to leave the stage and live as a gentleman. His farewell performance was given at Drury Lane on 26 February 1851. He retired to Sherborne, then Cheltenham, where he died in 1873. A two-volume edition of his diaries appeared in 1875/76, edited by Sir William Pollock. Although this was a labour of love on Pollock's part, it did lasting damage to Macready's reputation by revealing his contempt for his own profession and many of the people he had worked with.

John Oxenford (1812 – 1877) joined the staff of *The Times* in 1839, replacing Michael Nugent as dramatic critic, a position he retained until his retirement in 1875. The stature of *The Times*, combined with his long tenure, made him the most influential dramatic critic, and managers always provided him with his own box on first nights. He had a penetrating mind and an encyclopaedic knowledge of dramatic literature, but John Thadeus Delane, legendary editor of *The Times*, told him to avoid the sort of criticism that would lead to letters of complaint, as he did not want space in *The Times* to be occupied by a subject that was of little interest to most readers. As a result, Oxenford's reviews were bland and often amounted to little more than a summary of the plot. He justified this blandness by saying that his tender-heartedness would not allow anyone mentioned in his reviews to go home to find his wife and children in tears. However his impartiality was also compromised by the fact that he was a prolific author and translator of farces, melodramas, libretti and ballets that he sold to the managers who provided him with his first-night box. He further compromised his position by accepting 'retainers' from managers to read plays in advance and suggest improvements, thus virtually guaranteeing a good review in *The Times*. He was a scholar and a linguist with a profound grasp of German literature and thought. His work on Schopenhauer established the philosopher's reputation, not only in Britain but in Germany, while his translation of Goethe's *Autobiography* is still in print. He had a keen awareness of the cultural significance of Drury Lane and supported Chatterton's attempts to restore the theatre to its position as the home of the poetic or 'legitimate' drama. After Oxenford's death, a committee was formed to erect a statue of him in Drury Lane but this came to nothing, although he was commemorated by a stained-glass window in Southwark's Roman Catholic Cathedral, Oxenford having become a Catholic two years before his death. His farce *A Day Well Spent* eventually became *Hello Dolly!*

Samuel Phelps (1804 – 1878) made his London debut as Shylock at the Haymarket Theatre in August 1837 and then joined Macready's company at Covent Garden from 1837 to 1839. His performances were highly acclaimed, with the result that Macready, who saw him as a rival, confined him to secondary roles. In spite of this, Phelps agreed to be part of Macready's company once again at Drury Lane between 1841 and 1843. The Theatres Regulation Act of 1843 abolished the 'patent privileges' that gave Covent Garden and Drury Lane the exclusive right to perform plays in London, and Phelps took advantage of the new freedom by entering into a triumvirate with Thomas Greenwood, the lessee of Sadler's Wells Theatre in Islington, and the actor Mary Amelia Warner, to run Sadler's Wells as a 'legitimate' theatre. This inaugurated an eighteen-year regime that remains one of the highlights of the history of the London stage. Phelps staged all of Shakespeare's plays bar six, including rarely performed works like *Pericles* and *Love's Labour's Lost*, as well as plays by Shakespeare's contemporaries and modern plays. Phelps has a good claim to being the first 'director', as we would understand the term. Unlike the actor-managers who were only interested in shining themselves and surrounded themselves with nonentities, Phelps believed that everything in the production should serve the needs of the play. He wanted all of the actors to be good and he trained them in the delivery of their parts, so Sadler's Wells became effectively an acting school. He was prepared to accept small parts, and he rescued *A Midsummer Night's Dream* from years of neglect by playing Bottom, deemed too small a part by other actor-managers, and making it one of his greatest successes. Following the retirement of Greenwood in 1860, Phelps found the strain of being artistic director and business manager too much, so the Sadler's Wells management came to an end in 1862. Phelps accepted a position in the company set up by the French actor Charles Fechter at the Lyceum but soon realised that Fechter was playing the old actor-manager's trick of hiring his greatest rival to keep him off the stage. Phelps left Fechter and became effectively artistic director at Drury Lane just as Chatterton was managing to wrest control from Edmund Falconer. The first two seasons at Drury Lane were a triumph for Phelps and he continued successfully to manage Chatterton's programme of 'legitimacy' until 1868 when *King o' Scots* (in which Phelps played two parts) signalled a change of artistic direction. Sidelined by the programme of historical spectaculars and melodramas that Chatterton introduced, Phelps made his last appearance at Drury Lane in *Rebecca*, the 1871 autumn drama. In 1872 he appeared in a series of 'legitimate' plays for Chatterton at the Princess's Theatre but had to withdraw for health reasons. He fell out with Chatterton and never worked for him again. He eventually made up his feud with Chatterton and agreed to appear in *The Winter's Tale* in 1878, followed by a series of farewell performances, but his health deteriorated and he died without re-appearing at the Lane.

Clement Scott (1841 - 1904) was dramatic critic of *The Sunday Times* until protests from actors and managers about his caustic style led to his departure. He then became dramatic critic of *The Weekly Dispatch* and *The London Figaro*, from both of which Chatterton tried to get him sacked for writing hostile reviews. He joined the team of critics at *The Daily Telegraph* in 1871 and in 1878 he took over from E. L. Blanchard as chief dramatic critic. He inherited John Oxenford's mantle as the leader of *corps dramatique*, always granted his own box on first nights. He championed the managements of Henry Irving and of Squire and Marie Bancroft, believing that they were raising standards in the theatre both artistically and morally. He advocated what he called Free Trade in the theatre, by which he meant freedom for the critic to criticise and for the manager to put on whatever sort of entertainment he wanted, provided it was decent. However his claims to independence were undermined by his close relationships with Irving, the Bancrofts and other managers. He refused to accept outright bribes, but he adapted plays for the Bancrofts. His reviews were popular because they were so readable: he either loved or loathed a production. He saw himself as the defender of Victorian values and detested trends towards realism, especially in the plays of Ibsen which he compared to an open sewer. He resigned from *The Daily Telegraph* in 1898 following hostile reaction to the publication of an interview in which he had implied that women on the stage were immoral. His theatrical autobiography, *The Drama of Yesterday and Today*, published in 1899, contained a number of hostile references to Chatterton, thirteen years after his death.

E. T. (Edward Tyrrel) Smith (1804 – 1877) was, at different times, a policeman, restaurateur, auctioneer, picture-dealer, newspaper proprietor, pub landlord and bill discounter. He took the lease of the Marylebone Theatre in 1850 for two years, then became lessee of the Theatre Royal, Drury Lane in 1852. After a difficult start, he made the theatre profitable for the first time in many years with a mixture of opera and circuses and managed both to pay his rent and to generate dividends for shareholders. He saved the theatre from demolition, which was being recommended to the Duke of Bedford, its owner, by his London agent. He remained lessee of Drury Lane for ten years. During that time he took over the Royal Panopticon in Leicester Square and rebuilt it as the Alhambra Music Hall. He took over Her Majesty's Theatre in 1860 but had to beat a hasty retreat when he couldn't pay the rent. He ran Cremorne Gardens from 1861 to 1869; Astley's Theatre from 1863 to 1864; and the Lyceum Theatre from 1867 to 1869. There were numerous other theatre, music hall and catering ventures. Although some of his projects lost money, his backers knew that he was honest and didn't resent the failures. He was well liked and respected, especially for his charitable work.

Benjamin Webster (1798 – 1882) was born into a theatrical family and went on the stage at an early age. In 1837 he took over the Haymarket Theatre where he built on the theatre's reputation as the house for good productions of good plays, especially comedies. He brought together a strong company by paying his actors well and he was similarly generous towards playwrights. When he took over the Haymarket it was only allowed to open in the summer when the patent houses of Covent Garden and Drury Lane were closed, but he celebrated the passing of the 1843 Theatres Regulation Act, which abolished the 'patent privileges', with a season that ran continuously for seventeen months. In 1844 Webster acquired the lease of the Adelphi Theatre and installed his mistress Madame Céleste to run it. In 1852 Webster acquired the freehold of the building and in 1853 sold the lease of the Haymarket in order to concentrate on running the Adelphi with Madame Céleste. There was a falling-out between Webster and Céleste, who left to take over the Lyceum from Edmund Falconer. In 1860, Webster, in need of a hit, entered into an arrangement with Dion Boucicault to present the London premiere of *The Colleen Bawn* that left him as effectively the front-of-house manager of his own theatre. The relationship between Webster and Boucicault deteriorated until Webster banned Boucicault from the Adelphi and Boucicault took a four-month lease on Drury Lane to continue presenting his plays. In 1869 Webster took on the lease of the Princess's Theatre in Oxford Street. He struggled to run the two theatres and it was rumoured that he was on the verge of bankruptcy. Chatterton entered into a partnership with him, paying off Webster's debts and planning to run the Adelphi and the Princess's together with Drury Lane. There was friction between the two men and Chatterton persuaded Webster to sell him the leases of both the Princess's and the Adelphi and withdraw from management. In 1878 Webster took legal action against Chatterton, claiming that he had been misled over the terms of their agreement. The judge threw out the case, but Webster brought it to court again in 1879. Once again, it was thrown out. Webster was probably suffering from dementia by this stage. He died three years later.

Bibliography

Shirley Allen (1971) *Samuel Phelps and the Sadler's Wells Theatre*, Middleton, Conn: Wesleyan University Press

James Anderson (1902) *An Actor's Life*, London: The Walter Scott Publishing Co Ltd

Matthew Arnold (1879) *Mixed Essays*, London: Smith Elder

Matthew Arnold (1882) *Irish Essays and Others*, London: Smith, Elder and Co, 1882. 'The French Play in London' first appeared in *The Nineteenth Century*, XXX, August 1879, 228-243.

H. Barton Baker (1904 reprinted 1969) *History of the London Stage and its Famous Players*, 1576-1903, New York: Benjamin Bloom

Squire and Marie Bancroft (1909) *The Bancrofts: Recollections of Sixty Years*, London: John Murray

John and Michael Banim (1825) *Tales by the O'Hara Family*, London: W. Simpkin and R. Marshall, 3 vols

J. H. Barnes (1914) *Forty Years on the Stage: Others (Principally) and Myself*, London: Chapman and Hall)

Daniel Barrett, (November 1988) '"Shakespeare spelt ruin and Byron bankruptcy": Shakespeare at Chatterton's Drury Lane', *Theatre Survey*, 29:2, 155-74

Edward Leman Blanchard (1891) *The Life and Reminiscences of E. L. Blanchard*, Clement Scott & Cecil Howard (eds.) London: Hutchinson & Co., 2 vols

J. B. Booth (1943) *The Days We Knew*, London: T. Werner Laurie

Michael R. Booth (1981) *Victorian Spectacular Theatre 1850 – 1910*, London: Routledge & Kegan Paul

Michael R. Booth (1995) *Theatre in the Victorian Age*, Cambridge: Cambridge University Press

Percy Bradshaw (1958) *Brother Savages and Guests: A History of the Savage Club 1857 – 1957*, London: W. H. Allen

Alfred Bunn (1840) *The Stage: Both Before and Behind the Curtain, From 'Observations Taken on the Spot'*, 2 vols, Philadelphia: Lea and Blanchard

Lord Byron (1835-1836) *The Works of Lord Byron with his Letters and Journals and his Life by Thomas Moore Esq*, London: John Murray, 17 vols

Byron's Letters and Journals (1973-1982) (ed. Leslie A. Marchand) London: John Murray, 12 vols

Marvin Carlson (1985) *The Italian Shakespearians: Performances by Ristori, Salvini and Rossi in England and America*, Washington: Folger Books

Carol J. Carlyle (2000) *Helen Faucit: Fire and Ice on the Victorian Stage*, London: The Society for Theatre Research

Carol J. Carlisle (2004) 'Faucit, Helen [*real name* Helena Faucit Saville or Savill; *married name* Helena Martin, Lady Martin] (1814–1898)', *Oxford Dictionary of National Biography*, Oxford University Press

John William Cole (1859) *The Life and Theatrical Times of Charles Kean, FSA, including a summary of the English stage for the last fifty years and a detailed account of the management of the Princess's Theatre from 1850 to 1859*, London: Richard Bentley, 2 vols

John Coleman (assisted by Edward Coleman) (1886) *Memoirs of Samuel Phelps*, London: Remington and Co.

John Coleman (1888) *Players and Playwrights I Have Known*, London: Chatto & Windus, 2 vols

John Coleman (1904) *Fifty Years of an Actor's Life*, London: Hutchinson and Co., 2 vols

Dutton Cook (1883) *Nights at the Play: A View of the English Stage*, London: Chatto & Windus, 2 vols

Jim Davis and Victor Emeljanow (2001) *Reflecting the Audience: London theatregoing, 1840-1880*, Hatfield: University of Hertfordshire Press

Jim Davis (ed.) (2010) *Victorian Pantomime: A Collection of Critical Essays*, Basingstoke: Palgrave Macmillan

Tracy C. Davis (2000) *The Economics of the British Stage 1800 – 1914*, Cambridge: Cambridge University Press

Basil Dean (1956) *The Theatre at War*, London: George Harrap

Basil Dean (1970) *Seven Ages: an autobiography 1888-1927*, London: Hutchinson

Charles Dickens (1965 - 2002) *The Letters of Charles Dickens* (ed. Madeline House & Graham Storey) Oxford: The Clarendon Press, 12 vols

John Doran (1881) *In and about Drury Lane and Other Papers, Reprinted from the pages of the 'Temple Bar' Magazine*, London: Richard Bentley and Son, 2 vols

John Dryden (1962) *John Dryden: Of Dramatic Poesy and Other Critical Essays* (ed. George Watson) London: J. M. Dent and Sons Ltd, 2 vols

Barry Duncan (1964) *The St James's Theatre: Its strange and complete history 1835 - 1957*, London: Barrie and Rockliff

Falconer v. Chatterton, Complaint and Answer, (1866) London: Murray and Co. printers. The only known copy is in the Houghton Library of Harvard University, Cambridge, Mass. Thr 465.20.140

Helena Faucit (Lady Martin) (1885) *On Some of Shakespeare's Female Characters*, Edinburgh & London: William Blackwood & Sons

Richard Fawkes (1979) *Dion Boucicault: a biography*, London: Quarter Books

Percy Fitzgerald (1913) *Memories of Charles Dickens*, Bristol & London: J. W. Arrowsmith and Simpkin, Marshall, Hamilton, Kent & Co

Richard Foulkes (1984) *The Shakespeare Tercentenary of 1864*, London: The Society for Theatre Research

Richard Foulkes (1997) *Church and Stage in Victorian England*, Cambridge: Cambridge University Press

Basil Francis (1950) *Fanny Kelly of Drury Lane*, London: Rockliff

Roger Fulford (1967) *Samuel Whitbread, 1764-1815: A study in opposition*, London: Macmillan

Harry Furniss (1924) *Some Victorian Men*, London: John Lane The Bodley Head Ltd

Gorel Garlick (2003) *To Serve the Purpose of the Drama: the theatre designs and plays of Samuel Beazley 1786-1851*, London: Society for Theatre Research

Gorel Garlick (2016) *Charles John Phipps FSA: Architect to the Victorian theatre*, Great Shelford, Cambridge: Entertainment Technology Press

George Godwin (1878) 'On the Desirability of Obtaining a National Theatre not wholly controlled by the Prevailing Popular Taste: A paper read at the Cheltenham Congress of the Social Science Association (Art Department) October 1878', London: Wyman and Sons

Andrew Halliday (1865), *Every Day Papers*, London: Tinsley Brothers, 2 vols

Augustus Harris (1885) 'The National Theatre', *The Fortnightly Review*, vol. XXXVIII, July-December 1885, 630-636

Joseph Hatton (1892) 'The Battle of London' in *Cigarette Papers for After-Dinner Smoking*, London: Hutchinson and Co., 48-66

Frederick Hawkins (1897) 'John Oxenford', *The Theatre*, series 4, vol. XXX, 80-90

Robert Hogan (editor in chief) (1996) *Dictionary of Irish Literature*, Revised and Expanded Edition, London: Aldwych Press, 2 vols. Entry on John and Michael Banim by Mark D. Hawthorne, 1:115-116.

John Hollingshead (1895) *My Lifetime*, London: Sampson Low, Marston & Company, 2 vols

Michael Holroyd (2009) *A Strange Eventful History: the Dramatic Lives of Ellen Terry, Henry Irving and their Remarkable Families*, London: Vintage Books

Margaret J. Howell (1982) *Byron Tonight: A poet's plays on the nineteenth-century stage*, Windlesham: Springwood Books

Derek Hudson (1972) *Munby: Man of Two Worlds, The Life and Diaries of Arthur J. Munby 1828 – 1910*, London: John Murray

Joseph Knight (1893) *Theatrical Notes*, London: Lawrence & Bullen

Henry James (1949) *The Scenic Art: Notes on Acting and the Drama 1872 – 1901*, London: Rupert Hart-Davis

Charles Lamb Kenney (1864a) *Mr Phelps and the Critics of His Correspondence with the Stratford Committee*, London: T. H. Lacy (pamphlet)

Charles Lamb Kenney (1864b) *The Legitimate Drama at Drury Lane Theatre* (pamphlet)

Charles Lamb Kenney (1875a) *A Memoir of Michael William Balfe*, London: Tinsley Brothers

Charles Lamb Kenney (1875b) *Poets and Profits at Drury Lane Theatre: A theatrical narrative*, (pamphlet) London: Aubert's Steam Printing Works

Charles Lamb Kenney (1878) *Drury Lane Theatre: Season 1878-79*, (pamphlet)

Charles Lamb Kenney (1880?) *The Life and Career of Dion Boucicault written by his schoolfellow Charles Lamb Kenney*, New York: The Graphic Company, undated, probably 1880

Derek Hudson (1972) *Munby: Man of Two Worlds, The Life and Diaries of Arthur J. Munby 1828 – 1910*, London: John Murray

Richard Leacroft (1973) *The Development of the English Playhouse*, London: Eyre Methuen

Robin H. Legge (1895) 'John Oxenford 1812 – 1877', *Dictionary of National Biography*, vol. 43, ed. Sidney Lee, 12-13

S. R. Littlewood (1939) *Dramatic Criticism*, London: Sir Isaac Pitman and Sons Ltd

The London Stage 1660-1800: A calendar of plays, entertainments & afterpieces together with casts, box-receipts and contemporary comment compiled from the playbills, newspapers and theatrical diaries of the period, edited in five parts by Emmett L. Avery, Arthur H. Scouten, George Winchester Stone, Jr and Charles Beecher Hogan, 11 vols, Carbondale, Illinois: Southern Illinois University Press, 1960-68

Deirdre McFeely (2012) *Dion Boucicault: Irish Identity on Stage*, Cambridge: Cambridge University Press

James Mapleson (1966) *The Mapleson Memoirs: The Career of an Operatic Impresario 1858-1888*, ed. Harold Rosenthal, London: Putnam

Gail Marshall (ed.) (2012) *Shakespeare in the Nineteenth Century*, Cambridge: CUP

Henry Morley (1866), *The Journal of a London Theatregoer from 1851 to 1866*, London: George Routledge and Sons, reprinted in facsimile by Leicester University Press, 1974

Mowbray Morris (1882) *Essays in Theatrical Criticism*, London: Remington and Co.

Christopher Murray (1975) *Robert William Elliston, Manager*, London: Society for Theatre Research

Allardyce Nicoll (1927) *The Development of the Theatre: A study of theatrical art from the beginnings to the present day*, London: George G. Harrap, fourth edition 1958

Harry William Pedicord (1954) *The Theatrical Public in the Time of Garrick*, Carbondale and Edwardsville: Southern Illinois University Press

W. May Phelps & Johnston Forbes-Robertson (1886) *The Life and Life-Work of Samuel Phelps*, London: Sampson Low, Marston, Searle & Rivington

J.R. Planché (1872), *The Recollections and Reflections of J.R. Planché*, 2 vols, Cambridge: Cambridge University Press, [2011]

Augustus Pugin & John Britton (1838) *Illustrations of the Public Buildings of London: with historical and descriptive accounts of each edifice*, Second edition edited and enlarged by W. H. Leeds, London: John Weale Architectural Library, 2 vols

Report from the Select Committee on Dramatic Literature (1832) London: House of Commons

Report from the Select Committee on Theatrical Licences and Regulations (1866) London: House of Commons

Jeffrey Richards (2005) *Sir Henry Irving: A Victorian Actor and his World*, London: Hambledon

Jeffrey Richards (2015) *The Golden Age of Pantomime: Slapstick, Spectacle and Subversion in Victorian England*, London: I. B. Tauris

Johnston Forbes Robertson (1925) *A Player Under Three Reigns*, London: T. Fisher Unwin

Daniel Rosenthal (2013) *The National Theatre Story*, London: Oberon Books

Tommaso Salvini (1893) *Leaves From the Autobiography of Tommaso Salvini*, London: T. Fisher Unwin

Clement Scott (1899) *The Drama of Yesterday and Today*, London: Macmillan, 2 vols

Mrs Clement Scott (1919) *Old Days in Bohemian London: Recollections of Clement Scott*, London: Hutchinson and Co.

F. H. W. Sheppard (General Editor) (1960) *Survey of London XXIX: The Parish of Westminster Part One, South of Piccadilly*, London: The Athlone Press

F.H.W. Sheppard (General Editor) (1970) *Survey of London XXXV: The Theatre Royal Drury Lane and the Royal Opera House Covent Garden*, London: The Athlone Press

F.H.W. Sheppard (General Editor) (1970) *Survey of London XXXVI: The Parish of St Paul Covent Garden*, London: The Athlone Press

Robert M. Sillard, (1901) *Barry Sullivan and his Contemporaries: A histrionic record*, London: T. Fisher Unwin, 2 vols

Michael Slater (2002) *Douglas Jerrold 1803-1857*, London: Duckworth

Richard Southern (1950) 'The Problem of A. B.'s Theatre Drawings', *Theatre Notebook*, vol. 4, October 1949 – July 1950, No. 7, London: Ifan Kyrle Fletcher on behalf of the Society for Theatre Research, 58 - 62

John Russell Stephens (1980) *The Censorship of English Drama 1824-1901*, Cambridge: Cambridge University Press

Klaus Stierstorfer (2004) 'Oxenford, John (1812–1877)', *Oxford Dictionary of National Biography*, Oxford University Press

Edward Stirling (1881) *Old Drury Lane: Fifty years' recollections of author, actor and manager*, 2 vols., London: Chatto & Windus

Freddie Stockdale (1998) *Emperors of Song: Three Great Impresarios*, London: John Murray

Jill A. Sullivan (2011) *The Politics of the Pantomime: Regional identity in the theatre 1860-1900*, Hatfield: University of Hertfordshire Press/ Society for Theatre Research

Julia Swindells & David Francis Taylor (eds) (2014) *The Oxford Handbook of The Georgian Theatre, 1737 – 1832*, Oxford: Oxford University Press

William Tinsley (1900) *Random Recollections of an Old Publisher*, London: Simpkin, Marshall, Hamilton Kent & Co, 2 vols

J. C. Trewin (1960) *Benson and the Bensonians*, London: Barrie and Rockliff

Basil Walsh (2008) *Michael W. Balfe: A unique Victorian composer*, Dublin: Irish Academic Press

Geneviève Ward and Richard Whiteing (1918) *Both Sides of the Curtain*, London: Cassell and Co Ltd

Margaret Webster (1969) *The Same Only Different: Five Generations of a Great Theatre Family*, London: Victor Gollancz

Robert Whelan (2013) *The Other National Theatre: 350 Years of Shows in Drury Lane*, London: Jacob Tonson

Geoffrey Whitworth (1951) *The Making of a National Theatre*, London: Faber and Faber

Benjamin Dean Wyatt (1813) *Observations on the Design for the Theatre Royal, Drury Lane, as Executed in the Year 1812: Accompanied by plans, elevations and sections of the same*, London: The Architectural Library

Edmund Yates, *Edmund Yates: His Recollections and Experiences* (1884) London: Richard Bentley and Sons, 2 vols

Notes

PREFACE

1. One of the peculiarities of Coleman's autobiography is the almost complete absence of dates, including the year of his own birth. It can be deduced from references to historical events in the text.
2. Blanchard, 2:532. Coleman does not mention this in his autobiography.
3. John Coleman, *Curly: An Actor's Story*, London: Chatto and Windus, 1885
4. Robert Whelan, *The Other National Theatre: 350 years of shows in Drury Lane*, London: Jacob Tonson, 2013

1: THE YOUTH OF CHATTERTON

1. Letter from FBC to his uncle Charles in India dated 4 May 1858. Uncle Frederick described himself as 'Harpist to H.R.H. the Duchess of Gloucester and the Courts of France and Belgium' (*The Times*, 11 October 1852, 4).
2. Coleman (1888) 2:327. Most of this chapter is derived from pp. 326-34 of Coleman's version of Chatterton's first-person narrative.
3. Coleman (1888) 2:329. This was presumably J. C. Moore's *Penny Shakespeare* that began to appear in sixty parts in 1845, when Chatterton would have been eleven. (Christopher Decker, 'Shakespeare Editions' in Marshall, 29)
4. By 1871 there were 308 amateur dramatic societies with 5,500 members in London alone. (Davis [2000] 231)
5. Letter dated 31 December 1855 from Richard Bryant, FBC's uncle by marriage, to FBC's uncle Charles, living in India. Bryant tells his brother-in-law that Edward Chatterton had also managed to get him a job at Drury Lane.

2: THE LYCEUM YEARS

1. 'Lyceum Theatre', *The Times*, 16 September 1856, 10
2. 'Sadler's Wells Theatre', *The Times*, 23 April 1856, 10
3. Classified advertisements, *The Times*, 13 September 1856, 6
4. Edward Chatterton had been in charge of the box office at Drury Lane since September 1853. E. T. Smith, the lessee of Drury Lane from 1852 to 1862, was in the habit of including Edward Chatterton's name in the classified advertisements at a time when no other box office manager was mentioned by name.
5. On 4 March 1868 Chatterton made Drury Lane available for a benefit performance to raise funds for May.
6. Edward Chatterton managed to negotiate a benefit for himself at Drury Lane on 18 March 1858, but he had a far higher profile than any other box office manager in London.
7. Chatterton told Coleman that: 'as I had a little *nous* in financing, I got him over many of his troubles; but they were too strong for him, or he was too weak to grapple with them'. (Coleman [1888] 2:335)
8. 'Lyceum Theatre', *The Times*, Monday 8 December 1856, 9
9. *The Times*, 9 April 1858 9; 28 May 11; 17 September 1858 9. Dillon's counsel denied that he had made any such statement, which suggests hypersensitivity on Chatterton's part.
10. Letter from Chatterton to his uncle Charles in India dated 4 May 1858
11. 'Lyceum Theatre', *The Times*, 27 August 1858, 10. On 13 September there was a second *Times* review owing to a change of leading lady which once again praised the play 'in spite of all its defects' and reported full houses 'where there was once a

very melancholy series of scantily occupied benches'. (*The Times*, 13 September 1858, 7)
12 *The Times*, 28 December 1858, 7
13 'What the World Says', *The World*, 21 June 1882, 14
14 Coleman (1888) 2:338
15 'You must not take a theatre too far west,' Dion Boucicault told the 1866 Select Committee on Theatrical Licences when asked about the lack of success of the St James's Theatre. 'It must be in the centre of the pleasure-seeking population.' (Report 1866 4481)
16 'St James's Theatre', *The Times*, 3 October 1859, 7
17 'St James's Theatre', *The Times*, 6 October 1859, 10.
18 On 19 January Oxenford would review another of his own pieces at the St James's, *My Name is Norval*. Described as a tragic ballet, it was actually a burlesque with lots of dancing by Lydia Thompson. It formed a curtain-raiser to the pantomime. (*The Times*, 19 January 1860, 12)
19 'A Dramatic Ogre', Letter to the Editor, signed 'Fair and Square', *The Era*, 20 November 1864, 10
20 Yates 1:309
21 Open letter from 'Audax' to Douglas Jerrold published in *The Theatrical Journal* of 7 March 1855 and cited in Slater, 244.
22 *Report from the Select Committee on Theatrical Licences and Regulations* (1866) 4560. 'At the same time that I was writing the criticisms in the *Morning Chronicle*,' Brooks told the Committee, 'I was bringing out pieces. It may be wrong, but it is not human nature to be in daily intercourse with people, profiting by their labour, and possibly being in social relations with them, and then go off to your desk and say, Mr Brown's acting is weak, and Mr Johnson's declamation is vulgar. I felt myself disqualified from giving that form of opinion; I could not do justice either to the public or to the actor.'
23 Hawkins 88. A report of Oxenford's funeral in *The Era* (4 March 1877, 7) carried a list of sixty-eight pieces, but the list was incomplete.
24 Oxenford gave 1839 as the first year of his employment at *The Times* in a speech to the Junior Garrick Club in 1873. He succeeded Michael Nugent as dramatic critic and was assisted, initially by Charles Lamb Kenney who joined him in 1841, then by James Davison, to whom he handed over all musical coverage in 1849. ('Dinner and Presentation of Portrait to John Oxenford Esq.', *The Era*, 9 March 1873, 4; Kenney [1880?]; Hawkins, 82)
25 Yates, 1:309
26 'Dinner and Presentation of Portrait to John Oxenford Esq.', *The Era*, 9 March 1873, 4
27 Blanchard recorded meeting him at Chatterton's annual dinner at The Hawthorns in Clapham Road on 2 July 1874. (Blanchard, 2:440)
28 Hollingshead, 1:202.
29 Burnand was delighted to be offered £25 in advance and one pound per night for every night over twenty-five. (Duncan, 109) It ran for sixty performances.
30 'Those who recollect the condition into which the house had fallen when it was taken by Mr F. B. Chatterton will properly estimate his improvements,' said *The Times*. 'The crowded state of the theatre last night shows that its newly acquired popularity has not abated.' ('St James's Theatre', *The Times*, 17 November 1859, 10)
31 Coleman (1888) 2:339.
32 Kenney (1875a) 146-7
33 *The Chatham News and North Kent Spectator*, 24 November 1860
34 *The Chatham News and North Kent Spectator*, 15 December 1860
35 *The Chatham News and North Kent Spectator*, 29 December 1860

36 On 17 December 1860
37 On 10 January 1861
38 On 14 January 1861
39 'The Uncommercial Traveller', *All The Year Round*, 30 June 1860, 276. Published in book form as 'Dullborough Town' in *The Uncommercial Traveller*.
40 Even the walk back to London can be seen as a sort of tribute to Dickens, whose fondness for long walks once caused him to walk from London to his house at Gad's Hill in Kent. In *Great Expectations*, which was being serialised in *All The Year Round* during Chatterton's management in Rochester, the hero Pip walks from Rochester to London in chapter XLIV. However, this chapter was first published in the magazine on 1 June 1861, five months after Chatterton and Sinclair made the journey on foot.
41 Coleman (1888) 2:340
42 Coleman (1888) 2:341
43 The sub-title of the play comes from a popular Irish air of which Falconer used the first four lines in much of the publicity:
Ah! The moment was sad when my love and I parted
Savourneen Deelish, Eileen Oge!
As I kissed off her tears, I was nigh broken-hearted
Savourneen Deelish, Eileen Oge!
'Savourneen Deelish, Eileen Oge' means 'young Eileen, the faithful sweetheart'.
44 *The Times*, classified advertisements, 5 September 1861, 6 and daily for several weeks
45 On 8 November 1872, when Chatterton was running the Adelphi and the Princess's as well as Drury Lane, he placed thirty advertisements in the classified columns of *The Times*: fourteen for Drury Lane of which five were press quotes for *The Lady of the Lake* (adapted by Andrew Halliday from Sir Walter Scott); thirteen for the Adelphi of which seven were press quotes for *Mabel's Life* (by H. J. Byron); and three for Shakespeare's *Hamlet* at the Princess's. These occupied more than half of a column.
46 *The Times*, classified advertisements, 8 Nov 1861, 6
47 The real Peep o' Day boys were a rural Protestant guerrilla force that carried out attacks on Catholics during the sectarian struggles of the 1790s. Falconer changed them from Protestants to Catholics.
48 Edmund Falconer, *Peep o' Day*, Act IV, scene II
49 'The Lyceum', *The Times*, 11 November 1861, 4
50 Banim, 3:1
51 'The Christmas Pantomimes, Burlesques &c', *The Times*, 27 December 1861, 7. The royal family were shown in the scene depicting Dundag Bay.
52 '1. The Lower Lake from Castle Lough - 2. Kenmure Cottage in Glena Bay - 3. Dundag Bay in the Middle Lake - 4. The Old Weir Bridge - 5. The Eagle's Nest - 6. Muckross Abbey by Moonlight changing to the True Lovers' Retreat on Magical Emerald Isle, on which the Water Fairies rise to dance by moonlight on the Lakes.' (*The Times*, classified advertisements, 26 December 1861, 6)
53 'The Christmas Pantomimes, Burlesques &c', *The Times*, 27 December 1861, 7
54 'The scenery is magnificent. No less emphatic phrase could do adequate justice to the splendour and beauty of scenes that one and all deserve to be classed among the grandest stage pictures which the magic pencils of Messrs Grieve and Telbin have as yet produced.' *Morning Post*; 'Scarcely anything so effective and, at the same time, so beautiful [as the quarry scene] has ever been exhibited. The audience not only applauded but absolutely rose and shouted their

delight.' *Morning Herald.* (*The Times*, classified advertisements, 18 November 1861, 6)
55 *The Times*, classified advertisements, 11 January 1862, 6
56 Falconer had worked with Balfe before as the lyricist for two of his operas: *The Rose of Castille* in 1857 and *Satanella* in 1858.
57 The actual anniversary had been the day before, a Sunday. It is sometimes claimed that Tom Taylor's play *Our American Cousin* was the first play to run continuously for a year in London. *Peep o' Day* opened on 9 November 1861 and *Our American Cousin* opened at the Haymarket Theatre on the following Monday. Both plays ran continuously until Christmas when *Our American Cousin*, which had not been doing particularly good business, was withdrawn to make way for the Haymarket's Christmas programme. It resumed performances on 27 January 1862, by which time *Punch* had taken up the character of Lord Dundreary with a dramatic effect on the play's popularity (Report, 1866, 3535). Both plays ran continuously throughout 1862, with both managements publishing the ordinal numbers of their performances, but *Peep o' Day* was always numerically ahead of *Our American Cousin* because of the latter's 'missing' month around Christmas. *Peep o' Day* closed on 23 December 1862; *Our American Cousin* ran until 1 April 1863, by which time it had reached 396 performances (compared with 346 of *Peep o' Day*). It had definitely run for more than one year, whichever way the calculation is made, but it came second to *Peep o' Day* in the achievement.

3: A STROLL DOWN DRURY LANE

1 From a short memoir, probably written by Sheridan's son-in-law, quoted in Fulford, 278
2 William Pedicord (1–18) examined all of the surviving evidence relating to the capacity of Garrick's Drury Lane and concluded that Garrick and Lacy started their management in 1747 with a capacity of 1,001. They added surrounding buildings to the theatre and were able to increase this to 2,362 by 1763. Before putting the theatre on the market, Garrick had his friend the architect Robert Adam make alterations and improvements which may have resulted in a slight decrease in the capacity.
3 'It was originally estimated that Drury Lane should hold 3,919, although the final capacity is usually given as 3,611.' (Leacroft, 135)
4 Sheppard (1970) *Survey of London* XXXV, 97
5 Richard Brinsley Peake (1841) *Memoirs of the Colman Family*, 2: 20, quoted in The London Stage, Pt 5, iii, 1473.
6 Richard Cumberland (1807) *Memoirs*, 2: 384
7 J. R. Planché (1879) *The Extravaganzas of J. R. Planché*, London: Samuel French, vol. 2, 13
8 Bunn, 2:223
9 Bunn, 2:229
10 Anderson, 208; 'Public Amusements', *Lloyd's Weekly Newspaper*, 26 June 1853; 'Drury Lane Theatre', *The Times*, 20 October 1853, 7
11 The details of Jullien's lease emerged in the Court of Bankruptcy where he testified that he took on Drury Lane in August 1847 at a rental of £3,500 per annum. He paid at the rate of £20 a night, starting as soon as the promenade concerts began in August. (*The Times*, 18 August 1848, 7)
12 Anderson, 170
13 Anderson, 201
14 Bedford Office London, Annual Report, 1852, 5, quoted in Sheppard (1970) *Survey of London* XXXV, 26

15 Sheppard (1970) *Survey of London XXXV*, 26; Report (1866) evidence of Edward Tyrell Smith, 131, #3674
16 Coleman (1886) 212
17 George Augustus Sala, 'Echoes of the Week', *The Illustrated London News*, 8 December 1877, 554
18 Ward and Whiteing, 223
19 'The Christmas Pantomimes etc: Drury Lane', *The Times*, 28 December 1852, 8
20 From Smith's obituaries: George Augustus Sala, 'Echoes of the Week', *The Illustrated London News*, 8 December 1877, 554; 'The Late Mr E. T. Smith', *Touchstone or the New Era*, 1 December 1877, 13
21 Yates, 2:124
22 Ward and Whiteing, 222
23 In October 1853 Smith announced the last performances of the Shakespearean season by the Irish actor Gustavus Brooke, to be followed by 'another and very different field of operation [which] presents itself to the manager's enterprise in catering for the tastes and requirements of his patrons, the British public' – an American equestrian troupe with acrobats, clowns, performing dogs and monkeys. (*The Times*, 17 October 1853, 8; & 30 November 1853, 6)
24 'Drury Lane Theatre', *The Times*, 29 October 1859, 9; Falconer v. Chatterton, 4
25 Stirling, 1: 267. Edward Stirling was an actor, stage manager and general factotum at Drury Lane during the 1850s, 1860s and 1870s, and claimed to have been present at the dinner at which this exchange took place.
26 See Fawkes, 120-32
27 *The Times*, 10 November 1862, 8

4: A PARTNERSHIP AT THE NATIONAL THEATRE

1 Coleman (1888) 2:342
2 *Falconer v. Chatterton*, Complaint 4-5. The details of the financial arrangements between Falconer and Chatterton at the Lyceum and Drury Lane are taken from this pamphlet, published by Chatterton in March 1866, following a legal dispute with Falconer in September 1865, which contains both Falconer's complaint against Chatterton and Chatterton's answer to the complaint. These documents were presented to the court which ruled in favour of Chatterton, whose case was more convincing. When Chatterton published the pamphlet and circulated it to the Company of Proprietors and members of the profession, he was threatened with contempt of court. He escaped prosecution but had to promise not to circulate any more copies. ('Falconer v. Chatterton', *The Times*, 16 March 1866, 11) The only known copy of this pamphlet is now in the Houghton Library of Harvard University.
3 Chatterton would later say he couldn't confirm the figure of £8,000, but that Falconer had spent 'an unnecessary sum of money'. *Falconer v. Chatterton*, Answer 10
4 'Meeting of the Proprietors of Drury Lane Theatre', *The Era*, 1 February 1863
5 'Drury Lane Theatre', *The Times*, 22 December 1862, 9
6 'Meeting of the Proprietors of Drury Lane Theatre', *The Era*, 1 February 1863
7 Falconer said that the budget for the first season was £1,500, but Chatterton, who actually had to raise the money, said that it was £1,300. (*Falconer v. Chatterton*, Complaint 7 and Answer 11)
8 'Time in his course has built up the pantomime into an institution as venerable as Magna Charta, as sacred as The Bill of Rights, as dearly cherished as Habeas Corpus. The Pantomime is considered as worthy of the boards of Old Drury as the works of Shakespeare himself. Indeed,

Shakespeare, mighty magician as he is, could not make the theatrical ends meet without the Clown's string of sausages to eke them out... Pantomime did not attain to all the rights and privileges of a British householder until it took up its abode in Drury Lane.' ('Boxing Night at the Theatres: Drury Lane', *The Era*, 29 December 1867, 10)

9. 'Velocipede', 'Correspondence', *The Entr'Acte*, 9 December 1871, 6
10. 'The Theatres', *The Illustrated London News*, 30 December 1865, 655
11. 'The Theatres: The Pantomimes', *The Illustrated London News*, 2 January 1875, 19
12. 'The Pantomimes', *The Athenaeum*, 2 January 1874, 29
13. 'Mr E. L. Blanchard and the Censor', *The Era*, 22 November 1874, 15
14. 'The Christmas Novelties: Drury Lane', *The Era*, 31 December 1876
15. E. L. Blanchard, *Beauty and the Beast*, Lord Chamberlain's copy of the script in the British Library: Add MS 53081 L
16. Blanchard recorded in his diary for 24 December 1858 receiving £30 in total for Robin Hood. He was paid in three instalments for *Little Goody Two Shoes*: £25 on 13 January 1863; £25 on 7 February 1863 and £26 on 21 March 1863. (Blanchard, 1:210; 1:274; 1:276; 1:277) He would receive £100 for the 1870/1871 pantomime *The Dragon of Wantley*. (Blanchard 2:390; 2:394)
17. Frank L. Emmanuel, 'William Roxby Beverley', *Walker's Quarterly 2* (January 1921) 10, cited in Richards (2015) 127; 'The Christmas Pantomimes, Burlesques etc: Drury Lane', *The Times*, 27 December 1860, 7, cited in Richards (2015) 144; 'London Theatres: Drury Lane', *The Entr'Acte*, 17 October 1874, 4
18. W. J. Lawrence, 'Beverly, William Roxby (1810?–1889)', rev. C. D. Watkinson, *Oxford Dictionary of National Biography*, Oxford University Press, 2004; online edn, May 2013. Beverley's name was spelt both with and without the third 'e' during his lifetime. It is without the 'e' on his tombstone (Richards [2015] 419n.) but as the town from which the name derived has the third 'e', that spelling is used throughout this book.
19. Planché, 2:135
20. *The Era*, 1 January 1860, reviewing *Jack and the Beanstalk* (Drury Lane, 1859) cited in Richards (2015) 143
21. 'Celebrities at Home CCXXVI: Mr Beverley in Russell Square', *The World*, 22 December 1880, 3 - 5
22. Oscar Wilde, 'Shakespeare on Scenery', *Dramatic Review*, 14 March 1885, 99, reproduced in *The Complete Works of Oscar Wilde, 6, Journalism Part 1*, John Stokes and Mark W. Turner (eds.), Oxford: Oxford University Press, 2013, 44
23. Coleman (1888) 2:344
24. 'The Christmas Pantomimes, Burlesques etc.', *The Times*, 27 December 1863, 3
25. A committee was formed but the attempt came to nothing. (*The Era*, 1 April 1877, 6; *The Illustrated London News*, 7 April 1877, 331) Oxenford was, however, commemorated in a stained glass window in St George's Roman Catholic Cathedral in Southwark. Oxenford had been received into the Catholic church in the autumn of 1875, just as he was retiring from *The Times*, but it was extremely unusual to grant the privilege of a memorial window in the Cathedral to someone who was not a member of the clergy nor of an old Catholic family nor, as far as we know, a donor. The window was blown out by a bomb in World War II. ('Entre Nous', *Truth*, 22 March 1877, 354 and personal communication [25 November 2018] from Melanie Bunch, Hon. Archivist and Historian

26. The reviewer in *The Era* ('The Theatres etc.', 1 March 1863) claimed this was the largest crowd of extras ever deployed on the stage of Drury Lane.
27. 'Drury Lane Theatre', *The Times*, 24 February 1863, 12
28. Coleman (1888) 2:344
29. Morley, 264
30. Charles Dickens to Wilkie Collins, 22 April 1863, in Dickens, vol, 10, 1862 – 1864, 237
31. *Falconer v. Chatterton*, Answer, 25
32. Coleman (1888) 2:346
33. We do not know the exact date on which the lease was transferred to Falconer. When Falconer and Chatterton were both making their depositions to the court during their legal dispute three years later, the date was left as a blank in both Falconer's complaint and in Chatterton's answer.
34. *Falconer v. Chatterton*, Answer 14 & Coleman (1888) 347-50. Chatterton's account to Coleman is confused as to the timing of the transaction, which he suggests came in March 1864, instead of March 1863, but it corroborates the statements in the 'Complaint and Answer' depositions of 1866 in other respects.
35. Knowles fancied himself as a connoisseur and 'anything in the shape of a picture "fetched" [him], so he rose to the bait.' (Coleman [1888] 2:349) *Peep o' Day* opened at the Theatre Royal, Manchester, on 9 November 1863 where it ran successfully until Christmas. The panorama was exhibited before the play while the Falconer/ Balfe ballad *Killarney* was sung. Several of the original London cast appeared in this production.
36. *Falconer v. Chatterton*, Answer 19
37. Coleman (1888) 2:344-5
38. *The Times*, 1 October 1844, 5; *Punch*, 13 July 1844, cited in Allen, 84
39. When William Archer was campaigning for a National Theatre fifty years later he proposed that the theatre would keep all of Shakespeare's plays in its repertoire with the exception of *Troilus and Cressida* and *Titus Andronicus*. The eminent Victorian scholar James Halliwell was so disgusted by *Titus Andronicus* that he refused to accept it could have been written by Shakespeare. (William Archer, *The Theatrical 'World' of 1896*, London: Walter Scott, 1897, xlvii; Marshall, 26.)
40. *The Examiner*, 18 October 1856, cited in Allen, 148
41. Coleman (1886) 242 & Dickens, vol. 10, 1862 – 1864, 247 – 249. Being offered the Ghost would have brought back painful memories for Phelps who had been cast in the part by Macready when he was deliberately keeping Phelps in small parts to forestall any challenge to his pre-eminence during his Drury Lane management of 1841-43.
42. 'Music and the Drama: Drury Lane', *The Athenaeum*, 19 September 1863, 378
43. *Falconer v. Chatterton*, Answer 25
44. *Manfred*, act 3, scene 4, in *The Works of Lord Byron*, vol. 11, London: John Murray, 71
45. Letter from Byron in Venice to John Murray, 15 February 1817, reproduced in Leslie A. Marchand (ed.) (1976) *So Late Into The Night: Byron's Letters and Journals*, vol. 5, London: John Murray, 170
46. Preface to *Marino Faliero* in *The Works of Lord Byron*, vol. 12, 1835, 60n.
47. *The Times*, 13 October 1863, 4
48. Chatterton was about to commission a new score when the music librarian at Drury Lane told him that they had Sir Henry Bishop's manuscript score still in the theatre's music library. ('Drury Lane Theatre', *The Era*, 7

February 1869). The 1834 production was at Covent Garden at the time when Alfred Bunn was managing both theatres, which is how the score ended up in the Drury Lane library.

49 *The Times*, 13 October 1863, 4
50 *The Times*, 27 October 1863, 9
51 'Drury Lane Theatre', The Times, 3 November 1863, 5
52 Cook, 1:259, from Cook's review of *The Cataract of the Ganges* in March 1873
53 'The Theatres', *The Illustrated London News*, 27 September 1873, 290. The flyer referred to was promoting Shakespeare's *Antony and Cleopatra*. According to *The Era*, it had been circulating in London for two months before the production opened. ('Drury Lane Theatre', *The Era*, 28 September 1873, 12)
54 Flyer for *Manfred* contained in the Drury Lane box for 1863, Victoria and Albert Museum Theatre and Performance Collection. Also accessible online as part of the John Johnson Collection, Bodleian Library, Oxford, London Playbills Drury Lane box 1 (90)
55 Coleman (1888) 2:345
56 *The Times*, 27 October 1863, 9
57 'For a time he (Oxenford) was assisted by facetious Charles Kenney, who needed a little more good sense to retain his position.' (Hawkins, 82)
58 Kenney was fluent in French and was described by George Augustus Sala as 'the very best French-speaking Englishman that I ever came in contact with.' ('Echoes of the Week', *The Illustrated London News*, 14 December 1879, 559)
59 F. C. Burnand, *Records and reminiscences, personal and general*, 1904, 2:245 cited in Kurt Gänzl, 'Kenney, Charles Lamb (1821–1881)', *Oxford Dictionary of National Biography*, Oxford University Press, 2004

60 Hollingshead, 1:85-6
61 Ward, 61
62 Doran, 1:2
63 Richards, 182-3, drawing on the research of Jennie Bisset
64 'The Christmas Pantomimes, Burlesques etc: Drury Lane', *The Times*, 28 December 1863, 7
65 *The Chatham News and North Kent Spectator*, 2 March 1861
66 Blanchard, 1:286, diary entry dated 8 January 1864, but should be 9 January
67 'Drury Lane Theatre', *The Times*, 11 January 1864, 10
68 Halliday (1865) 'Shakespeare-Mad', I:175. First published in *All the Year Round*, 25 May 1864
69 The letter, dated 21 January 1864, is in the Shakespeare Centre Library in Stratford-upon-Avon. It is quoted in Kenney (1864a) 6 & Foulkes (1984) 15
70 Although *Henry IV* did not open until 28 March, the pamphlet carrying the correspondence must have been published before the middle of February as Charles Flower, chairman of the Stratford committee, had a letter in *The Era* of 14 February 1864 responding to the publication ('The Shakesperian Tercentenary Celebration at Stratford-upon-Avon', 9). He expressed disappointment that his committee's attempt to present three plays by Shakespeare to the highest possible standard had been obstructed by the professional jealousy of 'the foremost man in his profession'.
71 'Mr Phelps always studies, and he could not fail of some success', was typical of the grudging praise he elicited. ('*The Fortunes of Nigel* at Drury Lane', *The Spectator*, 3 October 1868, 1154)
72 Kenney (1864a) 7
73 Quoted in 'Echoes of the Week', *The Illustrated London News*, 20 February 1864, 190
74 Foulkes (1984) 15. Fechter claimed he

had asked the Stratford committee to defend him against Phelps's implication in the Drury Lane playbills that he had acquired the part of Hamlet by subterfuge. They declined to do this, and passed a resolution regretting the offence caused to Phelps. When Fechter resigned in protest the committee then 'placarded most of the chief railway stations' with allegations of breach of faith. ('Mr Fechter and the Stratford Committee', *The Era*, 17 April 1864, 15)

75 'The Theatres: Drury Lane', *The Illustrated London News*, 2 April 1864, 326
76 'Echoes of the Week', *The Illustrated London News*, 2 April 1864, 327 & 'The Battle of Shrewsbury', *The Illustrated London News*, 30 April 1864, 426
77 Blanchard, 1:288; diary entry for 28 March 1864
78 'The Theatres: Drury Lane', *The Illustrated London News*, 2 April 1864, 326
79 The 1863/64 Drury Lane pantomime *Sinbad the Sailor* contained a scene which 'shows the National Monument to Shakespeare – that is to be' ('Drury Lane', *The Athenaeum*, 2 January 1864, 27). As the monument was never to be, it would be fascinating to know what was depicted.
80 Copy in the John Johnson Collection of the Bodleian Library, London Playbills Drury Lane box 1 (92). Chatterton's negative comments about a physical monument didn't prevent him from making Drury Lane available for benefits on 30 June 1863 and 23 April 1864 to raise funds for 'a monument, embracing a bronze statue placed under a decorative canopy, in the style of the Poet's period' somewhere in London. (Classified advertisements, *The Times*, 23 April 1864, 10) The performances of *Macbeth* at Drury Lane in the week commencing 5 December 1864 were preceded by 'Addresses', written by five different poets and delivered by five different actors, soliciting support for a monument to Shakespeare to be erected on Primrose Hill by working-class members of the People's Shakespeare Movement. People were invited to become subscribers to the fund by donating anything from one penny upwards to collectors as they left the theatre. (Classified advertisement, *The Times*, 9 December 1864, 6) Samuel Phelps was President of the Council. (*Addresses delivered at the Theatre Royal, Drury Lane, in aid of the People's Shakespeare Memorial Fund*, London: Thomas Hailes, 1864 [?]) The addresses were all reproduced in *The Era* (11 December 1864, 10).
81 'Drury Lane Theatre', *The Times*, 23 May 1864, 12. The season ran for 205 nights and was Chatterton's longest at Drury Lane.
82 *Falconer v. Chatterton*, Answer 24
83 *Falconer v. Chatterton*, Answer 26
84 Copy in the John Johnson Collection of the Bodleian Library, London Playbills Drury Lane box 1 (97). First published 3 September 1864, it was reproduced in *The Era* of 4 September 1864, 8.
85 'Echoes of the Week', *The Illustrated London News*, 10 September 1864, 255
86 Falconer's farce *The O'Flahertys* opened on 17 October and ran for thirteen continuous performances and another seven non-continuous performances throughout the season as a curtain-raiser to various Shakespeare plays. Falconer played Thaddeus O'Flaherty. 'Very bad' according to Blanchard (Blanchard 1:298). *Love's Ordeal* opened on 3 May, also starring Falconer, and ran for seven performances. There was also a revival of Falconer's one-act

farce *Too Much for Good Nature*, originally produced at the Lyceum in 1858, which opened on 1 November and received ten performances.
87 Kenney (1864b) 3 – 4. Copy in the University of Nottingham Library
88 'Drury Lane Theatre', *The Times*, 3 October 1864, 10
89 'For scenery, and in a large measure for costumes, the resources of the house [Drury Lane] are sufficient without the need of going to further expense.' ('The Theatres', *The Illustrated London News*, 6 October 1866, 326)
90 'Musical and Dramatic Gossip', *The Athenaeum*, 27 May 1865, 725; 'Drury Lane', *The Era*, 12 March 1865, 11
91 Carlyle (2000) 201 & Carlyle (2004)
92 Coleman (1886) 188
93 Hudson, 238-9, diary entry for 23 March 1867
94 'Drury Lane', *The Times*, 18 October 1864, 12
95 'Drury Lane', *The Times*, 20 October 1864, 10
96 Carlyle (2000) 213. The theatre was closed on the day before the opening 'in consequence of the immense preparations necessary for the production of Shakespeare's tragedy of *Macbeth*', which was almost unheard of at Drury Lane for any production other than the pantomime.
97 There had been a holding paragraph on 4 November, promising 'a detailed notice' on another occasion – a favourite device of Oxenford's. (*The Times*, 4 November 1864, 4)
98 'Drury Lane', *The Times*, 7 November 1864, 4. In fact, Chatterton had no share in the lease at this stage.
99 From the season prospectus, copy in the John Johnson Collection of the Bodleian Library, London Playbills Drury Lane box 1 (97)
100 'Drury Lane Theatre, *The Times*, 4 February 1865, 9
101 'Drury Lane Theatre, *The Times*, 22 February 1865, 12
102 Many years later, when John Hollingshead was writing his memoirs, he described the failure of the Italian tragedian Ernesto Rossi in a season that he had co-produced at Drury Lane with Chatterton by saying that: 'His receipts was as bad as Milton's *Comus* at the same theatre. I cannot say more, except that these were dreadful.' (Hollingshead, 86-7)
103 F. B. Chatterton, Letter to the Editor, 'Formosa', *The Times*, 24 August 1869, 10
104 Blanchard 1:310, diary entry for 3 May 1865
105 'Drury Lane Theatre', *The Observer*, 21 May 1865
106 Drury Lane Theatre, *The Times*, 22 May 1865, 12
107 The Easter Amusements: Drury Lane', *The Era*, 23 April 1865, 10
108 'Mr Falconer has proved that the national theatre can be conducted on high principles, and that the public will patronise our standard drama when placed on the stage in a becoming style.' ('The Theatres', *The Illustrated London News*, 28 May 1864, 527)
109 'The Theatres', *The Illustrated London News*, 22 August 1863, 203; 'The Theatres', *The Illustrated London News*, 30 September 1865, 319
110 *Falconer v. Chatterton*, Complaint 20
111 *Falconer v. Chatterton*, Complaint 22
112 *Falconer v. Chatterton*, Answer 19
113 *Falconer v. Chatterton*, Answer 33
114 'Law Report: Court of Chancery', *The Times*, 23 September 1865, 11; & 'Drury Lane Theatre', *The Times*, 25 September 1865, 11
115 'Drury Lane Theatre', *The Times*, 25 September 1865, 11
116 Anderson, 273-4
117 'Drury Lane', *The Athenaeum*, 11

November 1865, 659
118 *The Times*, 3 November 1865, 6, classified advertisement. The playtext carries a list, supplied by Charles Kean, of the sources for the costumes. This list was presumably from his production at the Princess's Theatre in 1852. (*King John as performed at the Theatre Royal, Drury Lane, under the management of Mr F. B. Chatterton*, London: Thomas Hailes, 1867 (?) 10-11)
119 'Drury Lane', *The Athenaeum*, 11 November 1865, 659
120 'The Theatres', *The Illustrated London News*, 29 September 1866, 315-6
121 'Drury Lane Theatre', *The Times*, 6 November 1865, 5
122 Doran, 1: 8-9 & 17
123 'Returning from the pantomime', *The Illustrated London News*, 6 January 1866, 24. Matinees were called 'morning performances' even though they took place in the afternoon.
124 George Augustus Sala, 'Pantomime Children', *The Illustrated London News*, 26 December 1874, 606
125 'Drury Lane Theatre', *The Times*, 22 February 1866, 6
126 Anderson, 279
127 'The assignees had… felt it their duty to inquire into the facts, and, with the assistance of an able accountant, they closely investigated the books, and had come to the conclusion that there was no foundation whatever for the claim on Mr Chatterton; on the contrary, that there was a considerable balance in that gentleman's favour… there was no doubt that Mr Falconer in making the claim had done so under misapprehension, and as he had suffered a lengthened imprisonment it was probable that he had laboured under great mental excitement, and he has since obtained leave to remove from the proceedings the objectionable statements he had made in reference to Mr Chatterton.' ('Court of Bankruptcy, August 2, before Mr Commissioner Holroyd, In Re Edmund O'Rourke, otherwise Falconer', cited in *Falconer v. Chatterton*, 37)
128 'Court of Bankruptcy: In Re Edmund O'Rourke', *The Times*, 3 August 1866, 9; Coleman (1888) 2:351
129 Classified advertisement, *The Era*, 18 May 1866, 8
130 'Drury Lane Theatre', *The Morning Post*, 2 February 1867, 7
131 'Debenture Holders and Renters of Drury Lane Theatre', *The Era*, 24 February 1867. The figures were included in the arbitration of a dispute between Chatterton and Dion Boucicault with regard to an arrangement between the two of them for producing *Formosa* in 1869. They both accepted John Hollingsworth as the arbitrator. A copy of his ruling is to be found in the Special Collections, University of Kent Library.
132 Chatterton's manifesto forms the first of four pages of a pamphlet in the Theatre and Performance Collection of the Victoria and Albert Museum, Drury Lane box 1866. Pages two and three contain details of *King John* followed by *The Comedy of Errors*, *Macbeth* and *The Beggar's Opera*. The manifesto was also included in later playbills and programmes during the season. A playbill issued in November 1866 promoting the forthcoming production of *Faust* is in the John Johnson Collection of the Bodleian Library Oxford, London playbills, Drury Lane, box 1 (104), 'The Hunchback', accessible online.
133 'Re-opening of Drury Lane Theatre', *The Era*, 9 September 1866, 11; 'The

Theatres', *The Illustrated London News*, 29 September 1866, 315-6
134 Coleman (1888) 2:352-3
135 Coleman (1888) 2:352
136 Coleman (1888) 2:352

5: SOLE LESSEE AND MANAGER

1 The *Report from the Select Committee on Theatrical Licences and Regulations* (1866, 295) contains a table showing the capacities of the twenty-seven London theatres, with that of Drury Lane given as 3,800. Only the Britannia Theatre in Hoxton had a larger capacity than Drury Lane, at 3,923. The capacity of Covent Garden is given as 6,880, but this was for promenade concerts at which the majority of those attending were strolling around on the platform that covered the pit. For some reason the Covent Garden management didn't supply the figures for a seated audience.
2 'Drury Lane Theatre', *The Times*, 24 September 1866, 10
3 Charles and Henry Webb were not twins, but their resemblance was so strong that audiences were unable to tell them apart. ('The Theatres: Princess's', *The Illustrated London News*, 5 March 1864, 238)
4 A classified advertisement in *The Times* on 28 November 1866 states: 'The scenic department under the direction of Mr William Beverley, whose valuable services are now exclusively devoted to this theatre.' This wording is slightly but significantly different from that used in previous seasons. For many years Beverley had been working at Drury Lane in the winter and Covent Garden, where he designed operas for Frederick Gye, in the summer. ('Celebrities at Home CCXXVI: Mr Beverley in Russell Square', *The World*, 22 December 1880, 5)
5 See page 268, note 74, for the exceptions.
6 From Goethe's *Kunst und Altherthum* (Art and Antiquity) quoted in *The Works of Lord Byron*, vol. 11, 1836, 71n.
7 Murray, 107
8 'The Theatres', *The Illustrated London News*, 2 February 1867, 119
9 All quotations from the four-page promotional leaflet headed 'Theatre Royal, Drury Lane. Combination of Classical and Romantic Plays: Shakespeare, Goethe, Sheridan Knowles and Lord Lytton', December 1866, copy in the John Johnson Collection, Bodleian Library, University of Oxford, London Playbills Drury Lane Box 1 (104). Accessible online.
10 'Drury Lane Theatre', *The Times*, 22 October 1866, 7
11 Scott, 2:291
12 Coleman (1888) 2:353
13 Chatterton repeated this to Coleman, and Clement Scott, who had actually been at the first night, included the legend in his autobiography. (Scott 2:292-3)
14 Hollingshead, 1:185
15 'The Christmas Pantomimes, Burlesques etc: Drury Lane Theatre', *The Times*, 27 December 1866, 7
16 'Benefit for the five fatherless children of the late Henry Webb', *The Era*, 24 February 1867. On 13 February 1870 *The Era* reported the death of Charles, second son in the family, at the age of fourteen. Chatterton, J. L. Toole and John Billington were praised as organisers of the Webb Fund, 'which was so liberally contributed to by almost every member of the profession'. (5)
17 '"Mr Sims Reeves is indisposed" is an announcement that his admirers have heard so often', lamented *The Era* (3 November 1878, 6). In April 1864 he had been announced to appear in an all-star matinee of *The School for*

Scandal at Drury Lane to raise funds for the Royal Dramatic College, but when his 'indisposition' was announced from the stage, there was laughter followed by cries of 'humbug!' ('Royal Dramatic College', *The Times*, 14 April 1864, 14) His no-shows were so notorious that the posters for his concerts warned patrons that their money would not be returned if he failed to appear through indisposition. (Sir John Pollock, *Time's Chariot*, London: John Murray, 25)

18 Coleman (1888) 2:354; 'Mr F. B. Chatterton and Mr Sims Reeves: Court of Common Pleas – June 27', *The Era*, 30 June 1867, 6; 'Chatterton v. Reeves', *The Era*, 25 August 1867, 11
19 *The Examiner*, 20 April 1867
20 Kenney (1875b) 13
21 *The Daily News*, 19 April 1867
22 *The Wrexham Advertiser*, 20 April 1867
23 *The Colleen Bawn Settled at Last* opened at the Lyceum on 5 July 1862; *My Heart's in the Highlands* opened at Drury Lane on 9 November 1863 and *An April Fool* on 11 April 1864
24 'Nothing in the Papers', *The Illustrated London News*, 4 March 1871, 206. 'It is not easy to understand how an object that excites no interest whatever outside the walls of a theatre, when seen within them can attract thousands of eager spectators... unless it be on the fly-in-amber principle of admiring "how the devil it got there".' (Kenney [1875b] 15-16)
25 Blanchard, diary entry for 23 April 1867, 1:337
26 Andrew Halliday, *The Great City*, Act I. MS accessed in the Lord Chamberlain's collection of plays in the Manuscripts Department of the British Library.
27 '*The Fortunes of Nigel* at Drury Lane', *The Spectator*, 3 October 1868, 1153.

The article was specifically about Andrew Halliday's next Drury Lane drama, *King o' Scots*, a year after *The Great City*, but the writer was considering it in the context of 'the passion for having London scenes brought on the stage'. The taste for 'the hard, dry, copying of street scenes, with real hansoms and costermongers' barrows' (an obvious reference to *The Great City*) was dismissed as 'very pitiable and unsatisfactory', but the writer predicted that whenever 'the dramatist of the day' might appear, he would find in London's astonishing size and richness of experience a fitting topic for his genius.

28 'Opinions of the Press on the Triumphantly Successful Drama of The Great City', Bodleian Library, University of Oxford, John Johnson Collection, London Playbills Drury Lane box 1 (108), 5 August 1867. Accessible online.
29 This was above the capacity of 3,800 that Chatterton had provided to the House of Commons Select Committee on Theatrical Licences and Regulations of the year before. The difference was presumably accounted for by people who were standing.
30 Kenney (1875b) 16
31 *The Entr'Acte*, 15 May 1875, 9
32 Kenney (1875b) 16
33 Kenney (1875b) 17
34 George Augustus Sala, 'Echoes of the Week', *The Illustrated London News*, 29 December 1877, 618 & Fitzgerald, 43-5. Percy Fitzgerald, a friend of Dickens, was invited by Dickens to accompany him to Drury Lane. He left an account of the disappointing outing in his memoir of Dickens. John Oxenford described *The Miller and His Men* as the perfect toy theatre play and predicted that, for as long as boys are playing with toy theatres, it would be preserved from oblivion. (John

Oxenford, 'The Toy Theatre', *The Era Almanack* 1871, 67 – 8) He was right about that as toy theatre enthusiasts still perform it.

35 Journal entry in Ravenna, 12 January 1821, in Leslie A. Marchand (ed.) (1978) *Born For Opposition: Byron's Letters and Journals*, vol. 8, 22-3 and Letter from Ravenna to John Murray of 16 February 1821 in Leslie A. Marchand (ed.) (1978) *Born For Opposition: Byron's Letters and Journals*, vol. 8, 78

36 Letter from Ravenna to John Murray of 16 February 1821 in Leslie A. Marchand (ed.) (1978) *Born For Opposition: Byron's Letters and Journals*, vol. 8, 78

37 'The purse of Old Drury/ Was not burst, I assure ye, / With the weight of the treasure,/ When, in spite of displeasure,/ And legal injunction,/ Abjuring compunction,/ This play they enlisted,/ And to act it persisted,/ Till 'twas thoroughly hiss'd at.' (*Blackwood's Magazine*, 1822, cited in *The Works of Lord Byron*, vol. 12, London: John Murray, 1835, 215)

38 Letter from Ravenna to John Murray of 16 May 1821 in Leslie A. Marchand (ed.) (1978) *Born For Opposition: Byron's Letters and Journals*, vol. 8, 119

39 Cited in *The Works of Lord Byron*, vol. 12, 1835, 47-8

40 Quoted in John Gardner, 'The Case of Byron's Marino Faliero', in Swindells & Taylor, 483

41 Howell, 41

42 Classified advertisements, *The Times*, 8 November 1867, 6

43 'Drury Lane Theatre', *The Times*, 4 November 1867, 7

44 Dutton Cook, *Nights at the Play: A View of the English Stage*, London, 1883, 1:16-7, cited in Howell, 46-7

45 'The Theatres', *The Illustrated London News*, 9 November 1867, 518

46 'Annual Meeting of the Drury Lane Proprietors', *The Era*, 2 February 1868

47 Kenney (1875b) 18

48 Mapleson, 29 - 30

49 'Destruction of Her Majesty's Theatre by Fire', *The Illustrated London News*, 14 December 1867, 658

50 Mapleson, 73. In 1867 Chatterton was living at 3 Kennington Oval.

51 Frederick Chatterton, letter to *The Morning Post*, 2 March 1868

52 Seven years later Mapleson would publicly thank Chatterton for: 'so readily [placing] the magnificent theatre at his disposal on the destruction of Her Majesty's Theatre, notwithstanding the many advantageous offers he received from other quarters' (Classified advertising, *The Times*, 20 March 1875, 8).

53 *The Athenaeum*, 22 February 1868, cited in Richards (2015) 276

54 Diary entry by Lewis Carroll, 17 January 1866, cited in Richards (2015) 276

55 Cole, 1:125

56 It was written by 'Col. A. B. Richards, well-known as the originator of the present volunteer movement'. According to Kenney, he was described as 'a gentleman known to literature' by some of the papers, 'in which case literature had probably the advantage of most people'. (Kenney [1875b] 19) Kenney's pose was an affectation: Alfred Richards had been editor of *The Morning Advertiser* and proprietor of the Queen's Theatre in Longacre by the time Kenney was writing. (Scott, 2:472) *The Prisoner of Toulon* received only ten performances.

57 'Mr Chatterton has certainly done his best to elevate the national drama to its proper position.' ('Drury Lane Theatre', *The Era*, 29 March 1868, 14); 'The house was crowded, Mr F. B. Chatterton, the manager, taking his benefit, and for his energy in the cause of legitimate drama meriting

recognition'. ('The Theatres', *The Illustrated London News*, 28 March 1868, 314)
58 'Drury Lane Theatre (Last Night)', *The Era*, 22 March 1868 (Town Edition)
59 Mapleson, 13n.
60 A copy of Mapleson's pamphlet is to be found in the Victoria and Albert Museum Theatre Collection, Drury Lane box, 1868.
61 *Building News*, 3 April 1868, 226
62 Mapleson, 76

6: SUCCESS
1 Kenney (1875b) 17-19
2 Kenney (1875b) 19
3 Kenney (1875b) 21
4 'The Theatres', *The Illustrated London News*, 28 October 1871, 417/8
5 'Dibdin… could produce a dramatic version of any given novel in something under eight-and-forty hours after its publication; and his competitors did not require much more time in the concoction of their plays on the same subject.' Dutton Cook, 'King o' Scots', *Pall Mall Gazette*, October 1868, reprinted in Cook, 1:81
6 'Drury Lane Theatre', *The Era*, 4 October 1868, 14 (Country Edition)
7 'The King o' Scots', *The Illustrated London News*, 17 October 1868, 382
8 *The Era*, 14 March 1869, 10
9 *The Era*, 10 January 1869, 8
10 Coleman (1888) 2:356
11 'Drury Lane Theatre', *The Times*, 28 September 1868, 9
12 Details taken from a poster in the John Johnson Collection, University of Oxford, Bodleian Library, London playbills Drury Lane box 1 (116). Accessible online.
13 'The Theatres', *The Illustrated London News*, 6 March 1869, 251. 'The legitimate month, which, at this season of the year, is, with laudable perseverance, diligently gone through at the national theatre, Drury Lane, must not be suffered to pass without special attention.'
14 Phelps's nephew described Dillon's attempt to alternate Falstaff and Hotspur with his uncle as 'simply ludicrous'. (Phelps & Forbes-Robertson, 24)
15 'Drury Lane Theatre', *The Times*, 30 March 1869, 10
16 'The Theatres, *The Illustrated London News*, 19 February 1870, 207. Chatterton brought King back to Drury Lane for another two weeks of legitimate drama towards the close of the 1869/70 season, then kept him on to play the villain Varney in *Amy Robsart*. At Easter 1871 Chatterton cast him as Quasimodo in Andrew Halliday's *Notre Dame* at the Adelphi.
17 *The Era*, 3 January 1869, 12
18 *The Hull Packet and East Riding Times*, 21 May 1869
19 *The Era*, 1 November 1874, 11. The critic was reviewing the transfer of *Amy Robsart*. Other Drury Lane shows to transfer to the Standard included *Peep o' Day* (1870), *Formosa* (1870), *Rebecca* (1872 and 1873) and *The Cataract of the Ganges* (1873).
20 The dramatic critic of *The Illustrated London News* was also agitated on this point: 'Had Formosa remained at home she might have married her parents' potboy, or, at most, the neighbouring cheesemonger's apprentice, but now a gentleman of fortune and high breeding… humbly sues for the distinction of being her husband.' ('The Theatres', *The Illustrated London News*, 28 August 1869, 215)
21 'Formosa at Drury Lane Theatre', Letter to the Editor, *The Times*, 19 August 1869, 7
22 F. B. Chatterton, Letter to the Editor, 'Formosa', *The Times*, 24 August 1869, 10
23 Clement Scott attributed the epigram

24 Coleman (1888) 2:355
25 Leader, *The Times*, 24 August 1869, 7
26 Dion Boucicault, 'Formosa', Letter to the Editor, *The Times*, 26 August 1869, 6
27 Stephens, 82-3. The anomaly was excused on the grounds that, in an opera, 'the words are subsidiary to the music'.
28 Leader, *The Times*, 26 August 1869, 8-9
29 Yates 1:309
30 'The curiosity excited by the discussion of the moral influences of the piece seems to induce excursionists, on their return to town, to pay this theatre an early visit.' (*The Era*, 3 October 1869, 10)
31 Kenney (1875b) 24. Boucicault would later claim that his share of the profits came to 'over £3,000 for ninety nights', but Formosa ran for 117 nights. ('Dion Boucicault and *The Shaughraun*', *The Era*, 10 December 1876)
32 We know some of the details of the agreement because – inevitably where Boucicault was involved – there was a dispute over money. Boucicault claimed that Chatterton had overcharged the rent of Drury Lane against the takings for *Formosa*, which meant his share of the profits was reduced. They both agreed to accept John Hollingshead of the Gaiety Theatre as arbitrator, and he found in Boucicault's favour. Chatterton was paying £5,000 a year in rental up to a maximum of 200 nights, with additional payments for every night beyond this up to a maximum of £5,350 for a maximum of 270 nights. Chatterton had already reached an agreement for a summer season of opera in 1870, which, in addition to the fact that *Formosa* had opened the season in August 1869, meant that the theatre would be open for 48½ weeks in the year and the rent of £5,350 would be payable. This meant that the weekly average for the year was lower than that which Chatterton had charged against *Formosa*. A copy of Hollingshead's adjudication, dated 11 May 1870, is held in the Templeman Library Special Collections at the University of Kent at Canterbury.
33 'The Theatres', *The Illustrated London News*, 28 August 1869, 215
34 Stephens, 86-7
35 Kenney (1875b) 27
36 'The Theatres: Christmas Pantomimes and Burlesques', *The Illustrated London News*, 1 January 1870, 27. The critic claimed that no fewer than eight Vokes were appearing.
37 'Velocipede', *The Entr'Acte*, 5 February 1870. 6; 'Pantomimic talent seems to be as hereditary as gout in certain houses' was another critic's observation. ('The Pantomimes', *Pall Mall Gazette*, 1 January 1870) The Covent Garden pantomime featured the rival Payne family.
38 'Drama: Drury Lane Theatre', *The Athenaeum*, 19 February 1870, 270
39 *Amy Robsart* in 1871, 1872 & 1874; *Rebecca* in 1875; and *The Cataract of the Ganges* in 1873.
40 Coleman (1888) 2:354
41 It opened at the Princess's Theatre in Oxford Street in February and the Standard Theatre in Shoreditch in March 1870, with most of the original cast. The first out-of-London production had opened in Newcastle on 11 October 1869.
42 Richards (2015) 179
43 Coleman (1888) 2:355. The text actually has 'A profit of £3,000 in Lent', but this must have been a typographical error. The figure of £2,000 is given on the previous line, and it is the figure given by Kenney (1875b, 28) who was writing with the account books in front of him.

Coleman reports Chatterton saying that he engaged Edmund Falconer for his original part 'on liberal terms', but he was confusing revivals of this play: Falconer was still in the USA.

44 'Metropolitan Gossip', *The Preston Guardian*, 9 October 1869
45 'The Theatres', *The Illustrated London News*, 16 October 1869, 391; Coleman (1886) 251
46 Mapleson, 91
47 'The Theatres', *The Illustrated London News*, 29 October 1870, 455
48 Sheppard (1970) Survey of London XXXVI, 247. Webster's status as 'proprietor' first appears in *The Times* classified advertisements on Monday 12 April 1852, 4
49 See 'Theatre Royal, Adelphi (Rebuilding and Enlarging)', classified advertisement, *The Times*, 3 April 1856, 6,
50 *The Era*, 24 April 1870, 9
51 'Court of Common Pleas', *The Times*, 18 June 1870, 11; 'A Theatrical Slander Case', *The Era*, 19 June 1870, 5
52 The work was carried out under the supervision of Marsh Nelson as architect to the proprietors, and C. J. Phipps, the leading theatre architect of the day, as architect to Chatterton. Phipps had been acting for Chatterton in relation to the bodged work of the previous year, although he insisted in a letter to *Building News* that it had been carried out to a high standard and to his entire satisfaction (*Building News*, 22 April 1870, 331). Phipps would succeed Marsh Nelson as architect to the proprietors in 1879 (Garlick [2016] 93-3; *The Builder*, 13 December 1879, 1,369).
53 Andrew Halliday and Frederic Lawrance, *Kenilworth or Ye Queene, Ye Earle and Ye Maydenne*, London: Thomas Hailes Lacy, n.d., Scene 8, 45
54 'Drury Lane Theatre', *The Times*, 26 September 1870, 12
55 Anderson, 306. In 1835, when J. R. Planché adapted *La Juive* for Alfred Bunn as *The Jewess*, he altered the ending so that the heroine's true identity as a Christian is revealed *before* the bonfire on which she is to be burnt alive for heresy is lit. (Whelan, 356) Dion Boucicault saved his Colleen Bawn, who had been murdered both in his source novel *The Collegians* and in real life, while *The Athenaeum* (23 November 1861) blamed the cool reception of his play *The Octoroon* on the fact that 'the English do not like to see their heroines sacrificed'. Boucicault quickly rewrote the ending so that the heroine would survive, describing the new ending as 'composed by the public and edited by the author'.
56 'Drury Lane Theatre', *The Times*, 26 September 1870, 12
57 Classified advertisements, *The Times*, 27 September, 6
58 *The Observer*, 26 September 1870, cited in the classified advertisements, *The Times*, 27 September, 6
59 'Drury Lane Theatre', *The Times*, 26 September 1870, 12
60 As an afterpiece for the first seven performances, then as a curtain-raiser until Christmas. The other piece in the programme was a farce called *A Domestic Hercules*. The timings given for the first seven nights were: *A Domestic Hercules* 7.00 p.m.; *Amy Robsart* 7.45 p.m.; *Phobus' Fix* 11.00 p.m., ending 11.30 p.m, so Amy Robsart had a running-time of three-and-a-quarter hours.
61 Kenney (1875b) 30. Kenney remarks that this is just below the profits generated by *Formosa*, but on this occasion Chatterton didn't have to share them with the author. Andrew Halliday must have been on a fee or royalty.
62 Chatterton presented Victoria Vokes with a bracelet the next day to mark her great success in a role that was

totally different from anything she had played before. (*The Era*, 20 November 1870, 10)
63 'Velocipede', *The Entr'Acte*, 14 January 1871, 6
64 'Christmas Entertainments: The Theatres', *The Times*, 27 December 1870, 4
65 'Drama', *The Athenaeum*, 1 January 1870, 31. *The Entr'Acte* (5 February 1870, 6) complained that the advertising 'makes the stage of the national theatre like the gallery of the Agricultural Hall in cattle show week'.
66 'Nothing in the Papers', *The Illustrated London News*, 31 December 1870, 675
67 Classified advertisements, *The Times*, 20 March 1871, 8
68 In 1869, when the first of the coalition seasons was barely underway, the opera critic of *The Era* had complained about the monopoly and wished for its speedy destruction, otherwise opera impresarios would be able to get away with feeding the public an undiluted diet of Verdi instead of looking for interesting new works. ('The Opera and the Press', *The Era*, 25 July 1869, 10)
69 Mapleson claimed in his *Memoirs* that: 'It has amused me… to see how persistently Mr Gye endeavoured… to bring my career as operatic manager to an abrupt end.' (Mapleson, 89) It is hard to believe that Mapleson found it all that amusing at the time. Gye, on the other hand, regarded Mapleson as a slippery character whose word could not be relied on. 'If only you could have learned to do two things,' Gye told Mapleson years later, 'to tell the truth and to go straight, we could have made such a success of the amalgamation.' (Gabriella Dideriksen and Matthew Ringel, 'Frederick Gye and "The Dreadful Business of Opera Management"', *19th-Century Music*, vol. 19 no. 1, Summer 1995, 9)
70 *The Era* of 9 July 1871 (p.13) reproduced a call first made in *The Globe* to establish some sort of public body to prevent the waste of such a valuable site in central London. In December 1868 *The Builder* published a denial of a rumour that was circulating to the effect that the Earl of Dudley, who held the lease of Her Majesty's, only intended to reconstruct the shell, without fitting it out. However, this is exactly what happened. The theatre was not fitted out until Mapleson undertook the task at his own expense in 1877. (*The Era*, 6 December 1868, 6)
71 'Her Majesty's Opera, Theatre Royal, Drury Lane', *The Era*, 23 April 1871, 11
72 Mapleson, 92
73 Classified advertisements, *The Times*, 20 September 1871, 6, The text was taken from a handbill signed by Andrew Halliday in which he promised that 'every alteration [to Sir Walter Scott's story] has been made with a reverential hand, and with the view of doing as little violence as possible to the purpose of the glorious story'. (Victoria and Albert Museum Theatre Collection, Drury Lane box 1871)
74 'Velocipede', 'Correspondence', *The Entr'Acte*, 18 November 1871, 3. Halliday was the only living person apart from Dion Boucicault who challenged William Beverley in the battle of the font sizes, whose symbolic value means so much to people working in the theatre and so little to everyone else. On the publicity for *Amy Robsart* his name was in letters of the same size as Beverley's. For *The Lady of the Lake* (1872), *Antony and Cleopatra* (1873) and *Richard Coeur de Lion* (1874), Halliday's name would be the same size, and in some cases even larger, than Beverley's.

75 *The Daily Telegraph*, 25 September 1871
76 'Drury Lane Theatre', *The Times*, 26 September 1871, 4
77 Coleman (1888) 357. Halliday later claimed that it had taken £24,000 'at the doors' (Advertisement, *The Era*, 7 January 1877, 11). The acknowledgement of the £250 raised at the matinee of *Rebecca* on 6 December 1871 was printed in *The Era*, 17 December 1871, 11.
78 At Adelaide Neilson's benefit performance of *As You Like It* on 18 December, Chatterton had led the whole company in singing the same patriotic song, which was 'received with enthusiastic admiration'. He also had the audience on their feet and cheering when the band play the song on the first night of *On The Jury* at the Princess's on 16 December (*The Times*, 21 December 1871, 4)
79 'Mr Chatterton's Benefit', *The Era*, 24 March 1872, 12
80 'Drury Lane', *The Era*, 31 March 1872, 11
81 'The Theatres', *The Illustrated London News*, 30 March 1872, 319
82 Mapleson, 94
83 On 17 October and 22 October 1870 respectively
84 Coleman (1888) 2:358
85 The theatre historian Barton Baker regarded these endless farewell performances as a serious mistake: 'Madame Céleste, alas, reappeared upon the scene of her former triumphs, only to sadden old playgoers by comparisons between the past and the present, and to excite the incredulity of younger ones. And this was not her last appearance; again at the end of 1874 she exhibited the wreck of her fine powers to an unsympathising audience.' (Barton Baker, 435) Madame Céleste's final performance appears to have been as Miami in *Green Bushes* at the Adelphi on 16 October 1874. Ironically, it was not billed as her farewell performance, presumably because she intended to act again but was prevented, perhaps by ill health. She died from cancer in 1882.
86 *The Times*, 11 April 1871, 9
87 ''The Drama: Lyceum Theatre', *The Athenaeum*, 24 September 1870, 412-3 & 'The Lyceum Theatre', *The Times*, 19 September 1870, 6
88 'Princess's Theatre', *The Times*, 3 July 1871, 5
89 Coleman (1888) 2:352
90 Coleman (1888) 2:359
91 Coleman (1888) 2:370
92 The phrase 'double-barrelled benefit' to describe Chatterton's habit of giving himself not one but two benefits at the end of the season was coined in the theatrical weekly *The Entr'Acte* for Chatterton's benefit at the end of the 1872/73 season at Drury Lane. ('London Theatres: Drury Lane', *The Entr'Acte*, 12 April 1873, 4)

7: THE CRACKS BEGIN TO SHOW
1 *The Daily Telegraph*, 25 September 1871
2 'Drury Lane Theatre', *The Observer*, 23 September 1872, 6
3 Blanchard, 2:416, diary entry for 21 September 1872
4 In his account of the production (Kenney [1875b] 36-9) Charles Lamb Kenney described *The Lady of the Lake* as 'the reverse of profitable to the management'. His account was contradicted by Chatterton when he spoke to Coleman about *The Lady of the Lake*. Chatterton claimed (Coleman [1888] 2:357) that the production had made a profit of £4,000. He was speaking fifteen years after the event, without any papers to consult, and this may be one of the many confusions in his narrative. Kenney was writing three years after

the event, with the Drury Lane account books before him, and his account must have been approved for publication by Chatterton himself at the time.

5 Classified advertisement, *The Times*, 28 February 1873, 8

6 Webster claimed that he had often stood in for the leading man in the original production. ('"The Cataract of the Ganges" at Drury Lane', *The Era*, 16 February 1873, 4)

7 Review reprinted in Cook, 1:259-63

8 More of the original text was restored when the production transferred to the Standard and there was new scenery painted by Richard Douglass. The Drury Lane costumes and special effects were used but there was a different cast. (Kenney [1875b] 45; 'Drury Lane', *The Era*, 9 March 1873, 10; 'The Theatres', *The Illustrated London News*, 19 April 1873, 379)

9 Joseph Knight, 'Drama: The Week', *The Athenaeum*, 12 April 1873, 481)

10 The lease issued to Chatterton as sole lessee in 1866 actually expired on 30 June 1873, but as Mapleson's opera was already booked in, he had asked the proprietors in the autumn of 1872 to extend the period to 15 August 1873. This was agreed. The new five-year lease at the annual rent of £6,500 a year was to run from 18 August 1873. 'Drury Lane Renters', *The Era*, 24 August 1873

11 'Drury Lane Theatre', *The Times*, 1 April 1873, 8

12 'Railway and Other Companies', *The Times*, 22 August 1873, 5 & 'Drury Lane Renters', *The Era*, 13 April 1873

13 'Drury Lane Renters', *The Era*, 13 April 1873. See also 'Drury Lane', *The Times*, 25 February 1871, 12 & Drury Lane Renters', *The Era*, 24 August 1873.

14 'Railway and Other Companies', *The Times*, 21 July 1873, 8

15 Ristori was scheduled to appear as Marie Antoinette on 4 July, when a visit of the Shah of Persia was arranged at only one day's notice. It may have been felt that an Italian actress portraying a French queen in Italian would have been unsuitable for the Shah so a performance of extracts from operas was arranged instead. Ristori therefore gave one performance in the week after her benefit, which took place on 11 July. There was also one matinée, so there were eleven performances in all.

16 In his *Times* review (16 June 1873, 6), John Oxenford complained that the booklets were in English only, instead of Italian and English as formerly. Two days later a classified advertisement warned patrons against buying the booklets on sale outside the theatre as these were not accurate; only the booklets on sale in the auditorium for 2s. were authorised. Five days after that, Oxenford reassured his readers that the booklets were now bilingual. ('Madame Ristori', *The Times*, 23 June 1873, 10)

17 James Anderson saw Phelps as Othello in the first few days of the season and described it as: ' solid and correct (he always was) but slow and hard, and exhibited no more love and passion for Desdemona than a stewed prune.... sadly deficient in fire and electricity.' (Anderson, 312-3)

18 Phelps went to the Gaiety and, according to John Hollingshead: 'till the day of his lamented death, he considered himself... engaged to me, and never thought of any public appearance without consulting me.' Phelps told Hollingshead that he preferred the Gaiety to Drury Lane, which was too big. (Hollingshead, 2:77)

19 None in 1869/70; one in 1870/71 (Adelaide Neilson's benefit in *Romeo and Juliet* on 19 December); one in 1871/72 (Adelaide Neilson's benefit in

As You Like It on 18 December); two in 1872/73 (*King Lear* for Chatterton's benefits on 29 & 31 March).
20 Dryden, *Of Dramatic Poesy*, 2: 67
21 The Yale Edition of the Works of Samuel Johnson, VIII, *Johnson on Shakespeare*, New Haven & London: Yale University Press, 1968, 873; A. C. Bradley (1904) *Shakespearean Tragedy: Lectures on Hamlet, Othello, King Lear, Macbeth*, London: Macmillan and Co., 260
22 Phelps's biographer Shirley Allen called it 'one of the most important productions of a theatrical generation'. (Allen, 242)
23 'Drury Lane Theatre', *The Morning Post*, 21 July 1873, 3
24 'Drury Lane Theatre', *The Builder*, 27 September 1873, 771.
25 'The Theatres', *The Illustrated London News*, 27 September 1873, 290
26 'The Theatres: Drury Lane', *The Times*, 22 September 1873, 12
27 'The Theatres: Drury Lane', *The Times*, 22 September 1873, 12
28 Dutton Cook, review of *Antony and Cleopatra* in *The Pall Mall Gazette*, reprinted in Cook, 1:294
29 Anderson, 317
30 The theatrical paper *The Era* sarcastically observed that 'the public… fully appreciate such condescension' when she agreed to appear in a benefit performance for Henry Irving. ('Theatrical Gossip', *The Era*, 18 June 1876)
31 She had only been acting for a year, having made her debut at the Standard Theatre in East London on 14 September 1872 as Pauline in *The Lady of Lyons*. She caught Chatterton's eye playing Oliver Cromwell's daughter Elizabeth in *Cromwell* by Colonel A. B. Richards which opened at the Queen's Theatre on 21 December 1872. ('Ellen Wallis', *Touchstone*, 5 October 1878, 3)
32 'Presentation to Miss Wallis', *The Illustrated London News*, 19 October 1873, 9
33 'Miss Wallis as "Cleopatra" at Drury Lane Theatre', *The Era*, 19 October 1873, 9
34 Anderson, 318
35 The correspondence was sparked off by a very late review of Charles Kenney's pamphlet *Poets and Profits* that was published in *The Athenaeum* on 18 December 1875, 840. This revealed that the loss on *Antony and Cleopatra* had been between £4,000 and £5,000, which provoked Isabella Glyn to write saying that she was glad to learn that Chatterton had been punished for showing disrespect to Shakespeare. Her letter appeared in *The Athenaeum* on 1 January 1876, 30. Subsequent letters appeared on: 15 January, 100; 22 January 137-8; 29 January, 172; 12 February, 241; & 26 February, 307-8.
36 Anderson, 317. Five years later another critic would accuse Chatterton of putting on plays 'destined rather to win the applause of the injudicious many than of the judicious few'. ('Scrutator', 'A Winter's Tale', *Truth*, 10 October 1878, 409)
37 Classified advertisements, *The Times*, 6 November 1873, 6
38 F. B. Chatterton, Letter to the Editor, 'Formosa', *The Times*, 24 August 1869, 10
39 'A Dramatist on the Criticism of the Drama', Correspondence, *The Pall Mall Gazette*, 1 February 1869
40 Anderson, 319
41 Kenney (1875b) 44
42 W. E Gladstone, diary entry 1 December 1873, *The Gladstone Diaries*, vol. 8, ed. H. C. G. Matthew, Oxford: The Clarendon Press, 1982, 491
43 'Boxing Day Entertainments: Drury Lane', *The Times*, 27 December 1873, 5
44 Ruskin was not the first to make this

comparison. When Dr John Doran was writing his account of his visit to the last rehearsal of the 1865 pantomime he made the same point: 'Outside were blasphemy and drunkenness. Inside, boundless activity, order, hard work and cheerful hearts.' (Doran, 1:1)

45 'In this pantomime occurred the wondrous stage effect, which none who witnessed can forget, in the Mushroom Valley, where the fungi were seen to develop, according to their wont, with a rapidity of vegetation that has made them proverbial, and where others became transformed into hundreds of little children, their button tops forming the head gear of the army of little people.' (Kenney [1875b] 46.)

46 John Ruskin, *Fors Clavigera*, Letter 39, March 1874

47 See Jeffrey Richards, 'E. L. Blanchard and "The Golden Age of Pantomime"' in Davis (2010) 27

48 'Drury Lane Theatre', *The Times*, 4 February 1874, 7

49 Hollingsworth, 2:93

50 'London Theatres', *Entr'Acte*, 29 August 1874, 4. The architect James Buckle wrote of the Princess's in 1887 that: 'This theatre has probably had more uncomplimentary epithets bestowed upon it by lessees, actors and the public than any other London playhouse.' ('Mr Irving's "Safety Theatre"', *The Era*, 12 November 1887, 8)

51 'Theatrical Changes', *The Era*, 9 October 1870, 9

52 Chatterton paid Webster £5,950 for the transfer of the lease of the Princess's, as Webster was about to be declared bankrupt for that sum. ('The Adelphi in Litigation', *The Era*, 21 July 1878, 10)

53 'High Court of Justice, Chancery Division, Webster v. Chatterton', *The Times*, 19 July 1878, 4. Chatterton's lease came into effect on 17 January 1874.

54 The play had opened at the Adelphi on 5 December 1853 with the title *Thirst of Gold*. The title was changed to *The Prayer in the Storm* for this revival.

55 Stephens, 88-91

56 In 'The New National Opera House', J. H. Mapleson, Letter to the Editor, *The Times*, 4 August 1877, 10, Mapleson claimed that he had been paying £250 per week. On 28 August 1877 *The Times* printed a correction from Chatterton saying that Mapleson paid him £3,000 for a sixteen-week season, which works out at £187 10s. per week. Mapleson's seasons rarely ran for sixteen weeks, although he had to allow time to alter the arrangements in the auditorium and to clean the theatre, then restore the theatre to its previous seating arrangement afterwards, so he was probably calculating the rent based on the actual number of weeks during which he was putting on performances. However, the opera season really did run for sixteen weeks in 1874, so the payment may have been even higher than £3,000.

57 The irony was not lost on E. L. Blanchard who, in addition to writing the Drury Lane pantomime that year, wrote *Cinderella or Harlequin and the Little Glass Slipper* for the Crystal Palace. This began with a scene in The Curious Cabinet of Crotchets with characters dressed as musical instruments and the different types of music. 'Poor English opera – kept so in the distance/Folks have almost forgotten your existence', was represented by 'The Bohemian Girl', the eponymous heroine of Balfe's most famous opera. Italian opera was represented by Richard the Lionheart carrying a scroll saying 'Il Talismano'. 'Our famous Balfe Italian irons

required/To make his scholars smooth as he desired.'
58. Letter from Michael Balfe to Bill Davison, dated 23 February 1870, reproduced in Walsh, 168
59. *Illustrated Sporting and Dramatic News*, 13 June 1874; *The Times*, 10 June 1874, 5
60. 'The New National Opera House', Letter to the Editor, *The Times*, 4 August 1877, 10
61. Tinsley, 2:255
62. A classified advertisement in The Times (of 17 July 1871 [p.8] stated that £525 had already been raised. The statue cost in the region of £800.
63. Kenney (1875a) 308
64. Eventually there was a memorial to Balfe in Westminster Abbey, again by Mallempré, that was unveiled on 20 October 1882. It is a more modest, wall-mounted affair, with a profile of Balfe within an oval frame supported by books, musical instruments and the scores of *The Bohemian Girl* and *The Talisman*.
65. Anderson, 320
66. 'The London Theatres: Drury Lane', *The Entr'Acte*, 17 October 1874, 4
67. Kenney (1875b) 49
68. Anderson, 321 & 346. 'The legitimate drama is many fathoms deep, and poor Shakespeare, if not drowned, is at least a great way under water.' (323) Anderson's memoirs were serialised in the *Newcastle Weekly Chronicle* between January 1887 and April 1888, but they had been written several years earlier and the narrative ends at 1882. As a result, he doesn't mention his decision to break his own vow and do one more production. He played Tybalt in *Romeo and Juliet* at the Lyceum in the autumn of 1884.
69. 'Drama', *The Athenaeum*, 3 October 1874, 458
70. 'Queen's Theatre', *The Times*, 22 June 1874, 10
71. Ward, 62
72. Mapleson, 108-09
73. Classified advertising, *The Times*, 20 March 1875, 8
74. Chatterton's prices were stalls 7s. and dress circle 5s. Mapleson's prices for Salvini were stalls 12s. 6d. and dress circle 7s. 6d. His opera prices were stalls 21s. and dress circle 10s. 6d.
75. William Michael Rossetti, *Some Reminiscences*, New York, 1906, 2 vols, 1:189, cited in Carlson, 48; Henry James, *The Scenic Art*, New York: Hill & Wang, 1957, 172, cited in Carlson, 71
76. From a review, not attributed, but stuck onto a sheet in the Victoria and Albert Museum's Theatre Collection, Drury Lane Box 1875. The sheet carries several reviews, on both sides of the paper, all written in this wildly enthusiastic style.
77. Robert Speaight, *William Poel and the Elizabethan Revival*, Cambridge, Mass, 1954, 26, cited in Carlson, 51
78. 'Signor Salvini', *The Times*, Friday 4 June 1875, 7
79. Although her benefit performance on 11 July 1873 included her famous rendering of Lady Macbeth's sleepwalking scene in a mixed programme of items.
80. 'Mr Chatterton… did not think it right that in the great national theatre under his control I should be making so much money out of Shakespeare.' (Mapleson, 111)

8: INDIAN SUMMER
1. Kenney (1875b) 50
2. Kenney (1875b) vi
3. Kenney (1875b) 50
4. Kenney (1875b) 51
5. Kenney (1875b) viii
6. Kenney (1875b) ix
7. Kenney (1875b) iii
8. 'Drury Lane Theatre', *The Times*, 6 September 1874, 12
9. 'Dion Boucicault and *The Shaughraun*', *The Era*, 10 December 1876

10 Jefferson claimed in 1875 that he had played no other part since being in London ten years before and he didn't care if he played it for the rest of his life. ('Echoes of the Week', *The Illustrated London News*, 6 November 1875) It was described as: 'one of the most perfect performances the stage has ever known'. ('The Dramatic Season', *The World*, 2 August 1876, 10)

11 Coleman (1888) 360. Chatterton told Coleman that his three concurrent hits were *The Shaughraun, Rip van Winkle* and *Notre Dame*, but he was confusing Halliday's adaptations. *Notre Dame* had been a hit at the Adelphi in 1871.

12 Garlick (2003) 102

13 Sheppard (1970) *Survey of London* XXXV, 17-8 & 22

14 Andrew Halliday, 'English and American Theatres', *The Era*, 30 October 1870, cited in David and Emeljanow, 208

15 'The Rights of Drury Lane Renters', *The Era*, 7 December 1873; 'The Rights of Renters at Drury Lane Theatre', *The Era*, 22 November 1874; Letter from William Tegg, Hon. Secretary of the Renters' Committee, 'Original Correspondence', *The Era*, 22 November 1874; Reply from F. B. Chatterton, 'Original Correspondence', *The Era*, 13 December 1874; 'The Renters of Drury Lane Theatre', *The Era*, 12 December 1875

16 'The Renters of Old Drury', *The Era*, 19 December 1875

17 Letter to the Editor of *The Era*, 'The Drury Lane Renters – Dauney v. Chatterton', *The Era*, 13 December 1875. Augustus Harris claimed that a full house at Drury Lane should have been worth £500, but this was reduced to £350 once the renters had been provided with free seats. He was so frustrated by this that he decided to extinguish the privilege by buying all the renters' shares. 'The first night he took a full £500 in the house, the occasion was duly celebrated.' (Booth [1943] 113).

18 The full text of the letter is reproduced in McFeely, 184-6

19 George Augustus Sala mocked Boucicault's pretensions, saying that a cat can look at a king but it takes two to make a correspondence, and Disraeli had ignored the letter. Sala pretended to admire Boucicault's ability to make money out of absolutely anything and predicted a comedy for next season based on the Chartist Riots of 1848 that would earn him £150,000. ('Echoes of the Week', *The Illustrated London News*, 15 January 1876, 58)

20 For an account of the letter and Boucicault's involvement with Irish political causes see McFeely 116-38. Boucicault established the Boucicault Fund to receive the profits from benefit nights to be given in each town on the provincial tour of *The Shaughraun*. The fund supported the families of imprisoned Fenians and the men themselves when they were released. All prisoners were released between 1877 and 1878 following a petition by US President Grant and his cabinet.

21 Coleman (1888) 2:365

22 Classified advertisement, *The Times*, 11 January 1876, 8

23 Classified advertisements, *The Times*, 22 January 1876, 8

24 Coleman (1888) 2:365-9

25 Williamson published his correspondence with Chatterton in *The Era*. ('The Shaughraun', 19 November 1876)

26 'Boucicault v. Chatterton: Chancery Division', *The Times*, 17 November 1876, 8

27 'Boucicault v. Chatterton: Court of Appeal, *The Times*, 15 December 1876, 10

28 'Early in 1877, when I applied for the renewal of my lease of the Theatre Royal, Drury Lane, Mr Chatterton showed much ill-will, which I attributed to his jealousy at my previous success with Salvini, and to my having declined to allow him to engage the Italian tragedian on his own account.' Mapleson, 113
29 'Salvini v. Coleman: To The Editor of The Era', *The Era*, 2 July 1876
30 Reported in *The Athenaeum*, no. 2482, 22 May 1875, 699, cited in Carlson, 130
31 Mapleson, 111
32 'Signor Rossi' (by telegraph) (from a French correspondent) *The Times*, Monday 4 October 1875, 5. To make it worse, *The Times* carried another poor review of Rossi, this time as Hamlet, on Monday 18 October 1875. This reviewer said that Rossi should not make his debut at Drury Lane as Hamlet but should stick with Othello (10).
33 Carlson, 128. Madame Ristori's verdict on the two men was: 'Salvini, attractive, showy, fascinating, but melodramatic. Rossi, *magnifique*, a poet.' (Barnes, 138)
34 Coleman (1904) 2: 648
35 Hollingshead, 2: 86-7
36 Coleman (1904) 2: 648
37 Salvini, 171-72. Salvini claimed that he was troubled by a carbuncle between the shoulder blades and that he was given up for dead by the personal physician of the Prince of Wales. He discharged his company and returned Italy.
38 Coleman (1888) 2:370. Rossi took Hollingshead's advice and avoided Othello. Of his twenty-three performances, six were of Hamlet, six of Lear, six of Romeo and four of Macbeth. Henry James (53-4) observed that: 'For a stout middle-aged man one would say that Romeo was rather a snare.' The final performance (21 June) was Rossi's benefit at which he played scenes from several Shakespeare plays.
39 'The Dramatic Season', *The World*, 2 August 1876, 10
40 Hollingshead, 2: 86-7

9: DRURY LANE IN DECLINE
1 Anderson, 330
2 'King Henry V', *The World*, 20 September 1876
3 'Mr John Coleman's Bankruptcy', *The Era*, 4 March 1877, 13
4 *The Entr'Acte*, 7 November 1876, 7. This was the caption to a full-page cartoon of Coleman.
5 Coleman (1888) 2:388
6 'What the World Says', *The World*, 11 October 1876, 13
7 Anderson, 331
8 'King Richard III at Drury Lane', *The Spectator*, 4 November 1876, 1370-1
9 'The Degradation of the Stage', *The World*, 2 December 1874, 6
10 'The Ghost That Walks', 'The Modern Stage', *The World*, 23 December 1874, 14-15
11 'Correspondence: The Modern Stage', *The World*, 6 January 1875, 16 - 18
12 'Correspondence: The Drama and Dramatic Critics', *The World*, 13 January 1875, 16 - 17
13 'Correspondence: Drama and Dramatic Critics', *The World*, 20 January 1875, 16 & 27 January 1875, 16
14 'Dramatic Criticism', *The World*, 10 February 1875, 8. The article was unsigned but it carries the authority of the editor.
15 'Atlas', 'What the World Says', *The World*, 24 November 1875, 14. Oxenford's last review as dramatic critic of *The Times* was for Henry Irving's *Macbeth*. He struggled for a week to write it and resigned the day after it appeared on 2 October 1875. (Hawkins, 83)
16 *The Times* was very much a family

business in those days. It had been founded in 1785 by John Walter, who passed it to his son John Walter II, who passed it to his son John Walter III. William Delane, the father of John Thadeus, had been financial director of the paper from 1831 to 1847 and John Oxenford owed his position at *The Times* to the influence of his uncle Thomas Alsager, who wrote the City column until he was found to be 'jobbing' the paper to boost the value of shares that he held. He committed suicide.

17 Morris, 12
18 In November 1882 *The World* expressed mock outrage at the news that a theatre manager had laid on a 'jolly supper' for 'a few of the press and… two well-known newspaper writers… Who are these wretches?' *The World* wanted to know. The piece was headed: 'O tempora, O Mowbray! O chicken and champagne!' ('Atlas', 'What the World Says', *The World*, 22 November 1882, 13) According to the journalist J. B. Booth, Mowbray's departure from *The Times* was not much regretted by his professional colleagues. He was accused of parading his intolerant prejudices too blatantly, and his book was described as 'two hundred and twenty-six pages of aggressive biliousness' and 'a silly, prejudiced, unnecessary, and misleading work, written evidently by a soured and disappointed man'. (J. B. Booth [1943] *The Days We Knew*, London: T. Werner Laurie, 102, quoted in Richards [2005] 302)
19 Morris, 20
20 'Atlas', 'What the World Says', *The World*, 17 January 1877, 12 & 'What the World Says', *The World*, 11 August 1880, 13
21 'Nothing in the Papers', *The Illustrated London News*, 4 November 1871, 427
22 'Scrutator', *Truth*, 3 January 1878, 8
23 'Scrutator', *Truth*, 18 October 1877, 461-2
24 The only show to open at Drury Lane between *The Shaughraun* (which Oxenford reviewed) in autumn 1875 and *Richard III* in autumn 1876 was the 1875/76 pantomime, *Whittington and His Cat*, which Oxenford had probably reviewed. The review was too generous in tone to be Morris's and, although retired and in poor health, Oxenford continued to write occasional reviews for *The Times*. His enthusiasm for the Drury Lane pantomimes was well known, which would have made the invitation to review *Whittington and His Cat* a kindly one.
25 'The Theatres', *The Times*, 24 April 1876, 7
26 'Princess's Theatre', *The Times*, 22 May 1876, 10
27 'Drury Lane Theatre', *The Times*, 27 September 1876, 8
28 'Drury Lane Theatre', *The Times*, 26 February 1868, 10. Critics of other papers had not been so kind to the performance. According to *The Morning Post* (26 February 1868, 5), Sullivan ranted throughout: 'All that is subtle and intellectual in the character is of course lost amid this turbulent flood of noise.' *The Illustrated London News* damned with faint praise: 'The wonder is that, with his limitations of power, Mr Sullivan is able to repeat the traditions of the part with so much apparent energy; and his example shows how, by cultivation, a weak organ may receive an artificial development which shall answer most of the purposes required.' ('The Theatres', *The Illustrated London News*, 7 March 1868, 239)
29 The Drury Lane box for 1876 in the Theatre Collection of the Victoria and Albert Museum contains several programmes for *Richard III*, showing the switch in the text when Chatterton

replaced the Rimmel's advertisement with his own diatribe (probably written by Charles Lamb Kenney). Programmes consisted of one sheet of thin card, folded once to make four pages. The Rimmel's advertisement always appeared on the back page.

30 Classified advertisements, *The Times*, 30 September 1876, 8. Oxenford's review had actually appeared on 26 February 1868, not the 20th, and the quote ended 'British capital' not 'British stage'.

31 Knight, 149-50, review in *The Athenaeum* of 30 September 1876. Even in 1868, when Oxenford had praised Barry Sullivan's performance in the part, another critic had said of another production of Cibber's play that: 'the piece has long since lost its attraction, and would nowadays not pay the expense of its mounting'. ('The Theatres', *The Illustrated London News*, 22 August 1868, 187)

32 'Atlas', 'What the World Says', *The World*, 1 November 1876, 14. Henry Labouchere, the editor of *Truth*, for which he also wrote the dramatic criticism, liked to maintain a certain aloofness as a man of the world, and sarcastically observed of Mowbray's fierce denunciation that, once 'the critic of *The Times* [had] lectured Mr Chatterton for daring to do what every manager, with one exception, has done since the year 1700, it was not likely that any opportunity would be missed of making all Europe pause whilst Colley Cibber was cursed, and Nahum Tate was anathematised along with the Jackdaw of Rheims and other equally eminent personages'. Labouchere took the view that Shakespeare's play was a mess and that Colley Cibber's alterations made it much better for the audience. 'Scrutator' [Henry Labouchere], *Truth*, 8 February 1877, 170.

33 He described Shakespeare's text as being 'less fitted… for representation on the stage than almost any other generally acted play of the great poet', while Cibber's version was 'one of the most admirable and skilful instances of dramatic adaptations ever known'. (Cole, 2: 101)

34 'The Theatres', *The Illustrated London News*, 12 August 1876, 163 & 30 September 1876, 326

35 Austen Brereton (1908) *The Life of Henry Irving*, London: Longmans, Green & Co., 1:.167-8, cited in Richards (2005) 122

36 Classified advertisement, *The Times*, 29 January 1877, 8

37 The dramatic critic of *The World* agreed, concluding a very favourable review with the advice that: 'Mr Irving's physical powers should certainly not be subjected to the strain involved in nightly, or indeed very frequent, repetition of exertions that needs must be extremely severe; attempt should not be made to "run" *Richard III*.' ('The Theatre: Richard III', *The World*, 7 February 1877, 10)

38 Coleman (1888) 370. Sullivan missed the last few performances after Chatterton's old friend Henry Sinclair, who was playing the Earl of Richmond, nearly blinded him when he accidentally gashed Sullivan across the face during the swordfight on Bosworth Field. James Bennet had to take over the part.

39 There was a production of Cibber's *Richard III* which opened at the Olympic on 25 April 1892 for twelve performances. This seems to have been Cibber's absolute last gasp in London.

40 'Haska in Court', *The Era*, 11 March 187, 7; 'Drury Lane', *Touchstone or The New Era*, 14 April 1877, 4

41 'Drury Lane Theatre', *The Era*, 18 March 1877, 13

42 'Drama: The Week', *The Athenaeum*, 17 March 1877, 363 & 'The Theatre:

The Dramatic Season', *The World*, 15 August 1877, 9.

43 The Drury Lane box for 1877 in the Victoria and Albert Museum Theatre Collection contains a batch of reviews for *Haska*, none of them attributed to their respective newspapers apart from one in *The Figaro* (17 March 1877). This is the one that rebukes Chatterton for degrading Drury Lane.

44 'Rent of Drury Lane', *The Times*, 28 August 1877, 5; 'Drury Lane Theatre and Mr Mapleson', *Touchstone*, 1 September 1877, 12

45 Mapleson, 113

46 On 14 April 1877 Chatterton's paper *Touchstone* announced ruefully that Mapleson had surprised everyone by announcing his season at Her Majesty's when he might have had Drury Lane (9).

47 Sheppard (1960) Survey of London XXIX, 245; letter to the editor from Chas. Fredk. Fuller, *The Builder*, 23 January 1875, 82

48 Mapleson, 114

49 J. H. Mapleson, 'The New National Opera House', Letter to the Editor, *The Times*, 4 August 1877, 10

50 Mapleson, 109

51 The advertisement offering Drury Lane for four months from 7 April appeared in *The Times* of 15 March 1877, 8.

52 In 'The New National Opera House', J. H. Mapleson, Letter to the Editor, *The Times*, 4 August 1877, 10, Mapleson claimed that he had been paying £250 per week. On 28 August 1877 *The Times* printed a correction from Chatterton saying that Mapleson paid him £3,000 for a sixteen-week season, which works out at £187 10s. per week. Mapleson's seasons rarely ran for sixteen weeks, although he had to allow time to rearrange the auditorium and to clean the theatre, then restore the theatre to its previous seating arrangement afterwards, so he was probably calculating the rent based on the actual number of weeks during which he was putting on performances.

53 On 20 November 1864 a correspondent wrote to *The Era* (10) pointing out that twenty-one theatres in fifteen British cities were presenting plays by Boucicault, and asking why the critics were always so hostile towards a playwright who made the fortunes of managers and the reputations of actors. The anonymous writer, signing himself 'Fair and Square', concluded that it was because Boucicault was not a journalist, although many dramatic critics were playwrights and thus had the opportunity to praise their own works and denigrate those of a rival. It is quite possible that Boucicault wrote the letter himself.

54 '"Touchstone" and the "Era"', *Touchstone or The New Era*, 5 May 1877, 12

55 23 June 1877, 8; 30 June 1877, 11; 19 May 1877, 3-4; 2 June 1877, 7

56 'Scrutator' [Henry Labouchere], *Truth*, 26 July 1877, 108

57 Hollingshead 1:119

58 When Walter Gooch took over the lease of the Princess's from Chatterton in September 1877, advertisements for that theatre appeared in *The Era* again. However, there were no advertisements for Drury Lane or the Adelphi Theatre until 6 January 1878.

59 'Atlas', 'What the World Says', *The World*, 8 August 1877, 10

60 The disedifying sequence of events was reported as follows (all dates 1877). *The Era* 25 February, 12; 10 June, 6; 1 July, 5; 22 July, 5; 29 July, 10; 5 August, 5 & 9; 12 August, 5; 9 September, 12. *Touchstone* 12 May, 8; 2 June 3-4; 9 June, 7; 28 July, 9; 4 August, 3; 11 August, 2 & 8.

61 There were announcements in Chatterton's weekly paper *Touchstone*

on 7 and 14 July 1877 of the realistic drama to open on 15 September. On 21 July *Touchstone* carried a full-page advertisement for *England in the Days of Charles the Second*, to open on 22 September, although the announcement for the realistic drama opening on 15 September was still appearing on another page, so the decision must have been taken suddenly.

62 Halliday died on 10 April 1877 and was buried in Highgate Cemetery on 14 April. Chatterton was one of the pallbearers and one of the trustees of his estate. ('The Late Andrew Halliday', *Touchstone*, 9 February 1878, 6)

63 'The Theatre: Jane Shore', *The World*, 11 October 1876, 11. The words occur in a review of Wills's *Jane Shore* which went into the Princess's Theatre in October 1876. It had been touring the provinces as a vehicle for Miss Heath, an actress who had gone into management and who seems to have rented the Princess's from Chatterton for three months to show her production in London. When her sub-lease came to an end, Chatterton kept *Jane Shore* running until February, so it achieved 113 performances, but it was probably running at a loss while Chatterton negotiated the transfer of his lease to Walter Gooch in August 1877.

64 'Drury Lane Theatre', *The Observer*, 23 September 1877, 5

65 'The Theatre', *The World*, 26 September 1877, 10

66 Mowbray believed that the haste with which overnight reviews were written contributed to their poor quality, but his fellow-critics, no doubt stung by his suggestion that they would write good reviews for managers who poured alcohol down their throats, said that he was just too slow a writer to be successful as a journalist. (J. B. Booth [1943] *The Days We Knew*, quoted in Richards [2005] 102)

67 'Drury Lane Theatre', *The Times*, 27 September 1877, 4

68 'Drury Lane Theatre', *The Times*, 29 September 1877, 9

69 W. G. Wills, Letter to the Editor, *The Times*, 4 October 1877, 6. Wills failed to see the flaw in his own argument which was that, given his admission that he had jettisoned Scott's narrative in favour of his own, he was entirely responsible for the incomprehensible mess.

70 'Poets and Critics', *The World*, 10 October 1877, 14-15

71 'Atlas', 'What the World Says', *The World*, 24 October 1877, 10

72 'The Dramatic Season', *The World*, 14 August 1878, 9

73 'Drury Lane', *The Times*, 25 October 1877, 6

74 Morris, 16

75 John Hollingshead responded to a bad review of a production at the Gaiety Theatre: 'The *Times* newspaper, which now usually cultivates a certain toothpick after-dinner style of criticism, even went so far as to condemn the whole entertainment, the author, and the public, and to give directions for the management of the theatre which would land the manager in the Bankruptcy Court and the actor in the workhouse... The gift of prophecy is as rare as it is valuable, and if the gentleman who is now allowed to shake the tea-board thunder of the *Times* over the heads of theatrical managers really possesses this gift, he ought to be able to do much better than drudge for a newspaper.' (Hollingshead, 2: 97)

76 'Complimentary Benefit to Mr F. B. Chatterton', *The Era*, 17 February 1878, 6

77 Stirling, 1:314

78 'Drury Lane', *Touchstone*, 9 March 1878, 3-4 & 'Mr F. B. Chatterton's

Benefit', *The Era*, 10 March 1878, 6
79 'Dinner to Mr F. B. Chatterton', *The Era*, 17 March 1878, 6
80 In his speech at the Drury Lane benefit on 4 March, Chatterton had promised an Italian opera season 'by a new company at popular prices' on or before Easter Monday. This did not materialise and three weeks later he was advertising Drury Lane to let for three months from Easter. (*The Era*, 24 March 1878, 10)
81 'The Dramatic Season', *The World*, 14 August 1878, 9
82 The announcements about the benefit in *Touchstone* all referred to the fact that 'the present lease shortly expires', making this the perfect moment 'for professionally and publicly marking the estimation in which the Lessee and Manager is held'. (2 March 1878, 15)
83 'Theatrical and Musical Mems.', *The Entr'Acte*, 14 April 1877, 7

10: THE COLLAPSE

1 'Professional Gossip', *Touchstone*, 9 March 1878, 13; on the same day *The Illustrated London News* carried a denial of the story that had appeared in *Mayfair*. There was a similar rumour later in the year that Baroness Burdett-Coutts had lent Henry Irving money to take over the lease of the Lyceum Theatre. The Baroness was one of Irving's greatest admirers, but she denied ever having assisted him financially.
2 'Theatre Royal, Drury Lane', *The Era*, 28 July 1878
3 Joseph Hatton, 'The Battle of London', *Cigarette Papers for After-Dinner Smoking*, London: Hutchinson and Co., 1892, 54.
4 'The Dramatic Season', *The World*, 14 August 1878, 9
5 'The Adelphi Theatre, High Court of Justice, Chancery Division, Nov. 23rd. Kinnaird v Webster', *The Era*, 1 December 1878, 5
6 'The Adelphi in Litigation', *The Era*, 28 July 1878, 10
7 'High Court of Justice, Chancery Division, Webster v. Chatterton', *The Times*, 19 July 1878, 4; 'Webster v. Chatterton', *Touchstone*, 20 July 1878, 11; 'The Adelphi in Litigation', *The Era*, 21 July 1878, 10
8 Chatterton told Coleman twice that the Gatti brothers paid him £12,000 for the lease of the Adelphi. (Coleman [1888] 372 & 382) He may have been misremembering the sum, but it is possible that he made it a condition of transferring the lease that they should pay back the £2,000 he had borrowed from his bank the year before. Chatterton disliked owing money and would have scorned to use legal technicalities to get out of paying a debt.
9 Coleman (1888) 2:382
10 Charles Lamb Kenney, *Drury Lane Theatre: Season 1878-79*, 1878, 4, 6 & 7; pamphlet, copy in the Drury Lane box for 1878 in the Victoria and Albert Museum Theatre Collection; accessible online in the John Johnson Collection, Bodleian Library, University of Oxford.
11 There had been a benefit performance of *The School for Scandal* to raise funds for Kenney at the Gaiety Theatre on 20 June 1877 with Ellen Terry as Lady Teazle. It raised over £400 (*Touchstone*, 23 June 1877, 8). Kenney was known to be terminally ill and had been unable to work for the two years previous to this ('Mr Charles Lamb Kenney', *The Era*, 17 June 1877, 11).
12 'Atlas', 'What the World Says', *The World*, 31 August 1881, 13
13 It was at least the last thing he wrote under his own name. He was probably the author of the letter which appeared over Chatterton's name in *The Times* of 5 October (see page

210) which was singled out for ridicule by Edmund Yates in his 'What the World Says' column. Yates strongly implied that anyone who knew Chatterton would know he hadn't written the letter, with its 'fluency of expression and literary style at which his most intimate acquaintances must have been surprised. It was said of Goldsmith that he "wrote like an angel and talked like poor Poll", and in this respect at least Mr Chatterton may fairly be compared with Goldsmith.' ('Atlas', 'What the World Says', *The World*, 9 October 1878, 10)

14 From Kean's introduction to the printed version of his text, quoted in Nicoll, 193

15 The bear had been a feature of Kean's production, 'chasing the Antigonus of the time… with peculiar zest'. ('The Theatre: The Winter's Tale', *The World*, 2 October 1878, 9) Kean justified the appearance of a bear in Asia Minor by a quotation from the Second Book of Kings. (Cook, 2: 190-1)

16 'The Dramatic Season', *The World*, 13 August 1879, 8. '*The Winter's Tale* has not before been so liberally equipped by any Drury Lane manager, even when account has been taken of the production of the play by Macready in 1842, and by Mr James Anderson in 1850. The present performance, however, is gravely deficient in histrionic aptitude and intellectuality.' ('The Theatre: The Winter's Tale', *The World*, 2 October 1878, 9)

17 In 1871 she had decided against making her farewell appearance on the London stage as it was too 'degraded'. (Carlyle, 222)

18 Bancroft, 392. 'Bearable in many parts, and positively efficient in a few' was the lukewarm assessment of *The Morning Chronicle* of his Romeo on 29 January 1852. Twenty-five years later *The World* described him as: 'known to playgoers of this generation as a ponderous and rather torpid tragedian'. ('The Theatre', *The World*, 4 April 1877, 10) Joseph Knight said that he ranted throughout *Richard Coeur de Lion* at such volume as to demonstrate one of the legends surrounding 'the lion-hearted monarch, that Moslem horses were frightened of him for generations after'. ('Drama: The Week', *The Athenaeum*, 3 October 1874, 457-8)

19 'Scrutator', 'A Winter's Tale', *Truth*, 10 October 1878, 409

20 'Drama: The Week', *The Athenaeum*, 5 October 1878, 443, quoted in Knight, 237

21 James, 146-7, taken from 'The London Stage', *Scribner's Monthly*, January 1881

22 Anderson, 335-36

23 'Drama: The Week', *The Athenaeum*, 5 October 1878, 443, quoted in Knight, 237

24 'At the Play: In London', *The Theatre*, 1 November 1878, 300; *The London Figaro*, 5 October 1878, 11. According to *The Observer* (29 September 1878, 6): 'The chief glory of the acting is Mrs Vezin's… she throws the efforts of most of her colleagues into the shade.' 'Scrutator' in *Truth* (10 October 1878, 409) thought that: 'In the entire cast… there are only two artistes who soar above mediocrity. They are Mrs Hermann Vezin and Mr Ryder.' Ryder was playing Antigonus. He had played Polixenes in Charles Kean's 1856 production at the Princess's Theatre.

25 'The Theatre: The Winter's Tale', *The World*, 2 October 1878, 9; 'Theatres: Drury Lane', *The Illustrated London News*, 5 October 1878, 330; 'Scrutator', 'A Winter's Tale', *Truth*, 10 October 1878, 409

26 'Ellen Wallis' (profile) & 'Drury Lane' (review), *Touchstone*, 5 October 1878, 3 - 4. This issue – No. 79 – was the last to appear under Chatterton's

ownership. He sold it to Frederick de Burriatte who retained Edgar Ray as editor but dropped the sub-title 'The New Era' and changed the nature of the contents. There was still coverage of theatre and the arts, but much more about controversial political and social issues. The paper published excoriating profiles of Henry Labouchere MP, proprietor of *Truth*, and Edmund Yates, proprietor of *The World*, which caused the latter to storm into the *Touchstone* office with a big stick threatening to break the editor's back. He was bound over to keep the peace at Bow Street Police Court. ('"Touchstone" and "The World"', *Touchstone*, 23 November 1878, 14). The last issue of *Touchstone* appeared on 31 May 1879. (See Robert Whelan, 'Touchstone: A Forgotten Theatrical Newspaper', *Theatre Notebook*, 72:2, September 2018, 100-119)

27 'Scrutator', 'A Winter's Tale', *Truth*, 10 October 1878, 410
28 'The Church and the Stage', Letter to the Editor, *The Times*, 5 October 1878, 6
29 *The London Figaro*, 5 October 1878, 11
30 The acting was described as 'terribly bad' and – even worse from *The Builder's* point of view – Beverley had confused Greek and Roman architectural styles. (*The Builder*, 12 October 1878, 1,073)
31 Classified advertisement, *The Times*, 12 October 1878, 8. Chatterton inserted the same appeal into the next day's issue of *The Era*.
32 Coleman (1888) 2:375
33 'At the Play: In London', *The Theatre*, 1 December 1878, 374
34 The American scholar Daniel Barrett discovered in the Folger Shakespeare Library in Washington a letter dated 16 October 1878 written by Chatterton to Charles Flower accepting the position of director of the first season of plays to be performed in the Shakespeare Memorial Theatre. (Barrett, 168) Chatterton's appointment was announced in *Touchstone*, 19 October 1878 (5) and in *The Illustrated London News* on 9 November 1878 (447): 'The general arrangements are to be under the direction of Mr Chatterton, who is one of the governors of the association.'
35 *The Era*, 10 October 1875, 10.
36 Classified advertisement, *The Times*, 23 April 1875, 8
37 Edward Stirling, 'Closing of Drury Lane Theatre', *The Era*, 16 February 1879
38 'Atlas', 'What the World Says', *The World*, 12 February 1879, 10
39 'The Drury Lane Disaster', *The Theatre*, 1 March 1879, 78
40 Edward Stirling, 'Closing of Drury Lane Theatre', *The Era*, 16 February 1879
41 William Beverley, Letter to the Editor, *The Daily News*, 18 February 1879
42 Frederick Vokes, 'The Closing of Drury Lane Theatre', *The Era*, 23 February 1879. Realising that the events portrayed his family in a poor light, Fred Vokes tried to put forward another version of events, but it was contradicted by those who had been at the meeting. Thirty-two members of the company, including James Guiver (treasurer), Edward Stirling (stage manager), Carl Meyder (musical director), John Cormack (dance director) and other long-serving members of the company, signed a letter confirming that the Vokes and Lauri the clown were the only people who refused to accept the reduction in pay. The letter also stated that the Vokes family were receiving £130 per week (nearly £16,000 in modern terms) as opposed to £25 per week in their earlier days.

('Correspondence: Closing of Drury Lane Theatre', *Touchstone*, 15 February 1879)
43 'The Drury Lane Disaster', *The Theatre*, 1 March 1879, 81
44 Court of Bankruptcy in re: F. B. Chatterton, *The Times*, 3 April 1879, 4
45 Anderson, 338-9
46 The dividend for 1879 fell to £7 as the proprietors held back a larger than usual sum in reserve owing to the serious arears of rent by December 1878. 'Drury Lane Theatre' (Report of the annual meeting of proprietors), *The Times*, 19 July 1879, 13 & 'Drury Lane Theatre' (report of the annual meeting of renters), *The Times*, 28 July 1879, 6; 'Drury Lane Theatre', *The Morning Post*, 28 July 1879
47 'Drury Lane Theatre' (report of the annual meeting of renters), *The Times*, 28 July 1879, 6
48 Anderson, 208
49 'Atlas', 'What the World Says', *The World*, 12 February 1879, 10
50 'The Dramatic Season', *The World*, 13 August 1879, 8
51 'The Drury Lane Disaster', *The Theatre*, 1 March 1879, 81
52 'Scrutator', 'Drury Lane Theatre', *Truth*, 13 February 1879, 193
53 Hatton, 52-9
54 Tinsley, 2:129-32
55 Coleman (1888) 2:381
56 'Banquet to Mr Chatterton', *Touchstone or The New Era*, 16 March 1868, 10
57 Squire Bancroft recorded in his memoirs a distressing incident involving Webster. Bancroft and his wife had agreed to perform a few scenes from Bulwer Lytton's comedy *Money*, originally produced in 1840 and revived by the Bancrofts with great success, for a large-scale actor's benefit. Webster unwisely allowed himself to be persuaded to play the part he had created in the original production nearly forty years before. As he stood in the wings awaiting his cue, he panicked, saying he didn't know where he was or what he was supposed to do. Marie Bancroft had to steer him through the scene. (Bancroft, 133) His appearance as Richard Pride (his original part) in a revival of the melodrama *Janet Pride* at the Adelphi in 1874 had been embarrassing as he forgot his lines, left long pauses, then gabbled out whatever he could remember. ('London Theatres', *Entr'Acte*, 15 August 1874, 4)
58 'High Court of Justice, Nov. 29, Chancery Division', *The Times*, 1 December 1879, 4 ; 'Webster v. Chatterton', *The Times*, 4 December 1879, 4
59 The edition of *Touchstone* for 1 March 1879 (2 -3) carried a long profile of Chatterton, written in the most sympathetic tone and probably with his co-operation, which cited the partnership with Webster as a contributory factor to the collapse of his management. 'Indeed, we might almost go to the length of saying that but for his connection with these theatres, the catastrophe that has just overtaken him might have been averted.'
60 Coleman (1888) 2:373
61 At the Adelphi he had *Notre Dame* (255 performances), *Nicholas Nickleby* (191) *The Prayer in the Storm* (169), *The Wandering Jew* (152) and *Little Goody Two Shoes* (151); at the Princess's *Rip van Winkle* (214), *Lost in London* (126), *Eileen Oge* (117) and *Haunted Houses* (93).
62 'Merry-go-Round', *The Entr'Acte*, 23 March 1879, 4
63 Webster, 87-8. The entry for Webster in the Oxford Dictionary of National Biography, originally written by Chatterton's contemporary, the dramatic critic Joseph Knight, still claims that Webster's 'partnership [at

the Adelphi] with Chatterton failed on the grounds of his associate's extravagance.'

11: THE LAST YEARS

1. George Augustus Sala, 'Echoes of the Week', *The Illustrated London News*, 1 March 1879, 198. Sala had earlier described himself and Chatterton as 'veteran cronies'. ('Echoes of the Week', *The Illustrated London News*, 29 December 1877, 618)
2. George Augustus Sala, 'Echoes of the Week', The Illustrated London News, 8 March 1879, 223. Edward Stirling, the stage manager for many years at Drury Lane, put the combined figure at £800 in his memoirs written two years after the event. (Stirling, 1:317) Stirling's figure is probably more accurate, given the notorious difficulty involved in collected monies promised to charitable appeals.
3. Charles Lowndes, Letter to the Editor, 'The Shakespeare Memorial', *The Era*, 9 February 1879, 12. Nevertheless, Chatterton's name does not appear in Sally Beauman's *The Royal Shakespeare Company: A History of Ten Decades* (1982).
4. 'The Shakespeare Memorial', *The Era*, 27 April 1879
5. 'For Self and Shakespeare', *The World*, 30 April 1879, 8. Scorn for the Shakespeare Memorial Theatre was general in the London media, and particularly virulent at *The Daily Telegraph*. *The Figaro* was pessimistic about the prospects for a theatre 'buried away in the provinces out of sight of everyone, save the Yankee tourist and the antiquary'. ('Before and Behind the Curtain', *The Figaro*, 28 April 1875)
6. 'Mr F. B. Chatterton's Benefit', *The Morning Post*, 24 February 1880, 3
7. Hatton, 59
8. The description comes from H.G. Hibbert, *A Playgoer's Memories*, London: Grant Richards, 1920, 78, quoted in Jeffrey Richards, 'E.L. Blanchard and "The golden age of pantomime"', in Davis (2010) 31.
9. Classified advertisements, *The Times*, 15 January 1881, 8
10. Coleman (1888) 2:382
11. 'Circumstances in connection with my complimentary benefit at the end of the season led to a rupture with the Gattis which I have never ceased to deplore. It is a simple act of justice to say that a more liberal, large-hearted pair of men I have never met.' (Coleman [1888] 2:382)
12. Classified advertisements, *The Times*, 12 October 1881, 8
13. Chatterton wrote a letter to *The Era* ('The Closure of Sadler's Wells', 14 January 1882) listing the takings for the nineteen performances of *The Forty Thieves*.
14. Coleman (1888) 2:386
15. 'Law Intelligence', *Daily News*, 21 January 1882
16. Ward and Whiteing, 234
17. Coleman (1888) 2:386
18. 'Death of Mr F. B. Chatterton', *The Era*, 20 February 1886
19. Coleman (1888) 2:391
20. 'Mr F. B. Chatterton's Benefit', *The Era*, 7 March 1885; Coleman (1888) 391
21. *The Morning Post*, 20 July 1885, 3; ' Our London Letter', *Leicester Chronicle and Leicestershire Mercury*, 30 May 1885, 5
22. Coleman (1888) 2:397
23. George Augustus Sala, 'Echoes of the Week', *The Illustrated London News*, 8 December 1877, 554
24. Coleman (1888) 2:384-5

12: MAN AND MANAGER

1. *The Entr'Acte*, 16 December 1876, 6 & 28 July 1877
2. Coleman (1888) 2:376
3. 1873 (eighty-three performances), 1876 (sixty-six performances) and 1877 (twenty-four performances).
4. Tinsley, 2:186-7. *The Era* (5 December

1875) observed that: 'it is a matter for some regret that the beneficiaire has expressed disappointment at the smallness of the sum realised'.
5   Yates, 1: 186
6   Coleman (1888) 2:389
7   In 1868, 1870 and 1874 the Italian opera season had already started in Passion Week. In 1878 he let *Haska* run throughout the week as he had accepted £1,000 from Henry Spicer to stage it, and presumably felt he had to allow the author a chance to recoup some money.
8   F. B. Chatterton, 'Ash Wednesday', Letter to the Editor, *The Times*, 12 February 1875, 8. Hollingshead's letter had appeared on 30 January 1875, 8, co-signed by 491 people. The restriction was abolished in 1886.
9   F. B. Chatterton, 'The Church and the Stage', Letter to the Editor, *The Times*, 5 October 1878, 6
10 Coleman (1888) 2:325
11 Ward and Whiteing, 233
12 'Mr F. B. Chatterton', *Touchstone*, 1 March 1879, 4
13 Coleman (1888) 2:388
14 Yates, 1: 186. ' the marvellous Boy / The sleepless Soul that perished in his pride' comes from 'Resolution and Independence' by William Wordsworth (1802).
15 'Scrutator' (Henry Labouchere), 'Managers', *Truth*, 11 January 1877, 39-41.
16 Report of the annual meeting of the Drury Lane renters held on 4 August 1877, *The Era*, 5 August 1877
17 Report of the annual meeting of proprietors, *The Times*, 18 July 1872, 8
18 Report of the annual meeting of proprietors, *The Times*, 23 July 1877, 6
19 Arthur Murphy (1801) *The Life of David Garrick Esq*, vol. 2, 201
20 James, 119, from 'The London Theatres', dated 24 May 1879 and published in *The Nation*, 12 June 1879; Arnold (1879) 77, 'Equality', delivered as a lecture to the Royal Institution on 8 February 1878 and printed in the March edition of *The Fortnightly Review*, then included in *Mixed Essays*
21 'Scrutator' (Henry Labouchere), 'Managers', *Truth*, 11 January 1877, 39-41
22 'Scrutator' (Henry Labouchere), 'The National Theatre', *Truth*, 25 October 1877, 488
23 'Scrutator' (Henry Labouchere), 'Orders', *Truth*, 10 January 1878, 40
24 'Scrutator' (Henry Labouchere), 'An Impresario Malgré Lui', *Truth*, 29 November 1877, 639-40
25 'Scrutator' (Henry Labouchere), *Truth*, 16 August 1877, 200 & 22 February 1877, 230-1
26 This point was made by Joseph Knight in his review of a production of *King Lear* at Drury Lane which he described as 'the last degradation of which the tragic art is susceptible'. Knight discussed the lack of any real opportunity for actors to learn their craft and came to the depressing conclusion that, in the absence of any state subsidy for a British equivalent of the Comédie Française, no improvement was likely. ('Drama', *The Athenaeum*, 12 April 1873, 481-2)
27 *The Daily News*, 22 April 1879
28 Allen, 202
29 'Music and the Drama: Drury Lane', *The Athenaeum*, 27 February 1869, 316
30 All quotations from reviews written by Joseph Knight for *The Athenaeum*: 30 September 1871, 441; 24 April 1869, 579; 26 December 1874, 891; 12 April 1873, 481
31 '*The Fortunes of Nigel* at Drury Lane', *The Spectator*, 3 October 1868, 1154
32 Ward and Whiteing, 233
33 Leigh Hunt, *Autobiography*, ed. R. Ingpen, London: Macmillan, 1903, 1:152, quoted in Davis and Emeljanow, 199.
34 Morley, 6-7
35 'Nothing in the Papers', *The*

Illustrated London News, 23 January 1869, 83

36 For example, Henry Morley's review of *Manfred* for *The Examiner* in 1863: '*Manfred* has the best of successes, it brings what it should be the aim of every manager to bring, the educated classes back into the theatre.' Reprinted in Morley, 346

37 In *Poets and Profits*, Kenney wrote of 'the exhausting drain which was being inflicted on the treasury by this course of legitimacy' which left behind 'a marked deficit as a memento of the reward to be expected in the disinterested pursuit of classical literature'. He was describing the 'legitimate month' in the early part of 1868. (Kenney [1875b] 19)

38 'Atlas', 'What the World Says', *The World*, 12 February 1879, 10

39 Joseph Knight, 'Drama: the Week', *The Athenaeum*, 24 April 1875, 561, reprinted in Knight, 26-7. The remark occurred in the course of a bad review for the Bancrofts' production of *The Merchant of Venice* at the Prince of Wales's Theatre in which Knight reflected on the failure of *Antony and Cleopatra* two years before and criticised 'the attempt to convert [Shakespeare's] plays into spectacular entertainments, however it may suit the ignorant pleasure-seekers who [flock] to Drury Lane'.

40 Scrutator (Henry Labouchere), 'Managers', *Truth*, 11 January 1877, 39-41

41 'Scrutator' (Henry Labouchere), *Truth*, 14 March 1878, 331

42 Holroyd, 112-3. Isabel Bateman eventually became the Reverend Mother of the Community of St Mary the Virgin in Wantage, an Anglican order (Foulkes [1997] 164).

43 William Archer (1886) *About The Theatre*, London: T. Fisher Unwin, 241, cited in Richards (2005) 126; W. H. Hudson writing in the *Dramatic Review*, 9 January 1886, cited in Booth (1981) 96-7

44 'The Theatre: The Winter's Tale', *The World*, 2 October 1878, 9

45 Anderson, 320. The Anderson quote related to *Richard Coeur de Lion* in 1874. The cast for *Amy Robsart* were called for Saturday 10 September 1870, two weeks before the first performance (*The Era*, 4 September 1870, 8). The cast for *Rebecca* were called for Saturday 9 September, two weeks before the first performance (*The Era*, 3 September 1871, 8). The cast for *The Winter's Tale* were called for noon on Monday 16 September 1878. The production opened on the Saturday of the following week (*Touchstone*, 14 September 1878, 8).

46 'The Theatre: The Dramatic Season', *The World*, 13 August 1879, 8

47 'A Gain to Art', *The Theatre*, September 1879, 66

48 'The Vision of Truth. Canto the Third: The Dramatic Circle', *Truth*, 26 December 1878, 13. There is a special area in Hell reserved for the punishment of adapters who have mangled the work of great authors. Sir Walter Scott is sitting on the head of W. G. Wills, who had adapted *England in the Days of Charles the Second* in 1877 from Scott's *Peveril of the Peak*.

49 'A Gain to Art', *The Theatre*, September 1879, 67

50 'The Dramatic Season', *The World*, 14 August 1878, 9

51 Francis, 190. Basil Francis had this story from Mrs Gilchrist Frend, who had been a friend of Mary Greville, Fanny Kelly's lifelong companion and possibly her daughter. Fanny Kelly is described as being almost ninety at the time of the visit. As her ninetieth birthday fell in December 1880, nearly two years after Chatterton had left Drury Lane, the visit must have occurred during his last months as lessee.

EPILOGUE: DRURY LANE AS THE NATIONAL THEATRE

1 James, 3-4, from 'The Parisian Stage'

dated December 1872 and published in *The Nation*, 9 January 1873
2. James, 125, from 'The Comédie Française in London', dated 12 July 1879 and published in *The Nation*, 31 July 1879
3. Hollingshead, 2:114
4. At the conclusion of the season, Hollingshead announced that the forty-two performances (thirty-six evening and six matinees, had grossed £19,805 14s. 6d., an average of £472 per performance. ('Theatrical Gossip', *The Era*, Sunday 20 July 1879)
5. Matthew Arnold, 'The French Play in London', *The Nineteenth Century*, XXX, August 1879, 228-243, 237. Arnold's article was reprinted in *Irish Essays and Others*, London: Smith, Elder and Co, 1882, 208-243. All further page numbers are from the book version.
6. Arnold (1882) 239
7. Arnold (1882) 240-1
8. George Augustus Sala, 'The Stage Which May Be Coming', *Touchstone*, 12 January 1878, 3-4
9. Arnold (1882) 241
10. 'Mr F. B. Chatterton's Benefit', *The Standard*, 4 March 1879, 3
11. 'Drury Lane Theatre', *The Era*, 9 November 1879
12. When he was later criticised for putting on such a weak production so early in his management, Harris's response was: 'If you had to pay a thousand pounds for rent, and hadn't got it, and if a friend turned up and offered to find the shekels if you'd produce *Madame Angot* – what would you do?' This story was told by John Coleman in a programme note called 'The Romance of Drury Lane' that he wrote for his production in 1896 of a play called *The Duchess of Coolgardie*.
13. Harris (1885) 630
14. Harris (1885) 634-35
15. Harris (1885) 634-35
16. Whitworth, 26-9
17. Coleman (1904) 2: 690. The Lord Mayor's banquet was held on Tuesday 24 October 1876 in the afternoon, to allow members of the profession who were working to attend. An account was printed in *The Era*, 29 October 1876, 12. The playwright W. G. Wills also called for a National Theatre, drawing attention to the level of support for the visual arts compared with the stage.
18. John Coleman (1891) 'A National Theatre: an appeal to the London County Council', *The Nineteenth Century*, December 1901, 50, 991-1000. The article re-appeared as a chapter in Coleman (1904) under the title 'The Need for a National Theatre'. All page numbers are taken from the book version.
19. Coleman (1904) 2: 692.
20. Coleman (1904) 2: 696
21. Coleman (1904) 2: 704
22. Coleman (1904) 2: 705
23. Coleman (1904) 2: 706
24. Coleman (1904) 2: 708
25. Rosenthal, 23. William Bridges-Adams, who ran the Shakespeare Memorial Theatre in Stratford-upon-Avon from 1919 to 1934, said that, in the years before World War I, the National Theatre committee had enough money to buy Her Majesty's Theatre in the Haymarket outright, but they refused, dazzled by the vision of a brand new building. 'Their vision of bricks and mortar... was their undoing.' (*A Bridges-Adams Letter Book* [1971] ed. Robert Speaight, London: Society for Theatre Research, letter to Laurence Irving dated 2 May 1961)
26. Dean (1970), 227.
27. Dean (1956) 537. Dean used the fact that the Queen had actually laid the foundation stone on a site next to County Hall that everyone knew was not going to be used as proof of the incompetence of the National Theatre movement.
28. Dean (1956) 538.
29. Dean (1956) 539.

Index

Adelphi Theatre, 9, 14, 17, 22, 53, 101, 177, 178, 201, 205
    Webster acquires the lease, 109, 245; Webster acquires the freehold, 14, 109-11, 117, 137, 245; Webster sells lease to Chatterton, 137; Chatterton mortgages lease, 186-7; Webster claims Chatterton defrauded him, 186, 198-9, 283-4n.; Chatterton involved with management of, 109-11, 117-9, 121, 123, 127, 137-8, 167, 209, 242, 283n.; The Gatti brothers and Thomas Clarke take over the lease, 186-7, 198; *The Colleen Bawn* produced at, 20, 22, 38, 155, 159, 174, 239, 245; transfer of *The Shaughraun* to, 155-8
Albert, Prince Consort, 26, 60, 64, 131, 176, 204
Anderson, James, 112, 163, 164, 189-91, 222, 238, 281n.
    management of Drury Lane, 35-6; regards Drury Lane as cursed, 74, 144, 196; management of the Surrey Theatre, 71; acts at Drury Lane for Chatterton, 71, 102, 131-3, 143-4; stops acting, 144
Archer, William, 191-2, 221, 232, 257n.
Arnold, Matthew, 214, 226-7
Arnold, Samuel, 21, 28
Aspull, George, 6
Aspull, William, 6, 208

Balfe, Michael, 27, 140-2, 146
Banim, John and Michael, 22, 26
Bancroft, Squire and Marie, 115, 217, 219, 244, 283n., 286n.
Barker, Harley Granville, 232
Barnum, Phineas T., 101
Bateman, Colonel, 170, 221
Bateman, Mrs, 170-1, 221
Bateman, Isabel, 170, 221, 286n.
Bazalgette, Sir Joseph, 145
Bedford, Dukes of, 29-31, 36
Bernard, Bayle, 78, 86-8, 119

Betterton, Thomas, 183
Betty, William, 2
Beverley, William Roxby, 42-44, 54, 58-9, 64, 66, 67, 71, 75, 79, 80, 83, 87-8, 95-6, 102, 112, 125, 130, 141-2, 155, 172, 180, 183, 189, 203, 204, 238
    size of name on posters, 43, 78, 115, 268n.; in charge of the scenic department at Drury Lane, 62-3; under exclusive contract to Drury Lane for the pantomime, 65; for all performances, 78, 141, 202, 262n.; designs toy theatre production of *The Miller and his Men* for Charles Dickens, 85; criticises the Vokes for not supporting Chatterton, 195, 200
Blanchard, Edward Leman, 55-6, 58-9, 68, 83, 119, 125-6, 238-9
    writes Drury Lane pantomimes, 41-2, 54, 80, 116, 135, 145, 182, 183,194, 206, 228; dramatic critic for *The Daily Telegraph*, 165, 244
Boucicault, Agnes (née Robertson), 38, 158
Boucicault, Dion, 53, 83, 110, 133, 174-5, 193, 239-40
    rents Drury Lane from E. T. Smith, 37-8, 62; and the Shakespeare/Byron epigram, 103, 108, 149, 150-1; organises the statue of Balfe, 141-2; tries to make speech on last night of *The Shaughraun*, 156-8; tries to prevent production of *The Shaughraun*, 159, 174, 208
    PLAYS: *After Dark*, 174-5; *Arrah-na-Pogue*, 159; *The Colleen Bawn*, 20, 22, 25, 38, 62, 155, 159, 172, 174, 209; *The Corsican Brothers*, 172; *Faust and Margaret*, 78, 119; *Formosa*, 100-8, 111, 128, 149, 175, 183, 202, 220; *Janet Pride*, 118, 283n.; *The Octoroon*, 38, 159, 239, 267n.; *Rip van Winkle*, 152, 159, 174; *The Relief of Lucknow*, 38; *The Shaughraun*, 149, 151-2, 155-9;

Index

The Streets of London, 103, 159, 174
Braddon, Mary Elizabeth, 138
Braham, John, 14
Brooks, Shirley, 16
Browning, Robert, 147
Buckstone, John, 11, 118
Bulwer Lytton, Edward, 63, 66-7, 86, 216, 220, 283n.
Bunn, Alfred, 33, 36, 109, 140, 153
Burdett Coutts, Baroness, 185, 280n.
Burnand, Frank, 17, 118, 203, 204, 252n.
Byron, H. J., 121, 183, 203
Byron, Lord, 4, 67, 128
   unsuitability of his plays for performance, 50-51, 67, 78, 86, 87; iconic status of, 87, 102, 183, 217; and bankruptcy epigram, iii, 4, 102-4, 115, 133, 149-50, 169
   PLAYS: *Manfred*, 50-53, 54, 56, 78, 99, 104, 138, 190; *Marino Faliero* (*The Doge of Venice*), 85-9, 93

Carroll, Lewis, 92
Carte, Richard D'Oyly, 3, 140
Céleste, Madame Céline, 14, 109, 117-8, 127
Charles II, 31, 32
Chatterton, Amelia (mother of FBC), 5, 206, 209
Chatterton, Edward Andrew (father of FBC), 5, 6, 7, 13, 21, 152, 206, 209
   box office manager at Drury Lane, 7, 10, 251n.; supports FBC at the St James's Theatre, 14, 17
Chatterton, Frederick (grandfather of FBC), 5
Chatterton, Frederick (uncle of FBC), 5, 19, 58, 67, 81, 114, 251n.

Chatterton, Frederick Balsir (FBC)
   PERSONAL LIFE: birth, parents, siblings, 5-6, 209; education 5-6; harpist, 5-7; marriage to Mary Ann Williams, 7, 205, 206, 209-10; children, 124, 209-10; moves to 193 Clapham Road, 124; separation from his wife, 205, 209-11; possible nervous breakdown, 210-11; death, 206
   CAREER: house manager at Drury Lane, 1, 7; acting manager at the Lyceum, 9; benefit performances for, 10-1, 13, 19, 75, 81-3, 84, 93, 114, 116-7, 123, 126, 128, 182-4, 200, 202, 203, 205-6; takes on the management of the Lyceum with Edmund Falconer, 12; becomes lessee of the St James's Theatre, 14; becomes lessee of the Theatre Royal, Rochester, 18-20; takes on the management of the Lyceum with Falconer for a second time, 20; uses newspaper advertising and circulars in marketing, 21-23, 52-53, 79, 202-4, 211; takes on management of Drury Lane with Falconer, 28, 39, 150; renegotiates terms with Falconer, 46-47, 60-61; takes control of artistic policy at Drury Lane, 47, 50, 52, 53, 68; fights Falconer's legal action, 69-71; undertakes to pay the debts of the partnership, 74; becomes sole lessee of Drury Lane in 1866, 69, 75, 77; sub-lets Drury Lane for summer season of opera, 90-1, 93-4; concocts a hybrid between 'legitimacy' and 'sensation', 95-7; becomes lessee of the Theatre Royal, Hull, 98-9; and the 'Shakespeare spelt ruin' epigram, 102-4, 108, 115, 133, 149-50, 163, 167, 169, 170, 195, 202; and legal action against Phelps, 108; and management of Adelphi and Princess's Theatres, 109-11, 117-123, 127-8, 136-40, 152, 167, 174-5, 198-9, 209; has lease of Drury Lane renewed in 1873, 126, 128; feud with Boucicault, 155-8; rivalry with Coleman's management of the Queen's, 161-4; objects to Mowbray Morris's hostile reviews, 166-9; disposes of the lease of the Princess's, 174, 187; produces all-children pantomimes, 175; uses *Touchstone* to promote his interests, 176, 179, 191; feuds with *The Era* over the Royal Dramatic College, 175-8, 184; is given a complimentary dinner to mark his achievements, 183-4; has lease of Drury Lane renewed in 1878, 184-6; disposes of lease of the Adelphi, 186-7;

bankruptcy of, 195-6; fails in his attempt to have his lease of Drury Lane renewed in 1879, 196-8; is invited to direct the opening festival at the Shakespeare Memorial Theatre, 193-4, 200, 282n.; closes Drury Lane, 195; produces pantomime at Covent Garden, 202-3; management of Sadler's Wells, 204-5, 211; welcomes Fanny Kelly to Drury Lane, 223-4
Chatterton, Horace (brother of FBC), 6, 54, 178, 205, 208
Chatterton, Isabella (sister of FBC), 6
Chatterton, John Balsir (uncle of FBC), 5
Chatterton, Kate (sister of FBC), 6, 7, 81, 114
Chatterton, Mary (daughter of FBC), 124, 176, 205
Chatterton, Mary Ann (née Williams, wife of FBC), 7, 124, 205, 206, 209
Chatterton, Percy (brother of FBC), 6
Chatterton, Thomas (poet/forger, no relation), 205, 211
Cibber, Colley, 167-71, 277n.
Coleman, John, 1-4, 11, 18, 21, 36, 39, 46, 53, 108, 121, 123, 193, 204-5, 210-1, 231, 240
   relationship with Chatterton, 1-4, 7, 161-2, 205-7; management of Theatre Royal, Hull, 98-9; management of Queen's Theatre, 160-4, 167, 170, 231; campaigns for a National Theatre, 231-2
      BOOKS: *Fifty Years of an Actor's Life*, 2, 232; *Memoirs of Samuel Phelps*, 3; *Players and Playwrights I Have Known*, 3-4, 11
      PLAYS: *The Shadow of the Sword*, 3; *Uncle Tom's Cabin*, 2
Coleridge, Samuel Taylor, 130
Collins, Arthur, 4
Conquest, Benjamin, 12
Conquest, Clara, 12
Covent Garden estate, 29-30, 107, 234
Covent Garden Theatre, 31-4, 51, 83, 113, 117, 129, 146, 197, 200, 202, 206, 211, 226, 239, 241
   Macready's appearances at, 47, 62-3, 169, 238, 242, 243; and the patent privileges, 44-5, 48, 90, 109, 183, 219, 226, 243, 245; as an opera house, 90-1, 97, 108, 114, 115, 117, 137, 140, 146, 174, 197, 232-4, 239, 241, 262n.

Dauney, Alexander, 154-5
Davenant, Sir William, 31, 226
Dean, Basil, 232-4
Delane, John Thadeus, 17, 105, 166, 243, 276n.
Dickens, Charles, 19, 28, 46, 50, 83, 85, 152, 202, 205
Dillon, Charles, 18, 19, 24, 98, 138, 190, 193, 218, 222, 240
   management of the Lyceum, 8-12
Disraeli, Benjamin, 156
Donne, William, 105, 139
Drury Lane, Theatre Royal
   closure during Passion Week, 46, 56, 67, 82, 121, 158, 172, 210, 284-5n.
   Company of Proprietors of, 30-31, 33-4, 40-41, 46, 75, 89, 197
      rent charged by, 34, 198, 212
   fourth estate, Drury Lane described as, 214
   'legitimate month' at, 98, 100, 107, 218, 220, 265n., 286n.
   new renters of, 196
      dividends paid to, 74, 126-7, 153, 213-4; right to free admission, 127, 140, 152-5, 174, 214
   opera seasons at, 93-4, 97, 108-9, 114, 116, 127, 140-1, 145-8, 159-61, 173-4, 182, 212
   pantomime
      supremacy of, 41-42; matinees of, 66, 73, 112; appearance of children in, 74; advertisement scenes banned from, 113; as afterpiece or mainpiece, 35, 65-7, 81, 92, 98, 107, 114, 125, 135, 145
   patent privileges of, 31-2, 44-5, 48, 90, 109, 183, 219, 226, 243, 245
   presents Shakespeare from Easter to Christmas 1864, 65;
   reconstruction/redecoration of the auditorium, 40, 110-11
      for opera seasons, 91, 93-4, 114
   re-use of stock scenery, 62-3, 68, 141

Index

ticket prices, 62, 93-4, 147, 273n.
PLAYS (other than those by Shakespeare [q.v.] and Falconer [q.v.]): *Amy Robsart*, 111-6, 125, 128, 181, 193, 204; *The Beggar's Opera*, 75; *The Belles of the Kitchen*, 105-6, 114, 121; *Belphegor*, 93, 193; *The Cataract of the Ganges*, 125-6, 154; *The Colleen Bawn*, 38, 62, 172, 209, 239; *Comus*, 67-68, 70, 71, 103; *The Corsican Brothers*, 172; *Don Caesar de Bazan*, 45; *The Doge of Venice*, 85-9, 93, 95, 104; *England in the Days of Charles the Second*, 178-81, 184, 199; *Faust*, 78-9, 81, 82, 85, 86, 95, 121; *La Fille de Madame Angot*, 229; *Formosa*, 100-08, 111, 128, 183, 202, 220; *The Four Mowbrays*, 56; *Fun in a Fog*, 126; *The Great City*, 83-5, 93, 95, 99, 105, 121, 178, 183; *I'm Not Myself At All*, 107; *The Jealous Wife*, 193; *King o' Scots*, 95-7, 100, 121, 218; *The Lady of the Lake*, 20, 124-5, 142; *Manfred*, 50-53, 54, 56, 78, 99, 104, 138; *A Man of Two Lives*, 98, 100; *The Miller and His Men*, 85-6; *My Wife's Out*, 97; *Nitocris*, 1, 8; *The Prisoner of Toulon*, 93; *Richard Coeur de Lion*, 141-4; *Rebecca*, 114-6, 128, 134, 145, 149; *Rob Roy*, 81, 93; *Rule Britannia*, 113; *The School for Scandal*, 81, 99, 136; *The Shaughraun*, 149, 151-2; *The World*, 229; *The Wrong Man in the Right Place*, 119, 121-2
PANTOMIMES: *Harlequin and Good Queen Bess* (1849/50) 35; *Humpty Dumpty* (1850/51) 36; *Little Goody Two Shoes* (1862/3) 41-2, 44-5; *Sinbad the Sailor* (1863/4) 54-5; *Hop o' My Thumb* (1864/5) 65-6, 73; *Little King Pippin* (1865/6) 72-3, 74, 92; *Number Nip* (1866/7) 80-81; *Jack the Giant Killer* (1867/8), 92, 95; *Puss in Boots* (1868/9) 74, 97, 98; *Beauty and the Beast* (1869/70), 42, 107; *The Dragon of Wantley* (1870/1), 113-4, 121; *Tom Thumb* (1871/2), 116; *The Children in the Wood* (1872/3), 125; *Jack in the Box* (1873/4), 134-5, 137; *Aladdin* (1874/5), 74, 145; *Whittington and His Cat* (1875/6), 155; *The Forty Thieves* (1876/7), 171; *The White Cat* (1877/8), 182; *Cinderella* (1878/9), 194-5; *Bluebeard* (1879/80), 228-9; *Mother Goose* (1880/81), 203; *Aladdin* (1884/5), 205

Dryden, John, 129
Dumas, Alexandre (the elder), 35
Dumas, Alexandre (the younger), 104, 139-40
Dykwynkyn, *see* Keene, Richard Wynne

Edward, Prince of Wales (later Edward VII), 114, 116, 140-1
Elliston, Robert, 78, 86-7, 109, 125
Etty, William, 130

Falconer, Edmund (Edmund O'Rourke), 240-1
  and the management of the Lyceum, 12-4, 245; plays Danny Mann in *The Colleen Bawn*, 20, 209, 240; takes on the management of the Lyceum for a second time, 20; as a lyricist/librettist, 28, 240, 254n.; becomes lessee of Drury Lane, 28, 38-41, 275n.; alcoholism, 39, 46-7, 61, 69, 70, 121; renegotiation of terms with Chatterton, 46-7, 50, 60-1; legal action against Chatterton, 69-71, 255n., 261n.; bankruptcy, 74, 75; takes on management of Her Majesty's, 79-80; goes to America, 80; returns to Britain, 120; benefit with original cast of *The Colleen Bawn*, 209
  PLAYS: *The Cagot*, 11; *Bonnie Dundee*, 45-46; *Eileen Oge*, 120-1, 209, 241, 253n.; *Extremes*, 12-13, 14, 46; *Innisfallen*, 120; *Francesca, A Dream of Venice*, 14; *Love's Ordeal*, 68, 259-60n.; *Nature's Above Art*, 50; *Next of Kin*, 44-5; *Night and Morn*, 55-6; *The O'Flahertys*, 68, 259n.; *Oonagh*, 79-80, 120; *Peep o' Day*, 21-28, 39, 46, 47, 75, 107-8, 119, 120-1, 137, 156-8, 174, 204, 209, 240-1, 253n., 266-7n.; *Too Much for Good Nature*, 260n.; *Woman or Love Against the World*, 20-22, 27, 28

Faucit, Helen, 63-64, 65, 67, 68, 71, 79, 102, 104, 136, 194, 201, 218
   becomes Mrs Theodore Martin then Lady Martin, 63-4, 131, 189
Fechter, Charles, 28, 47, 49-50, 57- 58, 59, 116, 118
Flower, Charles, 193-4, 200, 258n., 282n.
Flower, Edward Fordham, 193

Garrick, David, 29, 30, 32, 56, 79, 129, 142, 168, 183, 188, 214, 241, 254n.
Gatti, Agostino, 186-7, 198, 200, 202-3, 211
Gatti, Stefano, 186-7, 198, 200, 202-3, 206, 211
Gilbert, W. S., 165, 215, 219
Gladstone, William, 134
Glyn, Isabella, 129, 132
Goethe, 78-9, 85, 89, 102, 119, 128, 183, 217, 243
Goldsmith, Oliver, 139
Greenwood, Tom, 6, 48, 49
Grieve, Thomas, 44
Guiver, James, 123, 138, 195
Gye, Frederick, 90-91, 97, 117, 146

Halliday, Andrew, 83-5, 95-6, 111, 115, 116, 118-9, 129, 131-2, 136, 152, 154, 178-9, 181, 183, 197, 202, 222
Harris, Augustus (junior), 3, 4, 41, 84, 185, 205-6, 239, 240, 241
   becomes lessee of Drury Lane, 196-8, 202, 211; disregards the National Theatre status of Drury Lane, 228-30
Harris, Augustus (senior), 28, 197
Haymarket, Theatre Royal, 32, 65, 109, 117-8
Her Majesty's Theatre, 31, 36, 37, 79, 90, 99, 137, 140, 153, 241, 244
   fire and rebuilding, 10, 90-1, 93-4, 114, 117, 146, 173, 264n., 268n.
Hollingshead, John, 53, 136, 177, 182, 184, 203, 210, 270n.
   co-presents Rossi at Drury Lane with Chatterton, 160-2; presents the Comédie Française at the Gaiety, 225-6, 266n.
Hugo, Victor, 97-8, 118
Hunt, Leigh, 219

Irving, Henry, 58, 139, 170-1, 178, 185, 211, 223, 225, 244, 277n.
   restores Shakespeare's text in Richard III, 171, 176; assists at benefit performances for Chatterton, 182, 202, 203; status of Lyceum under, 221-2

James, Henry, 147, 190, 214, 225
Jarrett, Henry, 91, 108
Jennings, Henry, 7
Johnson, Samuel, 4, 129
Jonson, Ben, 180
Jullien, Louis, 13, 34-36

Kean, Charles, 11, 65, 78, 119, 169, 176-7, 188-9, 239, 281n.
Kean, Edmund, 142, 168, 183
Keene, Richard Wynne (Dykwynkyn), 54-55, 58, 67, 71, 79, 80, 89
Kelly, Fanny, 223-4
Kemble, John Philip, 129, 188
Kenney, Charles Lamb, 18, 53-54, 58, 59-60, 61, 77, 103, 124, 126, 130, 141, 142, 143, 187-8, 203, 239, 241-2
   Poets and Profits at Drury Lane Theatre, 82, 124, 149-51, 271n.
Kenney, James, 18, 53
Killigrew, Thomas, 31, 226
Killarney
   ballet, 27-28, 137; Telbin's panorama of, 26-27, 43, 44, 47, 119, 137; song, 27
King, T. C., 98
Knight, Joseph, 144, 190, 193, 218, 285n.
Knowles, John, 47
Knowles, Sheridan, 13, 17, 99, 107, 216, 220

Labouchere, Henry, 211, 214, 220-1, 277n., 282n.
   management of the Queen's Theatre, 215-6
Lamb, Charles, 17
Ledger, Edward, 175-8
Lennox, Lord William, 182-3, 198, 200
Litton, Marie, 229, 230
Lord Chamberlain
   powers of theatre licensing and censorship, 41, 48, 80, 86, 90, 102, 104, 105, 139-40, 215
Lyceum Theatre, 8, 32, 120

Index

management of Madame Vestris and Charles Mathews, 42-44; management of Charles Dillon, 8-12; managements of Falconer and Chatterton, 12-4, 20-8; management of Colonel Bateman, 170; management of Henry Irving, 171, 221-2

Macready, William Charles, 58, 62, 168, 169, 231, 242
  management of Covent Garden, 47-9, 63-4, 75-6, 188, 190, 243; management of Drury Lane, 47-9, 63-4, 67, 69, 87, 103, 131, 243, 257n., 281n.
Mapleson, James, 90-91, 93-4, 97, 108-9, 114, 117, 140-1, 196-7
  presents Ristori, 127, 147-8; tries to build Embankment opera house, 145-6, 159-60, 173-4; presents Salvini, 146-8, 160-2
Mathews, Charles, 136
Milton, John, 67-68, 70, 71, 102, 217
Moojen, Frederick, 204, 206
Moore, Maggie, 158-9, 167
Morley, Henry, 220
Morris, Mowbray, 144-5, 164, 166-9, 171, 179-80, 181-2, 276n.

National Standard Theatre, 99-100, 108, 126, 222
Neilson, Adelaide, 112-4, 115, 189
Nelson, Marsh, 40, 110-11
Nilsson, Christine, 117, 140, 142

Olivier, Laurence, 169
Olympic Theatre, 3
Otway, Thomas, 87
Oxenford, John, 9, 13, 53, 56, 65, 88, 98, 131, 136, 145, 151-2, 168-9, 243
  champions the status of Drury Lane, 44-5, 52, 60, 64-5, 68, 72, 77, 80-1, 97, 111, 113, 115, 151; combines dramatic criticism with authorship of plays, 15-17, 52, 165; is accused of corruption and leaves The Times, 164-7
  PLAYS: *Beauty or the Beast*, 52 *A Day Well Spent/Hello Dolly!*, 16, 243; *Gone to Texas*, 52; *Magic Toys*, 15; *My Fellow Clerk*, 19; *My Name is Norval*, 252n.; *A Young Lad From The Country*, 65

Phelps, Edward, 3, 79
Phelps, Samuel, 3, 102, 104, 116, 131, 136, 163, 211, 240, 243-4, 270n.
  member of Macready's companies at Covent Garden and Drury Lane, 47-48, 64, 257n.; management of Sadler's Wells, 2, 9, 11, 48-49, 51, 62, 65, 129, 132, 169, 171, 188, 217, 231; member of Fechter's company at the Lyceum, 47, 49-50; as artistic director at Drury Lane, 50, 62, 68, 199, 218, 220; opens at Drury Lane in *Manfred*, 50-1; plays Manfred in Shoreditch, 99; dispute with Stratford tercentenary committee, 57-59, 194, 201, 259n.; relationship with Helen Faucit, 63-64, 67, 68, 218; appears for Chatterton at Drury Lane, 55, 65, 68, 71, 75, 78, 79, 81, 86, 89, 92-3, 95-6, 98, 115, 218; appears for Chatterton in Hull, 99; appears for Chatterton at the Princess's, 119-21, 127-8; disputes with Chatterton, 108, 112, 128, 170, 189, 209, 220; agrees to make farewell performances at Drury Lane, 190; style of acting, 58, 218, 258n., 265n, 270n.
Planché, J. R., 33, 42-43
Poel, William, 147
Princess's Theatre, 42, 59, 77, 103, 107, 137, 188, 190, 197, 239
  Charles Kean's management of, 11, 65, 78, 119, 163, 169, 188-9, 239, 261n., 281n.; Charles Fechter at, 28; Webster's involvement with, 110, 117, 121, 123, 128, 136-7, 187, 245, 272n.; Chatterton's involvement with, 17, 109-10, 117, 119-23, 127-8, 136-9, 152, 167, 174, 190, 199, 209, 241, 244, 279n., 283n.; Walter Gooch acquires lease of, 174, 187, 278n.; seasons of French plays at, 123, 128, 139-40; an unpopular house, 136, 272n.

Queen's Theatre, 3, 160-4, 167, 231, 240

Rachel, 147
Reeves, Sims, 81, 83, 262n.
Reynolds, Frederick, 137

Rignold, George, 228, 230
Ristori, Adelaide, 127, 147, 148, 161, 270n.
Robertson, Tom, 115
Roselle, Percy, 55, 56, 65, 72, 80, 92
Rossi, Ernesto, 160-2
Rousby, Mr and Mrs, 126
Roxby, Robert, 44, 54, 80
Royal Academy of Dramatic Art, 217
Royal Dramatic College, 175-8, 184, 218
Ruskin, John, 134-5

Sadler's Wells Theatre, 6, 9
Sala, George Augustus, 74, 200, 207, 227
Salvini, Tommaso, 146-8, 160-2
Scott, Clement, 80
Scott, Sir Walter, 23, 127, 149, 179, 183, 199, 220, 244
    The Fortunes of Nigel (see also Drury Lane, plays, *King o' Scots*) 95; *Ivanhoe* (see also Drury Lane, plays, *Rebecca*) 114-5; *Kenilworth* (see also Drury Lane, plays, *Amy Robsart*), 111; *The Lady of the Lake* (see also Drury Lane, plays, *The Lady of the Lake*), 124; *Peveril of the Peak* (see also Drury Lane, plays, *England*) 178-9; *Rob Roy*, 81, 93, 95; *The Talisman* (see also Drury Lane, plays, *Richard Coeur de Lion*) 140, 142
Shakespeare Memorial Theatre, 193-4, 200, 217, 282n.
Shakespeare, William, 4, 32, 37, 48, 79, 102, 142, 183, 202, 217
    tercentenary, 56-60, 193-4, 201; Jubilee of 1769, 56; spelt ruin, iii, 4, 102-4, 108, 115, 133, 149-50, 163, 167, 169, 170, 195; fails to observe the classical unities, 129
    PLAYS: *Antony and Cleopatra*, 128-34, 143, 145, 148, 170, 221-2, 238; *As You Like It*, 63, 67, 79, 93, 194, 229-30; *Comedy of Errors, The*, 59, 77, 79, 81, 193; *Cymbeline*, 57, 63, 64, 65, 67, 68, 71; *Hamlet*, 18, 28, 50, 57-8, 93, 98, 114, 116, 127, 128, 143-4, 147, 161, 170, 171, 221, 223, 259n., 275n.; *Henry IV Part 1*, 56-60, 62-3, 64, 98, 258n.; *Henry IV Part 2*, 62-3, 64, 93, 96, 163; *Henry V*, 163-4, 167, 228, 230, 231, 240; *Henry VI*, 49; *Henry VIII*, 65-66, 93, 190; *Julius Caesar*, 61, 71; *King John*, 71-72, 77-78, 86; *King Lear*, 93, 126, 171, 285n.; *Love's Labours Lost*, 49; *Macbeth*, 18, 57, 63, 64-65, 67, 71, 78, 82, 86, 98, 99,103, 127, 128, 132, 147, 161, 171, 181, 193, 218, 259n., 260n., 275n.; *The Merchant of Venice*, 35, 81, 93, 127, 193, 202, 238, 286n.; *The Merry Wives of Windsor*, 143; *A Midsummer Night's Dream*, 49, 85, 99, 233, 243; *Much Ado About Nothing*, 201; *Othello*, 7, 11, 19, 57, 63, 64, 65, 93, 98, 108, 127, 146-8, 160-01, 171, 193, 270n.; *Pericles*, 49, 243; *Richard II*, 49; *Richard III*, 18, 93, 164, 167-71, 176, 179, 181, 183, 190, 199, 203, 222, 242, 276-7n.; *Romeo and Juliet*, 59, 63, 67, 113,143-4,183, 273n.; *The Taming of the Shrew*, 79; *Titus Andronicus*, 49, 257n.; *Troilus and Cressida*, 49, 257n.; *Twelfth Night*, 59; *The Winter's Tale*, 36, 63, 188-93, 199, 221, 222, 233, 238, 244, 281n.
Shaw, George Bernard, 151, 233
Sheridan, Richard Brinsley, 29-32, 81, 98, 153, 183, 214, 220, 223
    The School for Scandal, 29, 71, 93, 99, 128, 136, 202, 229, 233, 262n., 280n.
Sinclair, Henry, 20
Smith, Edward Tyrell, 42, 80, 104, 126, 207, 212, 239, 244-5
    lowers the status of Drury Lane, 36-38, 53, 214, 227, 255n.; sub-lets Drury Lane to Boucicault, 38; pricing regime at Drury Lane, 62; transfers lease of Drury Lane to Falconer, 38-41, 46-47, 240; introduces matinees of pantomime, 66, 73, 112; management of Her Majesty's, 90
Soane, George, 78
Spicer, Henry
    Haska, 171-2; *The Lords of Ellingham*, 7, 171
Stirling, Edward, 80, 180, 195, 222, 255n.
Sullivan, Barry, 18, 77-8, 86, 93, 102, 164, 167-8, 170, 171, 181, 190, 200-1, 202, 222, 276n., 277n.

Telbin, William, 26, 27, 44, 47, 119, 137
Terry, Ellen, 92, 139, 178, 182, 202, 203
  becomes Irving's leading lady at the Lyceum, 221
Theatres Regulation Act (1843), 31-2, 48, 90, 219, 226, 243, 245
Thompson, Lydia, 14
Tinsley, William, 138, 141, 197-8
Toole, J. L., 116, 202, 203
Tree, Herbert Beerbohm, 3
Trollope, Anthony, 164

Vaughan, Kate, 134-5, 137, 143
Verdi, Giuseppe, 104
Vezin, Mrs Hermann, 79, 116, 191, 202
Victoria, Queen, 5, 25, 26, 64, 124, 137, 204
Vining, George, 110
Vokes family, 105-7, 112, 114, 119, 121-2, 135, 149, 171, 182, 194-5, 202
Vokes, Fawdon, 105, 107, 195
Vokes, Fred, 105,107,112, 116, 135, 195
Vokes, Frederick (senior), 106, 126
Vokes, Jessie, 105, 195
Vokes, Victoria, 105, 194-5

Wagner, Richard, 54, 108, 146
Ward, Geneviève, 136-7, 145, 210, 218
Wallis, Ellen, 131-2, 135, 142-3, 191
Warner, Amelia, 48, 49, 63
Webb, Charles, 9, 77, 262n.
Webb, Henry, 77, 81, 262n.
Webster, Benjamin, 9, 114, 116, 121, 126, 127, 128, 137, 177, 197, 245
  relationship with Madame Céleste, 14, 109, 117-8; partnership with Chatterton, 109-11, 117, 123, 136-7, 209, 283n.; and the Haymarket Theatre, 109, 117-8, 239; and the Adelphi Theatre, 14, 22, 38, 117-8, 137, 267n.; and the Princess's Theatre, 110, 117, 121, 123, 128, 136-7, 187, 245, 272n.; retirement benefit, 136; takes legal action against Chatterton, 186-7, 198-9; senility of, 199, 283n.
Webster, George, 9
Webster, Margaret, 136, 199
Wells, Sir Mordaunt, 182, 196
Whitbread, 30-31

Wilde, Oscar, 44, 151
Wilder, Thornton, 16
Wilkinson, Tait, 2
Williams, Samuel, 7
Williamson, James, 158-9, 167, 208
Wills, W. G., 138-9, 178-81, 197, 279n., 286n.
Wood, George, 108-9
World, The, (see also Yates, Edmund), 164-6, 169, 172, 180-1, 184, 194, 197, 201-2, 214-5, 222
Wren, Sir Christopher, 29

Yates, Edmund, 16, 164-5, 166, 169, 201-2, 209, 211, 220, 280-1n., 282n.